Pet Assisted Therapy:

A Loving Intervention and an Emerging Profession:
Leading to a Friendlier, Healthier, and more Peaceful World

by

Pearl Salotto

Pet Assisted Therapy:

A Loving Intervention and an Emerging Profession:
Leading to a Friendlier, Healthier, and more Peaceful World

Library of Congress Control Number 2001 135561
ISBN 0-9713676-0-4

Printed in Canada
First Edition 2001
2nd Printing 2004
3rd Printing 2007

Published by
D. J. PUBLICATIONS
Norton, MA
www.djppat.com

Produced by
PPC BOOKS
Redington Shores, FL

To D. J. – "Dog of Joy", in deepest appreciation of her love – which allowed me to be – The Best That I Could Be – through the times of pain and the times of joy.

To Dutchess, whose abiding love held a family together and allowed us all to "survive."

To my kids and grandkids – Ruthie, Frank, Anthony, Lori, Peter, Stacey, Ross, Francesca, and Joseph, whose love and support makes life worthwhile and whose passion for family pets has served as a "shining star" to me – ever keeping me focused on the multifaceted benefits of the Human Animal Companion Bond

To my mother whose respect for all living things inspired in me a spirit of reverence for life.

To Maj-En, who joined the family three years ago and has eagerly joined us in putting his "paws on the path" to this profession.

To Joy, my seven year old kitty cat, who has not put her "paws on the path" to this profession but has, nonetheless, added a great dimension to my joy and happiness over the years, by her ability to make me laugh through the many hysterical places on which she poses and by her ability to calm me down as I watch her relaxing and simply enjoying life.

To Jewel, my year and half old Persian, who similarly enriches my life. She is an incredible purr-er through brushing, hugging, veterinary checks, and most especially when she sleeps on the shelf near my pillow at night.

To Panda Girl, the Great Pyrennes I always wanted, who is helping, along, with Maj-En, to carry on D. J.'s legacy.

To Vera Jeschke, whose relationship with D. J. was instrumental toward my understanding of the "power "of this career. Photo credit courtesy of the <u>Democrat and Chronicle</u>, Rochester, New York

To *LaVaune Hutchins*, for use of her mother, Vera's, photograph which appears on the cover of this book. LaVaune believes that her Mother and Dad would have loved this book and would thrill at the thought of the happiness that the reading of this book would bring to others.

TABLE OF CONTENTS

Chapter 5: Animals Helping Us Expand Our Horizons and Reach Our Potential

PART III: Ethics

Chapter 6: Ethical Issues in Pet Assisted Therapy

PREFACE

Jeff Bettger *has a Ph.D. in experimental psychology. As a researcher at the Salk Institute, he currently studies the acquisition of American Sign Language by children who are deaf. Dr. Bettger's academic career has been paralleled with a wide range of volunteer activities. Through these activities, he has learned that the human brain provides for life, but that the human heart provides for quality of life.*

Thomas M. Vallie *worked in mental health for twenty five years before retiring in 1992. At that time he was Chief of Children's Services at Rochester Psychiatric Center in Rochester, NY. He holds a Master's Degree in Rehabilitation Counseling. Now residing with his wife Elizabeth in Hendersonville, NC. Mr. Vallie is preparing to write on the effects of oppressive work situations on people.*

> *After reading any newspaper or watching any news program, it is abundantly clear that the world faces severe and widespread problems. Most of these problems can be directly attributed to human despair, loneliness, and hopelessness. We desperately need effective and far-reaching solutions. Pet Assisted Therapy holds great promise as being one such solution. Documented success stories with clients representing the full range of age, health, and environment clearly demonstrate the diverse applications of this unique therapeutic approach. Pet Assisted Therapy Facilitation goes far beyond merely soothing a problem's surface manifestations. Human/Animal contact in a structured program seems to rekindle the primal spark deep within us all, indicating that we are indeed ALIVE, IMPORTANT, and unconditionally LOVED!*

Dr. Jeff Bettger

Much has been said and written about the decline of positive values in our society. The essays that follow speak about a movement, which contradicts decline in its own quiet way, person and pet to person, on the frontlines of human care and compassion.

There are plenty of victims. When asked to explain the decline of cultural values, most people can offer only fragmentary ideas, blaming greed, breakup of families, global economics, drugs, pollution, or the loss of religious convictions. While most can't present a convincing explanation, any of us can point to the devastating effects of decline in the injured lives of real people we know.

Ours is a violent world where real and potential dangers seem to lurk on every side. The smallest child and the most senior of our neighbors are in jeopardy in a society that appears to have lost its ability to protect, nurture and preserve them.

By far, the worst hurts are not from physical assaults, environmental poisons or economic disasters. The more destructive forces attack the human spirit. To paraphrase Mother Teresa of Calcutta: Though there are many who suffer from physical illness, many more suffer from rejection, loneliness and the loss of human contact and respect. She is correct in saying that these conditions are more devastating because they attack the core of a person's being, value, and meaningful purpose in life. They occur, sadly, within families and among people who should provide nurture, but do not. The greatest suffering is to be without love.

Pet Assisted Therapy Facilitators (PATF) count themselves among a growing number of professionals and lay persons, paid and volunteer, who open doors closed by fear and pain. Pet Assisted Therapy is a fledgling profession, which will take its place in the healing and rehabilitative arts. It is founded on simple, human values and lessons learned from those who appreciate the worth of pets in the human experience.

To mention a few:

— The smallest kindness can awaken a heart turned cold by neglect or isolation
— Everyone needs understanding, compassion and recognition as a person of value
— Pets arouse positive memories and feelings in nearly everyone, even the most injured or withdrawn
— Compassion is nonviolent and in fact, contradicts violence and heals scars brought on by a violent world
— Pets are a bridge for many back to the human family and to human contact
— Animals can teach us all something about patience, about cheerful dependence, acceptance, obedience and persistent loyalty
— There is a place for every kind of help and care where injured, suffering or marginalized people are treated or nurtured.

The victims of cultural and social violence can be helped. Pet Assisted Therapy is one proven means by which basic human kindness, understanding and compassion can challenge cultural and social decline, one person at a time.

Pioneers like Pearl Salotto inspire us with a vision of a less violent world and awaken in us the importance of "little things" that turn out to be not so little, like the value of pets to the human spirit. Pet Assisted Therapy is becoming a vital partner in the habilitation and rehabilitation of injured people who await the human touch that comes by way of affectionate pets and their partners.

Thomas M. Vallie, MS

FOREWORD

Jerrold Tannenbaum is Professor in the Department of Population Health and Reproduction at the School of Veterinary Medicine, University of California at Davis. He teaches undergraduate and veterinary school courses in veterinary and animal law and ethics and lectures on various issues in ethics, law, and bioethics. The author of numerous papers on veterinary and animal law and ethics, he speaks frequently to veterinarians, veterinary students, scientists, and humane societies on ethical and legal issues relating to animals and veterinary practice. Mr. Tannenbaum is the author of Veterinary Ethics, a required text at veterinary schools in the United States and Canada.

Very few people are true pioneers. Very few books are truly indispensable. Pearl Salotto is a pioneer, and this is an indispensable book.

It may not be accurate to say that Pearl Salotto invented Pet Assisted Therapy – although she was among the handful of far-sighted people who were the first to make Pet Assisted Therapy a serious field. It may not be fair to say that Pearl Salotto was the first to appreciate the role a family pet can have in therapy work – although few have done more to promote this important part of the practice of Pet Assisted Therapy.

Pearl Salotto is an outspoken advocate for two things that are crucial to the development of Pet Assisted Therapy as an effective and essential health care intervention.. First, Pearl Salotto has been advocating for and teaching PAT within the university community for over a decade. She understood long ago that the information and techniques Pet Assisted Therapy Facilitators are developing are too important to be left to informal dissemination and anecdote. The facts must be selected, marshaled, and presented in a way that informs and inspires. There must be courses, and a curriculum, including lectures, readings, real examples, and practical experience. In this respect, Pet Assisted Therapy is no different from nursing or medicine. Pearl has never ceased to raise this call. Her current college course is among the models for Pet Assisted Therapy educators around the world. She has developed innovative curricula in Pet Assisted Therapy for high school and middle school students. Her D. J. "Respect for Living Things" Elementary School Program, as part of the school day, is unique primarily because of Pearl's ability to provide opportunities for the children to bond with D. J. and observe Pearl's relationship with D. J. as family. Pearl Salotto was among the first to make the call for the professionalization of Pet Assisted Therapy. Many people take their animals to health care facilities, and Pearl would be the first to applaud and encourage this. As time goes by, more academics are becoming interested in studying the psychological and health benefits of Pet Assisted Therapy, and Pearl would be the first to welcome this. However, for Pearl Salotto, Pet Assisted Therapy is a profession. It is her life's calling, as medicine is the life calling of the physician and healing animals the life calling of the veterinarian. Pearl understood long ago that if Pet Assisted Therapy is to fulfill its potential, it must have its own practitioners who are expert in its application. Pearl also understood that if Pet Assisted Therapy is to gain the confidence and cooperation of patients and the other health care professions – medicine, nursing, psychology, and social work – it too must be a profession. It must be practiced by people who gain expertise through a lifetime of observing, learning, and helping. Like other professions, it must train its own practitioners, hold them to the highest standards of competence, and imbue them with a distinctive and funda- mental set of values.

Pearl has set about making Pet Assisted Therapy into a true profession. She has practiced Pet Assisted Therapy tirelessly. She has promoted the benefits of Pet As- sisted Therapy to health care professionals and educators. She, along with others D. J. and this profession have inspired, have lobbied legislators and regulators to gain re- spect and protection for Pet Assisted Therapy and therapy animals. She has taught hundreds of students. She has served as a role model to others who want to make this unique healing art their life's calling. And she has produced this wonderful book.

Finally, with the publication of this book, along with the many other important books in this field, colleges and universities that want to teach Pet Assisted Therapy – and surely they should all want to teach it! – will be able to do so. The instructor and student will find a range of topics that cover the essentials and provide stimulus for further study. There is a useful selection of scientific studies that show the importance of empirical research to the field. There are superb discussions of Pet-Assisted Therapy directed at some of its most important beneficiaries: the elderly, adults and children with disabilities, patients at rehabilitation hospitals, and persons with emotional or mental challenges. The code of ethics for Pet Therapy, written by Pearl Salotto, is the most comprehensive proposed code available and can serve as a beginning for the consideration and adoption of an ethical code for this emerging profession. A signifi- cant portion of the book addresses the teaching of Pet Assisted Therapy, and provides guidance through first-hand accounts and sample curricula that can be put into place at the elementary, middle school, high school, and undergraduate level. There are also discussions of the broader role of Pet Assisted Therapy in promoting respect for all living things.

What makes this book so useful, so engaging, and so accessible to teachers, students, and practitioners of Pet Assisted Therapy is its wide range of authors. Social scientists, physicians, veterinarians, educators, students, animal owners, and those touched and inspired by assistance animals are represented here. The volume presents not just an overview of the field of Pet Assisted Therapy, but also a sense of the people who engage in and are affected by it. The truly human – and humane – soul of the field emerges from these pages.

To teachers who know in their hearts that Pet Assisted Therapy must be devel- oped and taught, I say use this book in your classes. To students who are thinking about working in the field, I say read this book and be inspired by it. To pet owners who are active or considering becoming active with their animals in therapy work, I say use this book as a guide. To health care professionals and educators, I say study this book and understand clearly its message: Pet Assisted Therapy is a unique and effective modality that can help and humanize all who are touched by it.

Also present in this book, and in Pearl Salotto's tireless work to develop her profession, are the animals that are the essence of Pet Assisted Therapy. In particular, the reader will learn about Pearl's beloved D. J. D. J. inspired Pearl to do her good work, helped her develop knowledge and techniques that are now firmly embedded in Pet Assisted Therapy, provided instruction and inspiration to Pearl's students and apprentices, accompanied Pearl in her therapy and educational sessions, and was a friend in good times and bad. Pearl believes that D. J. was meant to do these things. Anyone who has had the privilege and pleasure of knowing Pearl and seeing those she has helped knows this is so. D. J. now rests in peace, but her inspiration lives on in Pearl Salotto's work and in her therapy pets Maj-En and Panda Girl. D. J.'s legacy also lives on through the work and programs of those she touched. D. J. contributed mightily to the growing profession of Pet Assisted Therapy of which this book will be a part.

INTRODUCTION

I hope with the publication of this book – twelve years in the making – that the vision contained herein – the idea that animals and people together – via the profession of Pet Assisted Therapy – will help to bring about a friendlier, healthier, and more peaceful world – can move a little bit closer to reality.

I am confident that readers of *Loving Intervention*, will recognize that this powerful bond between pets and people, has the potential to impact in a positive way many of society's issues and problems, from depression to loneliness, from violence to substance abuse, from racism to suicide, from school violence to premature sexual involvement, from abuse of animals and children to recidivism in prisons.

Therefore, it is with great joy and with great humility, that I offer this edited treatise to college students and health care workers and educators, to criminologists and counselors to social scientists, ethicists, and advocates for children, animals, and individuals who are elderly, to service-learning teachers and society's leaders, as well as the general public, who wish to learn how professional PAT, at every level of society, can help move us closer toward our mutual goal of a more compassionate, caring, and respectful world.

Through discussion of the history and research in Part I of *Loving Intervention*, through the eloquent words of several dozen authors in Part II, demonstrating how PAT in a variety of settings and with a variety of animals, can enhance and change the lives of many, in a deep and profound way, that affects not only the individual and the pet, but families and society as well, and through Part III which offers suggested curriculum for all levels, protocol for PAT in treatment facilities, as well as an extensive section on ethics, (which combined with education provides a solid foundation for any profession) the reader will come to understand the potential impact of PAT in hospitals, nursing homes, and assisted-living settings, schools of all levels, hospice centers, shelters, prisons, as well as councils on drug and violence prevention, and governmental bodies, among others.

Readers will come away heartened and excited, if not surprised, that a wagging tail or a paw extended in friendship, can open up a child's heart, that a depressed or dependent person in a hospital can find a new lease in life, via a canine or feline friend, that a prisoner's years of anger and rage can be dissipated by a fish or a bird in his/her cell or that a policeman or counselor's knowledge of the link of abuse can help prevent further violence.

Much to my amazement, I too found out, not only that animals and people are good for each other, which I have always intuitively known (I had wanted, for example to be a trainer for seeing eye or hearing ear dogs), but that there was an emerging profession based on this concept, via a certificate program at Mercy College in New York, a first in the nation.

I found out about pets providing therapy for the first time when, incredibly, a relative stranger placed in my hand one day, while I was teaching school in the Bronx, a brochure describing such a program. This chance occurrence happened about the same time, the spring of 1986, when my children had just bought me, the gift of a lifetime, a thirteen week old Samoyed pup, Nafrostas Sweet D. J.

I didn't realize at the time, but she and I were about to embark on a path that not only changed our lives and the lives of many others, but also would result, twelve years later, in the publication of this book.

I had come from a family where I was raised by a mother who cherished every living thing from the snowflakes to the sunrise/sunset, from the birds to the flowers, from the tiniest caterpillar to a baby lion cub – that my sisters and I were privileged to touch in a life-changing moment, in a back room at the Lincoln Park Zoo, in Chicago.

At the time of being given the Mercy College PAT brochure and D. J. coming to our family, I was also attempting to break away from a marriage where our beloved pet Dutchess, had provided my three children and myself love, constancy, meaning, companionship, opportunities to nurture, run, play, and laugh in a family where one of the necessary pieces was missing – a loving father and husband.

Enrolling, that fall, in this four course certificate program, I experienced for the first time the incredibly powerful bond between people all ages who love animals. Additionally, in this program the respectful support of my professor, Dr. Steve Daniels, opened doors for me to gain the confidence to find my way with loving, but untrained, nine month old D. J. in mostly uncharted territory.

In Course I of this program, a whole new world was opened up for me, by reading Dr. Leo Bustad's "The Importance of Animals to the Well-Being of People," Jerry Tannenbaum's "The Human Companion Animal Bond: Cliché or Challenge?" and Phil Arkow's "Loving Bond." Maybe our world would be a better place, if these were required readings in all our high schools and universities.

In Course II, D. J. was evaluated by my professor, where I got my first glimpse into temperament testing. I sat in the back of the room as D. J. related lovingly to my professor, then a stranger to her, enjoying his grooming and petting. She responded appropriately by startling and then lovingly returning, when a loud noise was made by an assistant about twenty feet away. Similarly, when a cart was rolled in front of her, she looked and startled, but displayed no fear or aggression, and again was eager to return and relate lovingly to the professor. The temperament evaluation is intended to rule out the potential for aggressive behavior if there is an unexpected event or noise occurring in a facility. However, of course, we all recognize that temperament evaluation is an on-going process.

During this program, I also had the life-changing experience of witnessing, for the first time, D. J.'s spontaneous eagerness and joy in sharing her love with young and old, in class field trips to a nursing home and a residential treatment facility for teenagers. I will always remember a young lady at one of these facilities who, while hugging D. J., said "No one ever got to like me so fast" or the other young lady who literally jumped in the air, exclaiming "now I can go to bed happy." I also remember a lady at the nursing home who asked if D. J. was a guard dog and when I said no, she quickly responded "I knew that. She is a love dog" or another lady who asked me how often I bathe D. J. and when I said, "not very often," she said "I know you were only teasing me. I know you bathe her every day."

Through these early experiences, to our subsequent experiences over the last twelve years, in nursing homes and schools, D. J.'s love for people and their reactions back to her, has opened up for me, a great opportunity, my lifetime dream of wanting to help make the world a better place. Little did I realize then, that I was to not only work with D. J. in the field, but that I would become a strong national voice, raising the call, for the professionalization of PAT.

Both amazed and overwhelmed at the impact, of D. J.'s loving touch, at our first job in New York in 1988 and heartbroken by the plight of these individuals' loneliness, I slowly began to realize that I would devote the rest of my life to doing all in my power to seeing that every lonely individual, who could benefit from interacting with a loving animal, would have the opportunity to do so.

It became clear to me, coming from a family that placed a high value on education, that this interaction we call PAT, needed to develop from the previously voluntary effort – into a formal profession. This meant that universities across this land needed to educate enough PATs for every facility to have one on staff, working as part of the treatment team as do nurses, social workers, physical therapists, etc.

And thus the light that D. J. brought to patients' eyes and faces, also lit the way for me to help pioneer this "loving intervention" into a formal profession.

I realized that university programs needed to include a solid academic body of knowledge, through course work, as well extensive field experiences. As in other degree programs for various therapies, these two components provide an educational foundation for individuals to set up quality PAT programs, for the standardization of ethics and guidelines in the field, and for future licensure and credentialing.

The early years, with D. J., in which I saw, felt, learned, and recognized what I need to learn allowed me to develop a clear mission and philosophy. This personal experience with D. J. also gave me the background to work cooperatively with others, locally and nationally. I had developed a clear picture of my vision of this profession – which included three key aspects: a) the therapy pet must be family; b) the therapy pet's eagerness and well-being must be the foundation of any interaction; c) this field needs a strong educational component in order to develop as a profession. Numerous experiences that I had with D. J. allowed me to develop a state-of-the-art university curriculum. Thus, with D. J. as my inspiration and teacher, I gained the experience and the passion to inspire and teach others.

Through D. J.'s example I came to define PAT as – the sharing the love of our family therapy pets with those in need of a loving touch, in an interaction in which both the client, the therapy pet and society benefit. Through D. J.'s example, I was able to experience a profile of a true therapy pet. Additionally, my love for D. J. allowed me to realize the need for safeguards in the field, for I would not allow her to get hurt. So – experiencing PAT with D. J. – defined the field for me and allowed me to realize what PAT is and should be. Through working with D. J., it also became clear to me that it is the loving bond between the therapy pet and the PATF, which not only assures the ethics in the field, but the connection from which the magic of this profession springs, because the sharing and trust between the client and the facilitator is grounded in their common love for the pet.

D. J. not only inspired me to develop my philosophy and mission, but she taught me many practical things that I needed to learn to work effectively as a PATF and to teach others. For example, when D. J. spontaneously jumped on a chair one day to get closer to a client, I realized that clients did not need a pet sitting in their lap in order to relate. I learned that PATFs can never be distracted, even momentarily, because you may find your pet licking medication off a client's hand. I learned that the bond between D. J. and myself allowed patients to more easily trust me. I learned the need for understanding what diseases (zoonotic) could be passed between clients and therapy pets. I discovered the limitless love of therapy pets who never turn their back on anyone and their amazing flexibility in their eagerness to relate anywhere – in hospitals or churches, in classrooms or statehouses, in school hallways or TV stations, in parking lots or elevators, on therapy mats or chairs or patient beds. I found that the bond between patient and client must be maintained by regular visits, if at all possible, and yet, that a single positive interaction can be life changing. I found out that I need to know the patient before the interaction starts (functioning level, interests, talents, needs). I found out that I needed to understand medical terminology and how to write treatment plans. I learned the endless myriad of benefits that can accrue from therapy interactions. I learned the need for time limits and the need to have alternative activities available if the pet is tired. I recognized the need for good judgment and that a PATF needs enough confidence not to be embarrassed if schedules have to be changed, due to the needs of their therapy pet. I learned that work can be fun, as well as meaningful. I learned the indescribable joy that a therapy pet feels when anticipating going to work, as evidenced by D. J.'s squeals of joy as we approached familiar facilities. There were occasions when the volume of D. J.'s eager howls even kept me from getting lost. I learned, most of all, that every institution needed PAT. I learned that in this 'rush-rush' world of deadlines and timecards, Pet Assisted Therapy Facilitators must take the time to thank and appreciate, pet and play with, their beloved therapy pet after leaving a hospital or school, before they head off to the next obligation, never taking their pet for granted.

My feelings for D. J., born on my birthday and meant to go down in history, are beyond my facility with words to describe. The highest compliment I can give anyone, is that I feel toward them, like I do toward D. J.

D. J. has shown me the way in this profession. My feelings go deeper than love and deeper than bonding.

Before I got D. J., I read in a Samoyed book that – "To a Samoyed, every day is Christmas." What the author

*did not say was that the love of life that Samoyeds have
– is contagious – and has allowed me to feel that everyday is Christmas, as well.*

Our working in teamship makes this profession a great gift. Our sharing of souls makes life worthwhile.

As I look upon D. J. with enhanced, enriched, and expanded appreciation with each passing day, the words of Dolly Parton's beautiful song sings through my heart today and forever – "The Sweetest Thing I've Ever Known Is Loving You."

In addition to what I learned from D. J., the interactions between D. J. and my grandchildren, as they grew up together, have provided an unique and special dimension from which my appreciation for the impact of pets in the family grew and blossomed. From Stacey at one year old, circling through the kitchen into the dining room, living room, and back, time and again, just learning to walk with D. J. following her, ever so carefully, intuitively knowing that she was unsteady on her feet, to Ross putting a pillow on the floor for D. J. and another one for himself, and wouldn't you know it, growing up into a boy who cherishes and has time for each and every living thing he encounters, to Frankie's joy, appreciation, and understanding in her eyes as she, D. J. and I sat on the floor together, as she observed my joy as D. J. was giving me her paw time and again. Could this have contributed to the development of empathy in this one year old? The list of interactions spans D. J.'s lifetime, with countless walks, dog training classes, and simply enjoying quality family time together, precious moments – life affirming interactions of tenderness, fun, sacrifice, sharing, and learning between my grandchildren and D. J., not only was good for each of them – but allowed me to realize, through watching those I love – love each other – what the real potential of this field is all about.

Ross with Panda Girl - Love at Grandma's house.

In addition to what I learned from D. J. in the field and from my grandchildren's interactions with D. J., my mosaic of experiences was rounded out by my attending my first of many Delta Society National Conferences in 1987, where, lucky for our readers, I befriended many leaders in the field. These individuals not only inspired me, by being giants in the field, but also by their willingness to talk with, listen to, and teach newcomers in the field, including myself. I continue to be inspired and humbled by my friends and colleagues in this field (many of whom are authors in this book) who continue to devote their lives to working toward a better world for all living things.

And for the authors who are no longer with us – Dr. Leo Bustad and Dr. Cathy Bontke – I know that their work and their love for people and animals will shine on, in the hearts of those they touched, including, through their words in this book.

Readers of this book may be inspired to join with the authors of *Loving Intervention* to help take this profession to the next level. Readers, I trust, will recognize that this field will help professionals, whether or not they like animals, to understand the impact of animals on the clients with whom they work. For example, if a physical therapist cannot motivate a patient to walk or stretch an arm, maybe a pet can. If a mental health professional cannot motivate an individual to come to a counseling session, perhaps a pet in the office might. If a nurse encounters a patient in a hospital concerned about a pet at home or who wants their pet to visit with the rest of their family, perhaps this nurse will have a new awareness of the healing potential of such interaction. If a service-learning teacher is looking for opportunities in which students can truly make a difference, to their community and themselves, perhaps they will consider including PAT in their school curriculum. If an Empathy Building Task Force includes a PATF then, perhaps the final document could include childrens' relating to pets as one method of building empathy. If city/state governments had an annual D.J. Respect for Living Things Day, all citizens might grow in their respect and commitment to people and animals. If Health Departments across this land issued guidelines on PAT, countless individuals in nursing homes and hospitals would benefit. If a policeman recognizes that a child's life is in danger, as well as the pets, if there is abuse to either in the family, perhaps lives can be saved. If educators at all levels recognize that students who learn respect for animals will be more committed in all their relationships over a life-time, then indeed, maybe we will come a little closer to that peaceful world we all want.

Linda Jones with Maj-En - When D.J. and Maj-En entered my classroom for the first time; I did not realize what a magical door had opened. As the Service Learning Teacher and Coordinator, I was always seeking projects/programs to integrate into the curriculum. PAT became a unique and innovative program, which connected perfectly with high academic standards, as well as the New Standards from the National Center on Education and the Economy (NCEE).

In addition to our readers being inspired by our authors, as I have, I am sure they will also be inspired, as I am, by the ever flowing love, of not only D. J., but other therapy pets, including those who are no longer with us (including Jingles, Holly, Jake, Jetta, Cuddles, Sabrina, Clover, Tiffany, and Patterson), all of whom, not only heal, and help, and teach, but inspire us to be better people.

As Dr. Gus Thorton so eloquently stated, as he placed the medallion on D. J.'s neck, for winning the first Rhode Island Veterinary Medical Association Animal Hall of Fame Award: "In a world increasingly overwhelmed by violence, it is important to honor the animals who work so hard to try to make us better humans."

D.J. sitting proudly between Dr. Mary Coffee, Pearl, and Dr. Gus Thorton, (who presented the medallion to her) at the Double Tree Hotel in Newport, Rhode Island, after receiving the first annual Rhode Island Veterinary Medical Association (RIVMA) Companion Animal Hall of Fame Award in December of 1995. Courtesy of RIVMA

As my experiences have grown, so has my vision of the many possibilities of pets in our lives and of this profession. When I entered the field in 1987, I thought of PAT as a form of treatment in hospitals, nursing homes, agencies, and prisons. My realization of the much broader potential of this field has grown and is growing, with each passing day and with each new interaction. I now realize the overwhelming power of animals in our lives – in our families, schools, neighborhoods, and communities – which can definitely lead to a friendlier, healthier, and more peaceful world.

I now realize that one of the benefits is that relating to animals is a "leveling" experience – an experience of a gentler world, without hierarchies, wherein each of us – professionals or patients, parents or strangers, children or adults – can find a renewed recognition of each other's humanity – in our common love for our pets. For this reason alone, PAT should be taught at all educational levels. The eye-opening example of unconditional love that our therapy pets set, and allow us to experience with each other, can help all of our future citizens and leaders recognize – our common bond of humanity. This experience, this powerful connection over animals, can also turn strangers and even enemies into friends, with a new found connection over a mutual appreciation of a pet.

In order for the potential for pets in our lives to be realized and maximized, the profession of PAT needs to take a firm hold in universities across this land and to organize in order to self-regulate and set standards. The readers having experienced, through the following words and articles in this book, how D. J.'s and the other therapy pet's loving presence and positive affect in so many lives and the amazing variety and breadth of the good that has come, can only imagine the potential that would occur when the presence of therapy pets and their professional PATFs with whom they work, becomes fully accepted. Therefore, for all the good that PAT has done and will do and all the tragedies it will prevent, I offer *Loving Intervention* to those who wish to share this dream of a better world for people and animals via the profession of PAT and who will in turn, take up the call, enriching the lives of those with whom they come in contact, while at the same time helping to pass on this good work to the next generation, through their teaching, inspiring, envisioning, writing, and living. To this end I share my love for my pets, my vision of this profession and my life's work.

ACKNOWLEDGMENTS

If anyone has ever embarked on a new path in life, one with a potential for tremendous meaning, but also with many obstacles – the greatest gift that one could receive for their journey would be a "true friend," who stands firmly at one's side, through the good times and bad, always ready to listen, to suggest and to help and most importantly to support and validate. Such a true friend has been, and is, my daughter-in-law Lori. I fear that this book would not have been published if it had not been for Lori. From the first days in 1993, when I literally spread out hundreds of scribbled notes on her living room floor until the present time, as we are nearing the final stages before publication (9 years later) she has always been there listening, typing, retyping, editing, and reediting patiently.

Lori with D.J. - D.J. thanks you and so do I! Photo credit: Anthony Salotto

Love and appreciation also to my son Anthony for his support of my profession, from his first adorable smile when he saw my business card (Wags to Smiles) to the many photographs he has taken of my grandchildren with D. J. – from the many drives to and from airports as I went to many conferences (including his overnight stay with D. J. as I was snowbound at the Character Education conference in Washington), to the many trips to my house to go walking in the woods with my grandchildren and my pets and taking Stacey and Ross, with Maj-En, to puppy kindergarten and puppy gymnastics. And topping it off, with a gift of a lifetime – getting D. J., Maj-En and professional PAT on the Internet.

Love and appreciation also to my daughter Ruthie for being the person she is. Ruthie has always been there for me, caring about what I care about, from the first heartwarming note that I found waiting for me at home when I first brought home my thirteen week old puppy, D. J., until today, she has always cared about and put herself on the line for my pets and my profession. Through all her words and deeds and in all of her life's choices and interactions, she continues to pass on family values to her daughter Frankie and son Joseph, simply by living life with respect and kindness to others.

Love and appreciation to my youngest son Peter whose lifelong tenderness toward animals holds up a vision in which all living things are respected and whose interest in helping animals, including injured wild animals, personalized for me, the need for all universities to offer such educational opportunities for students in search of a meaningful career.

Love and appreciation to my grandchildren – Stacey, Ross, Frankie, and Joseph – who have enjoyed my pets, learned from my pets, played with my pets, helped train my pets, and participated in numerous activities surrounding my pets and profession, including videos, TV shoots, and statewide seminars. They have tremendously enhanced the lives of my pets by participating in numerous family interactions with them over many years. Most of all, I have learned the need for children to have meaningful interactions with animals, as I have observed through the years my grandchildren's interactions with my pets.

I also wish to acknowledge my heartfelt appreciation to all of the authors of this book, and to the therapy pets described herein, as well as to other friends and colleagues in the field, including: Sue Arruda, Sheri Bernard, Henry Boezi, Richard Bolig, Salty Brine, Ginny Campbell, Gerry Capitisto, Dr. Mary Coffee, Dave Colletti, Penni Cooke, Sue Corr, Betsy Dennigan, Denise and John DeSanty, Wayne Farrington, Mary Ionata, Judy Johns, Paul T. Jones, Jr., Dr. Josephine Kellerher, Marilyn Larkins, Judge Howard Lipsey, Donna Mangiante, Ann Marie Musiol, Slyvia Natalie, Carol Noonan, Gilberto Norbrega, Ann O'Kleasky, Mario Papito, Dr. Americo Petrocelli, Gail and Tom Richardson, Barbara Rockerfeller, Paul Sherlock, Jerry Tannenbaum, Hugh Tebeault, Priscilla Trudeau, Tony Vasquez, Nancy and Bob Whitcomb, Helene and Bill White, and Ken White. There are numerous other individuals who have been touched by D. J. and have supported this profession for whom I will be eternally grateful. These include people whose names I never knew, but whose impact I carry today, such as the secretary on the phone who said, "keep on doing what you are doing. Keep on making people happy."

Heartfelt appreciation to all who helped in some point in the proofreading of this book: Lori, Cathy Saideman, Tom Vallie, Hugh Tebeault, Gina Santoro, and Karen Trouve. I also wish to acknowledge M. J. Munro for compiling the index.

PART I

THEORY OF PET ASSISTED THERAPY

CHAPTER 1

THE HISTORY OF PET ASSISTED THERAPY
(Pearl Salotto)

Pearl Salotto

Loving relationships between people and animals have been taking place throughout history and the effects of this relationship are continually reflected in every aspect of our culture. Documented evidence of this relationship dates back at least 12,000 years, to an archeological find in Northern Israel, of a human skeleton clutching a puppy.[1]

It was not until 1790, however, that evidence of animals working as therapy facilitators was recorded at the York Retreat, founded by William Tuke and the Society of Friends in England. Individuals with mental illness were treated, not with punitive measures, but with kindness. This program became a forerunner of compassionate care and positive reinforcement for individuals with metal illness. It was found that relating to small animals, as well as tending gardens, helped patients gain a sense of well-being and, therefore, control.[2]

In 1867, a treatment facility for individuals with epilepsy, Bethel, opened in Bielefeld, West Germany. Bethel eventually expanded to serve individuals with a variety of health conditions. It is still in existence today serving thousands of patients. Therapeutic horseback riding, a wild game park and farm animals are an integral part of the healing process at this treatment facility. The Bielefeld philosophy is one of community where patients, staff, and animals (dogs, cats and birds) live together. Dr. Leo Bustad, an early pioneer in people-pet relationships, stated that visiting Bethel was among the most remarkable experiences in his life.[3]

Recognition of society's need to protect animals emerged from a series of social justice reform movements in the U.S. and Europe during the Victorian era, along with the recognition of the need to protect women, children, inmates and debtors. In 1822, the Royal Society for the Prevention of Cruelty to Animals (SPCA) was founded in England. Similar organizations soon followed in Germany, France, Norway and Russia. In 1866, the American SPCA was founded in New York. In 1886, George Angell started the Massachusetts SPCA pioneering the idea that humane education might be the long-range solution to better treatment of animals. In 1889, the American Humane Association (AHA) was founded to protect children and animals. Subsequently, a group broke off from the AHA and became the Humane Society of the United States (HSUS).

In 1918, Edith and Milton Latham started the Latham Foundation with the mission to promote, foster, encourage, and further the principles of humaneness, kindness, and benevolence to all living creatures." (Latham Letter, Winter 1998) Edith and Milton had grown up in a compassionate and educated family. While they had many luxuries as children, their greatest "treasures" were their cats, dogs, and horses. They were outraged at the treatment of animals in their society and felt that the way to a better world for all living things was through educating children. Over the next 30 years, Edith tried through a variety of ways to reach children, including Kindness Clubs and

---

[1] Cusak, Odean, & Smith, Elaine (1984). *Pets and the Elderly, The Therapeutic Bond* (2). New York: Hayworth Press.

[2] Arkow, Phil (1993). *"Pet Therapy": A Study and Resource Guide for the Use of Companion Animals in Selected Therapies* (7th ed.). Stratford, New Jersey: published by author: 37 Hillside Rd., Stratford, NJ 08084.

[3] Cusak & Smith, pp.2.

Essay Contests, through the Brother Buzz talk show and Withit television series, and through connecting with children's authors, including Gwyn Tebault. A newsletter, the "Latham Letter", and numerous other humane materials, particularly films and videos, have had and continue to have a significant and powerful effect on society. Latham continues, under the able and loving leadership of Hugh Tebault, to live up to its mission of "promoting respect for all life through education."[4]

In the early fifties, what one might call 'the birth of pet therapy' took place in the office of New York psychologist, Dr. Boris Levinson. A troubled young teen, who had up to this point been totally non-communicative, happened to come into Dr. Levinson's waiting room early. He sat down on the floor next to Dr. Levinson's loving dog, Jingles, and poured his heart out. As the amazed doctor entered the room and joined the young teen and dog on the floor, healing finally began. The kernel of an idea, that pets can "heal," came to the doctor.[5] This idea would later be tried successfully with other patients. Dr. Levinson wrote two historic books, "Pets and Child Development" and "Pet-Oriented Psychotherapy." He also shared his findings at psychiatric conferences. Jingles not only "opened pathways" into the hearts and minds of disturbed youngsters, but also into the human service profession.

Another significant development in the field occurred in the 1970's, when two brothers who adored and respected each other, raised their voices on behalf of people-pet relations. A young veterinarian, Dr. Bill McCulloch had read Dr. Levinson's work and approached his professor, Dr. Robert Anderson (of the School of Public Health at the University of Michigan), with his interest in the Human Companion Animal Bond (HCAB). It had become clear to him that the health of one's pet was a major public health issue. As pets are part of the family, their well-being or lack of it, has a huge effect on people's quality of life. He realized that veterinarians had a responsibility to the owners of pets, as well as to the pets. He felt that a veterinarian's compassion to the owner is a critical component of veterinary care. With his brother, Dr. Michael McCulloch, a psychiatrist in Portland, Oregon, a unique link was born, tying human mental and physical health to veterinary medicine. Mike McCulloch began to "prescribe" pets for his patients and in the few short years, until his tragic death, he left a great legacy for society. He saw pets as helping to fulfill the Hippocratic Oath - "Heal when possible - Comfort always." (L. Bustad and A. Katcher et. al., personal communication at the Delta Society Conference, 1987)

During roughly the same time period from 1975-85, Dr. Leo Bustad, Dean Emeritus of the College of Veterinary Medicine at Washington State University, became a leading voice for compassion, reverence for life and promotion of people-pet relationships. He developed and taught a course on Reverence for Life at the Washington State University College of Veterinary Medicine in Pullman, Washington. He also developed guidelines for the "Bustad Buddies" Animal Assisted Therapy program at Pullman Memorial Hospital. He has traveled the world speaking on behalf of the HCAB and his People Pet Partnership Program. This PPP program led to the development of several groundbreaking therapy programs in schools, hospitals and prisons. He was

---

[4] Evans, Elliot (Winter 1993). A Historic Perspective - The Early Years. *The Latham Letter*. 14 (1), cover, 4.
[5] Cusak & Smith, pp. 3.

also influential in starting the Pet Assisted Therapy program at Tacoma Lutheran Nursing Home in Washington, which is known for being the first in the country to have a staff person responsible for the facilitation of Pet Assisted Therapy. Dr. Bustad has written numerous books and articles, as well as, mentored and befriended many starting in the field. (L. Bustad and A. Katcher et. al., personal communication at the Delta Society Conference, 1987)

Meanwhile, Drs. Elizabeth and Sam Corson, of Ohio State University, had met Dr. Leo Bustad and others at conferences dating back to the 1979 *Pets and Society* conference in Vancouver, Canada. The Corsons had also read Dr. Levinson's work and they "rather accidentally" saw first hand the powerful and positive connections between animals and people. They had been working with patients who had been non-communicative and bedridden for years. These individuals had been unresponsive to traditional therapies. When some of these patients heard dogs barking, who were living on another floor of the building as part of a research project, they asked to see them. After much thought, the Corsons carefully designed a therapy program with the dogs. Nearly all the patients, who participated in the program, were transformed and were subsequently discharged. The Corsons felt that the impressive results were due to the fact that the dogs had become friends of the patients, without judging or criticizing them. The dogs had been able to serve as "loving links" for those individuals who had previously lost their desire and/or ability to interact with people.[6]

Meanwhile, psychiatrist Dr. Aaron Katcher, of the University of Pennsylvania at Philadelphia, along with his graduate student, Erika Friedmann and others, demonstrated, through their historic research in 1977, that interacting with a pet lowers the person's blood pressure, whereas interacting with a person, even in one's own family, raises it. In another historic research project, Dr. Katcher and his team demonstrated that individuals suffering from a severe heart attack (myocardial infarction) who had a pet waiting for them at home upon their release, were three times more likely to be alive the following year - compared to those who went home to only family members of the human variety. The researchers were so surprised that they re-did the research and again found - that the pet was the significant variable.[7]

In the 1970's, the Center to Study Human-Animal Relationships and Environments (Censhare) was founded at the University of Minnesota to take a multidisciplinary look at relationships between animals and people. Centers to study people-pet relationships sprung up at several locations around the country. Among these were the University of Pennsylvania at Philadelphia, directed by Dr. Aaron Katcher and Alan Beck, an ongoing voice in the call for scientific inquiry into the field of HCAB. Other centers were located at UCLA-Davis, directed by Lynette Hart and at Tufts University Veterinary School - The Center for Animals and Public Policy directed by Dr. Andrew Rowan.

This Human-Animal Companion bond is eloquently described by Jerry Tannenbaum, Esq., past professor of Ethics at Tufts University Veterinary School. In his article, *The Human/Companion Animal Bond: Cliché or Challenge?,* he describes

---

[6] Cusak & Smith, pp. 3.
[7] Delta Society Conferences (1987-1992). Information received at a variety of conferences.

the HCAB as a voluntary, mutual and on-going relationship between an animal and a person which is a central priority in each of their lives.[8]

Another early pioneer in PAT was David Lee, a social worker at Lima State Hospital in Ohio for prisoners with mental illnesses. He allowed some of these individuals to tend to a wounded bird, and discovered that previously violent, depressed and suicidal inmates suddenly began to cooperate and work together, finding new meaning in life. His much expanded program of today has been regularly evaluated by humane groups, which have found that the animals enjoy a loving home at Lima, and help the prisoners as well. (Conversations with Leo Bustad, Aaron Katcher and others at The Delta Society Conference in 1987.[9])

Another significant step occurred when Dr. Lynn Anderson became the HCAB specialist for the U.S. Army. He was cognizant of the importance of pets in the family and took this into account when families were transferred. He also attempted to start a Pet Assisted Therapy program at Brooke Army Medical Center. On one occasion he brought comfort to a little girl with cancer by bringing her puppy to her hospital room. This child, who had not smiled, laughed or spoken in months, immediately brightened.[10]

Linda Tellington-Jones, a pioneer in understanding and communicating with animals, has raised all of our horizons, through her Tellington TTouch. This enables the HACB to be enhanced, through quality time spent on the pet's emotional and physical well-being. As a result of this closer and "healthier" relationship between the facilitator and his/her therapy pet, they are able to work more effectively in teamship. She has traveled the world to bring positive change to animals, both family pets and wild animals, who are sick, depressed, aggressive, and injured.[11]

Phil Arkow, as Director of the Pikes Peak Humane Society in the 1970's, was one of the first to develop a "Petmobile" to enrich the lives of individuals in nursing homes. He wrote two books which greatly enhanced the development of PAT: "The Loving Bond" and "Pet Therapy: A Study and Resource Guide for the Use of Companion Animals in Selected Therapies." Mr. Arkow continues his positive influence in the field and is today the national chairperson for the Latham Foundation's Committee on the Prevention of Child and Animal Abuse.[12]

In the late 1970's Dr. Bustad, both Drs. McCulloch and Dr. Katcher, formed the Delta Group as a subgroup of the Latham Foundation, according to Hugh Tebault, Sr. This group eventually became an independent organization in 1980 calling themselves the Delta Society, with Dr. Bustad as its first president. Their mission is "to promote animals helping people improve their health, independence, and quality of life." (Delta's newsletter *Interactions*, 1997) The Delta Society gathered a huge library of resources

---

[8] Tannenbaum, Jerrold, M.A., J.D. (1995). *Veterinary Ethics: Animal Welfare, Client Relations, Competition and Collegiality*, (2nd ed.). St. Louis: Mosby Yearbook Inc.

[9] Delta Resource Packet on Pet Therapy in Prisoners.

[10] Delta Society (mid 1980s). Pets and Our Health [Video]. (Available from the Delta Society, 289 Perimeter Road East, Renton, WA 98055-1329 or deltasociety.org.)

[11] Tellington-Jones, Linda, & Taylor, Sybil, (1995). *The Tellington TTouch*. New York: Penguin Books.

[12] Arkow, pp. 12.

on the HCAB, publishes a quarterly newsletter called *Interactions* and a scientific journal called *Anthrozoos*. Delta holds annual national conferences to provide opportunities for people committed to the human-companion animal bond to gather, network, share, and learn. A highlight of these national conferences was The "Jingles" Awards. These awards were given to those special therapy and service animals who have helped spread the magic of this profession as surely as Jingles infused young hearts with love and hope. Delta also belongs to the International Association of Human Animal Interaction Organizations which holds periodic international conferences on the HCAB. [13]

Early educational initiatives in PAT on university campuses came from Linda Case as she taught a course to nurses at Mennonite College in Illinois on the HCAB. Additionally, several PATF certificate programs at universities were developed. The first certificate program was developed by Dr. Steve Daniel, Dr. Jack Burke, and his wife Jean in 1980 at Mercy College in Dobbs Ferry, New York, which made history when it was approved for college credit by the New York State Education Department. In 1990, Pearl Salotto developed a certificate program at the State University of New York at Brockport College in their department of Continuing Education. She now teaches her program, The D. J. Pet Assisted Therapy University Certificate Program, in Rhode Island. Recently several other certificate programs have been started. In 1995 Dr. Aaron Katcher started a certificate program at Harkum College in Bryn Mawr, Pennsylvania, and in 1996 Phil Arkow did likewise at Camden Community College in Camden, New Jersey.

In addition to certificate programs, organizations, and conferences there are ongoing research projects in the field. Recent research studies have substantiated the positive relationship between animals and pets. A study conducted in 1990 by Judy Siegel, published in the *Journal of Personality and Social Psychology*, showed that pet owners go to doctors less often. A 1991 study by Cindy Wilson, published in the *Journal of Nervous and Mental Disease*, indicated that pets alleviate anxiety and have a relaxing effect on college students. James Serpell also, in a 1991 study, reported that dog owners experience fewer minor health problems. Warwick A. Anderson's 1992 Australian study on survival after cardiovascular disease provided additional documentation confirming the health benefits of pets. In Karen Allen's 1994 research article, entitled *The Value of Service Dogs for People With Severe Ambulatory Disabilities,* she documented that service dogs not only enhance quality of life, independence and community involvement on the part of individuals with disabilities, but are cost effective as well, by cutting down significantly on the hours that these individuals need patient care. Recent research (1995), *Pet Ownership, Social Support, and One Year Survival After Acute Myocardial Infarction in the Cardiac Arrhythmia Suppression Trial (CAST),* by Erica Friedmann Ph.D., and Sue A. Thomas, RN, states that "The current study provides strong evidence that pet ownership, and dog ownership in particular, promotes cardiovascular health independent of social support and the physiologic severity of the illness."

Also, in recent years - the Latham Foundation, HSUS, and AHS have published

---

[13] Delta Society Conferences (1987-1992). Information received at a variety of conferences.

research on the link of abuse between animals and people. Several states have run conferences to educate professionals about this tragic connection, including a 1995 conference in Rhode Island, "From the Tangled Threads of Violence Weave a Silver Web of Hope." This conference focused on the positive side of people-pet connections (Pet Assisted Therapy), in addition to the tragic link of abuse. As an outgrowth of this conference, the Windwalker Humane Coalition for Professional Pet Assisted Therapy was established. One of Windwalker's major accomplishments has been facilitating the introduction of legislation in 1997 leading to the establishment of an official state-wide commission to study this link of abuse. In 2000 Windwalker successfully facili- tated the passage of legislation giving therapy pets the same rights as service dogs. In 2001 Windwalker teamed up with Feinstein High School for Public Service to suc- cessfully pass legislation in which Rhode Island became the first state to include guard- ian, along with owner, in all state regulations regarding companion animals. Another significant accomplishment of the Windwalker Humane Coalition has been the facili- tation of a study group at the Rhode Island Department of Health. This led to the dissemination, to all of it licensees, of guidelines on professional PAT, voluntary PAT, resident pets and family pet visits. Windwalker is also known for its annual D.J. Re- spect for Living Things Day, as well as standards for credentialling in PPAT.

It is to be hoped that by the time further books on PATF are published, the field will have developed to the point where PAT will be widely recognized as a legitimate, reputable therapy eligible for third-party reimbursement from the insurance field, as with other forms of human service. As Dr. Andrew Rowan semi-humorously stated in his editorial, *The Health Benefits of Human-Animal Interactions,* published in Anthrozoos, "The strong indications of benefits to individuals provided by Friedmann, et al (1980) and Anderson, et al (1992) would have generated enormous research inter- est if the intervention (pet ownership) could have been patented and sold as a drug." Hopefully, this book will help society to see that this loving living intervention, while not a pill or capsule, is a valid and powerful form of treatment that requires us all to sit up and take notice.

CHAPTER 2

SCIENTIFIC RESEARCH IN PET ASSISTED THERAPY

Section 1:
THE EFFECTS OF A CANINE CO-THERAPIST ON INDIVIDUAL THERAPY SESSIONS WITH ELEMENTARY SCHOOL CHILDREN WITH SBH (SEVERE BEHAVIORALLY HANDICAPPED)

<u>Barbara J. Wood</u>, Ph.D., A.C.S.W., L.I.S.W., is an Associate Professor of Social Work. She started work with her pet dog, Holly, as a therapeutic bridge with emotionally disturbed, inner-city children, over ten years ago. She lives with her husband, pet dog Holly, two cats and a Quarter Horse mare, in Columbus, Ohio.

The beneficial therapeutic effect of companion animals on residential populations has received increasing popular and academic attention. The foundation for this work was laid by Levinson and Jingles (Levinson, 1969) to the work of Samuel and Elizabeth Corson (Corson, 1980). Corson described the improved communications and behavior of children/patients facilitated by a canine co-therapist. The question that intrigued me was whether a canine co-therapist would have similar beneficial effects on emotionally disturbed children in a public school setting.

Initial interest and support for a pilot project was positive and enthusiastic. Consequently a formal proposal, which included faculty, staff and student interest, the teachers union sanction and a veterinarian's certification of good health and temperament, along with parental permission slips for the students, was submitted to the school administration. It was approved for the second semester.

Dogs were domesticated about 12,000 years ago and currently in the United States there are about one hundred million cats and dogs. Sixty percent of American households have pets. Households with pets are mostly the households that have children. Thirty six percent of U.S. homes have children and thirty seven percent have dogs. Clearly human-animal bonding has been going on for thousands of years (the beneficial effect was noted by the Greeks and Romans) and is currently a significant element in American life. However, serious consideration of this phenomenon received little attention, except for some isolated institutional settings until after World War II.

Boris M. Levinson, a psychologist, "discovered the value of using a dog in therapy sessions with a disturbed child. Levinson's dog, Jingles, was with him when a child and his mother arrived early for their appointment. In prior sessions, the child remained nonverbal; thus, the child's response to Jingles caused Levinson to recognize the possible benefit of using a dog as a communication link between therapist and child."

Previous findings include:

1. The presence of animals lowers blood pressure and reduces stress.
2. The presence of animals penetrates the isolation of autistic children and for many children is the only contact left with nature in urbanized America.

3. Pets draw out the nurturing and emotional side of men.

4. Those who had a good relationship with pets empathized more with other people than children who had not.

5. Children with pets are less aggressive with their peers than are children who do not have pets.

6. Troubled teenagers are more likely to open up when a therapist brings a dog along. "Patients sometimes express their feelings through the animal. They'll say, 'Your dog looks pretty sad' meaning 'I'm pretty sad.'"

Success with other populations and in other settings has been reported. Would Pet Facilitated Therapy work with a SBH public school population where the therapy sessions took place in the school during regular school hours?

Methodology:

Most human-animal bonding therapies used in institutional settings obtained animals through their local Humane Society. This procedure had several drawbacks for the school setting. The temperament of such animals is not well known and consistent care for the animal is problematic over evenings, weekends and vacations. Consequently, I proposed that the animal to be used be a dog that was privately owned.

The dog is a brown, short-haired, mixed breed, spayed female. "Holly" is seven years old, weighs twenty pounds, is of even temperament and was examined by a veterinarian. Since Holly already had a permanent home, the problem of consistent care was solved and if the project was terminated she could readily retire to her previous position as my house pet.

Location:

The SBH (Severe Behaviorally Handicap) students in this study were all inner city youths who attended a public elementary school (grades one through seven), which serves SBH students exclusively and is located in a large (approximately 70,000 pupils), urban school system in central Ohio. The once weekly therapy sessions took place in the school during regular school hours. A small classroom had been set aside for the counseling room, and for each session Holly was present during the class period.

Subjects:

There are very few girls referred to the SBH school. Also, there were more students in the initial counseled and non-counseled match group. However, some students moved out of the district, some left the school program due to changes in custody, and some returned to regular school during the academic year. Consequently, the fourteen students that remained in the final research study were all male and attended the SBH school the entire academic year.

Seven students, who had been recommended by the teachers for therapy, were matched with seven students (also selected by teachers) who did not receive therapy.

The match group was chosen to be the equivalent of the therapy group on age, race, sex and functional level. Four of the therapy and match group were African American and three each were Caucasian. There was no greater variance in age between the groups than three months. The functional levels were within standard deviation parameters. The counseled group received therapy without Holly the first semester and with Holly the second semester. The match group received no therapy with or without Holly the first and second semester during the academic year.

Instrumentation:

The SBH school focuses on improved school behavior and has a behavioral modification approach to achieve this goal. Consequently the entire SBH school program is a type of treatment milieu compared to a regular school. The school measures behavior using the BES (Behavior Evaluation Scale). Some referring schools may use other behavior standardized measurements.

The Behavior Evaluation Scale (BES) was specifically developed to aid in the decision-making and programming "for children and adolescents with behavior disorders/emotional disturbances." (Behavior Evaluation Scale, p. 2, 1983). Of the six primary purposes of the BES, two are "to document progress resulting from intervention, and to collect data for research purposes." The BES is designed for use with students at all grade levels (K-12) and was standardized on data collected from ten states, one of which was Ohio. The BES has fifty two items which are divided into five subscales dealing with an inability to learn, unsatisfactory interpersonal relations, inappropriate types of behavior or feelings, pervasive mood of unhappiness or depression, and physical symptoms or fears associated with personal or school problems. A Behavior Quotient, is a composite of the weighted sub scales. The BES was completed for the study sample by each student's teacher.

There is no standardized equivalence scale to convert other rating scales to the BES. Consequently, three masters degreed social workers were requested to review and compare the other testing scales to the BES. Their conversion scores were averaged and used as the "BES" scores. Of the forty-two behavioral measures (fourteen students rated three times - pre-entry, first semester, and second semester), only six measures were "converted" BES scores.

BES scores were collected on each student before they entered the SBH school (prior to counseling), at the end of the first semester (after therapy sessions without Holly), and at the end of the second semester (after therapy with Holly). BES scores were similarly compiled for the match group.

Findings:

With the BES scores, the higher number indicates behavioral improvement. The BES score for the counseled group before coming to the SBH school was 447 and the BES score for the match group before coming to the SBH school was 338.

The BES score for the treatment group, which received counseling only, the first semester, was 593. The BES score for the second semester (received counseling with

Pet Facilitation) was 602. The non-counseled match group's first semester BES score was 551 and the second semester, it was 513. The Pet Facilitated Therapy group improved their scores by nine points and the non-counseled group lost 38 behavior points. The difference between the groups was 47 points.

   Attendance is also recorded on a standard form which is completed daily by the student's teacher. The academic year has 180 student days. For seven students in each group that makes a total of 1260 possible days to attend school. The counseled group without Pet Facilitation missed 101 days the first semester and 84 days the second semester (counseling with the dog), for a total of 185 missed for the entire academic year. The non-counseled group missed 114 days the first semester and 149 days the second semester for a total of 263 absent days.

   The absence rate for the counseled group (pre-Holly) was 16.0% for the first semester and 13.3% for the second semester (with Holly), for a year total of 14.7% absence rate. The non-counseled group was absent 18.1% the first semester and was absent 2.6% the second semester for a total of 20.9% for the school year. The counseled group with Holly was 10.3% less absent compared to the non-counseled match group. The group that received counseling and pet-facilitated therapy throughout the entire year was absent 6.2% less than the match group during the school year.

Discussion:

   The authors of the BES, in their discussion of reliability, claim a sensitivity in their scale of a ten day interval. This may have had an effect on the BES scores. The administration of the first semester BES scales was completed after the students had recently returned from Christmas vacation and may have been in a good behavioral period. The administration of the BES at the end of the second semester was completed the week before summer vacation. The end of the school year for students has historically been an "I don't care anymore attitude," which may have depressed the end of the year scores. If this is so, the pet-facilitated therapy group reversed the downward trend in the BES end year scores.

   SBH students have a background of school difficulties. Their experience of school is a negative one and, consequently, they have low motivation toward good attendance. Younger SBH students are often sent to school even when they are sick, presumably to provide respite from the behavioral problems for their caretakers at least during school hours. As the students get older, however, the desire to avoid school that all SBH students have, is able to be acted upon. The older SBH students may leave home in the morning, but they do not go to school. Near the end of the year, attendance becomes a real problem, as caretakers are worn from the go-to-school struggle and are less able to enforce attendance and the older students develop "Spring Fever" and skip school even more frequently. Hence absences tend to increase during the second semester of the school year. Hence, the fact that the pet-facilitated group not only did not follow the trend of poorer attendance, but reversed it by 10.3%, is even more meaningful.

Summary:

Many previous reports on Pet Facilitated Therapy are based on anecdotal informa-tion. This study compared two groups of SBH students in a public elementary school. One group received counseling without Pet Facilitation for the first semester and coun-seling with Pet Facilitation for the second semester. The match group did not receive any counseling either semester. The semester that the group received counseling with Pet Facilitation made modest gains in behavior (8%) and improved attendance by 10.3%.

Section 2:
THE EFFECTS OF TWO THERAPY PETS, D.J. AND INCA, WITH PRESCHOOL CHILDREN WITH DEVELOPMENTAL CHALLENGES
(Pearl Salotto)

Does Pet Assisted Therapy have a noticeable impact on children with developmental disabilities? This question can in part be measured by a six week internship program on the part of two Pet Assisted Therapy Facilitators (Pearl Salotto and another Mercy College student) and two pet therapy dogs (D. J. and Inca), working with children with developmental disabilities.

Can we see changes in children as young as toddler age, two to four years old, in a relatively short period of treatment time? The answer is a definite yes. The following results occurred, working once a week for an hour and a half. This internship, part of Mercy College's PATF Certificate Program, consisted of a PAT program for a group of twenty preschool children with developmental disabilities.

Were our goals (increasing nurturing skills, increasing confidence and self-esteem, increasing understanding of proper treatment of animals, and knowledge of how to care for animals, decreasing fear of animals, increasing cooperation, verbalization, and concentration, as well as bringing joyous experiences) being met? The answer is a definite yes, as indicated by the attached results (including pre-assessment, post-assessment and evaluation). Virtually every child had some positive results from the Pet Assisted Therapy program. While there was a wide variation in the degree of the results, neither the astounding progress of many youngsters, nor some minimal progress in each and every youngster, was surprising. It was heartwarming and rewarding - but not surprising. How could kids not be positively affected by loving dogs?

Pet Assisted Therapy's moving results with children who are emotionally disturbed and with individuals who are elderly, are echoed in this program, loudly and clearly with these beautiful children. It was the gentleness and the loving concern of the teachers, the aides, and the volunteers that paved the way for the children to benefit from our Pet Assisted Therapy program.

In our first session, the teachers sat on the floor holding the children in their laps and gently guiding tiny, eager, yet fearful hands toward their first touch of soft fur, only when the child seemed ready to do so. This was truly the foundation for the success of the entire program.

Little hands touching loving dogs allowed us to, from the very beginning, objectively measure and subjectively recognize visible effects, personality changes, and the acquisition of, hopefully, permanent positive internal feelings in the children of respect for all living things.

The most significant changes were in the area of overcoming fear of dogs; increasing understanding that animals are living things and should be treated with respect, care and love; increasing reality orientation; increasing confidence; increasing experiences of joy, and increasing the ability to look forward to pleasurable experiences.

Some changes were noticed in verbalization abilities. The changes in the children regarding improvement in attitude toward school, attitude toward other children and adults were not significant, as the children rated high in these in the pre- as well as the post-assessment. Most of the children seemed to like school.

The major gratifying changes occurred in the following areas:

1. Decreased fear of animals: In 14 out of 20 children there was a decreased fear of animals, which according to a 1-10 scale, ten children changed between 3 and 8 points on the scale, four children changed 1 or 2 points and out of the remaining six children, four had no prior fear of animals and two children refused during the whole Pet Assisted Therapy program to touch the animals, although one of the children threw crackers to the dogs and smiled while they ate the food.

2. Treatment of animals: In this category the results were unbelievably rewarding and gratifying with 19 out of 20 of the children showing some improvement and 11 out of 20 showing improvement of over 4 points on a 1-10 scale.

3. Nurturing skills: In this category 9 out of 20 children showed improvement of 2 or more points.

In the area of increased self-confidence, 8 out of 20 children showed an improvement of 2 to 4 points and two others showed a 1 point improvement. In the area of reality orientation, 8 out of 20 children showed some improvement and similarly some improvement was seen in the area of verbal skills.

In the evaluation questionnaire, it was noted that many children mentioned the dogs when walking past the room used for Pet Assisted Therapy. Additional comments were that the children enjoyed feeding the dogs, and that they looked forward with great enthusiasm to seeing the dogs. In one case it was noted that a parent had commented that she had noticed a decreased fear of animals on the part of the child, who was not given to communicating very much. Another comment made was that many of the children had increased their ability to concentrate and focus. Teachers commented that a follow-up pet therapy internship would be a good idea, as well as follow-up art projects and stories about animals.

Teachers also commented that if the program had run for more than six weeks or for more hours per week, even more changes would be anticipated. The changes resulting from the program are significant, considering the small amount of contact hours.

Kids also learned about cooperation when taking turns feeding or brushing the therapy dogs. Kids visibly displayed joy in the gentle acceptance they received from the dogs. Once again, animals in general - D. J. and Inca - in particular, have proven to be "kids best friend."

Astounding and joyous changes were seen in specific children. One little girl, initially, had to be held in the teacher's arms, as the fear was so great that she could not even remain on the floor with them. Subsequently, she reached out a timid hand from her secure spot in the teacher's arms. The following week this same child marched right into the Pet Assisted Therapy room and reached out a "confident" hand spontaneously touching D. J. Can this striking improvement be measured by assessment charts?

Pearl Salotto

YES - but the feelings of the moment defy words.

One little girl, at the beginning of the Pet Assisted Therapy program, thought the therapy dogs were merely pieces of property on which she could release her negativism toward adults. When her little fingers moved toward the dogs to pinch or poke she was immediately removed from the animals and had to sit alone. She soon learned that she needed to give gentleness to the therapy animals in order to feel Inca's loving kiss or hold D. J.'s paw.

Another boy, approached the dogs in a carefree, joyous and relaxed manner during the first Pet Assisted Therapy session and continued loving every minute of it, throughout the entire six weeks. Another boy sat rigidly on a chair, refusing to move even with the gentle prodding of his teacher. By the last week of the program he had accomplished it all, feeling comfortable and happy while petting, walking, brushing and feeding the therapy dogs.

If there was any doubt about the effects of the PAT program, they would have been easily dispelled at the site of the million dollar smiles on the faces of these twenty children. As they enthusiastically approached Inca and D. J., they would say "Dog! Dog! Dog!" – this out of basically nonverbal children. Without question, the internship program accomplished its goal and hopefully gave the children the first of many positive and life affirming experiences with animals and the world around them.

It seems more than fitting to this author to end this paper by giving proper credit to the therapy dogs, without whom there would have been no program! This internship experience taught me what therapy pets can give, allowing me to realize what we owed back to our therapy partners. This paved the way for my future work in ethics.

The exquisite gentleness and "understanding" of the dogs in the Pet Assisted Therapy program, D. J. - a two year old female Samoyed and Inca - a three year old Weimar, touches the heart, as I think nothing else does. Throughout this internship, these two dogs lovingly interacted with the children despite excruciating one hundred degree heat and by being approached by no less than twenty strange children and adults in less than one and a half hours. Despite "backward brushing, close "fisted" feeding (during which the dogs would smell and lick and WAIT until the child opened the hand) and paws being inadvertently stepped on when a child mistakenly backed into a dog, D. J. and Inca alway treated the children gently. Even though the children were not always being calm and quiet, and did not hold the leash, in the manner in which the dogs were used to, these two therapy dogs knew that the children were being loving. (There was no question in the dogs' mind that there was any harm intended.) How did the dogs know that? Does anyone think dogs do not think and feel and understand? Hats off to these two dogs - beautiful in spirit, as well as in body and to all other living creatures who enrich our lives in ways beyond measure.

Assessment Chart

	Attitude toward School		Relationship to Other Children		Relationship to Adults		Fear of Animals		Knowledge of Proper Treatment & Respect of Animals		Nurturing Skills		Reality Awareness		Increased Self-Confidence		Increased Self-Esteem	
	Pre	Post	Pre	Post	Pre	Post	Pre	Post	Pre	Post	Pre	Post	Pre	Post	Pre	Post	Pre	Post
Child # 1	8	9	7	8	9	9	5	2	0	6	8	8	5	8	6	8	6	8
Child # 2	10	10	9	9	9	10	3	1	0	5	8	8	8	9	9	9	9	9
Child # 3	10	10	7	8	8	8	2	1	3	7	6	8	7	9	7	7	8	8
Child # 4	10	10	9	9	9	9	2	1	0	6	9	9	8	9	8	9	8	9
Child # 5	10	10	10	10	10	10	10	4	0	8	9	9	10	10	9	10	9	10
Child # 6	10	10	10	10	10	10	10	9	0	0	8	8	8	9	9	9	9	9
3 sessions only																		
Child # 7	8	9	3	5	5	5	5	2	2	8	4	8	7	7	5	9		
Child # 8	9	9	9	9	9	9	7	1	2	7	5	7	9	9	6	9		
Child # 9	8	8	7	8	9	9	8	2	1	7	3	7	8	9	5	8		
Child # 10	9	9	7	8	8	9	5	2	5	8	7	9	9	10	5	9		
Child # 11	9	9	5	8	8	8	7	2	2	6	5	6	7	9	5	7		
Child # 12	6	8	4	7	5	7	8	2	2	5	3	5	7	8	5	7		
Child # 13	10	10	9	9	10	10	1	1	5	7	5	5	7	7	8	8		
Child # 14	10	10	7	7	10	10	1	1	3	5	6	6	8	8	8	8	8	8
Child # 15	10	10	7	7	10	10	1	1	5	7	5	5	8	8	7	7	8	7
Child # 16	5	5	4	4	4	4	1	1	1	3	0	0	3	3	5	5	7	5
Child # 17	10	10	10	10	8	8	1	1	5	6	7	7	8	8	8	8	5	8
Child # 18	10	10	7	7	7	7	1	1	5	9	5	7	8	8	8	8	8	8
Child # 19	10	10	6	6	10	10	10	6	5	7	5	5	8	8	7	7	7	7
Child # 20	7	8	4	7	5	8	9	1	1	6	4	6	8	8	6	9	7	7

19

Section 3:
ANIMAL ASSISTED THERAPY AND THE ELDERLY: EFFECTS ON PSYCHOLOGICAL WELL-BEING

Jean Burke, MA, LAHT, [1] Dr. Stephen A. Daniel, Ph. D. [2]
Dr. Jack Burke, D.V.M., Cecilia Tweedy, M.G.A., M.H.A.

Jean Burke is an Assistant Professor of Veterinary Technology at Mercy College, Dobbs Ferry, New York. Jean holds a Masters Degree and is a licensed Veterinary Technician. She is very active in Pet Assisted Therapy research, has lectured nationally on the subject and co-authored the first Certificate Program in Pet Assisted Therapy. Aside from her research and academic responsibilities, Jean is a practicing veterinary technician.

Jack Burke D.V.M., a graduate of Cornell University Veterinary College, has served as a Professor and Director of Veterinary Technology at Mercy College, Dobbs Ferry, New York since 1981. He is recognized as an early researcher in the Pet Assisted Therapy field. In 1984 he co-authored the first college level Certificate Program in Pet Assisted Therapy at Mercy College. Dr. Burke is also a veterinary practitioner with a special interest in animal behavior.

Stephen A. Daniel received his Ph.D. in experimental psychology with a specialty in psychopharmacology from the University of Minnesota in 1978. He then completed a two-year postdoctoral fellowship in behavioral toxicology. In 1980, he was hired as an assistant professor of psychology at Mercy College and was promoted in 1984 to an associate professor. In 1985, he became a licensed psychologist in New York State. Dr. Daniel, along with Dr. Jack Burke and Professor Jean Burke, has been involved with the establishment, implementation and continued success of the unique New York State approved Pet-Assisted Therapy Facilitation Certificate Program. Established in 1984, this program helps to certify Animal-Assisted Therapists by offering courses in psychology, animal behavior and training, and Animal-Assisted Therapy and requiring a one-semester internship. The Burkes and Dr. Daniel have published and presented several papers on the importance of education programs in Animal-Assisted Therapy programs, animal behavior issues in the field and data on the efficacy of Animal-Assisted Therapy programs with several different populations. There have been many graduates of the program, including Ms. Pearl Salotto.

Cecilia E. Tweedy received her M.P.H. with a concentration in Gerontology from

---

[1] Department of Veterinary Technology, Mercy College, 555 Broadway, Dobbs Ferry, NY 10522.
[2] Department of Psychology, Mercy College, 555 Broadway, Dobbs Ferry, NY 10522.

the New School for Social Research and also holds a Certificate in Social Work from Fordham University. She spent 13 years as Director of Social Services at Hudson View Nursing Home in Yonkers, NY and 4 years as a hospital administrator at Julia C. Butterfield Memorial Hospital in Cold Springs, NY. She was a pioneer in establishing Pet-Facilitated Therapy programs in long-term care facilities and worked on legislation in New York State to allow animals in long-term care facilities. She has worked with Jean Burke, Stephen A. Daniels, and Jack Burke to establish visitation and resident Animal-Assisted Therapy programs.

Pet Facilitated Therapy has been employed in a variety of institutional settings with elderly patients (Bustad, 1980; Corson and Corson, 1981), psychiatric patients (Thompson, et al, 1983), and children (Condoret, 1983; Robin, et al, 1983). The most frequent reported use of pet therapy programs, both visitation and resident pet programs, have been with the elderly.

There are several reasons for this fact. Many people in nursing homes were previously pet owners and contact with animals, even on a limited basis, allows for fond memories. In addition, the animals provide a context for social interactions and discussion. The animal visits also provide orientation to the "here and now," an orientation that is important in any therapeutic environment. Finally, the animal can help people who are lonely and will love them uncritically. Other specific characteristics of nursing homes and nursing home characteristics that are addressed by Pet Facilitated Therapy are discussed by Corson and Corson (1980).

The present study has been designed somewhat differently than other studies. There was assessment of psychological and social factors that are important therapeutically. Changes in individual patient's affect and verbalization characteristics have been reported by Corson and Corson (1980). Other investigators have assessed the effects on blood pressure and survival rates (Friedman, et al, 1980). Secondly, assessment was completed four times during the visitation program – once before the program began, twice during the program, and once a month after the visitation program had ended. Finally, this program was an interdisciplinary effort involving the Veterinary Technology and Psychology Departments at Mercy College. The Veterinary Technology department provided well-trained and well-vaccinated pets, in order to minimize the likelihood of accidents, disease or any other problems. In addition, sensitivity and ability to work with animals was provided by volunteers from this department. The Psychology department provided sensitivity to the client population, as well as the ability to analyze changes seen in the patients. In addition, the Psychology department has an active Animal Behavior program, which is an important component of the Pet Therapy program.

The purpose of this study was to assess changes across a variety of behavioral categories as a result of a pet visitation program in a nursing home. Protocols were employed that were similar to those recommended by Bustad (1980) and Lee, et al, (1983). By using well-trained "celebrity" animals, it was possible to avoid many of the potential problems (bites, scratches, accidents).

Methodology

Subjects: Participants were chosen from each floor of the Hudson View Nursing Home on the basis of interest and previous ownership of pets. The study had thirty-six participants who were present during all four phases of the project. They ranged in age from 35 to 93. However, most participants were between 70 and 82. There were 20% males (N=8) and 80% females (N=26).

Instruments: A twelve question survey was developed specifically for this program and for the geriatric client population. The questions were asked about the patients' 1) activity 2) responsiveness 3) sociability 4) cooperativeness 5) interaction with other patients and 6) amount of smiling. Each question was followed by a five point scale in which an observer could measure the ability to engage in these behaviors, movements or activities on a continuing basis from rarely to frequently.

For ten weeks, four animals (two small dogs and two cats), accompanied their trainer, and visited the nursing home one day a week for approximately ninety minutes. The visits occurred at the same time of day (12:30 - 2:30 p.m.) on Tuesdays or Wednesdays. At the same time, eight to ten student volunteers from the Mercy College Veterinary Technology and Psychology department accompanied the animals, trainer and other personnel on the visits.

The students brought the participants to the solarium and the pets and students would meet them there. Each participant could then interact with the pet and the volunteer student animal handlers. After each animal was on one of the four floors for forty-five minutes, animals were exchanged between floors, so that each floor had a visit from a dog and a cat. In order for some possible memory and bonding between students or pet and clients to occur, student and pets consistently visited the same floors week after week.

After the sessions with the clients ended, students, supervisors and social service staff from the nursing home met to discuss the visit and air out any problems that were occurring during the visits.

The pets that visited the nursing home were professional animals that have participated in commercials and television programs. They were trained and owned by a professional animal behaviorist. They were trained to excrete on command and were habituated to being petted by large groups of people for long periods of time and therefore, could remain calm during visits.

In addition, a member of our research team is a licensed veterinarian and could check for physical or potential zoonotic problems with the animals.

The assessment part of the study was divided into four phases. Social service and nursing filled out the survey for each participant in the study, at four different times, but not during the visits.

A different staff member filled out the survey in each phase. In addition, these staff members did not know who was participating in the study and why the surveys were being compiled. The four phases were:

Phase I (Pre):   The surveys were completed prior to the visit of the pets or Mercy College volunteer students or staff..

Phase II (5-week):   The surveys were completed after the fifth week of the pet and student visits.

Phase III (10-wk):   The surveys were immediately completed after the tenth (next to last) week of pet and student visits.

Phase IV (Post):   The surveys were completed one month after the last visit by the students and pets.

Statistical Analysis: The data was entered on a Digital Equipment Corporation System 20 Computer and analyzed with the SPSS Software Package (Nie, et al, 1975). The data was analyzed by a randomized block (repeated measures) analysis of variance. Planned comparisons were made between the four phases of the study by the Scheffe Test of planned comparisons. In all cases, the level of significance was $P < .01$.

Results

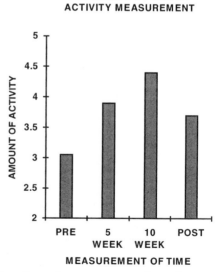

PET THERAPY PROJECT ACTIVITY MEASUREMENT

Figure 1 shows differences in initiation of activity as a function of the four phases. This treatment effect on this scale was highly significant ($F(3,105) = 21.00 P < .01$). Pairwise comparisons, using the Scheffe procedure revealed that there were significant ($P < .01$) differences between the Pre - 5 week and Pre - 10 week survey results. In general, participants would participate when encouraged before the visits began. They increased initiation of activity greatly during the visits; more initiation was seen after 10 weeks than after 5 weeks. However, activity levels did not remain elevated after the program, compared to when the program began

Figure 1 shows amount of activity as a function of measurement phase (see text for details). On the ordinate, 1 = no participation, 3 = participation when encouraged and 5 = initiation of activity. These data are the mean of 36 subjects. *'s represent significant differences from the "pre" measurement time ($P < .01$).

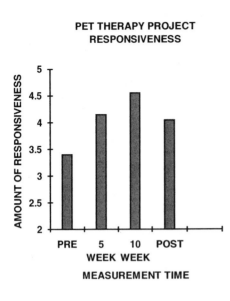

PET THERAPY PROJECT RESPONSIVENESS

Figure 2 shows changes in responsiveness as a function of the four phases. This treatment effect on this scale was highly significant (F (3,105) = 18.63; P < .01). Pairwise comparisons revealed that there were significant differences (P < .01) between the Pre - 5 week, Pre - 10 week and Pre - Post survey results. As a whole, the participants were aware but withdrawn before the program began, but became much more alert and active to their surroundings through the course of the study. Again, the responsiveness was greater after 10 weeks than 5 weeks. Responsiveness remained significantly greater than before the study, even a month after the visits had ended.

Figure 2 shows responsiveness to the environment as a function of measurement phase. On the ordinate, 1 = unawareness of surroundings, 3 = awareness, but withdrawn and 5 = alertness and awareness of surroundings.

These data are the mean of 36 subjects. *'s represent significant differences from the "pre" measurement time (P < .01).

Figure 3 shows differences in socialization as a function of the four phases. This treatment effect was highly significant (F (3,105) = 26.55; P < .01). Pairwise comparisons revealed that there were significant differences (P < .01) between the Pre - 5 week, Pre - 10 week and Pre - Post survey results. As a whole, the participants would respond to contact from others, but would not initiate contact before the study began. As the study progressed, the participants more actively sought the company of others and initiated socialization. Active socialization continued at a higher rate even a month after the study ended.

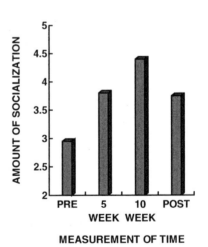

PET THERAPY PROJECT SOCIALIZATION

Figure 3 shows socialization as a function of measurement phase. On the ordinate, 1 = isolation from others, 3 = responsiveness to contact from others and 5 = actively seeks company of others.

Figure 4 shows changes in cooperativeness as a function of the four phases (F (3,105) = 26.8; P < .01). Pairwise comparisons showed significant increases in cooperativeness (P < .01) between Pre - 5 week, Pre - 10 week and Pre - Post survey results. As a whole, the participants were slightly willing to cooperate if asked to, before the study began. After 5 and 10 weeks of the program, the participants were willing to offer assistance to others. The effect lasted for a month after the study.

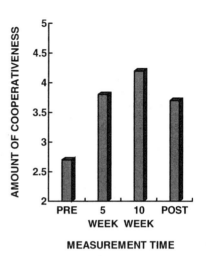

**PET THERAPY PROJECT
COOPERATIVENESS**

Figure 4 shows cooperativeness as a function of measurement phase. On the ordinate, 1 = never helps others, 3 = willing to help if asked and 5 = offers assistance to others. These data are the mean of 36 subjects. *'s represent significant differences from the "pre" measurement time (P < .01).

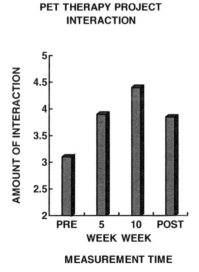

**PET THERAPY PROJECT
INTERACTION**

Figure 5 shows changes in interaction with others as a function of the four phases. Interaction changed significantly across the four phases (F (3,105) = 26.62; P < .01). Pairwise comparisons showed significant increases in interaction (P < .01) between Pre - 5 week, Pre - 10 week and Pre - Post survey results. As a group, the participants would interact briefly with others before the study began. After 5 or 10 weeks of the program, the participants were much more likely to participate in group games or activities. The effect one month after the program ended was still significantly higher than before the program began.

Figure 5 shows interaction with others as a function of measurement phase. On the ordinate, 1 = does not respond to others, 3 = interacts briefly with others and 5 = interacts in group games or activity. These data are the mean of 36 subjects. *'s represent significant differences from the "pre" measurement time (P < .01).

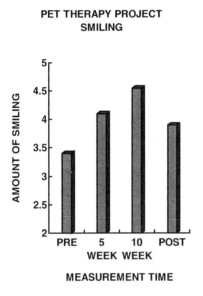

**PET THERAPY PROJECT
SMILING**

AMOUNT OF SMILING

MEASUREMENT TIME

Figure 6 shows the amount of smiling as a function of the four phases. Smiling changed significantly across the four phases (F (3,105) = 20.26; P < .01). Pairwise comparisons showed significant increases (P < .01) in Pre - 5 week and Pre - 10 week comparisons. As a group, the participants would smile rarely-to-sometimes before the study began. After 5 to 10 weeks of the program the participants smiled often. After the study ended, their amount of smiling was no different from when the program began.

Figure 6 shows amount of [smiling] as a function of measurement phase. On the ordinate, 1 = never smiles or shows pleasure, 3 = rarely smiles or shows pleasure and 5 = often smiles and shows pleasure, when appropriate. These data are the mean of 36 subjects. *'s represent significant differences from the "pre" measurement time (P < .01).

Discussion

The measured psychological changes, due to the pet visitation program were large and dramatic. All measured psychological factors changed as a result of the pet visitation. What was more surprising was that in four of the six scales (responsiveness to the environment, socialization, cooperativeness and interaction with others), significant elevations were noted when measured one month after the visitation program ended. In addition, by using this particular research design, the recommendation of Bustad and Hines (1983), Corson and Corson (1981), and McCulloch (1983) were followed. What may have differentiated the longer-lasting effects from the other shorter-lasting effects (amount of activity and amount of smiling) is that the longer-lasting effects were more social in nature and therefore, by definition, more dependent on other people. Activity and smiling are scales that are measured more solitarily and individual components seemed to be more program-dependent. The visitation program may have affected many people and the effects may have been more synergistic with those socially measured activities (responsiveness, socialization, cooperativeness and interaction with others).

Obviously, there may be many other factors than the pet visits themselves that may account for these data. The first factor may have been that the staff may have measured what the researchers wanted them to measure (Hawthorne effect). There are several factors which militate against this interpretation. Firstly, different staff members on different floors filled out the assessment forms each time. Secondly, since the staff were not directly involved in the program (the student/volunteers brought the patients to the area of interaction), they did not know what phase the study was in, nor who was participating or why the surveys were being taken.

To ensure that these factors would not be an interpretative problem, the study would have had to involve a non-involved "blind" observer, with treatment and control groups. In this study, the ethical, temporal, and financial limitations did not allow for this expensive luxury.

A second set of factors had to do with the student and faculty volunteers. Every time the pet visits occurred, the volunteers accompanied them. It is difficult to say whether the pets alone, the people alone, or the combination of the people and pets caused the measured changes observed in this study. However, observations from this study and data from other work the present investigators have done, indicate that the effect is a combination of the pets and the people.

The student volunteers entered the program never having had contact with people who are elderly and sick or lived in an institution. The students began the program with quite a bit of fear and apprehension. These student volunteers each changed in their own way and they are no longer afraid of the elderly. The animals served as the focal point or as McCulloch (1983) states, the "social lubricant" through which the two generations could interact. (Corson and Corson, 1981). The continued presence of the animals provided a context for the visit and the conversations. Although the changes in the students were not assessed scientifically, these changes also appeared to be large and dramatic.

These data suggest that much research needs to be done in this area. The use of a control group and observers not aware of the different conditions and patient populations are important. In addition, the use of multiple measurements, physiological and pharmacological, as well as psychological changes, could be very useful and important. It is also important to verify, with similar measurement techniques, the generality of these findings to other populations. Finally, as Daniel, Burke and Burke (in press) suggest education programs in this area are important that take into account the staff, the patient, the animal and the therapist.

We wish to thank Bashkim Dibra for providing well trained dogs and cats and giving generously of his time for this investigation. We also wish to thank the staff of Hudson View Nursing Home for their support and encouragement. Dean James Melville and Dr. Frances Mahoney of Mercy College provided much needed logistical, financial and moral support. In addition, we wish to thank Ms. Diane Granville for her assistance in preparation of the assessment scales.

Section 4:
THE HEALTH BENEFITS OF PETS – REVIEW OF NATIONAL INSTITUTES OF HEALTH STUDY

The principal sponsors were the NIH Division of Research Services and the Office of Medical Applications of Research. Other sponsors were the NIH Clinical Center; National Center for Nursing Research; National Heart, Lung, and Blood Institute; National Institute on Aging; National Institute of Child Health and Human Development; the Centers for Disease Control; and the Food and Drug Administration.

Overview

More than half of all U. S. households have a companion animal. Pets are more common in households with children, yet there are more pets than children in American households. There are more than fifty-one million dogs, fifty-six million cats, forty-five million birds, seventy-five million small mammals and reptiles and uncounted millions of aquarium fish.

It is important at this time to assess whether these populations have any beneficial impact on physical, social and psychological health.

To this end, the National Institutes of Health convened a Technology Assessment Workshop on The Health Benefits of Pets on September 10-11, 1987. After a day-and-a-half of presentations by experts in relevant fields, a working group drafted the following report to provide the scientific community with a synthesis of the current knowledge and a framework for future research, and to provide the public with the information it needs to make informed decisions regarding the health benefits of pets.

Throughout history animals have played a significant role in human customs, legends, and religions. Primitive people have found that human-animal relationships were important to their very survival, and pet-keeping was common in hunter-gatherer societies. In our own time, the great increase in pet ownership may reflect a largely urban population's often unsatisfied need for intimacy, nurturance, and contact with nature. However, it is impossible to determine when animals first were used specifically to promote physical and psychological health. The use of horseback riding for people with serious disabilities has been reported for centuries. In 1792, animals were incorporated into the treatment of mental patients at the York Retreat, England, as part of an enlightened approach attempting to reduce the use of harsh drugs and restraints. The first suggested use of animals in a therapeutic setting in the United States was in 1919 at St. Elizabeth's Hospital in Washington, D. C., when Superintendent Dr. WA White received a letter from Secretary of the Interior F.K. Lane suggesting the use of dogs as companions for the psychiatric hospital's resident patients. Following this, the earliest extensive use of companion animals in the United States occurred from 1944 to 1945 at an Army Air Corps Convalescent Hospital at Pawling, New York. Patients recovering from war experiences were encouraged to work at the hospital's farm with hogs, cattle, horses, and poultry. After the war, modest efforts began in using animals in outpatient psychotherapy. During the 1970's, numerous case studies of animals facilitating therapy with children and senior citizens were reported.

The Role of Pets in Cardiovascular Health

The role of social support in cardiovascular health - a question not yet resolved despite considerable research - provides a rational framework for studying the possible benefits of pets beyond mere enjoyment and affection.

Since psychological factors can elicit strong and immediate responses from the cardiovascular system, many studies are attempting to determine whether such influences ultimately affect the risk of developing cardiovascular diseases. The description of a "coronary-prone behavior pattern," or Type A behavior, and its link to the probability of developing overt disease provided hope that, with careful training, individuals could exercise additional control over somatic illness by altering their lifestyle. Relaxation, meditation, and stress management have become recognized therapies for attempting to reduce blood pressure before pharmacological methods are prescribed. It therefore seems reasonable that pets who provide faithful companionship to many people, also might promote greater psychosocial stability for their owners, and thus a measure of protection from heart disease. Systematic research addressing this issue is scarce, and it has been difficult to draw definitive conclusions from the few studies with small sample sizes that have been completed. A selection of these, providing direct, as well as indirect evidence relevant to this hypothesis, was reported at this conference.

A plausible physiological basis for a beneficial influence of pets is provided by studies of heart rate in Old World monkeys and research of blood pressure in college students. There is now objective evidence, based on direct examination of coronary arteries, that monkeys housed in benign social environments and more frequently engaged in affiliative behaviors, develop less severe coronary disease than monkeys repeatedly exposed to dominance-competitive interactions. It is possible that this decrease in atherosclerosis is directly related to the much lower heart rates that have been observed in these animals by means of telemetry, especially at times when they are engaged in social interactions with each other. Decreased coronary disease in animals with genetically lowered heart rates also has been reported by others.

Since elevated blood pressure is also associated with higher risk of developing significant coronary heart disease, demonstration that the presence of an unfamiliar dog lowers systolic blood pressure (but not diastolic blood pressure or heart rate) in college students is only partially encouraging findings for proponents of a link between health and pet ownership. The experiment should be repeated, using the subjects' own pets rather than an unfamiliar animal, which may evoke a degree of anxiety in some people. A number of studies have reported that domesticated animals can influence physiological measures such as heart rate and blood pressure acutely, but conclusive data are needed to demonstrate that the magnitude of these effects is sufficient to be clinically significant and endure over a sufficiently long period of time to be beneficial. One approach would be a cross-sectional study showing lowered heart rates or blood pressures in pet owners than in nonowners, although the problem of self-selection still remains. Experimental designs that randomly assign pets to some individuals and not to others for a period of time would be ideal, although more difficult and costly.

However suggestive the findings from studies of human physiology may be, the final link will have to come from clinical studies that demonstrate a direct relationship between pet ownership and either the incidence of , recurrence of, or mortality from heart disease in people. Results from one such study, presented at this conference, found that postmyocardial infarction survival rates were much higher among pet owners than among nonowners. However, as in the case of other social variables, only a small proportion (3.5 percent) of the difference in mortality was attributable to pet ownership itself. Because determining severity of disease is not yet an exact science, it is conceivable that all MI patients who owned a pet were in relatively better health, as reflected by their ability to care for a household pet. It is therefore important to conduct rigorous prospective studies in which the effects of placing a pet with a randomly chosen sample of post-MI patients would be examined.

In spite of the current insufficiency of data conclusively linking pet ownership to cardiovascular health, the evidence provided at this conference is sufficiently encouraging and intriguing to be worthy of serious follow up. Those who own pets would surely be delighted to learn that they reap unexpected health and financial benefits (from lower health care costs) in addition to enjoying the companionship of the family cat or dog.

Conference participants agreed that definitive conclusions on possible benefits of companion animals would require much larger sample sizes and more rigorous experimental designs than studies conducted thus far. Reexamination of data from one or more of the existing large epidemiological studies or collection of relevant follow-up data seeking to link incidence of disease with presence or absence of household pets could be a useful forerunner to costly *de novo* population studies. Alternatively, future national health surveys might include questions related to pet ownership among the demographic data collected so that the relationship of household pets to a variety of illness' and conditions also could be determined.

Pet ownership is a very personal decision reflecting an individual preference; this can bias the outcome of nonrandomized studies. Not only does ability to care for a pet imply better health, it also may reflect availability of more discretionary income, which may result in more investment in health care. A companion animal may not necessarily be appropriate for everyone; however, withholding a pet from someone who wants one could be as much a source of distress as forcing one upon someone who does not.

Conference participants accepted that many questions would have to be examined when attempting to resolve these issues. Given the present state of knowledge, the best judge of risks or benefits of pet ownership for optimal cardiovascular health is the individual. Hopefully, research developments will provide better guidance in the future.

The Role of Pets in Child Development

A number of empirical studies have investigated how children interact with pets and how they view their relationships with animals, including pets. These studies have taken two basic forms: (1) observational studies of actual interaction between child and pet and (2) interviews with children in which their attitudes and beliefs regarding animals in general, and their own pet in particular, were examined.

These studies have demonstrated major developmental changes in how children interact with pets. For example, toddlers (2 to 3 years old) are more likely to hit, poke, or grab their pets (behaviors that might be considered aggressive) than are older children. Three- to four-year old children tend to pet their animals more than engage in other behaviors, while 5- and 6-year-olds generally hug, stroke, massage their pets, suggesting both more sophisticated and "gentle" physical contact patterns and more empathetic social relationships. These age-based changes in patterns of behavioral interactions with pets are generally parallel to the developmental changes in interaction patterns that children have with familiar humans, including parents, siblings, and peers.

Examination of children's attitudes toward pets reveals that many of them ascribe a rich range of social attributes to these animals. Some of these attributes - especially love and affection, companionship, intimacy, and nurturance - also are used in the children's description of their relationships with other specific people, but other attributes - for example, ownership and entertainment - are uniquely ascribed to pets. Consider the attributes of companionship and love and affection. Most children rate their own pets very high on both characteristics while they rate neighborhood animals high on companionship but not on love and affection. (By way of comparison, siblings tend to be rated high on companionship but not on love and affection, while the reverse is the case for ratings of grandparents.) Taken as a whole, these results suggest that, children's relationships with familiar animals, especially pets, are unique and different from their relationship with pets typically is complementary to these other relationships rather than a substitute for any one type of human relationship.

Of course, children differ in their attitudes and relationships toward pets, and some of these differences can be related to factors such as family size, presence or absence of younger siblings, and family income (most of the studies to date have been limited to samples of children from stable, suburban middle-class families, and generalization to other groups of children may not be valid). The long-term consequences for children of establishing such relationships with pets and other animals have not been studied to date in any detail, although a number of studies of children in diverse family circumstances suggest that, at least for some, the presence of a pet is greatly beneficial. On the one hand, it has been suggested that exposure to pets should facilitate the establishment and maintenance of relationships with peers, especially in grade and high school. On the other hand, there has been some concern that children who establish too intense a relationship with a pet may suffer in the development of sophisticated and meaningful relationships with other people. More research is needed to determine what such long-term consequences might be and to identify any conditions, situations, or characteristics of particular children whose specific relationships with their pets put them at risk for developing problems in subsequent social, emotional, and cognitive development. Prospective longitudinal studies in home or neighborhood settings would be very useful in this regard.

Health Correlates of Pets in Older Persons

In addition to examination of the effects of the human-companion animal bond among children and special populations of chronically ill or disabled adults, there has been widespread consideration of the benefits of companion animals for older persons.

Pearl Salotto

Interdisciplinary researchers in veterinary medicine, public health, and the behavioral sciences have begun to explore the health correlates of the human-animal bond and to examine the benefits of a wide range of pet-facilitated therapies on the health and functioning of the elderly. The assumption of a salutary effect of pet ownership on the health of older persons is based on a growing body of literature suggesting the importance of social life changes affecting health or social situations.

Two types of research predominate in this area. A few large-scale epidemiological studies are examining the association of pet ownership and attachment with the health and well-being of older persons living independently in the community. However, most researchers are involved in applied intervention studies examining the effect of pet-facilitated therapy or animal visitation programs on older persons in long-term care settings.

Data from a national probability sample of 1,232 older persons living in the community reveal a lack of influence of pet variables on health outcomes in the general population of older persons: (1) no direct association was found between pet variables (pet ownership and attachment) and reported illness status or levels of depression, (2) no support was found for the hypothesized protective buffering role of pet ownership/attachment, and (3) there was stability in basic conclusions across subgroup analyses based on sex, age, and pet characteristics.

However, a benefit of pet ownership and attachment in combating depression, but no general illness status, was found among older persons in situations of personal stress who were without adequate human social support (e.g., bereaved persons with no close source of human support). Significant health benefits of human-animal interactions in the general population of older persons may be limited to persons in special "at-risk" circumstances. There is also new research examining the relationship between pet ownership, psychosocial variables, and health care utilization. These data collectively suggest that pet ownership may reduce the demand for care for medically nonserious problems.

Studies of health benefits of pet programs for nursing home and health center residents often are flawed methodologically or reported incompletely. Yet the cumulative weight of these studies strongly suggests that psychosocial benefits can be gained from animal visitation programs for at least some older persons in such settings. For example, the presence of animals in institutional settings is associated with the tendency of older persons to smile and talk more, reach out toward people and objects, exhibit more alertness and attention, and experience more symptoms of well-being and less depression. Pet programs have proven superior in producing psychosocial benefits in comparison to some other alternative therapies (e.g., arts and crafts programs, friendly visitor programs, and conventional psychotherapy).

PART II

PRACTICE OF PET ASSISTED THERAPY

CHAPTER 3

PET ASSISTED THERAPY IN HEALTH CARE

Section 1:
PET ASSISTED THERAPY AND INDIVIDUALS WHO ARE ELDERLY

Article 1:
PROGRAMMING QUALITY SERVICES FOR OLDER ADULTS IN LONG-TERM CARE FACILITIES

__Ann M. Rancourt__, Ph.D., was an Associate Professor and Coordinator of the Department of Recreation and Leisure Studies at SUNY Brockport in Brockport, NY.

Abstract: The purpose of this paper is to serve as a catalyst for discussion about the provision of quality services for older adults in long-term care facilities. Those 65 and older today represent 12% of the population.[1] By the year 2030 those 65 and older will represent 20% of the American population. Approximately 5% of older adults are institutionalized. For those who are institutionalized, quality of life experiences are dependent on care-providers. If quality of life is to be improved for people in long-term care settings, there needs to be a change not only in the types of services provided, but in the way services are provided. At the heart of quality is the provision for meaningful relationships. Programs that lay the foundation for meaningful interactions are needed. It is the role of the care-provider to strive to provide opportunities for activities and experiences that are meaningful and engaging.

Keywords: Quality Services, Older Adults, Long-Term Care.

All of us begin life by needing to be taken care of – to be fed, housed, clothed, loved, supported and to be provided with opportunities that will help us grow into self and away from self and into self again. We need to have opportunities to explore and discover, to challenge ourselves, to socially interact and bond, to love and to feel connected. We begin to ride the carousel and reach for the golden ring.

From the first, we seek to control our environment and we are rewarded when we begin to manipulate and master things in ways that allow us to have control and effect change. As we grow, we come to see the myriad of roles that we can potentially assume and we begin to assume those roles. We become brothers and sisters, friends, co-workers, homemakers, mothers and fathers, aunts and uncles, husbands and wives, significant others, grandmothers and grandfathers. Somewhere along the way we are deemed competent and deserved of respect; we are productive members of a productive society. We laugh, we cry, we live, we bury our dead. Our children and nephews and nieces grow, and we grow older. Some of us stay alive and well until the day we die; some of us are dead long before someone pronounces it so.

We change, things change, not that things are better or worse, but that things are different. The differences result in some loses and some gains and the seconds turn into minutes, the minutes hours, the hours days, the days months, the months years. It seems we have only blinked and we are twenty and forty and sixty and eighty.

At age 41, it is hard to believe twenty years have passed since I was 21. As fast as these twenty years have come and gone, I will blink and I will be 61. I cherish my interdependence, the moments of my life, my growth and I hope it will remain so until I exit this place on my journey through time and space. I will try to take care of myself, I will try to eat well and to exercise and to effectively cope and manage the stress in my life so that I will remain, as well as I can, until the day I die.

But I may become ill and unable to care for myself. I have no children to care for me, so I may come to rely on strangers to feed, house, clothe, bathe, love, support and walk with me – to touch me. I may need strangers to provide me with opportunities to help me grow into myself, to explore and discover, to challenge me, to allow me to socially interact and to bond, to allow me to share love and to feel connected, to allow me to have control in my environment, and to be treated with the dignity each of us is worthy of. My life may end in such a way that I may indeed have come full circle, continuing to reach for the golden ring. And it may be you I come in contact with, it may be you I come to trust with my soul, my being as fragile and as strong as it is.

Today 5000 Americans turned 65 and tomorrow 5000 more will. In 1990, 31 million people will be 65 or older. That is 6 million more than 10 years ago and 13 million more than in 1965. Those 65 and older today represent 12% of the population (more than the entire population of Canada) (Horn & Meer, 1989). By the year 2030 those 65 and older will represent 20% of the American population. Today there are 2.7 million people over 85, by 2012 there will be 7 million; they represent the fastest growing segment of the population (Henderson, 1989). Seventy percent of those over 85 are *1990* women and 82% of them are widowed. Those over 85 presently have an average eighth grade education. The world of the very old is disproportionately a world of women with little advanced formal education (Horn & Meer, 1989).

Today most older people over 65 live in their own homes or apartments, with 15% of the men living alone, and 41% of the women living alone. "Elderly women represent the fastest growing and single poorest segment of American society" (Minkler & Stone, 1989, p. 109). Only 5% of older adults are institutionalized in nursing homes, but 5% of 35 million people is 1,750,000 people – too many to warehouse, too many to hide, too many to forget about – too much life to waste.

Of that 5% in nursing homes and long-term care settings, who are we talking about? They are our brothers, our sisters, our mothers and fathers, our aunts and uncles, our husbands, wives and significant others, our neighbors, our friends. They are us! They are as alike and as different as each sunrise and sunset. It is their *sameness and uniqueness* that makes each of them - them, just as it is with us. They are people who were and are competent and deserved of respect. They were responsible as parents and siblings and spouses and friends and workers. They made contributions, they rode the carousel and now they are in the hands of strangers relying on them to do the right thing.

Some have lost physiological, biological, and/or cognitive functioning. Few, if any, have lost the ability to feel, though those feelings may be masked. Some are very different people because of the losses; but none are so different that they do not need: (a) affirmation of dignity and worth; (b) to be loved and to love; (c) to be in control and to have a say about their lives. They are adults, they are not children. There is much to learn from them. We should journey to them; their journey should not always be to us.

Pearl Salotto

Older persons in nursing homes have been characterized as "depressed, unhappy, intellectually ineffective, possessing a negative self-image, docile, submissive and having low interest in their surroundings" (Smith & Bengtson, 1989, p. 166). These are characteristics of what is known as the social breakdown syndrome; that results from a loss of privacy, personal possessions, friends, and which ultimately affects our capacity to care. Professionals need to ask if the provision of quality and meaningful services can effect those characteristics and balance the losses.

Quality services, quality care, quality assurance are currently very important in health care delivery. In some ways it is sad that we have come to a point where we must mandate quality care; that we cannot trust each other to care for each other. On the other hand, we can look positively on the suggestions and guidelines being presented that better prepare and assist professionals to provide care that is of high quality. Often at the very heart of the quality issue is money. Quality services typically cost money. Programs in long-term facilities are understaffed and staffs are underpaid. It is difficult to justify paying more for someone who works at McDonalds (Eagan, 1989) than we pay someone who cares for our older people. However, this society seems to pay lip service to valuing the human resource. We do not seem willing to pay to educate, maintain, habilitate or rehabilitate it, yet we continue to purport it as our most precious resource. If we want quality services we must be willing to pay for them. Those who provide those services need to demonstrate knowledge, competence and caring – and through such demonstration we will see a return on our investment.

As a professional in the human services, caring and love is one aspect in the provision of services. We are reminded that "all true love is grounded on esteem" (Buckingham, 1958, p. 150), and we should never forget what saved ET! Another aspect in the provision of human services is knowledge. We know that "real knowledge like everything else of value is not to be obtained easily" (Arnold, 1955, p. 316), and that "all wish to possess knowledge, but few, comparatively speaking, are willing to pay the price" (Juvenal, 1955, p. 319). Professionals responsible for providing quality services to human beings have got to be willing to pay the price. We must acquire the knowledge necessary to assure, as best we can, quality. We must seek to balance our capacity to care and our capacity to know.

We need to approach problems from a "what if?" perspective. As we seek to "master the possibilities," we focus on problems and limitations. There may be setbacks, but we continue to seek solutions. We need to insist on the highest standards as we provide services to our older people.

We should strive to remain energized, stimulated, and inspired, as difficult as that may be in a bureaucracy. We need to rely on our own knowledge, instinct and experiences. We cannot automatically accept that the system knows more than we do. We should listen, watch, learn, evaluate and determine the strength and weakness of the system. *We cannot march to the absurd simply because the tune is being played!* Our purpose as advocates *is not* to see that the system survives in its insanity; it is to see that people (for whom the system was created to serve) are served well.

Staff/participant ratios are critical to quality care and provisions of quality services to those in long-term care settings; in the 1990s, care-providers have got to fight for lower ratios. Large activity rooms and a full plate of activities do not and will not lead to nourishment or satisfaction for all. They do not necessarily enhance quality of life for older people.

In the 1990s, there should be a change not only in the types of services provided, but in the way services are provided. For example, on my birthday, I do not invite all members of the college (my institutional environment) to my party; I don't even invite members of my department. I choose to share my birthday with people who know me – I choose to share it with people with whom I share meaning. For quality services to exist we've got to move away from the large group/institution activities; we've got to increase the number of staff, and we've got to provide opportunities for the person and his/her nucleus of meaningful relationships to share experiences together. That is what quality is about – sharing experiences with those with whom we share meaningful relationships. Quality does not equate with participating in an activity. The types of opportunities and the way services will be provided are as diverse as the individuals housed under the one roof; the possibilities are limitless, we need only explore, discover and implement them.

We all have the capacity and power; vulnerability and need; we all have hidden potential! The problem with the medical model is that it focuses on what's wrong with us. For physicians that may be necessary, for those of us providing human services it can be limiting. It limits us to seeing what is wrong with someone rather than what is right with someone. Even those who are most ill or impaired may be capable of more than we imagine or expect. Let us not limit them by our doubts and lack of expectation. Let us assume roles as facilitators and enablers, not controllers. Let us **EMPOWER** the person any way we can! We need to affirm and reaffirm the strengths of the individual, while being cognizant of and gentle with the problems and limitations.

"Recreation activities which are regressive, which resemble busy work given to children, will not promote feelings of growth, achievement and self worth. On the contrary, they will only demoralize individuals, family and staff." (Greenblatt, 1988, et. al). When a human being is cut off from adequate stimuli, from sources of information, and the opportunity to interact, previously attained competence levels begin to disintegrate. Provision of activities in itself is not beneficial. Provision of meaningful experiences, and the way activities are presented and conducted are important variables relating to benefit and satisfaction.

Staff-patient relationships in nursing homes function to encourage dependency among residents and discourage independent behaviors. Recreation activities provide opportunities for interdependence and control and competence.

Research on autonomy is reasonably interpreted as indicating the role of the helpless elder is to a significant degree shaped by the immediate environment of the individual – its opportunities and constraints – "experiments with people showing extreme functional losses – residents and prospective residents of nursing homes have shown that these losses are reversed by modest increases in autonomy" (Rowe & Kahn, 1989, p. 29). Shary and Iso-Ahola (1989) in a study on autonomy in nursing homes found that residents experience helplessness and a loss of zest. They found profit-oriented facilities (because of focus on efficiency) did not compare favorably with not-for-profit facilities which were more focused on facilitating individual autonomy and control. They indicate that due to the typical care and treatment in nursing homes, residents erroneously infer incompetence in situations in which they have been previously successful. The two researchers support the premise that a sense of control has a definite and positive role in sustaining life. Our role, then, is to provide as much opportunity as we can for individuals to exercise personal choice, control, and responsibility. One can quickly see that a multitude of opportunities are needed to accommodate different levels of competence.

A study by Kelly et al. (1987) found activities which were most important to adults provided satisfying interactions with persons who are significant to us (family, friends), and which enhanced our sense of competence, worth, and personal expression. These researchers concluded that social bonding and companionship are central to subjective well being. It is not the numbers of people we interact with but the quality of the relationships that allow for mutual sharing.

Loneliness is a fact of life for many older persons. A common concern among those working in long-term facilities is the lack of opportunity to sit and talk (to do more than physically interact) with the people they serve. In examining Maslow's (1970) Need Hierarchy we might conclude that until the needs for love and belonging are met it many be useless to hope that older people in nursing homes will be motivated to sing and dance and exercise, to remain competent or to gain new competencies in the activities we provide. Until the need for love and belonging is met, they may not care about activities we promote to enhance self-esteem. We need to strive to provide opportunities that meet those unmet needs, particularly for love and belonging.

We must not just do *for* older people, we also need to do *with* them. It is important to most of us to give love, not only receive it. We need to ask if we are allowing our older people in nursing homes/long-term care settings to give. Could that be one reason pet therapy has proven to be so successful – because the older individual has once again been given the opportunity to love? Does that not also strike a chord for the potential for intergenerational programming?

Activity opportunities in the future need to focus on providing opportunities for meaningful interaction and experiences. The key to understanding someone is to know them and we need to facilitate that opportunity between and among people. We have to help people become connected. That means more than just organizing volunteers to come in every-once-in-a-while; it means facilitating the opportunity for friendship and meaningful relationships to evolve. It will take time and effort on the care-provider's part and on the part of the resident and the "new significant person." A match needs to be made and perhaps in some cases it will not be made. However, without meaningful relationships, the rest of it falls far second in the quest for quality of life. Three of the eight characteristics identified by Knapp (1986) as comprising a relationship are important to understanding the difference between *anyone* coming in and *interacting* with us and *someone* coming in and *sharing* with us. The *uniqueness* of a relationship focuses on an idiosyncratic communication system – that is, conversation is different between two people sharing a relationship than it is between two strangers or two acquaintances. The *depth* (characterized by the openness between two people) is different as is the *breadth*, being able to discuss a variety of topics/interests. It is the degree to which each of these exist that define the relationship and which makes it something to value as it enhances the quality of our life. Thus in the future at the heart of quality services in long-term care facilities is *the provision for meaningful relationships*.

Pets in programming and intergenerational programming should continue to be supported. Children's day care centers in nursing homes provide opportunity for generations to interact and share. A latchkey phone line program, linking those in the nursing home who have sufficient cognitive functioning with those children in the community who so desperately need to know someone is there for them, has potential benefits for those participating. These and similar programs seem to lay a foundation for meaningful interaction.

Older people, particularly those in long-term care facilities may experience significant physical, emotional, and social stress. Activities should be geared toward helping to alleviate this stress, toward maintaining homeostasis. It is common knowledge that aerobic activity releases endorphins positively affecting stress and depression. Laughter is said to have a similar effect. Thus, for those who are not mobile enough for, nor interested in aerobics, we should consider providing opportunities to laugh! We need to move beyond schedules or canned laughter (movies, comics, sketches, etc.). We need to create opportunities for moments of genuine laughter typically occurring between and among people who share something in common. Relaxation exercises also need to be a part of stress reduction activity programming.

Opportunities need to be provided for touch. We have come to be very cautious of who we touch and how we touch, but we all need to be touched; and most of us would probably agree it is more meaningful when we are touched by someone we share a meaningful relationship with. I am single and have been my whole life. It is difficult for most people I interact with to comprehend what it is like to go for days without being touched by another human being. I can personally attest to the value of a hug genuinely given. What a sad state of affairs it is at the end of the 20th century that there are older people in places called nursing homes who are only touched when someone needs to do something to them. Touch, then, should be an integral part of programming and provision of services.

We should also focus on activities and experiences that provide enjoyment for the moment. There are some older people in nursing homes who do not need to learn a new skill, don't need something that will carry over to tomorrow, and don't need something they might use as a stepping stone to trying something else next year. There is nothing wrong and indeed there is a lot to be said for an activity or experience that just for that moment brings us joy or satisfaction and for just that moment brightens and enhances the quality of one's life.

The goals have got to be different for an older person in a nursing home than they are, for example for a young man of 20 with a brain injury who is in a nursing home. We have got to recognize the differences and help those who pay for the services and establish the guidelines/standards to recognize the differences also. Just because we house X number of people under one roof does not mean one pot of soup will satisfy them all. The menus (services) need to be different and the meals (programs) need to be served differently. Let's get back to the basics and some common sense!

If we continue to provide activities the way we have been providing and do provide them, it's not going to make a significant dent in the quality of life of the residents of nursing homes. Obviously though something is better than nothing, something is not enough, particularly as it relates to the provision of quality services and enhancing quality of life. Providing a sensory stimulating environment doesn't mean much when you feel all alone, scared, confused, angry, not in control; when your place in the world is not valued, and your unique qualities as a human being are not recognized – or worse – ignored.

Quality care is more than custodial care, and if the government and those setting standards of quality are serious, resources must be provided that best facilitate that care. It should be understood by any care provider that an older person may perceive or feel *loss* of control, *loss* of love and belonging, *loss* of self-esteem, loss of self. Those losses must be balanced with gains. We have got to facilitate meaningful relationships, an opportunity to share experiences and activities with those whom we share meaning. We've got to, then, find something each can be successful at, that is purposeful. We've got to move away from negative expectations and the consequent self-fulfilling prophecies. We've got to accept each person for whom he or she is – we don't have to like them – but we've got to accept them. That acceptance cannot be based on their doing what we want them to do, but rather their being who they are. And from the most highly functioning and competent to the least – we've got to embrace personhood and be thankful we had the opportunity to experience each person as a unique human being!

In conclusion, it is not participating in life's activities that enhances life's satisfaction or quality of life; it is participating in meaningful activities and having meaningful experiences that enhance our life's quality. We must continue to strive to provide opportunities for activities and experiences that are meaningful and engaging.

Meaning and meaningful activities, then, are our goals, our purpose, and our challenge. What we bring or do not bring is all that these individuals we serve will or will not have. It is each of our individual effort that will contribute to or not contribute to the enhancement of someone else's quality of life. We must bring professional knowledge and human love and common sense. We bring what we are, we bring what we value, we bring ourselves. We must trust each other to do what's right!

* The U.S Census Bureau updates national statistics every ten years. The statistics in this article are based on the 1990 figures.

References:

Arnold, T., (1955), In T. Edwards, C.N. Catrevas, & J. Edwards, (Eds.). *The New Dictionary of Thoughts* (316). New York: Standard Book Company.

Buckingham. (1958). In *Treasury of Familiar Quotations* (150). New York: Avenel Books.

Eagan, A.B. (1989). Options for Aging. In H. Cox (Ed.), *Aging, 6th ed.* (175-180). Guilford, Conn.: Dushkin Publishing Group, Inc.

Greenblatt, F.S. (1988). *Therapeutic Recreation for Long-TermCare Facilities*. New York: Human Sciences Press.

Henderson, C. (1989). Old Glory: America Comes of Age. In H. Cox (Ed.), *Aging, 6th ed.* (19-22). Guilford, Conn.: Dushkin Publishing Group, Inc.

Horn, J.C., & Meer, J. (1989). The Vintage Years. In H. Cox (Ed.), *Aging, 6th ed.* (83-91). Guilford, Conn.: Dushkin Publishing Group, Inc.

Juvenal, (1955). In T. Edwards, C.N. Catrevas, & J. Edwards, (Eds.). *The New Dictionary of Thoughts* (319). New York: Standard Book Company.

Kelly, J.R., Steinkamp, M.W., & Kelly, J.R. (1987). Later-life Satisfaction: Does Leisure Contribute? *Leisure Sciences* 9(3), 189-200.

Knapp, M., (1978). *Social Intercourse: From Greeting to Goodbye*. Boston: Allyn & Bacon.

Maslow, A.H. (1970). *Motivation and Personality* (2nd ed.). New York: Harper and Row.

Minkler, M., & Stone, R. (1989). The Feminization of Poverty and Older Women. In H. Cox (Ed.), *Aging, 6th ed.* (104-110). Guilford, Conn.: Dushkin Publishing Group, Inc.

Rowe, J.W., & Kahn, R.L. (1989). Human Aging: Usual and Successful. In H. Cox (Ed.), *Aging, 6th ed.* (23-29). Guilford, Conn.: Dushkin Publishing Group, Inc.

Shary, J.M., & Iso-Ahola, S.E. (1989). Effects of a Control-relevant Intervention on Nursing Home Residents' Perceived Competence and Self-esteem. *Therapeutic Recreation Journal* , 1, 7-15.

Smith, K.F., & Bengtson, V.L. (1989). Positive Consequences of Institutionalization: Solidarity Between Elderly Parents and Their Middle-aged Children. In H. Cox (Ed.), *Aging, 6th ed.* (166-174). Guilford, Conn.: Dushkin Publishing Group, Inc.

Article 2:
ANIMALS AND INDIVIDUALS WHO ARE ELDERLY: CAN PETS FILL THE VOID?
(Pearl Salotto)

Pet Assisted Therapy programs in nursing homes can enrich the lives of individuals who are elderly in many ways. The joy of touching a soft, gentle, and responsive pet can bring a smile to those who don't often smile; can give unconditional love to those who believe they are unlovable, and can bring a new feeling of worth and reason to wake up in the morning to those whose lives are empty with loneliness. Regular visits, by the same temperament tested therapy pet can bring something to look forward to, to those who have no other meaningful relationships. These therapy pets can provide happy and joyous experiences to those who may not know or care what day it is, except when the pets are coming; they can give a feeling of being needed to those who feel useless; they can give something to talk about, to those who may not otherwise have anything to say.

A friend of mine once commented to me – that no nursing home, no matter how fancy, is a pleasant place in which to be. Unfortunately no truer words were ever said. By the time one enters a nursing home, individuals probably have had serious deterioration in health, thereby being unable to care for themselves. They may be confused or disoriented. They have perhaps lost their homes and their jobs either through retirement or inability to work.Whatever had kept them busy (job, volunteer work, raising a family) is now gone and they feel that they have lost their primary identity or role in society. Therefore, upon entering a nursing home, individuals have lost most of the control they had over their own lives.

Others now determine when and where they have meals, medication, and therapy. Chances are – any responsibilities they had over their life no longer exists. Their feelings of well-being continue to deteriorate as they become more dependent on the staff. Their opportunities to feel helpful or useful are minimal or non-existent. Their ability to nurture others might be lacking. As our society suffers from "ageism", most individuals fear the aging process and have difficulty maintaining their self-respect. Thus, feelings of despair, loneliness, pain and grief take over – and in truth there is little left to smile about. The fanciest of facilities doesn't mean an iota to a hurting soul, but rather as Dr. Ann Rancourt said previously – meaningful relationships are all that counts.

From my experience working in nursing homes, Donna Swanson's poem well describes the pain.

Minnie Remembers

God
My hands are old.
I've never said that out loud before
but they are.
I was so proud of them once.
They were soft

44

like the velvet smoothness of a firm, ripe
peach.
Now the softness is more like worn-out sheets
or withered leaves. When did these slender, graceful hands
become gnarled, shrunken claws?
When, God?
They lie here in my lap,
naked reminders of this worn-out
body that has served me too well!

How long has it been since someone touched me
Twenty years?
Twenty years I've been a widow.
Respected.
Smiled at.
But never touched.
never held so close that loneliness
was blotted out.

I remember how my mother used to hold me,
God,
When I was hurt in spirit or flesh,
she would gather me close,
stroke my silky hair
and caress my back with her warm hands.
O God, I'm so lonely!

I remember the first boy who ever kissed me.
We were both so new at that!
The taste of young lips and popcorn,
the feeling inside of mysteries to come.

I remember Hank and the babies.
How else can I remember them but together?
Out of the fumbling, awkward attempts of new
lovers came the babies.
And as they grew, so did our love.
And, God, Hank didn't seem to mind
if my body thickened and faded a little.
he still loved it. And he touched it.
And we didn't mind if we were no longer beautiful..
And the children hugged me a lot.
O God, I'm lonely!

God, why didn't we raise the kids to be silly
and affectionate, as well as

dignified and proper?
You see, they do their duty.
They drive up in their fine cars;
they come to my room to pay their respects.
They chatter brightly, and I reminisce.
But they don't touch me.
They call me "Mom" or "Mother"
or "Grandma."
Never Minnie.
My mother called me Minnie.
So did my friends.
Hank called me Minnie, too.
But they're gone.
And so is Minnie.
Only Grandma is here.
And God! She's lonely!

Used by permission of Donna Swanson, from MIND SONG, published by Donna Swanson, R.1 Box 159, Williamsport, IN 47993.

As society has become more aware of the tragedy of the plight of some individuals who are elderly, governmental and health care codes have come into place for individuals in long-term skilled nursing facilities and standards are constantly being upgraded by various accrediting bodies. Standards laid down by these groups require activity programs be available for individuals who are elderly for a certain number of hours per day during the week and also on weekends. Individual care plans must have an activity program based on the individual's needs. This is in the law and is annually checked. Long-term health care facilities found not in compliance are fined. However, this doesn't really seem to be rectifying the pain of individuals who are elderly living in such facilities. Music and Art Therapy in the past twenty years have come to be recognized as significant and meaningful. However, neither a music therapist bringing joyous song once a week (as wonderful and meaningful as this is) nor other good programs seem to fill the void.

Possible lack of funding for quality programming, and staff shortages make implementation of programs difficult. Many staff, although overworked, are truly caring, yet the tremendous emotional void remains in the lives of many individuals in these facilities.

While most nursing homes do their very best to assure a high quality of life for their residents, one can occasionally walk into a long-term skilled health care facility and see people with their heads lying on hard tables in the middle of the day or others laying back in Geri Chairs – mumbling, staring, or crying out in anguish or (just as painfully) sitting on their bed, whiling away the endless hours. (Arms that used to cradle, minds that used to be active, and bodies that used to move.) As in the words of my friend, "I know God brought you and DJ here – because I didn't have the slightest idea what I was going to do for the next four hours until dinner,"

Lady A's bond with D. J. is beautiful, but the situation is still heart wrenching. Her interaction with D. J. is joyous, but one hour a week isn't enough. Time weighs heavily on her, with nothing breaking the monotony except the next meal. Despite her blindness, this lady, recognizes and loves D. J. Despite her blindness and hearing loss, she waits for me, telling me that on Mondays she doesn't even turn on her radio as she is afraid she won't hear my knock at her door. Her smiles and exclamations of joy in the presence of D. J. defy words. Her conversations deal with her family and her despair at her blindness. She wants to know about my family (remembering my granddaughter Stacey even though she has never met her, but would like to) and my career as a PAT, in which she is very interested. These conversations allow her to focus on something other than her own problems.

The benefits of this program to her, include the joy of touching and feeling a living creature; the knowledge that she is special and that I will always find her, even if her door is locked and she doesn't hear my knock; her sharing of past memories, and the knowledge that our coming is something she can look forward to in the future. She says that D. J. is a celebrity here, which she is, but we also celebrate all those like this magnificent lady, who despite their own losses, are nonetheless thinking of others, as when she tells me that even if I have to cut her visit short, D. J. needs to visit her other friends., as well.

Are pets in nursing homes the answer to the void? Probably not – but they might come closer to alleviating the pain than anything I know of, with the exception of not being in the institution at all. The void could probably only be filled by individuals living out their lives within the loving arms of their family, which would of course include their pets.

The PAT programs that work in these facilities must be professionally planned and implemented, involving interaction on a regular basis with the same therapy pet, that has been temperament tested and medically screened. Pets have been an integral part of most families. Therefore, when one experiences multiple losses, upon entering a skilled nursing facility, therapy animals can soften the world a little. They can help lead to a life review, as animals lead to reminiscing and many other benefits. When PAT is part of the treatment or health care plan, medical referrals are filed, PAT objectives become part of the treatment plan and interactions are documented. "Pet Facilitated Therapy," due to bonding with the therapy animal, can then become a powerful motivator toward goals in mobility, range of motion, language, socialization, independence, enhanced self-esteem and enhanced quality and meaning in life.

I have spent the last several years working with individuals who are elderly in institutional settings. I have observed many interactions and have seen the benefits reaped by the individual's interactions with my therapy dog D. J. I have seen faces of joy abound. I have seen the glorious benefits of therapeutic touch [sensory stimulation]. I have heard, almost without exception, wherever D. J. and I go, stories pour forth – of family, pets, and happy memories. The joy of loving touch takes place not only within the designated Pet Assisted Therapy group, but with everyone and anyone we pass in client rooms, halls, and even elevators. This includes staff, clients, and family. I have observed that individuals who are said to be confused are incredibly focused during interactions with D. J. They become interested, involved, and enthusiastic.

It soon becomes apparent that, in the dog's presence – all of a sudden, these individuals are displaying caring and concern, not only for the dog's welfare and needs, but for each others. Memories come pouring forth. Animal interaction also motivates many people to come out of their rooms even if they are too ill, sad or depressed to come out for anything else. People who are normally passive, who show no reaction or emotion, become actively involved in interaction with D. J. To say that people "smile" in D. J.'s presence would be a gross understatement. D. J. serves as a focus for love, which allows the bond between her and an individual to grow stronger and stronger. The mutual love between D. J. and the individual then extends to include me as well, whereupon socialization, communication and friendship, which is therapy at its best, can take place. I have often thought that despite the ongoing disagreements among individuals in this field regarding professional definitions, that we could well solve the problem by simply using the title – "Pet Facilitated Friendship."

In addition to the universal benefits already described, D. J. and I have had numerous touching experiences. One lady at a nursing home said, "Could you leave D. J. here for a soft pillow tonight and pick her up in the morning." Another friend, who touchingly said as she was holding D. J.'s paw, "This is the sweetest touch I've felt in twenty years."

One beloved lady spoke to me as D. J. was sleeping across her feet. She opened up to me – as she had to no one else – about her recent loss of a family member. My interaction with her took place weekly over a year's period, as the bond – that she instantly felt with D. J. – grew and expanded to a bond of friendship, trust, openness, respect, and caring for me. Needless to say, I cared deeply for her, as well. (In the original Greek meaning of the word therapist, both parties benefited as a result of the treatment.)

D. J. gives Lady V gentle touch, softness, love, and continuity at a time when she is grieving, sad, sick, and trying desperately to "hang in there." She is trying to live up to her goals – being good to people, when another part of her wants to leave this world of pain and loneliness. She is content when she is petting D. J. or when D. J. sits proudly and happily against her legs to be petted. D. J. won't budge from her place against her – knowing her mission – knowing the joy she gives and the need she meets and receiving back all that she could ever want – through this lady's loving hands. Any distractions in the lobby or any movement of people have no appeal to D. J. D. J. and this lady are simply content with each other (see cover photo).

This lady has talked to me about so many things and shared with me so much of her life, as D. J. sleeps contentedly at her feet or sits proudly at her side. She has talked to me about her family and her childrens' families, their professions and interests. She has expressed grief over her losses and in an unforgettable moment she shared with me pictures that were fifty years old of when she was a bride. In the midst of those pictures was a newspaper clipping of herself and D. J., taken when our program was first started over a year ago. As D. J.'s picture is among her most cherished keepsakes, D. J.'s time with her, is among her most "cherished" times of the week. She once told me that if her loved ones in heaven could see her, they would know she was not alone.

This lady, D. J., and I have a bond, which is not only PAT at its best, but a beautiful and special relationship for all three of us with D. J. being "the tie that binds."

Another lady friend of D. J.'s and then mine, was moved to poetic responses observing interactions with D. J. Other individuals in the PAT group with this lady, would make comments like "Isn't she beautiful" or "I love D. J. so much." D. J. would extend her paw or give kisses, or wag her tail as if to say, "Thank you." My friend said, "D. J. is speaking lovingly back to us, as we are speaking lovingly of her."

Lady C opens her heart in the presence of D. J. She wants D. J. to have water, to go free in her room and to look out the window. She wants D. J. to be completely happy and relaxed. Her nurturing comes out in the presence of D. J. She talks about her love for all living things. Her poetry and creativity come out, leading her to say, "I never knew a dog that wasn't special" and "D. J. is speaking to me." She feels special in the presence of D. J., saying, "How special you make me feel when you stop by to visit with me." Her nurturing comes out in her caring, consideration, and thoughtfulness for me. She asks me if I have had lunch and she puts a sweater around my arms if she thinks I'm cold. I accept the sweater, even if I'm not cold, as I realize she needs these opportunities to give of herself to others. This lady says if I ever need to leave D. J. she would care for her. She even says if I need anything to let her know. She says she would like to hide D. J., so she could stay with her. She says D. J. could be a soft pillow.

This lady has asked to have D. J. loose in her room. When I hesitated, she said, "Why not? Why should she be on a leash? This is my room, no one's but mine and I want her to be free here." When I realized she had the right to make the decision and that I had complete faith in D. J.'s behavior, I removed the leash. D. J. took about two minutes to sniff around the room and then sat up against her and never moved for the remainder of the visit. The following week, this lady wanted D. J. to rest on her bed. I hesitated again, but realized pet policy allowed residents to make that decision. I laid my sweater on the bed and said, "Go Bed" to which D. J. eagerly responded. A half hour of PAT at its best followed. This lady and D. J. interacted in a relaxed and joyous manner. D. J. rolled over playfully on the bed and this wonderful lady laughed and talked delightfully about her love for living things and memories of her past and D. J. had the time of her life.

From the first moment - nothing but love - for D.J. and Clara. Clara Henderson was a resident of Wesley-On-East, Rochester, New York. Photo credit: Laurie Mercer, courtesy of Rochester Business Journal.

Tribute To Clara

This lady loves dogs.
This lady loves being in the presence of dogs.
This lady has a heart big enough to love all of God's creatures.
This lady is sweet and kind.
This lady is sharing and supportive and appreciative.
This lady is beautiful.
This lady makes our work seem worthwhile.

My dog, D. J. gives this special lady something to look forward to,
D. J. allows this lady to experience joy.
The poetry and gentleness in this lady comes out in the presence of D. J.
– but I have a feeling that this lady is gentle in spirit the rest of the time, as well.

It is my hope that D. J. allows this lady to forget her losses for awhile.
This lady believes that D. J. "speaks" to her with love,
as surely as D. J. is "touched" by her loving words and loving touches.

Pearl Salotto, 1988

Reflecting on this poem all these years later, I realize now that this lady's love for D. J, and D. J.'s love for her, would set me on a path that would embrace the rest of my life!

50

One lady, who needed to learn to manipulate her wheelchair with her arms, was so angry about her life, that she constantly refused to cooperate with therapists attempting to encourage her independence and mobility. She continued to refuse until, on one occasion, she saw D. J. across the room. I said, "Come on – I'll wait for you – it's your turn." She proceeded painstakingly, but determinedly, for the twenty minute trip across the activity room. Her joyous reward was relating to D. J.

Another lady there, who had not spoken a word since entering the nursing home, clearly loved D. J. and me. However, her joyous smiles always turned to a flood of tears, as her frustration and furor over her inability to speak overcame her. Then came that special day when a miracle happened. This lady was in a wheelchair and D. J. was on a chair, so the two of them could be close and in eye contact (per PAT policy.) As D. J. extended her paw to this lady, I said, "Is D. J. your friend?" and then "Are you D. J.'s friend?" She nodded affirmatively and joyously to both questions. D. J. was still holding the lady's hand with her paw. (True friends don't walk away from each other.) I quietly said to the lady, "Say FRIEND." She weakly, but determinedly uttered her first word since her stroke – saying FRIEND to D. J. Needless to say, amidst the sea of doctors and nurses standing around with tears in their eyes, perhaps more than one of them might have been wondering if, despite the fact that the type of interaction just witnessed was not in the medical textbooks when they went to school, the next generation of medical students should be reading about a remarkable "new treatment" based on a meaningful relationship with a canine friend.

Another remarkable reaction occurred with another friend of mine. She had never liked dogs, as her parents had told her to beware of them.

Lady H. happened to open her door as I was coming down the hall. When I asked her if she wanted to pet D. J. she said that she had never petted a dog in her life because she had grown up in the city and her parents had taught her never to touch a dog – as they were mostly stray and vicious. At this point, another lady told her, "But this is a wonderful dog and you would really love to pet her."

I explained to her that D. J. was a therapy dog and loved everyone. However, if she preferred not to touch her, that was fine, too. She could still visit with me. We visited for about fifteen minutes, with D. J. sitting calmly by my side in the hall. Our discussion did not focus on D. J. or dogs. We discussed many things and once she realized she enjoyed visiting with me, she suddenly said, "I'll try just one little pet." I guess at that instant of first contact with a soft gentle creature – eighty years of negative attitudes disappeared and the joy and amazement on her face was something I will never forget. She invited D. J. and me into her room and told me to be sure to come back again next week. In the weeks to come she always invited us into her room saying, "Of course I want you to visit. D. J. is my friend. D. J. is the nicest dog in the world. She must be in a class of her own because I trust her and I know she loves me."

This lady went on to say, "Would you think that I had never touched a dog in all my eighty years and now I can't wait to pet her. "This lady enjoys D. J. wherever we met – in her room, in the lobby or in the hallway. When others are around she exclaims, "all my life no one could get me to touch any dog, but now no one could keep me away."

Usually in PAT, the therapy animal paves the way for the human-to-human interaction. In this spectacular situation, the reverse was true.

Many more reactions and much joy has taken place over the years since I received a certificate in PAT from Mercy College. I gave up a teaching career to work full-time as a professional Pet Assisted Therapy Facilitator, which can only be described as a gift and a privilege. I recall one gentleman saying, "Wait here, please. I'll be right back." A staff person advised me that he was confused and would never remember to come back. I waited anyway and sure enough he returned, clutching a wrinkled picture of his wife and dog, both long deceased. Another gentleman, who instantly bonded with D. J., escorted D. J. and I up and down the hospital corridors, proclaiming to one and all that they wouldn't want to miss petting D. J. Or the lady in the hospital's activity room who threw open her arms welcoming D.J.'s kisses and exclaimed, "How did you know it was my birthday." Or another lady, who hollered across the room, "Watch out for her tail. It is under the leg of the rocking chair." When I turned to thank the staff person, I was told it was a client who alerted me and that she usually didn't get involved in anything.

If one's ability to react and care has been shut down due to despair, would it be too simplistic to suggest that the desire to share the love that is inside, might be re-awakened by an animal whose unconditional love touches a spark deep within.

As words defy description when trying to explain the good feelings that D. J. and individuals in nursing homes give to one another, suffice it to say that the smiles that D. J. and other therapy animals have brought, couldn't be tallied on a computer printout, but, rather where it counts – in many human hearts.

Article 3:
FOR A BETTER FUTURE – FOR INDIVIDUALS WHO ARE ELDERLY – VIA PET ASSISTED THERAPY

<u>Jan Hindley</u> recently received her <u>Master's Degree in Social Work</u> and is currently employed as a <u>Substance Abuse Counselor</u> at CODAC Treatment Agency. Having spent much of her life working towards the humane treatment of animals, she is a firm believer in the power of the human-animal bond to improve conditions for all living creatures, and plans to incorporate this belief in her social work career.

"Integrity vs despair" is how Erik Erikson described the inner conflict of old age. "Acceptance of oneself and one's role in life." "If this task is not accomplished, the individual may dedicate this time to unfinished tasks and feelings of despair and disgust." (Clinical Art Therapy, Landgarten). Unfortunately, these quotes accurately describe the plight of many of our elderly population.

Today the older population is the fastest growing segment of our society. It is estimated that 5% of individuals who are elderly live in some type of institutional care; many individuals who are elderly live with their families or spouse, and some live with friends. This leaves the majority of individuals who are elderly living alone. Many of the more fortunate are healthy and financially secure enough to find living alone satisfying and a good choice. Many, however, find themselves living alone because of unpredictable circumstances and would not chose this lifestyle. Many of these individuals who are elderly are not healthy or financially secure and because of this become isolated in their solitary homes.

Our government has seen the need to provide for these individuals who are elderly in part through home health care programs. These certified home health agencies offer skilled nursing, physical therapy, social work, homemaker/home health aide services, and nutrition counseling. These are Medicare-certified home health agencies. There are also volunteer agencies providing support for the isolated individuals who are elderly. One such program is the Neighborhood Friendly Visitor Program which provides companionship and friendly support to elderly who are homebound. Volunteers visit, read, write letters, and chat with individuals who are shut-in, who benefit from regular social contact. (1995 Pocket Manual of Elder Service).

Working with the geriatric population requires a special type of person. This person must be empathetic to the special needs of individuals who are elderly. He/she must be educated in the physical and emotional developmental stage of his/her client. He/she must be personally healthy, both physically and mentally, to withstand what Erikson warned of, "feelings of despair" in his/her client. The inclusion of Pet Assisted Therapy in working with elderly who are homebound could greatly benefit both the therapist and his/her client.

There are many special challenges facing the worker who has chosen to share his/her abilities and time with the geriatric population. Many workers and clients alike, find it difficult not to be too aware of the fact that this stage of life development precedes impending death. Individual men and women who are elderly also experience a role change that is beyond their control. This often results in a great feeling of loss, hopelessness, and helplessness. This segment of individuals who are elderly often lack the motivation to take care of themselves physically and emotionally due to the lack of contact with caring others. They feel they have become a burden to society and perhaps a burden to themselves, as well.

How can Pet Assisted Therapy aid in addressing these problems? Many of the steps needed are already in place. The presence of several different home health institutions is one entry possibility. By staffing their agencies with social workers or home health aides who are also certified Pet Assisted Therapists, agencies would be able to offer this service to appropriate clients at a minimal cost increase, as well as minimal change to their system's structure of providing care to its clients. These are two important issues when implementing change.

The needs of the clients, which would be addressed through the help of the worker and the therapy pet would include:

1. To learn to focus on the here and now of daily life and in doing so appreciating the opportunities available today. Pets can be excellent role models in living in the here and now. They accept each moment as it comes with eagerness and spontaneity. Witnessing this and discussing this with the worker may help an individual who is elderly embrace a new sense of enjoyment in his daily life.

2. To successfully complete a life-time review. The loss of role identity to the individual who is elderly (either through retirement from a job or career or the end of being a homemaker and head of family) often leads to a loss of self-esteem and depression. The therapy pet can facilitate communication with the client about past life experiences involving pets or animals which the worker and client can explore. By once more experiencing these memories the self-identity and self-pride of the client can be strengthened.

3. To improve overall wellness of the client: This may seem too broad a goal, however, there are many small steps that can be taken to accomplish this goal.
   a. Physically, the presence of an accepting, loving companion can reduce the level of stress the client may be feeling.
   b. The spontaneity and naturalness of the pet can bring comfort and humor into the visit.
   c. Through petting, brushing, playing games or walking the pet, the client can be motivated to be active, thus making use of both gross and fine motor skills.
   d. The sense of touch can be awakened by the feel of fur or a wet tongue or cold nose.
   e. Even the senses of smell, sight, and hearing can be touched by the presence of the therapy pet, perhaps making a memory link with the past. In this way cognitive well-being can also be increased. By having the client challenge his memory about past experiences or by teaching him new information about the therapy pet, the client is activating his thinking processes.

f. An important part of the clients wellness is certainly his emotional state. This is an area in which the therapy pet, the worker, and the client can make great progress. The validation of being accepted as a competent person who can not only accept the love and trust of the pet, but also return this love and trust, can bring about renewed self-worth. This love and trust can be "tried out" on the non-threatening therapy pet and hopefully, grow to include the worker and others.

g. Motivating the client to become open to life and to social supports in his environment is a crucial part of improving the quality of all aspects of life. Isolation and despair go hand-in-hand and there is a basic need in all of man, young or old, to connect with life. By offering a safe first step to making this connection, the therapy pet and worker can help the client face this life development stage with integrity.

The steps needed to implement Pet Assisted Therapy into the home health profession would include:

1. Contact possible agencies and help them to become aware of the benefits already being accomplished in institutionalized settings – such as nursing homes.
2. Be certified as a PAT, as well as knowledgeable in human services specializing in geriatrics.
3. Work with a certified therapy pet who has a temperament and physical qualities (size, non-shedding coat) that will be conducive to home visits.
4. Through staff meetings and consultations with family and client, design a list of clients who would seem appropriate for Pet Assisted Therapy.
5. Set up appointments with clients to discuss the program, including Pet Assisted Therapy in the treatment plan with the case managers.
6. Once Pet Assisted Therapy is in place, call before each visit to ensure pet is welcome and client's home is in a safe condition for the pet's visit.
7. Remember to let the pet work its magic with as little interference as is needed. The goal is to help the client learn to enjoy life in the here and now.

Section 2:
PET ASSISTED THERAPY AND INDIVIDUALS WITH DEVELOPMENTAL CHALLENGES

Article 1:
ANIMALS AND CHILDREN WITH DISABILITIES

Ruth E. Gallucci lives in Warwick, Rhode Island with her husband Frank, daughter Francesca, son Joseph, a cat, Mima, and a dog, Pashi. She has her Masters Degree in Special Education and her Certificate of Advanced Graduate Studies in Special Education Administration. Ruth has been a Special Education Teacher since 1988. She advocates for the rights of all people and animals. Ruth respects diversities in humanity and hopes to teach Francesca and Joseph the same. She wishes to thank her mother, Pearl Salotto, for her guidance in becoming the person she is today. Ruth strives to give her children everything her mother has given to her.

One cannot discuss disabilities in isolation from the people involved. Every individual with a disability is a person first, with his or her own strengths, weaknesses, likes, and dislikes. The disability is but one part of the person. Just as you would not like to be identified as "the woman with the big nose" or "the fat man," a person with a disability does not want to be called "that disabled person." When discussing an individual always use "person first" language. If you must refer to a person's disability it is more appropriate to say "the fourth grade boy who has developmental disabilities." Many people with disabilities will tell you that the largest handicap they face is that which is imposed on them by society. We must respect individual diversity and thus teach others to do the same.

There are three fundamental pieces of federal legislation, which along with state laws, protect individuals with disabilities. The first is Section 504 of the Rehabilitation Act of 1973, which prohibits recipients of federal funding from discriminating against qualified individuals with disabilities in programs, activities, services and employment. It ensures that schools receiving federal funds take the steps necessary to make their programs and services afford equal opportunity to people with disabilities. It also requires that individuals with disabilities be permitted to participate in programs and activities in the most integrated setting appropriate. The individual must be permitted to participate with whatever modifications he or she requires. The second piece of legislation was originally passed as the Education for All Handicapped Children Act in 1975. It is now entitled the Individuals with Disabilities Education Act, (IDEA). IDEA ensures a free and appropriate public education to each and every child with a disability. Schools must identify, evaluate, and develop individual education plans (IEPs). They must meet each child's needs in the least restrictive environment (LRE) and provide procedural safeguards to ensure their rights. This law allows for federal financial aid to states that meet its requirements. The last of the three laws is the Americans with Disabilities Act of 1990, (ADA). This law extends Section 504's mandate against discrimination to the private sector, and to state and local government agencies. Individuals with disabilities must be permitted to participate in regular programs if they choose to do so. However, separate programs are permitted when necessary to ensure equal opportunity. Public schools must meet program accessibility requirements. All three pieces of legislation have assisted individuals with disabilities in accessing their community in ways never before possible.

A child between the ages of 3 and 21, determined through evaluation to have a specific disability (as outlined in the IDEA), which adversely effects his or her educational performance, will be entitled to special educational services. More recently, part H of IDEA entitles infants and toddlers between 0 and 3 with disabilities to receive early intervention services. An individual's disability must be covered under IDEA in order to receive special educational services. These disabilities include specific learning disabilities, behavioral disorders, mental retardation, orthopedic impairments, other health impairments, speech or language impairments, visual impairments, multiple disabilities, autism, traumatic brain injury, deaf-blindness, and developmental delay (3-5 year olds). A child who does not qualify for services under IDEA may qualify for services under 504.

Understanding about the different disabilities will be of assistance when working with children receiving special education. A student with a learning disability has difficulty in one or more of the basic psychological processes involved in understanding or using language, spoken or written, which manifests itself in an imperfect ability to listen, think, speak, read, write, spell or do mathematical calculations. This individual will show a discrepancy between ability and performance levels. A student with behavioral disorders may display inappropriate behaviors or feelings under normal circumstances, feel unhappy or depressed to an abnormal degree, have a tendency to display physical symptoms or fears associated with personal or school problems, or have an inability to build or maintain satisfactory interpersonal relationships with peers and teachers. An individual with mental retardation has a significantly sub-average general intellectual functioning along with deficits in adaptive behavior. A child with an orthopedic impairment has a physical disability caused by a congenital anomaly, disease or other cause. Other health impairments refer to limited strength, vitality or alertness due to chronic or acute health problems, such as a heart condition, tuberculosis, rheumatic fever, asthma, sickle cell anemia, hemophilia, epilepsy, lead poisoning, leukemia or diabetes. A student with a hearing impairment will have either permanent or fluctuating hearing loss or deafness. A student with a speech or language impairment has a communication disorder, such as stuttering, impaired articulation, receptive or expressive language impairment or voice impairment. An individual with a visual impairment includes visual acuity ranging from 20/70 to 20/200 in the better eye after refraction, a significant loss of field of vision in both eyes or blindness. A child with multiple disabilities has a combination of disabilities, such as mental retardation and blindness or mental retardation and an orthopedic impairment, which causes severe educational difficulties. A student with autism has a developmental disability significantly affecting verbal and non-verbal communication and social interaction. The individual may engage in repetitive activities and movements, resist environmental or routine changes, and respond in an unusual manner to sensory experiences. An individual with a traumatic brain injury has an acquired injury to the brain caused by an external physical force, resulting in a total or partial functional disability and/or psychosocial maladjustment. The student's difficulties can involve cognition, language, memory, attention, reasoning, abstract thinking, judgment, problem-solving, sensory, perceptual and motor disabilities, psychosocial behavior, physical functions, information processing and speech. A student with deaf-blindness has concomitant hearing and visual impairments causing severe communication, developmental and educational problems. Finally, an individual with a developmental delay has a twenty-five percent (25%) delay and/or raw score equal to or greater than two standard deviations below the mean in one of the following areas of development, or a score equal to or greater than 1.5 standard deviations below the mean in two or more areas: social/emotional or behavioral adjustment, cognition, receptive or expressive language, visual perceptions, or fine or gross motor. Children between three and five are frequently considered to have a developmental delay if they meet the criteria or if they have a diagnosed physical or mental condition. Learning more about various disabilities will prove beneficial when working in special education; however, the best way to know an individual is by spending time with him or her. Remember, each child is unique.

Each child's special educational services begins with an Individual Education Plan (IEP), in which a team of professionals, including the parents, and student if appropriate, work together in forming goals and objectives specifically designed to meet the child's individual needs. The team will also decide what is required to meet these goals and objectives. A student with multiple disabilities, such as severe retardation and cerebral palsy may have goals which involve basic communication, socialization, mobility and daily living skills. A student with a behavioral disorder may have goals which focus on impulse control, following directions, and peer relations. Goals are written on a yearly basis with a focus on the long-term plan. What does the team hope the individual will be able to do in the future? What small steps can be taken at this point which can be of assistance? Finally, the team must decide what services the child requires to reach these goals. Will the child need speech therapy, occupational therapy, or physical therapy? Could Pet Assisted Therapy be of assistance? Could a pet motivate a child to learn? What outcomes could a pet assist a child in achieving? The benefits of pets are plentiful and are evident in the areas of cognition, speech and language, behavior, socialization and fine and gross motor development.

IDEA mandates that students needs are met in the "least restrictive environment" (LRE). This means that children should be educated within the regular classroom unless another placement is found necessary through the IEP process. Many people have asked why children with disabilities should be educated in the regular class. Many assume that they can get more in a small self-contained setting. Recent research, however, is proving that the skills children gain in the segregated setting are less beneficial to them after their school years than those gained in an integrated setting. The benefits to everyone involved are evident in true "inclusive schools." These benefits range from social to academic, from children with and without disabilities to parents and staff. In the inclusive environment, all people are accepted. Their diversity is celebrated and their strengths acknowledged. Children get the message that it's OK to have differences and that we are all human. Self-esteem is enhanced for those treated just like everyone else and for those who for the first time are able to lend a helping hand. Allowing students with disabilities to learn and grow in a typical environment has proven to be successful. The goals children with disabilities attain have more relevance to the everyday lives of children their age and more value in their future. A common culture is shared in which the children now have more in common. The differences tend to have less importance. Another benefit comes to the child who must struggle to complete classwork. They can gain the much needed practice by assisting their peers on similar tasks. The regular classroom curriculum can be adapted in a way to fit any child. A great deal of preparation and continued discussion must take place in order to make inclusive programs work; however, the outcomes are well worth the investment. Classroom teachers have noted the skills they have gained by working in a more collaborative environment with other professionals. When the culture of the school is that of acceptance of diversity everyone benefits.

After the school years have passed and individuals with disabilities enter their adult lives, they must have options like everyone else. In the past, people were sent to live in institutions and then to group homes. Today options are greater. Today there is more support for individuals with disabilities to live on their own, with chosen roommates or in groups. Federal and state programs allow individuals the options of living arrangements and the assistance needed to make it work. Hopefully through strong schooling and a well developed network of friends and family, the individual is ready to be a productive member of society and to actively participate in his or her community.

The sheltered workshop is no longer the only option for employment. Today people with disabilities are being employed in various locations and given the continued support needed to be successful.

Whether we talk about children or adults, or people with or without disabilities, we all have the same basic needs. We all thrive in a loving and respectful environment. Pets in the home, school and workplace can serve a very special role in our lives. That special cat or dog can provide the unconditional love we all so greatly desire. For the individual with disabilities, this may be truly difficult to find. Pet Assisted Therapy animals provide a calming affect on an otherwise stressful situation. They provide a motivation which can make all the difference in the world. All people deserve the best opportunity life has to offer. All of us can make a difference in our world, some simply need a caring hand along the way.

Could Dutchess have had anything to do with Ruthie becoming the person she is today?

Article 2:
D. J. AS PART OF TREATMENT WITH ADULTS WITH DEVELOPMENTAL CHALLENGES
(Pearl Salotto)

Professional Pet Assisted Therapy (PAT) programs in an adult day treatment setting can enhance the quality of life of individuals with developmental challenges in many ways. PAT can enhance the ability to move toward independence and accomplishment of treatment goals. Friendship with a therapy animal can be a powerful motivator, encouraging individuals to walk and talk, when in some cases there may be no other motivating factor. There are numerous activities in which the individual can be involved with the therapy pet such as brushing, feeding or walking. In the case of walking, of course, the PAT Facilitator, as well as a staff person, will assist. These activities will vary according to one's therapy pet involved in treatment. These interactions lead to a whole host of benefits, cutting across all domains, including physical, social, psychological, and cognitive. Remarkable benefits can occur while the individual is just having fun.

Many individuals spontaneously relate to the therapy animals. Their faces light up and they reach out and touch. Some individuals either spontaneously talk, saying "Dog" or "Soft," while others can be motivated to repeat words the facilitator or staff models. Individuals without the ability to speak, "speak" their joy through body language and in some cases learn to sign "dog" or "hug" or "brush" or "walk."

Some individuals I have worked with will spontaneously sit on the floor and hug or "immerse" their faces in the soft fur of my therapy pet D. J., a three year old Samoyed. Many individuals are gentle and even though they may be unable to answer when the facilitator asks if the pet is a living thing – their actions do speak louder than words.

There are other individuals whose hands need to be held, hand over hand, as they pet the therapy animal. The technique of hand over hand is done by taking the client's hand in the therapist's hand and guiding it to pet the therapy animal. This assures the therapy pet's safety. Other individuals need "hug over hug" so as not to squeeze too tightly in their enthusiasm.

Other individuals, who perhaps have had a life-long fear of animals, can be motivated to relate to the therapy pet one small step at a time. These individuals might be willing to look at the therapy pet through a glass door or over a gate. Eventually, over subsequent weeks and months, they might be willing to come closer and closer. Overcoming this terrible fear, through a program which goes slowly, at an individual's own pace, eventually can allow an individual to have many happy experiences. An individual may, therefore, be safer on community outings as he will, hopefully, no longer bolt if he sees an animal.

Initially, before individuals actually start PAT treatment, they need to have a medical referral on file recommending PAT. This referral would indicate that the individual has no known allergies to animals and no disease or behaviors which can harm the therapy pet. In addition, a PAT goal needs to be written, via overall treatment plan, to meet needs in specific domains. Also, individual assessments need to be made to determine attitudes toward animals and functioning level.

In addition, a PAT room needs to be designated. A written PAT policy needs to be in place, signed by administration, the PAT Facilitator, infection control personnel, and the PAT liaison. This policy specifies program guidelines, documentation and evaluation procedures, and an ethics statement which protects the well-being of all individuals and animals involved. The protocol needs to state that enough staff support will be provided and that the facilitator has the final say as to who is in the program, in order to ensure safety for all.

Once the background planning is in place, PAT sessions can begin. The individual and the therapy pet enjoy each other's company and eagerly interact in a variety of ways. One example of interaction could be the brushing of a therapy dog or cat. Other meaningful activities can include identifying the therapy pet's color, counting the therapy pet's feet, comparing body parts, etc. While the individual is having tremendous fun, PAT can be healing in many ways. Muscle tone is maintained or enhanced, as is range of motion in the fingers, hands, and arms. Pet Assisted Therapy is an ideal activity for individuals who need work on grasping. Concentration in an activity with the therapy pet, for a given number of seconds or minutes can also meet treatment goals for concentration or focusing. Many times an individual's motivation to accomplish their Daily Living Skills, i.e. brushing their own hair or teeth, is an outcome of the individual's helping the therapy pet to be appropriately groomed and cared for. The immeasurable benefit is the indescribable pride that the individual feels in "taking care of the therapy pet."

Activities, such as feeding the therapy pet or getting water, involve listening skills, and following directions such as walking, lifting, and pouring. Who could imagine the laughter and joy that occurs as patients are simply trying to meet fine motor goals by filling a pitcher and pouring it into D.J.'s bowl. D.J., in her enthusiasm, catches the stream of water in mid air. Nurturing a living creature, which is critical for feeling dignity and may not be frequently experienced, provides a major benefit. Above all, the individual experiences a pride and delight in these simple, but significant accomplishments.

Individuals with a treatment goal of walking a given number of feet or yards a day, may do so delightedly with the therapy pet. They may follow the therapy pet, who walks a few feet ahead with the Facilitator. They may also hold the therapy pet's leash. In these situations the Facilitator would also hold the leash and a staff person would hold the individual's arm. The benefits of renewed physical ability, exercise, fresh air, new awareness of body image (due to feeling the therapy dog's weight against their own), improved upper and lower body strength and balance, and joy to boot – what better programming could there be.

Many individuals love to play with the therapy pets. Therapy dogs, who are trained to retrieve and return balls, bean bags or dumbbells, can have a lot of fun returning objects to individual's laps, hands or placing them at their feet. Seeing a 100 year old individual, who has lived in a treatment center all her life, playing ball with my beloved D. J., is a sight to behold. While D. J. is not a natural retriever, she will eagerly return the ball for a piece of cheese or a "little hot dog." If PAT does nothing more than bring fun into lives, then it is more than worth it. Actually, PAT not only leads to fun, but transforms moods. Individuals who are upset may spontaneously lie near the therapy animal or the therapy animal may intuitively cuddle or nudge, thus changing gloomy feelings to joyous ones.

Pearl Salotto

For individuals whose treatment requires that they gain some independence by moving along on a "portable" board, following a beloved pet, is a joyful motivator. This can lead to an individual's ability to move along by pushing the moving board with his/her hands, as he/she lovingly follows the therapy pet. To the individual, this is not work, this is not therapy, this is the greatest thing in the world.

With individuals who laugh uncontrollably with joy, delight and pride, as the therapy dog chases the toy they have struggled to throw, jumps on the chair next to the wheelchair and deposits the toy back on the tray of the individual's chair, to be picked up and thrown again – this is PAT at its best. The individual knows that he/she is responsible for all the fun the therapy dog is having. The therapy dog is not just returning with the toy, but bringing it back to her or him. The dog and the individual have bonded. They have built up a relationship due to regularly, scheduled treatment sessions over many months, to which they both look forward.

Speaking of PAT at it's best – who can imagine a more heartwarming experience than an individual, so touched by the interaction, that she reaches out with two arms, one hugging the therapy pet and the other arm hugging the Facilitator. Love overflows in PAT sessions in many directions. Not only does the therapy animal love the client and the client love the therapy animal, but warmth, good feelings, and trust is shared between the Facilitator and the individual. The Facilitator's love for his/her therapy pet and his/her willingness to share her pet's love with others, is not missed by the individual. In many cases, it is this mutual love for the animal that initiates the closeness and trust between the Facilitator and the individual. In other cases, it is the model of love, respect and empathy for the feelings of the therapy pets, by the facilitator, that allows individuals to realize that animals have feelings and needs. When Facilitators are familiar with a individual's interests, strengths, needs, and functioning level, and accordingly plans the interaction, with specific written objectives, then cognitive, physical, and social-emotional gains can be made.

A major problem of institutionalized living is not being able to make choices. Therefore, it is tremendously important for staff to seek out opportunities for their individuals to make choices, thus displaying initiative. In PAT it is easy to find these opportunities – choosing to relate to the therapy animal, choosing which activity and in some cases, even choosing which of two therapy pets with whom to relate. It is great when an individual, who may not be able to voice his/her desires, can "speak" by moving his/her wheelchair from one therapy pet to the other.

It is clear that the love of a therapy pet, within the framework of a professional PAT program, with individuals with developmental disabilities, leads to a myriad of activities and outcomes, positive health benefits and improvement of quality of life. As staff and individuals alike share in the gifts of the unconditional love of the therapy animals, we are all reminded, that despite differences, we all share in the universal need for love.

Article 3:
EVERYBODY RIDES: THERAPEUTIC HORSEBACK RIDING

__Sue Epstein__ lives with her family on a small farm in Upstate New York. Sue gradu-
ated from SUNY Brockport with a degree in Sociology. The love of horses has al-
ways been a golden thread woven into the fabric of her life. As a child, they were
her friend and refuge; as a young adult, a volunteer opportunity to share her love
with people less fortunate. Now she shares this love with Margot, who owns two
ponies and shows her half-Arab, "Sugar Magnolia," quite successfully. Sue owns
the thoroughbred of her childhood dreams "Tiara." Besides horses; a dog, "Co-
coa," two cats, "Cookie" and "Twix," and a variety of fish and insects share the
Epstein home.

Alcoholics remember their first drink. I remember my first pony ride. I was four
years old. My friend's parents had rented a pony for her birthday party. After everyone
had taken two turns I begged for a third. Sitting there feeling like a princess, I tried to
figure out how to make this last forever. The boy who was leading me had clicked his
tongue a few times to make the pony move. I waited until he let go of the lead rope and
clicked. It worked!! The pony took off running!! I was exhilarated!! I loved it!! Of
course, the pony headed straight for home. The poor stable hand was terrified. Forty
years later I still remember with amazement that my mother was scared. My feelings
were of joy. I had absolutely no conception of why anyone should or would be scared.

It is fair to say that over the next ten years I became obsessed with riding and
horses. I understand now that horses give me the unconditional love which was not
part of my family. This is what makes riding therapeutic.

In this section I will discuss the history and development of Everybody Rides, a
therapeutic riding program in upstate New York. Also discussed will be some of the
riders' strengths, needs, disabilities, and benefits we have observed.

In January of 1979, while waiting for a meeting with a school superintendent, I
picked up a magazine and thumbed through it. A picture of a horse caught my attention. The article was about NARHA (North American Riding for the Handicapped
Association). I don't remember the meeting with the superintendent. I remember racing back to my office to call Washington, DC and to join NARHA. It was as if I had
met long lost relatives at my first NARHA workshop. All my life I knew that riding
was therapeutic. It was innate knowledge, not something that was ever put into words
or conceptualized. Life was not fun, growing up with a mother who was disabled with
MS and a father struggling to pay the bills. No one dared to feel joy or be happy.
Everything was out of control. Yelling and fighting were the norm. The stable down
the road was my refuge. When I rode, I was in control. I felt strong and powerful. At
home I felt like nothing and nobody. If I worked hard at the barn I was rewarded with
lessons, competence, blue ribbons, and most importantly, self-esteem.

The NARHA literature seemed to put my feelings into words. It was exciting to
learn that there were many programs springing up in various parts of the country where
horses work as a part of treatment. I have always believed that what got me through a
turbulent adolescence was riding horses everyday. Now I had a plan! I would start a

therapeutic riding program at the State Agricultural and Industrial School near Rushville, New York. The campus housed about 250 juvenile delinquent boys. The grounds and settings were perfect.

Armed with the facts and figures I had learned, at four days of intensive training presented by the NARHA, I approached the administration. Unfortunately for the boys, but fortunately for the Newark Developmental Disabilities Services Office, the plan was not accepted. Undaunted, I called Arlene Murphy, who was the Volunteer Coordinator at the DDSO in 1984. Her reception was of excitement.

Next I started twisting arms of everyone I knew who had a horse. With the help of Wayne County 4-H and all my friends, five adults and five children with various disabilities began horseback riding lessons. We met weekly in the pasture behind my house throughout that summer. We all worked hard, learned a lot, but mostly had fun. The benefits were apparent immediately. The adults who had just moved into a community residence, from an institution, were socializing with twenty community members who were volunteering. The children were interacting with each other as friends. Donna, a girl with emotional disabilities, said to Sandy, a girl without a leg, "Come on Sandy, if I can do this, so can you." All the cajoling from the adults had no bearing on Sandy's willingness to try to ride, but Donna's encouragement made all the difference. For once, Donna was helping someone else.

Throughout the first winter we continued to meet as a saddle club. We watched movies, cleaned tack, and learned parts of the horse. Dan Bailey, one of the riders and his mother named the program, "Everybody Rides." In 1987 I quit my job working with juvenile delinquents and came to work full-time as Volunteer Coordinator for the DDSO. My horses, Ambition and Sweetheart came with me. Ambition went blind several months after I bought her as a three year old. She had adapted well. She trusts her rider implicitly. She can be ridden on the trails and in the ring. Her four strong legs have carried many people who usually ride in a wheelchair to new heights of seeing the world and enjoying it.

The program skyrocketed from a small group of enthusiastic volunteers and ten riders to an integral part of the services provided by the Newark DDSO. We operate now with two paid instructors, a barn manager, an indoor equestrian center and over 300 riders. The accomplishments are an indication of the benefits to the riders and the support of the community for a unique program.

The riders range in age from 3 to 83. All of our riders have a developmental disability. A developmental disability is a lifetime mental or physical impairment which becomes apparent during childhood and can hamper an individual's ability to participate in the mainstream of society. Some riders are ambulatory and some use wheelchairs. Some can hear, speak and see, others cannot. Riders have cerebral palsy, epilepsy, and various levels of mental retardation.

Harold lived in an institution most of his adult life. He was referred to the Volunteer Department because of anti-social behavior. It was felt that a volunteer friend might give him some self-esteem and keep him busy. Reading the referral was scary. No volunteer would tolerate the kind of behavior Harold was exhibiting. I suggested Everybody Rides. Maybe if he could ride a horse, his self-esteem would improve. Maybe he would even make a friend from one of the volunteers. His reaction to riding was like mine. The attention of all the volunteers, the control he felt and the improve-

When not in front of a camera, Sovereign, loves to get a hug from a lovely young lady. Wendy Halstead gained self confidence, poise, assertiveness from her lessons on Sovereign.

ment to his physical strength changed his life. Harold started with a volunteer leading the horse and one walking on either side supporting him. Gradually the volunteers stepped aside and let him do more on his own. After two years of lessons he was riding independently. He seems to have been struggling within himself for this independence. Harold was our first rider to learn to canter. He had never earned this kind of recognition before. Besides controlling the horse, Harold learned to control himself. At the Special Olympic his behavior was exemplary. He won medals and made friends. He began to compete outside of the Special Olympics in open horse shows as the only rider who is disabled in the class. This self-control carried over to the rest of his life. Now he lives in an apartment, works in a restaurant [not a sheltered workshop], and has made a lot of friends.

Harold's riding is recreational. He learns equestrian skills, controls the horse and participates in competition. Agnes rides for educational reasons. She is 68 years old and attends a Senior Day Program. She lives in family care and has a mild mental retardation. Agnes is learning the letters of her name. Although she is 4'8", she feels strong, confident, competent, and tall, steering Ambition around the arena to the letters on the wall. In the classroom Agnes gets angry and frustrated learning her letters. It is difficult and she doesn't always relish the challenge. When riding Ambition, she doesn't mind. The volunteer who is leading Ambition, for Agnes, is the key to the situation. She must judge how much or how little to assist. Agnes understands how to use the reins to steer and stop. She is given the latitude to do what she can. The leader must be aware of when Agnes can do it herself and when she will need assistance. As you can see, the therapy overlaps the recreation and the recreation overlaps the therapy.

Safety is always a primary consideration. Every rider begins with three volunteers. The volunteer who handles the horse must have extensive experience with horses. She is responsible to control the horse when the rider cannot, even if the horse gets frightened. The volunteers on either side of the rider are called "sidewalkers." Their responsibility is for the rider. They provide as much or as little support as is necessary. For Harold, they walk next to him, spotting and giving confidence. For John, their support is necessary all the time.

John arrives at Everybody Rides in his wheelchair. He comes from his Day Treatment Program. John doesn't speak, but carries a communication book. A reporter from one of the local newspapers was there that day doing a story about our agency. When she was introduced to John he took out his communication book and pointed to a picture of a horse. She was astounded that a man with such extensive physical limitations was able to ride and was overwhelmed by his enthusiasm for this activity. John participates in hippotherapy – the movement of the horse is influencing his body. The goal is not for him to learn to control the horse. The rhythmic, swinging motion of the horse's gate produces similar movement patterns to what walking would produce if John could walk. He increases muscle strength and upper body control. A bucket hangs down over the arena. John loves baseball cards. It's a great game for him to get the baseball cards out of the bucket and keep them. Motivation is never a problem for John as long as he is riding one of his favorite horses.

Re-write

"Walk Ambition, please." is a simple three word sentence for many of us, but for some of the children who usually point to what they want, it is a major accomplishment. Ambition will stand still for a long time waiting to hear one of her riders tell her what to do. Then, with the help of the leader, she can take right off and her rider will have the immediate satisfaction of knowing that his/her command produced a response in this 1,000 pound animal. Sometimes, of course, we do just the opposite. The horse will keep trotting or walking, waiting for the rider to say "whoa." Speech goals are often part of a rider's program.

Overcoming fear is sometimes a goal in itself. David came and watched while his friends rode. He would put on the helmet and the boots and get close to the horse, but he screamed at every attempt we made to get him on. Although David doesn't express himself verbally, it was obvious that he was trying to overcome his fear. The horses fascinated him. He watched his friends ride, but he was terrified to get on. We tried the steps, we tried the mounting ramp and finally two hefty men boosted him up as he shrieked in terror. That day David rode around the ring twice, quiet sometimes, but screaming at other times. It is hard to say what made us insist that David ride. Usually if someone is so resistant we allow them the dignity to say no. There was something in David's eyes that made us all know that he wanted to ride. He just needed to overcome his fear. The next time David came to Everybody Rides, he walked up to the ramp and got on the horse. By the end of his eight-week session he was getting up by going on the steps and using the mounting block. A full year later, when it was his turn to ride again, David proudly walked up the steps, sat down sideways on the horse, swung his leg over and was ready to ride.

Everyone who had been involved in David's original lessons, glowed with pride. He had overcome a fear. The benefits had lasted. We never know what to expect, but our philosophy is to leave our expectations outside of the barn, because our riders surprise us with what they can accomplish. It is truly their abilities that count.

Article 4:
PET ASSISTED THERAPY HELPING PRE-SCHOOL CHILDREN WITH DEVELOPMENTAL DELAY

Alice Freeman is a school psychologist with the Warwick School Department. Previously she was an Adjunct Professor/Instructor in the Graduate Division of Special Education at Rhode Island College. She has a B.A. from Salve Regina College, M.Ed. from Rhode Island College, and has done graduate work in the School Psychology Department at the University of Rhode Island. Ms. Freeman has done presentations on sexual assault prevention, identification, and treatment of preschool and elementary school children and has participated in Family Court Reviews.

Pet Assisted Therapy (PAT) is increasingly being recognized as a diagnostically significant and therapeutic form of treatment. In addition to the elderly, prison, and elementary school age populations, PAT is extraordinarily effective in maximizing the physical, psychological, cognitive, and social domains of pre-school children (CH:3 to 5 years)

A program of Pet Assisted Therapy was implemented in a reversed mainstreamed program during the 1999-2000 school year. The classroom consisted of 7 preschool children with special needs and 5 children who were community peers. The quality of the children's growth through contact with a loving collie companion, and her outstanding Pet Assisted Therapy Facilitator was truly remarkable. The human/animal bond was a powerful motivator for goal-directed behavior with children with multiple disabilities; physical challenges and developmentally delayed behavioral control and adjustment, cognition, and speech and language impairment. A four year old child with moderate/severe delays verbalized her first complete sentence after the first session with "I love you doggie!"

For children with a profile of Reaction Attachment Disorder of Infancy or Early Childhood, PAT provides a positive focus, comfort level and a nurturing environment for the emergence of a bond of trust. Children on the autistic spectrum evidence a developmental disability significantly affecting verbal and non-verbal communication and social interaction that adversely affect a child's educational performance. The inclusion of PAT in their curriculum reduces problem behavior and facilitates engagement and learning in areas of social skills, communication, self-help activities, cognition, and play. What a superlative technique for children with autism to develop eye contact by the use of a smiling, loving therapy animal.

Children who have a fear of animals can be motivated to relate to the pet through approximation to the goal, i.e., "one step at a time." Observations reveal that a preschooler initially responded with a fearful semi-fetal position upon seeing a dog. Eventually, this child initiated a request to be a "special helper" in the care of said canine by brushing and feeding the pet.

PAT has a major impact on children who have been ultimately betrayed by sexual abuse perpetrated by trusted family members. A total of two preschooler verbalized abuse by a parent to a therapy dog in a shelter for victims of domestic assault. The pets of victims of domestic violence were provided with emergency shelter (no cost) through a cooperative program with a veterinarian. A vision for the future would be the inclusion of house pets in shelters.

An alarming statistic that is significant is the increase of preschool children who are cruel to animals. Research clearly reveals that cruelty to animals occurs concomitantly with other hostile behaviors such a fighting, stealing, destructiveness, and violence. By hurting animals, some preschool children may be rehearsing their own suicide attempts. A hospital program currently exists for children birth to three years who are diagnosed as suicidal and/or homicidal according to the Diagnostic and Statistical Manuel of Mental Disorders (DSM IV). Comprehensive research also reveals a link between animal abuse and violence toward people.

As animals are vulnerable to deeply troubled children, they can also help the children heal in a safe environment which protects both children and pets. Gradual desensitization and creative exposure to the pets over multiple sessions can precipitate respect for animals and all living things. This population also requires intensive, individual therapy.

It is evident that within the framework of professional PAT for preschool children, life's lessons on respect for all living things, health, self-esteem, positive interaction with others, self-improvement, and successful day to day living can be learned from our best animal friends.

Article 5:
"WHAT YOU NEED IS PET ASSISTED THERAPY"

Claire J. Senecal is the manager of Academic Records at Bryant College, Smithfield, Rhode Island. Although Claire's professional background is in business management, her desire to share her family pets' love with others led her to enroll in Ms. Salotto's "D.J. University Certificate Program for Professional Pet Assisted Therapy" at her local community college. Claire has been on the Volunteer Services for Animals' Board of Directors and is currently the president of the Windwalker Humane Coalition for Professional Pet Assisted Therapy.

ARC

In May of 1999, Suzanne Burman and I proposed a "one of a kind" concept to the administration at the Arc of Northern RI. Our proposal was to bring a "professional" Pet Assisted Therapy program to the residents and to document the results. Would it be a success? Would the residents actively participate? Would we be able to "break down" some of the barriers? And most importantly, would this program have a positive impact in the participants' lives? After reviewing our documentation since we began the program, we can confidently answer yes to all of the above questions.

Throughout the year, we have seen many small, gradual, behavioral changes. We have noticed a bond that formed not only with the therapy pets, but also among the participants themselves. As one of our participants prescribed to a peer who was having a bad day, "What you need is Pet Assisted Therapy!" This endorsement from a consumer who previously had a fear of dogs is tremendous praise indeed!

We Are Family

Suzanne Burman, my colleague, is also my sister. We enrolled together into the D.J. PAT University Certificate Program at our local community college in the fall of 1997. This PPAT program, taught by Ms. Pearl Salotto, consists of three courses: one semester of theory, the second semester of therapy pet training, and finally the third component is the completion of 100 internship and advocacy hours. Even though Suzanne and I had pursued totally different career paths, we had found a common link in our desire to share the love of our family pets with others in a therapeutic setting. Suzanne is a registered nurse and is on staff at the Arc of Northern Rhode Island. Her extensive experience in working with adults having developmental disabilities was critical in our development of this program. I have certainly learned a lot from her knowledge in the field.

Although my professional background is in management and business administration, the joy of my life is derived from sharing Pitou and Beano's unquestioning and unconditional love with our friends from the Arc. For over 30 years, I have had an involvement with dogs whether it was breeding, training, grooming or showing in the confirmation ring. But this is "as good as it gets!"

Rosie and Sam are part of Suzanne's family. Rosie is an all-American dog and was rescued from the local animal shelter. She is a patient and easy-going dog with lots of love to give. Sam, a Shih Tzu, has a little bit of a superiority complex, but not when it comes to dispensing affection. Sam has had several homes before being adopted by Suzanne and her family. He now has a permanent home!

My "grandchildren" are Pitou and Beano. Both are French Bulldogs and as my husband is found of saying, "These guys were bred to be therapy pets. They are so comical and affectionate!" I am, of course, in perfect agreement. Rosie, Sam, Pitou and Beano all have passed strict temperament tests administered by a professional dog trainer and have "graduated" from obedience training. Their training is on-going.

I truly believe that the "love connection" that we have, and that we share with others, is what makes our program truly successful.

The Love Connection

Our program, which we named **The Love Connection,** was conceived from our desire to offer adults with developmental disabilities the vast benefits of pet assisted therapy incorporated with instructional discussions about feelings, appropriate behavior, and how to care for ourselves and our therapy pets. If we were to do this properly, we knew that we had to limit our sessions to a small group. This also became an important consideration in our desire to ensure the safety of both our participants and our pets (see ethics). Our weekly discussions have not only proved beneficial to our participants, but have led to a strong friendship that has developed among the participants, Suzanne, and myself. This was not one of our original goals but it has become the best one!

The Program

Introduction

The purpose of this professional pet assisted therapy program is to provide regular therapy sessions between appropriate, consenting residents and a therapy pet. The sessions are designed to help in improving a client's physical and emotional well being. Each therapy session will be limited to two hours and meets once a week. Every session will have a specific format.

Goals

- To teach the participants that all living beings have feelings, thereby helping to develop a respect for the pets, themselves, and each other.
- To foster an environment in which the participants will talk about the general care of pets – such as feeding and grooming. This will lead to discussions about the importance of hygiene and nutrition in the participants' own lives.
- To provide an atmosphere of unconditional love resulting in an enhancement of the participants' self-esteem.
- To lead discussions about acceptable methods of nurturing and affection among the participants.

- To help improve the participants' physical health by incorporating activities, such as playing catch and walking the pets, into our treatment goals.
- To work on communication skills by leading the participants in discussions about the pets.
- To help improve the participants' social skills by interacting amongst themselves and the pets in an acceptable fashion.
- To provide a soothing environment that will serve to alleviate stress and anxiety. This will lower blood pressure and, therefore, improve general health for the participants. *supporting evidence?*

Guidelines

- Each session will be held in an acceptable designated area. The Arc Administration and the Pet Assisted Therapy Facilitators (PATFs) will mutually agree upon the session's duration.
- The sessions will require each participant to sign and submit an informed consent form. Medical clearance must also be obtained for every participant.
- The PATFs will meet with the proper house managers prior to the start of the sessions in order for the appropriate treatment goals to be established for each participant. The PATFs will maintain strict confidentiality.
- The therapy pets will be trained, temperament tested, and insured.
- All sessions will be attended and monitored by a professional pet assisted therapy facilitator. The PATF will ensure that a safe environment is provided to protect both the participants and the pets from harm and injury.
- Each session will consist of various activities including discussions about pets, story telling, general care of pets, responsibilities of pet owners, petting, grooming and play time with Rosie, Pitou, Beano, and Sam. Visual aids–such as books, pictures, games, and videos–will also be used.

Code of Ethics

- All therapy pets will receive ongoing and routine medical care.
- All therapy pets will be kept clean and properly groomed.
- All therapy pets will live in a loving and nurturing home with the PATFs.
- All therapy pets will meet the temperament and training standards established for pet assisted therapy animals by the Windwalker Humane Coalition for Professional Pet Assisted Therapy.
- All therapy pets will be closely monitored throughout the sessions.
- All therapy pets and participants in the program will be treated with the respect and dignity entitled to all living things and beings.
- All therapy pets and participants in the program will be protected from harm and danger at all times during each and every therapy session.

Pearl Salotto

Evaluation

Throughout the program's duration, an informed evaluation will be submitted to the administration. The written evaluation for each participant will include:

- The content of every therapy session.
- The manner in which each resident participated in the therapy session.
- If the assigned goals are being met, or if they are still realistic. Goals will be continually evaluated and/or developed.
- Whether or not each and every participant wishes to continue in the program.

Our procedure is to evaluate each participant on a weekly basis. The evaluation form that we use for the weekly report is more or less a check sheet with an area available for a more detailed comment on each participant's progress (see attached samples). On a monthly basis our observations are compiled into a more comprehensive document that allows us to evaluate whether our short and/or long-term goals are being met and if we are still on track. Our next process is to send each appropriate house manager a questionnaire for their assessment of the participants' progress since their enrollment into the program. When all of the documentation on each participant is compiled, we can either see a pattern of progress or a need to reassess our methodology. By continually assessing each person's progress, we are able to address his or her needs in a timely manner.

Pet Assisted Therapy

<u>*The Love Connection*</u>

Client Review Form

Name
_____

_____
Date

Behaviors
_____

_____

_____

Short Term
_____

_____

Long Term
_____

_____

Teaching Approach
_____

_____

_____

Current Status
_____

_____

_____

_____

The Love Connection
Weekly Evaluation Form

Name

_____

Date

[ ] Yes [ ] No Client made eye contact with pet

[ ] Yes [ ] No Client observed pet interaction with others

[ ] Yes [ ] No Interacted with pet

[ ] Yes [ ] No Verbalized

[ ] Yes [ ] No Spoke to others about the pet

[ ] Yes [ ] No Smiled/Laughed

[ ] Yes [ ] No Reached to touch pet
                    [ ] Assisted [ ] Not Attempted

[ ] Yes [ ] No Stroked/Petting
                    [ ] Assisted [ ] Not Attempted

[ ] Yes [ ] No Brushed pet
                    [ ] Assisted [ ] Not Attempted

[ ]Yes [ ] No Gave treats to pet
                    [ ] Assisted [ ] Not Attempted

[ ] Yes [ ] No Played with pet
                    [ ] Assisted [ ] Not Attempted

Summary/Comments

_____

_____

_____

_____

Lesson Plans

Our original vision for "The Love Connection" was to conduct a six-week teaching program for our participants and then to move on to another recommended group. We revised our plans when we discovered what a strong, positive impact the program had on our participants, and that life's little lessons are never ending. Most weeks, Suzanne and I find that we may start the sessions as instructors, but we end up learning much more than we might have thought possible from our friends at the Arc.

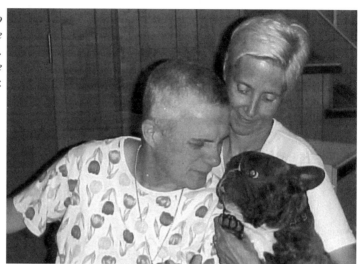

Resident with Beano and PPATF Claire Senecal) - Caring. Photo credit: George Beaubien, Jr.

<u>Week One – Establishing a Human/Companion Animal Bond</u>

Rosie, Pitou, Sam and Beano are introduced to the participants. The pets will visit with each of the participants. In turn, all of the participants are encouraged to pet the therapy dogs and offer them treats.

Questions for Discussion:

- How do you think that Rosie, Pitou, Beano, and Sam are like people? How do you think that they are different?
- How do you think that you should treat ALL living things? Do you think that everyone has the right to be treated with respect, concern, compassion, etc?
- How do certain things make you feel? What makes you feel happy, sad, scared, etc? Do you think that Rosie, Pitou, Beano and Sam have the same kind of feelings?
- How do you feel when Rosie, Pitou, Beano, or Sam is near you? Is it a good feeling? Do you feel happy?

The educational objective is for the participants to relate his/her own feelings with those of the therapy pets thereby making the human/companion animal connection.

Tools such as pictures of people smiling, laughing, crying, etc can be used along with pictures of animals playing and having a good time. We also took instant photos of the participants with the therapy pets. The participants were able to take the pictures home after the session. This helped to begin establishing the bond.

Week Two – Respecting Our Bodies

For this discussion, we will address the topic of good hygiene and respect of our bodies. We will talk about the need to take good care of ourselves, how we can prevent diseases, and the necessity of medical care.

Questions for Discussion

- Why do you think good hygiene is important? Do you know what hygiene is?
- Why do you think that it is important to keep your body clean?
- Would you want to be near Pitou, Rosie, Beano, or Sam if they didn't smell clean or if their nails were long and sharp?

The educational objective is for the participants to realize that by respecting their bodies and caring for their bodies properly they are helping themselves to stay healthy. We will talk about how both dogs and people need to get the proper medical care. Rosie, Sam, Pitou, and Beano go to the veterinarian's office every year for their examination and shots. People have to go to the doctor's office every year for their examination.

Legal ?

Tools such as a stethoscope, blood pressure cup, and a thermometer can be used to take the participants blood pressure, temperature, and to listen to their heartbeat. Then the participants can listen to the dog's heartbeat and talk about how it is different or similar.

Week Three – Nutrition and Exercise

For a portion of this session, the PPAT facilitator will encourage the participants to walk Rosie, Sam, Pitou, and/or Beano with our assistance. The participants will also play catch with the therapy pets. This will demonstrate "how the dogs get exercise."

Questions for Discussion:

- How do you think Rosie, Sam, Pitou and Beano get their exercise every day?
- How do you exercise?
- Why do you think exercise is important? How often should people exercise?
- How do you feel after exercising? Do you feel better?

To follow up our discussion of exercise, we will talk about the importance of good nutrition.

- Do you think it is healthy for the dogs to be overweight? Do you think it is good for people to be overweight?
- What did you eat today? What foods are good for you? What foods were not so good?
- What kind of food do you think Rosie, Sam, Pitou, and Beano eat? What kind of food do you think is bad for the dogs to eat?

The educational objective is for the participants to realize that their need for a good diet and daily exercise is not that different from the needs of the therapy pets. The participants will also learn that if they eat right and exercise they will live longer and healthier lives just as Rosie, Sam, Pitou and Beano will because we care and love them enough to make sure that their nutrition and exercise needs are being met.

Staff dietician kitchen

Tools such as clip art pictures of different foods, a poster of the food pyramid, and exercise tapes can be utilized. One of our lessons involved the participants making their own posters of good foods vs bad foods to take home with them. The PPAT facilitators helped the participants select clip art pictures of vegetables, fruits, etc. for good foods. Then we helped them complete the bad food area with clipart pictures of candies, soda, etc.

Week Four - Responsibilities

In this session we will discuss our duties and obligations. We need to be reliable when someone else is depending on us to perform a certain task.

Questions for Discussion: *What is a responsibility?*

- What types of things are you responsible for? Do you think that everyone has responsibilities?
- Do you think that it is a responsibility to own a pet? How do people take care of their dogs (daily walks, feeding, giving the dog attention, medical care)? Do you think that Rosie, Sam, Pitou and Beano are dependent on us?
- Do you go to work? Is that a responsibility? Do you think that Rosie, Sam, Pitou, and Beano have a job to do?

The educational objective is to make the participants realize that everyone is accountable for his/her actions and that all people and pets depend on one another. This dependence that we have on one another is a big responsibility. Rosie, Sam, Pitou and Beano have a responsibility also. They go to work as part of the Pet Assisted Therapy Program.

Tools such as photos of people at work (doctors, nurses, policemen, firemen, and construction workers) can be used to demonstrate the wide range of occupations that people perform. We also show a video of dogs at work. This video highlights dogs pulling sleds for transportation, dogs that work with the police to sniff drugs, and service dogs helping people with their daily chores.

Week Five – Communication

In this session, we will center the discussion on all types of communication – for people and for animals. We will also discuss the importance of communicating our thoughts and feelings in a proper way.

Questions for Discussion:

- Do you know of different ways that people communicate with one another?
- How do you think that people could communicate if they didn't understand one another such as if someone spoke another language? Do you think that drawing pictures would work? Could you draw a picture to tell me that you are hungry?
- Have you ever heard of sign language? When would you use sign language? (A demonstration of different signs could be shown to the participants along with what they mean.)
- How do you think that Rosie, Sam, Pitou, and Beano communicate? Have you ever heard a dog bark? Do you think that that would be a way of communicating? Did you know that dogs use "body language" to communicate? Explain what "body language" is and show examples.
- Do you think that yelling at someone is an appropriate way to communicate your anger? What would you think would be a better way?

The educational objective is to show the participants the different ways that people can communicate with one another and how we can improve this exchange. The lesson we hope to convey is how to let others know how we feel in an appropriate manner.

Tools such as stories and videos demonstrating the way that people and animals communicate can be utilized. We also brought supplies such as cut outs, crayons, and construction paper and encouraged the participants to make cards to give to the dogs to thank them for being their friends.

Week Six – Differences

For this week in the program, we will discuss how everyone is different. That difference is what makes everyone special.

Questions for Discussion:

- How do people look different? How tall are you? What color is your hair? What color are your eyes? Does everyone in this room look the same?

- Do Rosie, Sam, Pitou, and Beano look different? How do different types of dogs look? Do you know what a Poodle looks like? Have you ever seen a German Shepherd?
- How can each and every one of us make a difference in the world?

The educational objective is show to the participants that even though we may all look different; we all have the same kind of feelings. All of us, including Rosie, Sam, Pitou, and Beano, feel hurt, pain, joy, embarrassment, etc. Even though people may all look different, everyone needs and deserves to be loved and respected. *Be carefull*

The tool that we used to demonstrate our lesson was to take pictures of all of us and to talk about how we looked and how we felt about ourselves and about each other. The participants then took their pictures home to help them remember the good times we have together when they feel sad. *(?)*

The Games We Play

Although interacting with Rosie, Sam, Beano, and Pitou along with our weekly lesson is the most important function of our program, Suzanne and I have developed original games to encourage mental stimulation and social skills among our participants. Of course, the fun that we have playing the games is a huge bonus for all of us.

The first game that we created was a board game that we called the "Sam Game." The goal of this game is to bring Sam from the dog pound to a loving family home. A roll of the die determines how many spaces Sam will move towards home. Each of the participants moves a tiny Sam along the board and faces many obstacles along the way, such as Sam spots a fire hydrant, or a dogcatcher is nearby! If a participant lands on a yellow or a green square, he/she has to take the appropriately colored card. The cards have instructions for the participants to follow. A few of the instructions are:

- Please brush Sam because his coat is matted.
- Give Sam a hug.
- Play a game of ball with Sam.
- Tell Sam to sit.

The success of the "Sam Game" inspired us to create a game named after each of the therapy pets. The "Pitou Card Game" has a goal that is somewhat more challenging for our participants. The point of the "Pitou" game is for the players to match colors, numbers, and different breeds of dogs. The "winner" is the participant with the most matches at the end of the game. The "Rosie Game" is modeled after "Pin the Tail on the Donkey" and this game gives Suzanne and I an opportunity to discuss the different parts of Rosie's body in relation to our bodies.

The last game is a project under construction. The "Beano Game" will be similar to "Bingo." Beano is the last, but in no way is he the least!

The Beginning

Is there a need for professional Pet Assisted Therapy? I think that if you are reading this book, you have found the answer to that question. There are so many different populations that could benefit from PPAT! Previously, no such program for adults with developmental disabilities existed in our community. Our documentation and feedback from the administration at the Arc proves we have made a difference. The true sign of our success is that the participants are there every week and eagerly look forward to our program.

So where do we go from here? For Suzanne, Rosie, Sam, Pitou, Beano, and myself this is only the beginning of our journey. Suzanne and I have written and are currently proposing a second program to the administration at the Arc. This program will combine pet assisted therapy with service learning for our participants. Not only will they "get it," they will also "give it!" What better way to make a "**Love Connection**?"

I, for one, cannot erase those little "paw prints" from my heart.

Section 3:
PET ASSISTED THERAPY AT REHABILITATION HOSPITALS

Article 1:
ANIMAL ASSISTED THERAPY AT THE TEXAS INSTITUTE FOR REHABILITATION AND RESEARCH

Catherine F. Bontke, MD., was System Medical Director of Rehabilitation Services at the Rehabilitation Hospital in Connecticut and St. Francis Hospital. Prior to this Dr. Bontke was an Associate Professor of Physical Medicine and Rehabilitation at Baylor College of Medicine where she instituted an Animal Assisted Therapy program in 1986. She is a former member of the National Board of Directors of the Delta Society. She has also addressed the Windwalker Coalition at their summer 1997 seminar.

In 1986 I became Director of the Head Injury Program at the Texas Institute for Rehabilitation and Research (TIRR) which provides rehabilitation services and medical care to patients with severe closed head injuries. Many patients come to the program comatose and respond in very limited ways or not at all. Some patients have significant problems with the ability to think and remember, as well as with physical impairments which make it difficult for them to walk, talk, and care for themselves. Because of these patients' disabilities, their communication with humans is sometimes difficult, and often very limited.

In the summer of 1986 I received a call from a humane educator, Judy Hall, who worked at Special Pals, a not-for-profit animal shelter in Houston. I knew very little about animal-assisted therapy (AAT), but remembered my teenage years when I was disabled. My friend was Twiggy, a cat, who would lie on my bed, purr, and keep me company when I was unable to get up. These were special times for a very, very, unhappy teenager, and I hoped that my patients would benefit from having animals come into the hospital and "normalize" their experience. With the AAT program came a very special dog named Max, a golden-haired poodle, who knows exactly what he needs to do. To see Max work is a truly magical experience for families, visitors, staff, and patients. My patients have severe memory impairment, but most of them remember that Max is due to arrive on Monday night. The first time I witnessed Max in action was with a patient who was paralysed and comatose. He was sitting in a wheelchair with tracheotomy and nasogastric tubes in place, his head had been shaved, his eyes closed. He was able only to move his right hand, but not to our commands. Somehow Max knew. He put his head beneath the patient's right hand, and the patient began to stroke Max's head. This was the first purposeful movement this young man had made since his injury over three months before. Max rewarded him with a nuzzle. I was hooked, and Animal-Assisted Therapy became a regular part of our program.

AAT has expanded to other parts of the hospital. Two nights a week the animals and the human therapists visit patients with spinal cord injuries, the children's ward, individuals who have had amputations, and stroke patients. Everyone looks forward to the visits. Most of the evening staff (laboratory workers, nursing personnel and even maintenance) know that Monday and Thursday nights are special nights at TIRR. In the nearly three years of the program's existence, we have had only one scratched hand, and this was very superficial. When one of the dogs made a puddle underneath a head-injured patient's wheelchair, the patient, fearing the dog might get in trouble, tried to take the blame for the puddle, herself.

None of the worries voiced in the program's infancy, such as infection, have come to pass. Instead, very special things have happened. Because of much media coverage, the program has gained notoriety within the Houston area as an innovative and successful program. Some patients' families have actually chosen to come to our program for head-injury rehabilitation because of animal-assisted therapy. They think of us as a more humane place that is willing to take risks, a program "on the cutting edge."

Our risk is actually minimal because of the hard work and many hours of training volunteers, developing protocols and procedures, to develop a clear understanding of expectations in terms of therapeutic intervention, confidentiality, and animal and human health and welfare.

AAT, as a recognized therapeutic intervention, is still in its infancy, and much needs to be done to document its effectiveness as a therapeutic modality. More comprehensive education programs need to be developed with clear certification requirements for it to be a reimbursable therapy program. We all know the studies on the beneficial effects animals can have on general human health and spirit. But there is a vast difference between just knowing the benefits and developing a reimbursable therapeutic intervention.

AAT, in brightening lives, has a bright future. However, clear research to its benefits and limits must be accomplished, and a defined education protocol must be developed before the medical community can embrace this as one more way to help our patients lead happy, healthy lives.

Article 2:
THE IMPACT OF THERAPY DOGS IN REHABILITATION

<u>Mary and Bob Gadbois</u> have resided in East Lyme, Connecticut for 23 years. Rounding out the family are three Siberians Huskies. Mary is primarily a homemaker, but has volunteered for statewide and community citizen groups. She has been involved with getting legislation passed both on a state and national level and worked on environmental and taxpayer issues. Bob is a pipefitter out of Local 305 and works in construction. He, too, has done much volunteer work for groups, such as Mothers Against Drunk Driving and others. The majority of time is spent doing activities with their three Siberians: pet therapy, running/racing, obedience and public demonstrations. They have also been guest speakers in The D. J. Pet Assisted Therapy University Certificate Program and were the recipients of the 1996 Windwalker Humane Coalition's annual award.

Introduction:

For the past seven years I have been fortunate to do pet therapy with my husband Bob, and our three Siberian Huskies. Visits are done at nursing homes, convalescent/ nursing homes, social centers, a veteran's hospital, a children's hospital, a hospital treating the chronically ill, schools, day-care centers, and rehabilitation centers. Our Therapy Dogs – all registered with Therapy Dogs, Inc. – work with adults and children who are facing different types of problems such as cancer, mental illness, physical and/ or mental handicaps, Alzheimer's disease, and traumatic brain injury.

Sabrina and Tiffany, sisters who are now eight years old, were chosen and purchased from a breeder as puppies. They have always been house companions, working sled dogs, and have worked in obedience. At the age of one year they had the opportunity to participate in an outside demonstration and visit at the local Masonic Home. Seeing how much the people loved the dogs and how much the dogs loved the people convinced us that pet therapy was for us.

Our third Siberian, Clover, found herself in need of a good home at the age of six months. Hearing about her plight, we came to the rescue. Because it was important that she fit into the team, she was tried at pet therapy immediately. She was closely supervised so as to avoid any problems, and she passed with flying colors. It was obvious that she had received some obedience training, which, of course, also helped. Before too long she showed that she had experienced some kind of abuse, but with a little extra "TLC", patience, and love from us and the people she visited, she blossomed. Her flashbacks are now few and far between.

The training and experience gathered from working as sled dogs has helped all three dogs in their pet therapy work. They have been allowed to do the work they were meant to do, making them perfectly happy to accept their quieter and gentler side – that of therapy dog work. The commands used in racing are identical to those used when giving wheelchair rides and going for walks when on visits. Their exposure to dogs – lots of dogs – has been an asset. So has their public demonstrations (Winter

Pearl Salotto

Festivals, Carnivals, etc.) where they learned to accept all kinds of people and situations.

After Clover's serious knee surgery a few years ago, facing some limitations has become a way of life. Re-training her for therapy dog work was done, and she continues to have a very successful pet therapy career. With sled dog racing out of the picture, she still has never felt left out – she always is at the starting and finishing lines to view the other dogs. She also receives tons of attention and affection, keeping her part of the activities. The same holds true for Pet Therapy – other things are found for her to do to compensate for what she cannot do any longer.

Just recently Tiffany underwent the same type of knee injury and surgery. The same course of action is being pursued for her as has been for Clover. Just because she, too, can no longer do certain things does not mean she cannot be a Therapy Dog. The staff, as well as the residents/patients have already started giving her lots of extra love – letting her know she is very much wanted and needed. She has been repeatedly told that she can still give love, can't she!

Being well-rounded dogs has helped our Siberians to be able to reach out to people no matter what the circumstances. They feel useful. They display an eagerness to serve the people they meet. They are perfect for therapy dog work, and can work with anyone, in any situation. They are obedient, yet independent, patient, understanding, tolerant, and accepting – all attributes needed to work with physical therapy patients, with traumatic brain injury patients, and with hospitalized patients.

Therapy dogs working in teamship with the PAT and physical therapists can be a tremendous benefit to patients. They can be a reward when the patient performs exercises correctly and achieves a job well-done. They can have a soothing, relaxing, and calming affect on the patient who may be dealing with pain, anger, resentment, and/or hostility. They can motivate the patient so that the patient, by accident, does something he or she might have otherwise thought impossible. They can be a soft, cuddly body to pet, hold, hug and kiss when the patient simply wants and needs to relax. They can be the one to whom the patient can tell all his or her problems, while knowing that that "special friend" is listening. They can be the force to get the patient to physical therapy when the patient might otherwise avoid going.

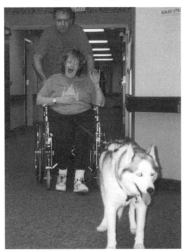

Jean, a resident at Bryde Brook Rehabilitation Center, gets the opportunity to be an Honorary Musher by taking a wheelchair ride with Sabrina with Bob ensuring everyone's safety.

The physical therapist can be the one who instructs the patient as to what moves or exercises are to be done. The therapist is the one who suggests how the therapy dog is to be placed, and gives cues to the PAT. It is the therapist who helps the patient to execute his or her directives while the PAT follows the cues. For the patient to achieve optimum results, the physical therapist and the PAT must work as a team.

The PAT can also help the patient by talking about his or her dog, by relating funny stories, etc. This can have a relaxing effect, bring a smile, and create a lighter moment for everyone.

When my husband and I did a physical therapy visit with our three Siberians at the rehabilitation center, for example, Bob kept two dogs at the back of the room in a "down/stay" position while I worked with the physical therapist and third dog. The dogs were rotated with each one having a turn. For some exercises, our dog was an integral part – the patient stretched her arm to pet Sabrina who could only be reached if she stretched her arm properly. For other exercises, like sitting up, there was a special reward – a big "Siberian hug" from our Sabrina. For a job well-done – the patient walked with Clover (the therapist pushed the wheelchair, the patient held the lead, and I assisted with Clover as she heeled next to the wheelchair).Telling her about Clover's puppy-like antics made her smile and relax, which certainly helped her to get through a difficult time. Letting the patient know she was not alone in what she was experiencing was accomplished by sharing with her Clover's story about her knee surgery, rehabilitation, and physical therapy, loss of racing career, and re-training for Pet Therapy. Giving her a wheelchair ride with Tiffany (and Bob's assistance) down the corridor, where she was a definite hit with all who watched, made for a happy ending to her session.

One other illustration of the effectiveness of therapy dogs in Physical Therapy is the results I have seen in young people at the children's hospital. I have seen "kids" who found it extremely hard or almost impossible to sit up, do so when one of our dogs was next to them. The physical therapist helped, but the catalyst was that they wanted to pet our Siberian. For "kids" who had a difficult time extending arms in normal day-to-day activities, or to even roll over when lying down, motivation to pet a dog could do it. Our therapy dogs helped make a difficult situation a little less difficult. They always generated smiles from everyone in the physical therapy room - "kids" and staff alike.

Our therapy dogs visit patients in a veteran's hospital, a children's hospital, and in a hospital focusing on individuals with terminal and chronic illnesses.

After we arrive at the hospital, we always stop at a small lounge near the elevator where the dogs are given water. Then, the dogs check in at the nurse's station where everyone spends a little one-on-one time visiting. The staff have gotten to know us and our dogs, so this time is very special. It gives the nursing staff a little break, a respite from their daily routines, a moment or two to chat and laugh and enjoy the dogs, and time to renew old friendships. It also gives them the opportunity to fill us in regarding the patients we will be seeing, the patients we should not see, and any other information we need to have, including screening for phobias and allergies.

The dogs go room to room, stopping to visit with anyone wanting to see them. For the patients able to visit without a nurse being present, we and the dogs do that. For other patients a nurse must be present.

Before leaving each floor (or wing) we always return to the nurse's station. We spend a few minutes with the staff so that the dogs can visit again. We alert the nurses to what was done, observations are shared, and information they might need to know is passed along.

This manner of doing pet therapy works very well. It allows the patients to spend private time with the dogs. It makes it possible for family members to share the dog's visits with their loved ones. It has made it easy for the nursing staff to be a part of the visits. It has given my husband and I the opportunity to spend quality time with everyone present. It lets the Therapy Dogs do their therapy. Nurses have even shared their supper sandwiches with the dogs.

The veteran's hospital our therapy dogs visit is part of a large complex which also includes a veteran's home. It is quite "neat" to know our dogs are allowed to pass the "NO PETS ALLOWED" sign posted next to the hospital door.

Although this hospital, as well as the other one, is state-run, visits are conducted quite differently. The pet therapy routine adopted here suits the patients we visit, as well as all the staff in this facility. It enables our dogs to spend quality time with the patients, nurses, family members and/or visitors, gives Bob and I time to really get to know the people, and makes it possible for our friend and volunteer, Scott Whittlesey, to work with Clover.

As a PAT, doing visits here, I work very closely with the Director of Volunteer Services. Our visits are on a regular monthly schedule under the auspices of the recreation therapy department. Groups and individuals visit with our Siberians in the public area on the first floor (called the Canteen), in two public areas on the second floor, and on the outside patio.

The receptionist also always announces that "The Therapy Dogs Have Arrived" and alerts the patients and staff as to where we will be and at what times. This makes it easy for us to connect with everyone. Additiontionally, Polaroid camera is available for photo taking of the patients and the dogs, something to which the patients really look forward.

At all our visits the dogs get to sit on chairs for petting by special friends, take walks with those patients desiring them, (with staff assistance) give wheelchair rides, and have playtime. The patients who have become best friends with the dog(s) always have a special treat – peanuts – to share with "their" dogs. The dogs, who never forget this, look all around the rooms, scanning all the faces until they find those friends, and they go right to them. They know they must sit and wait for their share, and they do just that. When a friend is missing, they cry because they cannot find him/her. It is an unbelievable and special relationship!

The visits are very much like family visits. The staff is available if we need them, but the dogs and the two of us get to do one-on-one visits. The nurses we see during the visits are always included in whatever is happening; for example, they push wheelchairs so that the patients can walk the dog with my assistance. I always make sure that the staff gets a **full report** regarding the entire visit either by phone or in writing later.

Visiting with everyone at the hospital is like visiting old friends! Every year the dogs (along with us) receive and accept their invitation for their Fall Carnival, where we as volunteers not only visit with all the patients, families and staff in an outside festive atmosphere, but we are also thanked for our efforts on their patient's behalf.

Along with everyone else at the cookout, our therapy dogs even get to have a hamburger and some chips.

Pet therapy at the children's hospital is done in a different manner. There, we work closely with volunteer services and even more closely with the Child-Life Department. Once we and our dogs went through orientation and were accepted, we were put on a once-a-month schedule. Yearly the dogs are "re-evaluated".

Upon arriving at the hospital for our visits, the dogs usually do a lot of visiting with staff, children, and their families outside. Once inside the lobby the dogs always find lots of children who want to visit with them there, too. Then, it is a must to stop at the hospital's offices to visit with all the staff who greet our dogs with much love, affection and attention. Tiffany, for example, has one special friend – she knows exactly where her office is and pulls my husband right to it. She knows a "hello" and cookies are waiting!

At the volunteer services' office we give the dogs water and put on their T-shirts. This cuts down on the dander and hair making it possible for the dogs to lay on beds or see kids right out of surgery. At the appropriate time the child-life therapist meets us and takes us upstairs to the children.

We go room-to-room, taking as much time as required per child. Sometimes visits even occur in the halls, and staff and families alike participate. The dogs are eager to do whatever is necessary to enable the children to pet them. Walks and wheelchair rides are sometimes the "prescription" of the day; other times it is having the dogs talk or sing; other times it is having them keep quiet.

We and our dogs are always greeted with a lot of enthusiasm by the staff and kids in the psychiatric unit, and although rooms may still be visited, the children quite often break up in small groups to visit with us. The children get to pick the dogs with whom they want to spend time. Many times each child has a turn going for a walk (with staff assistance), doing obedience, and/or performing tricks with "their" dog. Clover, for example, has a foam ball given to her by the children, and this is used for playing with her. On other occasions we all sit on the floor in small circles. While Bob and I chat with the children, the dogs are stretched out with the kids holding the leads. Some of the children may decide to "rest" on Sabrina, and she happily obliges. This makes for "quiet time" – a getting to really know each other time!

The children's hospital has a philosophy that they truly carry out, which is that they are one big, happy family. They have truly made Bob and I feel this, and they never hesitate to convey that to "their" Therapy Dogs (our Siberians and the other dogs involved in their program). Working with children means that we never make any move without a child-life therapist first okaying it. Nonetheless, these therapists always make us feel that it is a partnership, a team effort all the way. All the staff gives so much love to our dogs (and to us) that we cannot but feel it!

Visiting with patients with traumatic brain injury (TBI) is somewhat different than visiting with other patients. Visits are conducted based upon the condition of the patient. Some patients can be more fragile (physically, emotionally, and mentally); others less. Some patients with TBI may have severe limitations; others less. As a PAT, I have to always be constantly aware of these differences. Working closely with a therapeutic recreation director assures that these differences are taken into consideration and that the pet therapy program is varied when necessary to reflect this.

Pearl Salotto Traumatic Brain Injury

Having patients with TBI interact with our dogs may require a little more attention and patience on my part (and that of my husband). Noticing and acknowledging a blink of an eye, a smile, and/or nod of a head is extremely important because they are all significant accomplishments. When patients with TBI spell out the names of the dogs, a thank you for coming, or a question – again significant accomplishments – they expect us to pay attention and respond. Sometimes they let us know they want to pet a dog or feed that dog a cookie, but that they need assistance to do so.

Guiding our Siberians to just the right spot to enable the patients with TBI to reach out to them is what makes pet therapy work. With our help they are able to pet, to feed treats, to receive hugs and kisses and give kisses in return, to play and throw toys, to give obedience commands, and to hold leads. Many times patients with TBI cannot literally go to the dogs, so the dogs must go to the patients. For the patients who can take wheelchair rides and go for walks, so long as they are helped, this is done. Everyone in attendance knows it is a huge step forward, so the joy and pride at this accomplishment is shared by one and all. And when a patient in a coma expresses some type of reaction or response to the dogs being present, all the staff share that moment.

Our dogs visit with patients with TBI both individually and in groups. Nurses bring patients into the group and/or take us to specific rooms. Only a staff person should put down bed rails, remove wheelchair arms or pick up the hands of patients who are comatose to enable petting or feeding cookies. A team effort can accomplish miracles! With a little bit of time and energy on everyone's part, patients with TBI do respond favorably to our therapy dogs.

In conclusion let me ask – What is pet therapy? Does pet therapy work? Are there real benefits to patients from therapy dog visits? Is it worth the effort on the part of the staff to have therapy dogs come into their hospitals? Do staff, family members, and visitors receive benefits from visits? Is what our Siberians do considered pet therapy?

Based on the many years of doing pet therapy with our dogs I can, without a doubt, say that pet therapy is a program that is taken seriously by the staff. In physical therapy, as with patients with TBI, having therapy dogs as a part of the patients' treatment regimen has made a huge difference. Whatever my dogs do in these settings, it is therapy. Whether my dogs make patients smile and/or laugh, motivate patients to move muscles they thought they could not move, give companionship and love and friendship and affection, bring fun and joy, boost esteem and self-confidence, get patients to socialize with each other, and help patients and staff to share a common bond – the love for my dogs – it is most definitely therapy. And because of my dogs these patients have gotten to meet and know my husband and I, and we have all become extended family and friends.

At the children's hospital our dogs and different staff persons have each chosen each other as special friends. It is so nice to see Tiffany, for example, go off with the child-life therapist, and Tiffany always is on her best behavior for her friend. And Clover has kisses for her friends who also have kisses for her. One of the child-life therapists, on occasion, even holds a toddler on her lap enabling that small child to take a sled ride with my dogs when it otherwise would have been impossible.

When I see a patient with cancer hugging Sabrina (who sits until that patient is finished) with tears in his eyes, I know our dog has made a difference. When Clover makes a patient laugh, who previously was crying, I know our dog helped that patient. When a hospital patient diligently works on a collage made up of various news clips of our dogs, and the hospital proudly displays it, I see the difference in that patient's life made by our dogs. When a patient asks for Tiffany to please come and visit, the positive impact from our dogs is obvious. The pet therapy our dogs do has impacts reaching far beyond the visit at hand. For example, when a young women with TBI received a visit from Sabrina and Tiffany at the request of the staff, she responded with an instant smile, which amazed everyone because she had not displayed any reactions previously to this type of stimulation. We were asked to make certain that the dogs always visit her even if she was asleep.

In a tender moment two mothers of patients with TBI shared their thoughts with me regarding visits to their young adult children by our dogs. One mother took the time to write us a beautiful letter after her son returned home to New York. She could not thank us enough for visiting her son, for being so patient all the times he used his spelling board, for being so understanding of the fact that he chose to or not to speak to us when, in fact, he could speak. She also updated us on his progress, sent a photo of the dog she had gotten him, and even included a school paper. We have gotten to be good friends with another mother, who also shared her thoughts with me. She told me that, "Yes, the dogs' visits do help my daughter and do generate responses." She went on to say: "I'm sometimes the facilitator, talking about the dogs to her, helping her to pet and give the dogs cookies. The therapy dogs' enthusiasm is catching. Doctors say that sometimes her responses are reflexes; I prefer to think of them as smiles! Having more attention paid to my daughter makes me very happy. There are times people in nursing homes are forgotten, but this is not the case when the therapy dogs are visiting."

An ordinary Christmas was turned into an extraordinary one for some patients with TBI, because the nurses, aides, and recreational therapists realized the positive impact that therapy dogs make. Working with my husband and myself, lots of Christmas cheer was delivered by our sled dogs. The dogs were decked out with bells and bows as was our sled. One by one young TBI patients were lifted out of their wheelchairs and set in the sled by the staff. To a cheering audience and the sound of Christmas music each of these patients – smiling – took rides up and down the halls. Because the sled was cushioned with egg crating (serving to cradle them) no patient who wanted a ride was denied. The joy and fun shared by all was evident on everyone's faces. Although this therapy was certainly not traditional in nature, it was therapy most definitely. The affect on the lives of these young patients was noticeable for a very long time, with lots of smiles and laughter, not only occurring that night, but for many more nights to come.

An interesting perspective about the benefits to staff and residents/patients from visits by our therapy dogs is provided by Mary Joy White, a Staff RN at Bride Brook. Joy told me that "as a staff nurse working on a busy floor with non-stop things to do, I always think that anything appealing to your sight and feelings, or having a quick break to greet or even get a glimpse of someone or something you like, is just enough to perk up your day. Petting Sabrina's soft, white hair is a very good break. I think it is a wonderful therapy for the patients to see the dogs, pet or hug them. It makes the patients feel at home and close to nature and animals. These dogs are very fascinating, playful and lovable. I always think that the dogs get your attention no matter what kind of person you are. They make the patients energized and they then react by talking to the dogs or petting. To patients with TBI, these dogs serve as stimulation to their senses. Although patients with TBI lose consciousness or go into comas, knowing that there is a pet nearby is worth living for.

The words of one little girl who Tiffany visited in bed just after she had returned to her room from surgery will stay with Bob and I always. With Tiffany lying on her bed next to her, this little girl looked at her mom and said, "This is the best medicine I had all day."

Article 3:
PET ASSISTED THERAPY AT ST. JOSEPH CENTER FOR REHABILITATION

<u>Janet Accialioli</u> is a <u>Therapeutic Recreation Specialist</u>, TRS. She received her degree from the <u>University of Connecticut</u>. She has been working in Rehabilitation services for five years.

In December of 1993, the Saint Joseph Center for Rehabilitation started its Pet Therapy Program. After some months of preparation and contacts with Pearl Salotto – a national voice for professionalization of Pet Assisted Therapy – policy was written and the program began. The Rehab has always been open to having patient's animals visit from home. Pets are at times a major concern to the patients in the hospital, making sure they have someone taking care of them and that they can return to that caregiving roll when they return home.

Most of all, the patients miss their pets. For some, who may have lost a spouse, their pet is their closest friend. Patients who need to be comforted by the pet can be somewhat fulfilled with a visit by D. J.

The program was set up to meet other needs of the patient as well. Therapeutic goals can be worked on, with D. J. as the motivator. A patient with a body neglect (patient will ignore one side of the body) can be motivated to attend to the neglected side if they have to look or reach that way to see and pet D. J. The dog's fur may bring sensory input to a hand or arm which has decreased sensation. Some individuals with aphasia (a disorder in the brain which affects a person's ability to express, understand, read, or write language) try to communicate with the animal either by voice or other means, which may help to widen his/her means of communication to others. One patient, when introduced to the dog, began to whistle (a sound he had not produced before) and even began to sing a little song to get the dog's attention. The patient's family was present and was delighted with this breakthrough.

Our specialized Neuro Behavioral Unit may use pet therapy for other goals. A person who has had some form of brain injury may have periods of agitation, high anxiety, or even memory deficits. The dog may lead to relaxation. Sitting and petting an animal can be very soothing for these patients.

One patient who had memory deficits was able to remember some past events that revolved around pets he had and presently has, including what kind of animals and their names.

Pet therapy was also used as behavior modification with a patient who was uncooperative with therapy. If she attended therapy and participated, her reward was to attend pet therapy.

After a stroke a patient who has a paralyzed arm needs cues or assistance to use the paralyzed side. It is easier to use the arm that "works." Patients can integrate both arms to pet or brush D. J.

Another patient needing to work on balance was able to take the challenge of ambulating while walking the dog. (This is only under the condition that the staff person would be holding the patient's arm and the PAT would assist in holding the therapy dog's leash.) This allowed for a normal distraction and realistic environment to work on walking.

D. J. has also provided some therapy for the staff. There are staff who look forward to Monday to visit with D. J. One of the Aides will take time out of his day on Monday to set up the room for D. J.'s visit.

D. J. is always very calm and never makes a noise or ruckus. Only one time during therapy did D. J. actually bark – during a thunderstorm. It brought some excitement to Rehab for the day, as the administrative director came to see why D. J. was barking. D.J.'s barking at the thunder led to much healthy laughter, spontaneous language, and enhanced socialization, not to mention a wonderful discussion on why we don't inhibit our pets from their natural instincts.

The benefits of pet therapy are seen throughout Rehab, from not only the patients, but staff and family members too. Although our goals for therapy may be very specific, the benefits for each individual are wide ranged.

A resident with D.J. - A friend - helping out a friend. Courtesy of Struminsky Photography

Pet Therapy Program:

Editor's note: These guidelines are specific only to St. Joseph's. Other hospitals should adapt guidelines to meet their own patients' needs.

Purpose: To provide a therapeutic medium to enhance the quality of life of patients and to provide a mechanism which would lead to improvements in speech, socialization, communication, behavior, fine and gross motor skills, and ambulation.

General Guidelines:

1. Pet Assisted Therapy (PAT) will be provided by a professional educated in PAT, working with an approved therapy animal. (Appropriate documents to be filed)
2. Designated hospital liaison will work with PAT professional to determine appropriate area for interactions and to determine appropriate caseload.
3. All patients will have a medical referral.
4. All patients will have the choice to participate, or not to participate — and how they wish to structure the interaction.
5. All patients will have specific PAT short-term objectives as part of the treatment plan.
6. All interactions will be documented by the PAT professional.
7. Hospital liaison is responsible for notifying PAT professional of any hazards to animal, i.e. medical or behavioral changes in individual or environmental hazards.
8. PATF professional will be with therapy animal at all times and will be responsible for all animal care.
9. Hospital liaison will be present at all interactions, unless it is agreed upon by hospital and PAT professional that this is not necessary.
10. Any patient receiving treatment with a warm water medium (i.e. hot pack or whirlpool) is restricted from PAT.
11. Program evaluations will occur in a timely manner.

Infection Control Guidelines for Pet Assisted Therapy on Designated Unit:

1. Each therapy animal will be pre-scheduled.
2. All therapy animals will be dewormed, immunized (includes Rabies, Distemper, and Parvo virus), and free of disease.
3. A professional Pet Assisted Therapist (PAT) must bring in approved therapy animals.
4. A professional PAT must remain with the therapy animal at all times.
5. Therapy animals may be brought to one specific location or taken to individual patient rooms.

6. Therapy animals are not allowed in laundry, utensil storage areas, food preparation areas or nursing stations.
7. Prior to the visit, the hospital liaison will ascertain whether any patient may have allergies to animals and notify these patients of visit.

Risk Management Guidelines for Pet Assisted Therapy on Designated Units:

1. Each therapy animal is groomed professionally once a month with grooming in between maintained on regular basis by the PAT professional.
2. All therapy animals are toileted prior to and after therapy program. It is the responsibility of the PAT professional to clean up accidents, with ESD notified to sterilize areas after the spill.
3. All therapy animals will be immunized, dewormed, and free of disease.
4. Treatment area will be cleaned and sterilized after therapy program by hospital liaison.
5. Patients who are immunosuppressed (e.g. cancer, chemotherapy, multiple sclerosis, etc.) will not receive PAT.
6. Patients will receive "informed consent" about the risks and benefits of PAT, including the remote possibility of dog bites.

Section 4:
PET ASSISTED THERAPY AND INDIVIDUALS WITH EMOTIONAL/ MENTAL/BEHAVIORAL CHALLENGES

Article 1:
THE POTENTIAL IMPACT OF PETS IN MENTAL HEALTH

__Thomas M. Vallie__ worked in Mental Health for 25 years before retiring in 1992. At that time he was Chief of Children's Services at Rochester Psychiatric Center in Rochester, N.Y. He holds a Master's degree in Rehabilitation Counseling. Now residing with his wife Elizabeth in Hendersonville, NC, Mr. Vallie is preparing to write on the effects of oppressive work situations on people.

A World of Grief and Pain:
Flowers Bloom;
Even There. [1]

(Issa)

Hidden in the Haiku poem is a small moment of feeling from daily life. If we are willing, the vision of the past will draw us into a world of greater meaning that lies beyond.

So it is with mental illness. Those who suffer such, own a world of grief and pain. Yet mental and emotional illness does not own them; nor does it capture every aspect of their life and being. Flowers bloom, even there.

Views of Mental Illness

For the sake of this discussion, three views of mental illness will be presented. They are:

1) The Outsider View (stigma)
2) The Insider View (the sufferers side)
3) The Human View (where compassion overcomes fear)

There will be few scientific or learned definitions offered. For these one might consult The Diagnostic and Statistical Manual of Mental Disorders [2] or other psychiatric texts. Neither will there be found here discussion of specific psychiatric treatments, whether medical, chemical, psychological or social. These are not within the purpose or scope of this chapter and book.

---

[1] Price, Dorothy (ed.) (1987). *Silent Flowers, A New Collection of Japanese Haiku Poems*. Hallmark Editions.
[2] American Psychiatric Association (1987). DSM III R.

95

Rather, like the introductory haiku poem, a small moment of the mentally or emotionally troubled person will be presented. The reader may be drawn to explore what lies beyond.

The Outsider View - Stigma

Our lives run unavoidably on assumptions and stereotypes about people. These help us to interact successfully with many individuals each day. Erving Goffmann observes in his classic work Stigma[3] that in our ordinary interactions we ignore some undesirable attributes we notice in people which are incongruent with our stereotypes of what a given type of individual should be. However, when an attribute is deeply discrediting, then a stigma is attached to the person which disqualifies him from that first stereotype. A stigma, itself a negative stereotype, is an invisible mark of shame or disgrace applied to a whole class of people indiscriminately.

The stigma attached to mental and emotional illness is characterized by a cluster of discrediting ideas about "crazy" people. This stereotype holds that mental patients are dangerous, weak, incompetent, deviant, violent, and worthless. Even with the advent of AIDS, persons with mental and emotional illness remain the most feared and shunned of disabled persons. Certainly most persons with mental illness have some discrediting characteristics some of the time. The stereotype is rarely entirely true of a given person who suffers mental illness.

The Outsider View accepts the general stereotype of the mental patient even though his experience shows that friends, family and respected public figures have suffered mental or emotional problems! Strangely, we make exceptions for loved ones and those we favor while maintaining an unreasonable stereotype about the "mentally ill" group itself.

When confronted with a stranger who has a known history of mental illness, the Outsider sees a Charles Manson, not a person, but a bundle of preconceptions. He expects fear; expects the stigmatized person to go into an uncontrollable rage, injure someone, be incoherent and unable to follow simple directions. Not many people, certainly no Outsiders, have taken time to examine the misconceptions in their psychiatric stereotype and take steps to change.

News agencies seldom fail to report that a man who stole a car or beats his wife or had a gun, had "a history of mental illness." The media are examples of Outsiders who profit from sensationalizing a stereotype that plays to our fears.

Outsiders do not want to know that there are treatments, cures, and controls; that people with mental and emotional illness are human and normal in ways which exceed the limits of their illness. People who have cancer are not called "Cancerians", yet people who have mental illness are regarded as "Crazy", "Mental", "Psycho", in a way which fuses the illness inexorably with the person.

There is no shortage of Outsiders in our society. They persist even among some caregivers who should know better, but refuse to relinquish the stereotype. After all,

---

[3] Goffman, Erving (1963). *Stigma: Notes on management of spoiled Identity* (3). Englewood Cliffs, N.J.: Prentice-Hall.

taking care of "those patients" is their job.

Mentally ill and emotionally disturbed persons themselves are gullible to the stig-matizing stereotypes about their illness. They are no different from anyone in our cul-ture in accepting and operating under stereotypes. Ideas about "Crazies" preexist their own illness. As they see stereotypic symptoms in their own behaviors, they first dis-qualify themselves using the ordinary social point of view, then begin to cope with the ways others treat "that kind of person" which they have been shown to be. [4] Later, stigmatized persons may learn to "cover" their illness in order to "blend" or "pass into" society. All of this is from a basic acceptance of the stigma and stereotype of mental illness.

Returning to Issa's Haiku; the Outsider neither acknowledges the mentally ill person's grief and pain – for that would sidestep the stereotype – nor does he see the possibility of flowers blooming, especially there.

The Insider View - The Sufferer's Side

For many years I interviewed and sometimes supervised, students from high school to post-doctoral levels who undertook internships or fellowships at a psychiatric hos-pital. Early in their experiences, if not before acceptance into training, I usually asked the probing questions: "What is mental illness, and where does it come from?"; "What do you think mental and emotional illness feels like to the person afflicted?"; and "What does mental illness do to a person?"

The questions were meant to encourage the students to express themselves and begin to examine their own stereotypes, as well as to invite them to begin to cross over to the Insider Prospective. From the answers, a plan would evolve that would expose the students to the enduring human side of people with mental or emotional illness.

Though one suspected that some deep-seated unexamined prejudices lay under the surface, rarely did I hear them from a prospective student intern. Most often there were vague answers and no real understanding of the "world of grief and pain" to be found in the heart of a mentally afflicted person. Honest face to face interchange with patients changed most misconceptions.

Some were quick to attribute mental illness to an undefined chemical imbalance, indifferent mothers, cold fathers, or to blame a sick society which creates sick people. Few, except those who experienced mental illness in themselves or loved ones, could speak from a sufferer's experience or point of view.

Articulating an "Insiders" understanding is difficult for a person who has not ex-perienced mental illness himself. Yet it is possible to be a "wise" almost-insider by carefully listening to those so afflicted, by careful observation, and sympathetically comparing similar fears, feelings, and thoughts that are familiar, but muted in ones own "normal" experience.

So, what does the Insider experience in the depths of illness? Each individual's range of symptoms is more or less different in kind and degree from others. Here is a laundry list that touches some of the physical, emotional, intellectual, social, psycho-

---

[4] ibid; p. 80.1

logical, perceptual, and spiritual experience of mentally ill persons:

Terrible physical pain -	"My body aches all over every time I move. It's real I tell you!"
Sleeplessness -	"I haven't slept in two weeks. I can't!"
Lethargy, Hopelessness -	"She (referring to herself) can't get out of bed all day." "There isn't any reason to get up anyway."
Enemies Everywhere -	"Everyone is out to get me – look where I am."
Isolation, Deep Loneliness -	"No one understands me. I have no friends." "There is no one who cares that my heart is breaking."
Deep ambiguity -	"I can't make a decision on anything, don't you think?" "My feelings move from place to place all of the time."
Terror, Unknown Fears -	"There is no way to describe the horrible terror I feel." "The worst part is that I don't know what the terror is about."
Self Doubt and Blame -	"What they say about me seems true - I am crazy. It's all my fault."
Confusion -	"Every time I try to think I get all messed up and even forget what the question was."
Loss of Self Control -	"I can't trust myself – I do these things and can't stop until I lose it and have to be held down. It just comes on even when I try to control it."
Anger, Rage -	"I have the feeling that my anger is so strong that I will hurt and kill everyone in the world."
Abject Sadness -	"I cry all day – so sad – I don't know why."
Guilt -	"Sometimes I just feel dirty, from all the things I did, and will do again. I see why God is punishing me."

Social Skill Loss -	"Before, I could do lots of stuff – now I just forget what I am supposed to do – I couldn't hold a job or take someone on a date."
Self Destructive Acts, Urges -	"It would be better for everyone if I were dead."
Extreme Compulsiveness -	"If I don't jump up and touch the light switch at the same time thirty times in a row, I can't go to sleep. If I fail to start the other stuff over too."
Rejection -	"Nobody cares about me, not even my mother. She left me here, alone. They had a family reunion and didn't even tell me. No one wanted me around to screw up the party."
Fragmented Reality -	"The worst part was, nothing made sense any more. I was so afraid because nothing fit together or made sense."
Hallucinations -	"The voice tells me to hurt the teachers. It's a man's voice that comes whenever it wants. I have to do what it says."

One gets a taste of the grief and pain experienced by many mentally ill persons. The quotes only hint at the depth of confusion, chaos, and fear that may be experienced. Being an Insider is not all that desirable. But it is worthwhile to know that mentally ill persons act most often against themselves rather than aggressively toward others.

Besides the sufferers themselves, the accomplished Insiders are the family members and caregivers of those who suffer mental and emotional illness. They are often the only lifeline to a stable human world. They walk in the dark corridors of mental illness in hope of leading sufferers back to a safe, productive life. They truly know a world of grief and pain.

Human View - Where Compassion Overcomes Fear

Beyond stigma, past miracle drugs, aside from brain chemistry, bad parenting, deprivation, violence and abuse is a place where people of all sorts and diverse experiences find a human core. This is not some syrupy romantic idea you might find in a greeting card. The Outsider has not considered its existence. Even the Insider can numb the idea that "Flowers can bloom even there." But it is true nonetheless.

All human beings who are conscious and the least receptive share needs, feelings, talents, responsiveness, morality, and values in common. Not to say that we are all the same in character or depth. Yet we share the human spirit and being. We are talking here about the painful impact that the loss of human contact has on people.

Mental and emotional illness in its more severe forms, but in milder forms as well, attacks areas of the person which make us human - our ability to think and reason, to perceive clearly, and to be in control of one's emotions.

The person experiencing illness knows he is not thinking clearly or experiencing what others do, or acting and feeling like others. He feels directly the severe impact from the stigma of being "Crazy" and without worth or acceptability. He sees himself as useless, different, repulsive, incompetent, unlovable, even alien. A wedge is driven between the sufferer and the rest of us. All the while Outsiders and Insiders alike reinforce the sense of alienation, directly or inadvertently.

Yet the basic needs - to be touched - to have the respect of others - to be known by name- to have friends and associates - to belong to a social group or church - to be forgiven - to be wanted and thought of as interesting, talented, attractive - to have one's privacy - to be productive- to have a place on which to take a stand, all remain intact. They are the part of the human side that is most accessible to compassionate people.

The Human View looks beyond diagnosis, treatment strategies and therapies; beyond undesirable behaviors, disability and a host of characteristics that fuel stereotypes and stigma. The Human View looks beyond one's own fears and the terrified heart of the person with a mental illness. It knows by experience that the needs and longings of the person with a mental illness are no different from those found in one's own heart. Compassion is a knowing heart that reaches out to someone who suffers. In our Haiku equation, the Human View sees a world of grief and pain, yet encourages flowers to bloom, even there.

Keys to Compassionate Helping

Pet Assisted Therapy Facilitators, among many other ancillary helpers, whether voluntary or paid to give care, have a tremendous opportunity to render powerfully effective aid to troubled persons. They do so from the Human Viewpoint where compassion confronts fear and where hearts, whether of caregivers or care receivers, speak the same language.

Professional and assistant mental health workers play a primary role in diagnosing and treating persons with mental illness. Their efforts are to understand, to find chemical solutions, to repair and reintegrate brokenness, to teach and apply controls, and to focus many rehabilitation forces. Except where compassion informs and accompanies the professional at work, the Ancillary helper takes a different path. No need to try to compete with or duplicate the professional mental health worker's role, but to take guidance and accept direction.

The daily challenge is to be compassionate in difficult circumstances, and to return willingly the next day. The tools of the trade are few: friendliness, understanding, listening, generosity, peacefulness, kindness and a forgiving and loving heart. These characteristics flow from the life experience and hardships we all share. Those who learn to be compassionate for others out of their own grief and pain are best equipped to help the person who suffers a mental or emotional illness.

When human compassion is combined with a trained pet, then the tools of the trade are more than doubled - where one plus one equals three, four or five.

The relationship between a person and his/her pet and person suffering mental illness is focused on finding the most direct route to replacing negative feelings of worthlessness, unlovableness and failure with acceptance, friendship, and intrinsic worth.

A compassionate union with a pet can awaken a heart turned cold by neglect or isolation, and often does. A woman in her eighties, long mute and withdrawn, suddenly remembers and says, "I had a dog once. How she loved to fetch. I loved that mutt, and she loved me. Can I pet your dog?" Doors long closed were opened just a crack.

Everyone needs understanding, compassion and recognition. A boy in a children's psychiatric hospital improves his angry, aggressive behavior. "The pet lady is coming tomorrow. She lets me brush her dog. I'm real good at it."

Compassion is non violent and in fact contradicts violence and heals scars brought on by a violent world made more so for the mentally ill person. "Could I play with Bugsy the rabbit?", asks a young woman who became psychotic after being sexually abused. "Of all the pets she seems the gentlest and just lets me hold her."

Pets are a bridge back to the human family for mentally and emotionally damaged people. There needs to be a compassionate person standing fearlessly with that pet to help the troubled person to make the next step back from the chaos and oblivion.

Summary

We all use stereotypes to deal with people and situations every day. Mentally ill persons are most feared when stereotypes about them discredit and stigmatize the whole person. Outsiders, people who hold to stereotypes about "crazy" people, fail to see the pain and grief in the person suffering a mental or emotional illness. There is no recognition that afflicted persons have a human side full of needs and longings that go unanswered. They operate from a stereotype that stigmatizes.

Insiders see mental illness from the suffers side, with its terror, confusion and real pain. Yet insiders, even professional caregivers and the mentally ill person himself, may not go to the next level of understanding where human needs and longings are validated and compassionate caring is given and received.

The compassionate caregiver and ancillary helpers, like Pet Assisted Therapy Facilitators, have a unique opportunity to touch and heal hearts injured by the symptoms of mental illness, isolation and violence.

Article 2:
D. J. IS COMING TO SEE ME TODAY!
(Pearl Salotto)

In my work at a psychiatric facility for youngsters with "troubled" backgrounds, I found that the children responded, as all youngsters do, to my four-year old therapy dog D. J., with warmth and love. The best in them was brought out, in D. J.'s presence, with a little guidance and a lot of structure.

I started the Pet Therapy program at this facility (with a staff member always present) with a group of four or five children seated on chairs in a semi-circle, with D. J. and me about ten feet away. Initially, I led a discussion about whether or not animals are living things, how we know that and what are their needs as living creatures.

The children, despite a difficult past, seemed open to my rule that D. J. could only be treated gently. Even when not petting D. J., their presence in the room with her required them to be responsible, to be in control of their behavior, to be calm and quiet and to be respectful to all living things in the room. This meant they needed to be respectful to D. J., myself, their peers and their staff.

I proceeded in a slow, calm, encouraging and supportive manner. I told the children how gently they were petting D. J. and how happy they were making her. The staff and I demonstrated appropriate petting and allowed only one child at a time to come near D. J. At first the children petted her, then subsequently brushed her, gave her water and treats, that I brought in, and walked with her. I can honestly say that never did any of the youngsters hurt or attempt to hurt D. J. Only once in the year that I worked there, did staff have to remove any youngster. This was because that youngster raised his voice to another youngster. The benefits that the children received from this program were astronomical.

The following essay was my reflection on a comment that a child made to a staff person prior to my visit.

D. J. Is Coming To See Me Today

The benefits of the Saturday morning visits between four young boys, at a facility for disturbed children, and D. J., are boundless. We discussed the Golden Rule, as it applies to animals and people. Kids felt loved and gave and expressed love (verbally and behaviorally). Kids were running through the grass with the cool summer breeze – holding onto D.J.'s leash, (with me holding on as well.) The boys brushed D. J. gently, lovingly, appropriately - listening and following instructions. The youngsters alerted me to the fact that there was a hole in the fence – as their instinct to care for and nurture is coming forward in their concern for D.J.'s welfare. Kids told me D. J. needed to rest after running back and forth several times (not wanting to take advantage of her for their purpose.) One youngster climbed up and across the jungle gym and being greeted by D. J. with a waging tail as he jumped down, saying, "she waited for me – she likes me." Another youngster, not feeling well and resting on the grass, is amazed with D.J.'s intui-

tive licks of caring, that says "I hope you feel better."

Kids and a therapy dog enjoying each others company, in play and rest, mutually showing emotion and caring, outside, on a beautiful summer morning.

Interactions with D. J. provided a situation where kids could be calm, where they could have fun, and where they were motivated to control their behavior. These youngsters could nurture another living creature. They could care and love and feel proud and excited. They could look forward to something nice in their life, where they could excel, and receive compliments. They could feel D.J.'s very real love and return that love as they had bonded with her during the regularly scheduled visits.

I remember a comment a little boy made as we were running through the building to the outside yard. I had just told the children, "D. J. has to go to the bathroom." This child said, "If D. J. messes up, we will still love her." I used this loving and considerate comment to point out that people, as well as animals, mess up sometimes, but we still love them. Even though the children might have been told this before, all of a sudden the true meaning of the concept – that even if you make a mistake you are still good and lovable – came alive for them. The concept was no longer simply an intellectual statement, but rather a feeling coming from deep within, as the children had participated in a discussion arriving at that conclusion. Another unforgettable comment was when a youngster said, "I feel like I'm in heaven when I'm petting D. J. If I were her owner I would give her ice cream instead of dog food. There is no other dog in the world like her." I pointed out that this is true and it's also true that there is no other boy in the world just like you. By the look on that child's face, I felt the above scenario allowed him, possibly for the first time in his life, to feel a "positive" sense of his own identity. A youngster made the comment on one occasion, when we were playing outdoors, that D.J. needed to rest. Through the youngster's loving concern for D.J., it was easy for me to make the connection that when parents or staff say that children need to rest (or obey other rules), that it is for their good as well.

Lessons learned, feelings felt, esteem enhanced, fun-joy-safety are all positive and possible outcomes of a well planned, structured program, where administration, and staff provided the support, the therapy pet did just what comes naturally, and the PAT, educated in the field and in Human Services, although brand new in the field, exercised simple good judgment and common sense, sharing herself through her love for her pet and her desire to help the children.

Article 3:
THE BRIDGE OVER TROUBLED WATERS

__Laura Vear__ MA, holds a masters degree in Expressive Therapies and currently runs a Wellness and Recovery Center within Northern Rhode Island Community Services, where she oversees holistic treatment programs for people with mental illness. Laura also supervises interns for The D.J. Pet Assisted Therapy University Certificate Program as they provide professional services within the center. Previously, she had developed environmental education programs within various zoos and spearheaded early research into the therapeutic bond between humans and non-domestic animals.

Ellen left her small apartment in the city, a safe place where counselors were always available should she feel the need for support or reassurance. She walked the two blocks to her weekly session with Jill and Sassy, the therapy dogs. Ellen generally avoided going out of her apartment unless it was absolutely necessary, for she was uncomfortable around people she did not know well.

Carrying an empty soda container, Ellen smiled at the golden retrievers as she greeted the animals' owner, a pet-assisted therapist-in-training. Ellen then sat deeply in a chair and made eye contact with the therapist. The dogs stood near her, but appeared to accept that Ellen would not pet them, as she had not touched them in the two months that they had worked together. Ellen's gaze fell to Sassy, the younger dog, who was seated at her feet. The therapist-in-training, also the dog's owner, mentioned the softness of Sassy's ears. She had mentioned this to Ellen in the past, inviting her to touch the dog, but Ellen had always politely declined the offer. Yet, the therapy dogs always appeared happy to see Ellen, falling asleep near her feet, perhaps lulled by a sense of calmness generated by Ellen.

This was quite remarkable, since severe and persistent anxiety was one of the conditions that had initially caused Ellen to seek services. The relaxed young woman that almost melted into her chair, with two sleeping dogs at her feet, hardly fit the profile of an anxious person. The dogs' owner sat back and asked Ellen how her week had been. Ellen reached for Sassy and caressed the dog's ear before answering.

Contact.

Ellen had just reached a new experiential level of awareness, sure to change the dynamics of all future sessions with the therapy dogs. She was a person with little history of physical contact with others. A void would soon be filled, one that Ellen may never have known existed.

It is observations like these that still leave me breathless after nearly twenty years of work in a remarkable world that revolves around that most sacred bond between animals and humans. Ellen is not this person's real name, in accordance with confidentiality.

In my current position as an expressive therapist within a community mental health center, I have received support from all levels of management as I strive to include pet-assisted therapy into an environment designed for assisting people with on-going recovery from mental illness. I contrast this with a memory of my first job offer in the "traditional" mental health field. As my prior work in the zoo field was well-documented in my resume, the job offer had come with the comment "as long as you don't bring any goats to work."

My past work as an environmental education coordinator within various zoos allowed me countless opportunities to observe the animal-human bond in action. One particular interaction has always held a special place in my heart. While developing an animal-assisted therapy outreach program for a municipal zoo, the pilot project included introducing animals to patients that had been institutionalized, long-term, for chronic and persistent mental illnesses.

Within the confines of a locked ward, a small chinchilla rabbit found his/her way to the lap of a non-verbal, elderly man. I sat on the bed opposite him and watched this burly, silent man pet the rabbit with a gentleness that seemed foreign to his large hands. He continued to stroke the rabbit but appeared oblivious to my presence in the room. After several moments, his mouth began to move. I became aware of the word "nice" being repeated over and over, like a chant.

By staff report, this was the first word the man had spoken in over thirty years.

While exploring the concept of "misunderstood animals" within an urban zoo, I made a remarkable discovery amongst the people we label the institutionalized elderly. Much to the horror of nursing home staff, I always brought a large snake and a tarantula on the zoomobile when visiting individuals who are elderly. Staff consistently expressed concern that the animals would be too fearful for their delicate patients. It soon became clear that I was dealing with the fears of the support staff and their transference of these fears toward those in their care. When the "fearsome" animals were allowed into the site (which was more often then not), they elicited not fear, but understanding. The patients who are elderly greeted the snake and the spider with compassion, curiosity, and respect. As a civilized culture, we *maintain* our aged rather than revere them, as the so-called primitive cultures do. Individuals who are elderly and institutionalized display a level of empathy that comes from heart-felt experience.

Currently, I supervise interns from the D. J. Pet-assisted Therapy University Certificate Program. The interns provide their services to clients who suffer the symptoms of various mental illnesses. Many of these consumers are dually-diagnosed, meaning that they must also deal with a substance abuse problem along with the manifestations of their mental illness. For the purposes of this article, I will focus on the symptoms of anxiety, depression, and psychosis. The impact of pet-assisted therapy on symptom management is based on client report.

Anxiety can take many forms, including panic attacks, agoraphobia (marked fear of being alone or being in a public place where escape may be difficult or help unavailable), and obsessive compulsive disorder. Clients receiving pet-assisted therapy were asked to assess the following symptoms; feelings of panic, persistent fears, feeling restless or keyed up, irritability, compulsion to check things, avoidance of people/places that cause unease, feelings of detachment, exaggerated startle reflex, muscle tension, feelings of impending doom, and superstitious beliefs.

Depression is an affective disorder that can be a primary diagnosis or experienced as part of another mental disorder. Although many people can recognize the feelings of sadness, hopelessness, and discouragement that typically define depression, others may experience depression as the painful inability to experience pleasure in life. Clients receiving pet-assisted therapy were asked to assess the following symptoms; feelings of sadness, tearfulness, emptiness, lack of interest in activities usually enjoyed, decreases in appetite, unplanned weight loss, difficulty falling asleep, nightmares, excessive sleep patterns, fatigue, feelings of guilt, low self-esteem, and difficulty with concentration and decision making.

Psychosis is described as indicating a gross impairment in reality testing. Delusions and/or hallucinations are present and the person experiencing them lacks insight into their pathological makeup. Clients receiving pet-assisted therapy were asked to assess the following symptoms; auditory hallucinations, visual hallucinations, persecutory hallucinations, feelings of paranoia, thought broadcasting, and other delusional beliefs.

The accuracy of client report varied according to the intellectual functioning and the level of insight possessed by each individual. For instance, some clients experience psychosis, but are unable to recognize any hallucinations or delusional systems, as these symptoms are part of what they perceive as the real world. Other people may recognize that they experience things that have come to be known as hallucinations or delusions, but they are very guarded about sharing these perceptions with others.

In regards to depression, a marked improvement was noted in feelings of self-esteem. Most clients reported that they felt better about themselves when they were with the animals and, also, in between sessions. The same clients also noted a significant decrease in the amount of time that they felt sad and empty inside. Less than half of the clients noted improvement in the remaining symptoms of depression.

Anxiety, like depression, was experienced by all clients interviewed, to one degree or another. The most remarkable improvement was noted in the lessening of the symptoms of restlessness, irritability, agoraphobia, and feelings of impending doom. A significant number of clients also noted a lessening of persistent fear, feelings of unreality, and the startle reflex.

People appeared to have the most difficulty discussing and recognizing symptoms of psychosis. As mentioned before, insight is frequently limited in this area and clients are often guarded when it comes to discussing hallucinations and delusions. Only half of the people interviewed had active symptoms of psychosis, although all had experienced some symptoms at some stage of their illnesses. The majority of clients reporting psychosis related a decrease in auditory hallucinations, particularly the persecutory voices. They also noted a decrease in paranoia, thought-broadcasting, and other delusional beliefs. There did not appear to be a marked decrease in visual hallucinations.

When examined case by case, individual progress becomes quite remarkable. One woman reported improvement in 21 out of 22 of her symptoms as a result of pet-assisted therapy. A man reported that he was more interested in pleasurable activities now and had felt a major boost in his self-esteem since working with the therapy dogs. Another man who, at baseline, experiences severe symptoms of anxiety and psychosis, noted significant improvement in his most debilitating symptoms.

As an observer, I could easily add to the improvements recognized by the clients themselves. What I find most remarkable is that a group of people that generally lacks insight into their symptoms, due to the severity and chronicity of their mental illness, is able to identify areas of improvement. This may be related to the presence of the therapy dogs during the assessment process and the subsequent reduction in certain feelings of anxiety while in the company of the animals.

Pet-assisted therapy as an adjunct treatment modality for people with chronic and persistent mental illness is an avenue of symptom management that "does no harm." As evidenced by this article and the on-going work of others, pet-assisted therapy may be the prescription that helps many people cope with the psycho-social stressors that medication cannot remedy. As compassionate and non-judgmental listeners, animals create a bridge between the spiritual realm and the ego-driven world we have come to accept as society. It is a bridge that can be difficult to cross without the correct supports beneath it. The pet-assisted therapist, as an empathic listener, can be this supportive framework. The sacred relationship between a pet and his/her owner completes this bridge. . . and makes it a safe haven for others to travel upon.

Pearl Salotto   1975

Article 4:
PET ASSISTED THERAPY AT OAKWOOD CORRECTIONAL FACILITY

__David Lee__ graduated with a degree in Social Work in 1971. In 1968 he was drafted and sent to Vietnam as a medic. After serving eleven months he was wounded in a fire fight and was evacuated to Japan for four and a half months of surgery and recovery. He received two bronze stars for valor and the purple heart. David's interests include: humane issues, raising llamas on his farm, and doing whatever is necessary to be a good father to his seven year old daughter. David is married with two daughters, one twenty-two and one seven. He has successfully operated a Pet Therapy program at Oakwood Correctional Facility for almost twenty years. The program has always been well exposed and he was able to share the pet program on such shows as 60 Minutes, Those Amazing Animals, World News Tonight and several other documentaries.

Oakwood Correctional Facility (Formerly the Lima State Hospital for the criminally insane) houses the most dangerous criminal offenders in the State of Ohio.

All patients are prisoners who have become too dangerous to themselves or others, due to their mental illness, to be kept in prison. Many are high suicide risk and others are unpredictably violent. One would think this to be an unlikely location for companion animals, but they have resided here for over nineteen years. The companion therapist idea has proven to be one of the most effective programs available for working with depressed and suicidal patients. Please note that we do not permit pet animals to relate with assaultive or aggressive patients.

Relating to pets at this facility began in January 1975 as a ninety-day experiment. It started on one ward with three parakeets and an aquarium. The pets involved became very popular and soon other wards were requesting a similar program on their unit. Due to patient pressure and a reputation as a "hassle-free" program, pet therapy was soon expanded and was no longer just an experiment. Immediately several important things were discovered:

1. It gave patients something to do that could increase their self-esteem.
2. It provided the patients with a necessary diversion from normal routine.
3. It provided the patients with non-threatening, non-judgmental affection.
4. It gave patients companionship and reduced feelings of loneliness.

Within a year there were visible changes in many of the depressed, non-communicative patients. Instead of spending their day pacing the halls, many of the patients had discovered an interest object (the pet), who made no demands on them.

Larger institutions, such as Oakwood, are amenable to a large variety of pets, but many institutions may need to determine which pet might best serve their purposes.

When an institution first considers pets they usually think of dogs and cats. In the case of Oakwood, traditional pets were ruled out in favor of smaller pets (birds). The patients here are housed individually in 6x12 foot cells which would be small quarters to a dog or cat, but very large to a parakeet.

One of the most important aspects of working with pets as therapy is the close

108

physical proximity between the client and pet. Within the institution where space is limited the smaller pet appears to have the best results as they can stay with the client especially when he or she is troubled. Instinctively a troubled patient will retreat to his own area (cell) and the importance of having a companion at that time can be significant.

Pet therapy used successfully differs between long-term and short-term patients. When Oakwood was considered a long-time chronic institution, we worked with more personable pets, such as cats. As we became a short-term acute care hospital our emphasis changed to less personalized pets, such as goats, deer, geese, and rabbits. Working with less personalized pets provided a smoother transition for the patient so that upon recovery he could return to prison without a high attachment level.

Even though the pet program at Oakwood began somewhat by accident, it developed under a very structured set of guidelines due to the nature of the patients here.

In late 1974 a group of depressed and suicidal patients on one ward jointly risked punishment by hiding an injured wild bird in a mop room and feeding it scraps from the dining hall. It was unusual for these residents to be concerned about anything except their own problems. The bird died of its injuries, but the cohesion it created during its short stay was not forgotten and led to a now nineteen year old program.

During its history there were many successes and failures. For example, the attempt in 1981 to use a chimpanzee on one of the wards was a complete disaster. The eight-year old female had a violent temper and on several occasions "cleared the day hall." On another occasion working with wild turkeys as courtyard pets led to daily attacks on staff and patients. Eventually the turkeys were released into the wild.

Fortunately there were many many successes. Patients who were highly suicidal and depressed would literally change their behaviors. The program worked especially well with individuals who have a mild mental disability who are quick to learn repetitive chores and then feel a part of the team. The program's successes far outweigh the failures and it (the program) is felt by some to be the life-saver of the hospital.

There appears to be something about inmates of state facilities which makes them an appropriate target audience for a pet program. There is so much loneliness and rejection within individuals in an institution on whom pets can have a real impact. When a patient becomes very depressed there is some living thing to turn to, who is non-threatening. Much of this loneliness occurs when treatment staff are not present, such as over weekends or late at night. It is at these times that the pet truly earns its keep.

To actually set up a pet therapy program is not a simple matter and the program at Lima became even more complicated in 1984 when our hospital fell under JCAH (hospital accreditation).

The basics were followed:

1. Instructional write up
2. Start small
3. Cleanliness even to excess
4. Weekly documentation on each resident involved
5. Psychological testing before entry (depression scale) and the same testing after sixty days of involvement

6. No aggressive patients - only depressed and suicidal
7. Monthly reports to hospital administration and humane groups (So it is always clear to humane societies that the pets safety is the number one priority
8. Total openness of program to the press and any interested group

Our institution is proud to be the first institution of its kind to work with pets as a primary therapy in our patient recovery program. We maintain full JCHO accreditation and anyone who visits knows that TLC and humane care of our pets is our primary concern. It seems to follow that where there is a genuine concern for pets that concern for other people simply falls right into place.

In summary, the Pet Therapy Program, begun in January 1975, as a formal therapy program for patients/inmates who are depressed/suicidal has had a positive effect on participants and has been an excellent catalyst program for other interventions – pets range from parakeets and gerbils to llamas, goats and miniature deer.

Dave and "friends."

This program, the first of its kind in the United States, is, more than ever, a valuable form of therapy. It is well documented, both in writing and training, as well as through media exposure (60 Minutes, an HBO Special, Smithsonian, etc.)

This unique program providing patients with a "necessary diversion" and an opportunity to demonstrate "caring behaviors" has shown that the non-threatening, non-judgmental abilities of pets make them natural therapists.

Presently, there are over twenty-five pets living full time at Oakwood, including deer, goats, ducks, rabbits and llamas living outside and cockatiels, parakeets, finches, canaries, and a cat living inside.

In 1996-97 (Lima State) was officially transferred from the Department of Mental Health to the Department of Corrections. This meant a lot of changes–some good and some bad. They also were allowing the pets to stay so as not to upset all the employees and patients who were very protective of this program.

One of the changes was that some of the employees (cooks, custodial, and maintenance) were replaced with minimum-security inmates, many of whom were completing their sentences.

As these minimum-security inmates settled in, I proposed that these new inmates help develop Oakwoods Dog Program. So we began. The first phases were training and socializing dogs for the blind. The pilot dog organization (Lion's Club) supplied the pets, the food, and the vet needs. The dogs lived with the minimum-security inmates and went everywhere with them. This phase was so successful that we decided to enlarge and enhance the pup program by getting pups from the humane society and in a one year time frame trained these pups for people with special needs and for individuals who are elderly.

The premise was simple, many people in the community wanted a dog, but felt that housebreaking and training would be too much work. We focused on this and by the end of the year our dogs were command trained and ready for placement. We then turned our attention to training dogs to help individuals in wheelchairs and later to aid people who were hearing impaired. The difference between our Seeing Eye Program and our Assistance Dog Program was that after a year with us, the Seeing Eye dogs were taken to Columbus, Ohio for advance training and placement. The assistance dogs were placed directly with their permanent homes. Dawn's dog MOSES

The Seeing Eye dogs were so successfully trained that all of ours were placed (100%) where as the rate of success for dogs trained in a regular home was 80%.

By the time of my retirement, we were placing over 30 dogs a year to people in need. And also the prisoners received a new pup to train the very same day. What a natural winner. There were no losers. Individuals with disabilities got a quality dog to love, the dogs got a caring home, and the inmates got a chance to display caring and responsible behavior.

As I retired the program was in full swing and now two years later, it is still the prison's Number 1 program as well as being therapy for the psychiatric patients and the minimum security inmates.

I am so proud to have developed the various pet programs at Oakwood successful now for over 25 years.

I continue involvement especially at nursing homes where I work with our llamas and alpacas for therapy. My family is also heavily involved in school tours at our llama farm where we also have dogs, cats, deer, sheep, swans, and peacocks all of whom are eager to greet.

Animals have become a major part of my life, over the last 30 years and I am also amazed at the magical charm they have to help people. The companionship nonjudgmental and nonthreatening ways of pets is so valuable, I can only think that pet therapy is just beginning.

Pearl Salotto

Placement in 1997 include:

Champ (hearing ear) - placed with an 80 year old retired doctor with severe hearing loss.

Max (companion dog) - adopted out to an 82 year old (widow) in Bluffton, Ohio as a needed companion (4-2-97)

Brandy (companion dog) - adopted out to a family with a young child who suffers from chronic asthmatic problems (May 1997)

Lucky (companion dog) - adopted by a family whose little girl is wheelchair bound, due to birth defects (11-19-97)

Angel (companion dog) - adopted out to a family with a three year old daughter who has cerebral palsy and is wheelchair bound (12-3-97)

Sadie (companion dog) - adopted out to lady with multiple sclerosis who is dependent on a walker (12-9-97)

Midnight (companion dog) - adopted out as a full time resident at a nursing home in Spencerville, Ohio (12-18-97) (As of 2-2-98 the current resident dog is Max)

Shalom (companion dog) - adopted out to an elderly couple who are seeking a companion pet (12-97)

Article 5:   About 1990
PARTNERS IN HEALING...VIOLENCE

__Bob Walters__, 45, is a Tacoma native. He and his wife, Dixie, live on three acres of land with a variety of companion animals in the town of Eatonville, Washington, in the foothills of Mount Rainier. Bob received his __BA in Forest Management__ from Washington State University in 1972. He was a Naturalist and Operations Chief at Northwest Trek Wildlife Park near Tacoma for five years. In 1982, he became __Director of Education for the Humane Society for Tacoma and Pierce County__, a position he still holds. In 1989 he organized the Humane Coalition, a group of social service, humane and other violence-prevention agencies and the first of its kind, which is applying the growing evidence of the link between animal abuse and other human violence, toward creating greater public awareness and the impetus for action. He has spoken at regional and national conferences on the issue of cruelty, and is continuing to network on behalf of the coalition and the humane society.

It was already a sad day for the Mansfield family, in May of 1989. Dick and Candy, along with Dick's daughter, Sabrina, and Candy's three visiting nieces, had just completed a burial service for their Siamese/tabby cat, "Marbles" (named for his beautiful blue eyes). He had been hit by a car. They were walking back through a small, wooded area near their home in Tacoma, Washington, attempting to deal with the grief.

Suddenly they noticed the boy. He stood silently, trembling arms half-outstretched, naked, except for patches of mud. As Dick and Candy came closer to offer assistance, their bewilderment turned into a sickening realization that something terrible had happened to him. In his eyes was a look of unspeakable horror. Indeed, though his mouth was open, he did not, could not, speak.

Ever so carefully, Dick picked the boy up, carried him out of the woods and into their home, from where Candy had already called 911.

Why did this happen? Could it have been prevented? The man charged and later convicted for this brutal, sexual attack, Earl Shimer, had a record of crimes against children, but was free on parole. The police were aware of this, and were trying to keep a close eye on Shimer, but their hands were tied. When his neighbors were interviewed by local television reporters, they said he was well known for his cruelty, that years earlier, as a teenager, he had strung up cats and stuck firecrackers into the anuses of dogs and lit them.

News of this latest attack galvanized the citizens of Washington State to demand stronger laws against sexual predators. Other states have enacted similar measures.

The seven-year old boy survived the rape and mutilation, but if only his ordeal of pain and horror, which will undoubtedly stay with him forever, could have been prevented. Indeed, if only we could spare the countless victims from the pain of their abuse. What if Shrimer's early, dysfunctional behavior had prompted aggressive intervention and treatment? There is hope, if we heed the warning signs.

We have just scratched the surface of a profound human benefit, thanks to a better understanding of our relationship with other animals.

Pearl Salotto

In the epidemic of violence we are living in, animals are both victims and healers. Domestic violence, the nursery from which other violence sprouts, includes as the most common victims, the small and vulnerable. Companion animals are hurt and killed, just as humans are. The identity of the victim is in many cases a matter of coincidence.

Abused children may seek solace in the nonjudgmental, supportive response they get from the family pet. And as one study showed, they may even have a stronger bond than that of children living in normal, pet-owning families.

But where fear and pain are day-in and day-out experiences, a young child's malleable psyche is at greater risk of learning to control through violence. Some become abusive themselves or worse. Some seek abusive mates. Some transcend their painful youth, and become compassionate adults.

Even the average child, as experts in child development point out, is often hindered by inadequate or non-existent parenting, and the unrealistic expectations some parents have for their children's behavior. Add to this, racial prejudice, the incidence of drug and alcohol abuse, and poverty leading to desperation, and we have a massive social problem. What has been described as a lost generation of children is perhaps just the latest in a progression of self-perpetuating, lost generations.

Dr. Gail Melson, associate professor at Purdue University, says many children need to receive more nurturing from their parents, they lack opportunities to be nurturers - a key ingredient in developing self-esteem and social responsibility. "Child-rearing values within our society tend to focus on independence, initiation and assertion. The need for children to care for others, to learn how to contribute to the well-being of others outside of themselves, is not well recognized by parents or by educators…We are gradually coming to a new realization: nurturance develops during childhood, and this development is important both for optimal childhood functioning and for later adult functioning," says Melson.

Ironically, but not surprisingly, contact with animals is playing a key role in helping young children - victims of abuse and neglect, even young abusers - to improve both their social behavior and their outlook, by increasing their self-esteem and capacity for empathy, in short, the ingredients for nurturing. Miracles are being achieved by bringing animals in as helpers in therapies.

Green Chimneys, a rural farm facility for emotionally disturbed children in New York State, is well-known to professionals in Animal Assisted Treatment (AAT), for enabling these kids to break through their own emotional barriers and believe in themselves, by giving them a chance to care for and interact with farm animals and injured wildlife.

Why has it been so hard for most of us to accept the obvious? Philosophers, scientists, writers, even artists, have recorded it, defined it, have provided time-tested evidence that we are connected to everything around us, not just physically or spiritually, but by our actions.

Philosopher John Locke wrote in 1705, "[children] who delight in the Suffering and Destruction on inferior Creatures, will not be apt to be very compassionate or benign to those of their own kind." He even goes on to describe a custom of the times which reflected this belief: Our practice takes notice of this in the Exclusion of *Butchers* from Juries of Life and Death." Locke also points to the need to teach children

114

tenderness "to all sensible Creatures," in order to prevent violence.

English painter and engraver William Hogarth (1697-1764) famous for the social commentary in his art, produced a series of engravings, showing in painful detail, the stages of cruelty, beginning with the torture of animals, and culminating in murder.

In some of the earliest writings known to humanity, the ancient Egyptians recited funeral prayers to help ensure a successful journey for the deceased into the next world of eternal life. As the soul of the departed was weighed on the scales against the feather of Maat, goddess of truth and order, the litany describes acts of wickedness which had been avoided in this life, including causing harm to mankind, or to animals.

Much of the scientific documentation of the association between early abuse of animals and other forms of violence has relied on interviews with individuals involved - children, members of dysfunctional families, prison inmates and psychiatric patients. One of the first studies was conducted by Dr. D. Hellman and Dr. Nathan Blackman, and reported in the American Journal of Psychiatry in 1966. Further evidence has been gathered by psychiatrists, psychologists, veterinarians, and others. (see bibliography) With help from organizations such as the Geraldine R. Dogde Foundation, of Morristown, New Jersey, and the Latham Foundation, of Alameda, California, a number of studies and symposiums have helped to build greater awareness of the inseparable nature of all violent acts.

In *The Tangled Web of Animal Abuse: The Links Between Cruelty to Animals and Human Violence*, printed in The Humane Society News, Summer, 1986, Dr. Randall Lockwood and Guy R. Hodge wrote of the chilling anecdotal evidence which supported, and perhaps inspired, some of the later studies and their findings. They list Who's Who of serial killers and mass murderers known to have victimized animals earlier in their lives - David Berkowitz (the "Son of Sam"), Carroll Edward Cole, Albert DeSalvo (the "Boston Strangler"), James Huberty, Edmund Emil Kemper III and Brenda Spencer. The authors called for law enforcement, social services, the judicial system, and the public to take action, by looking at cruelty to animals as "a serious human problem," and creating a more comprehensive approach to violence prevention.

One such prevention program, "Project Empathy," was developed as a result of discussions held at the Guildford County Humane Society in Greensboro, North Carolina in 1987, and has also been applied by the Washington Humane Society in Washington, DC. Its goal was two-fold: to prevent recurrences of animal cruelty and to prevent escalation of past violence into aggression toward people.

Treatment would begin with an assessment of the individual's history, attitudes toward animals, and feelings about the act or acts for which he was referred for treatment. Next would come role playing, interactions with animals, videos, and other means of building empathy, followed by group sessions with similar offenders if possible. Changes in attitudes were assessed, as was the incidence of recidivism, through contact with probation officers.

But like other fledgling programs, this one was often thwarted by the sheer magnitude of violence the young clients were continuously exposed to, that prevention agencies were already having to deal with.

Another approach was initiated in the Puget Sound region in May 1989, after the assault on the Tacoma boy by Earl Shimer. Through contacts made by this writer, the

Pearl Salotto

Humane Coalition Against Violence was formed, and a think tank of twenty-five individuals in related fields was convened, eager to prevent violence.

They examined the significance of animal abuse in overall human violence, and identified ways to interrupt the generational cycle of abuse. Many recommendations came out of a coalition-sponsored conference in February of 1990. Some of them included cross-training, standardizing reporting methods, creating community awareness programs, updating and strengthening anti-cruelty laws, early intervention in cases of childhood animal abuse, linking treatment goals, involving animals in treatment, and establishing a national task force to attack the roots of violence. Through direct contacts and conferences, the coalition has enlisted teachers, counselors, social workers and others to be more alert for children's comments about, and actions toward animals.

Later that same year, another Humane Coalition Against Violence was founded in the San Francisco area. This coalition centered on the efforts of two people – Ken White, then Deputy Director of San Francisco's Department of Animal Care and Control, and Dr. Lynn Loar, Education Coordinator for the San Francisco Child Abuse Council. Together, White and Loar have conducted numerous training workshops on the link, and helped push through new legislation adding animal control and state humane officers to the list of mandated reporters of suspected child abuse.

The Garden Therapy Project at the Sonora County Humane Society in California, planned and developed with assistance from Dr. Loar, provides, like Green Chimneys, a sage, non-judgmental environment for at-risk children. They are referred by the YWCA Battered Women's Shelter to a bucolic, farm-like setting adjacent to the Society's animal shelter, where they learn safe, healthy touching, and nurturing, first by growing plants and eventually by interacting with animals.

The Toledo Humane Society in Ohio has established a Cooperative Child/Animal Abuse Prevention Program called Animal Advocates for Children. Under the guidance of Executive Director Mary Pat Boatfield, the program provides cross-training for cruelty investigations and child protection caseworkers, and is building a network for sharing case reports and referring individuals to appropriated treatment providers.

These local and regional programs offer the best hope for true violence prevention. They epitomize what is, in fact, becoming a national movement. The American Humane Association (AHA), with both child and animal protection divisions, has hosted two national summits, in 1991 and 1992, to address cooperative approaches to preventing child and animal abuse. While AHA's mission has always been the protection of children and animals, conference participants were reminded by the Geraldine R. Dodge Foundation Executive Director Scott McVay, that violence toward women must be considered in solving the entire puzzle of human violence.

According to figures released several years ago by the March of Dimes, 20% of all hospital emergency room visits by women resulted from battering. Three to four million women are battered yearly, and about four thousand of these cases result in death.

Animal control officers, social workers, teachers, the police, and counselors are being encouraged to ask about incidences of animal abuse. At the same time, a few community leaders are beginning to recognize the potential of AAT in preventing violence, school dropout, drug abuse, teen pregnancy, even rehabilitation of young offenders.

116

We are seeing a flourish of other community efforts to stem violent crime, and particularly youth violence. The approaches include tougher sentencing, teen curfews, boot camps, gun regulations, neighborhood watch groups, and alternative activities such as midnight basketball. Public schools are even beginning to teach self-protection, negotiating skills and anger management. But, while they represent worthwhile steps, most of these efforts fall short of including the treatment of animals in their scope of concern.

Sadly, many people, even in this parallel social movement, still ask the question: Should we really be that concerned about deliberate harm to animals? This not only reflects a callousness toward the fate of animals themselves, but denies the human benefits already being achieved through applications of the bond.

To understand the ties in our behavior toward any living being, is to see the need to stridently push for system-wide education in the value of kindness. Fighting anti-social behavior after it has begun is one thing, but without first imbuing a strong appreciation for the personal and social value of really caring about others, we are doomed to failure. Some of the training can be achieved through humane education curriculums in pre-school, primary and secondary school, even parenting classes, and other adult audiences.

In need of change is the societal acceptance, even glamorization of certain types of violence. Describing in 1971 how child abuse is actually encouraged by the *American way of life*, Pennsylvania Commissioner of Family Services, Richard Farrow, put it this way. "Our problem…seems to be one of identifying the abuse at an early stage and intervening on behalf of both parent and child. Our motives are good, even noble, but we really are too often locking the stable after the horse is stolen. We don't really prevent abuse; we seek to limit its extent and repetition…we as a nation believe in a certain amount of physical punishment as being good for children…" Such punitive approaches to child-rearing as beating, threats and fear tactics can only destroy self-esteem, and foster anti-social behavior.

Even as they push for the mainstreaming of humane education, humane societies, now more than ever, must link up with other agencies to find ways to eliminate our society's destructive obsessions with violence. We must ask what are the ingredients that contribute to the lure of violence? Simply growing up accustomed to its methods? Boredom or hopelessness? Greed that fuels the marketing of violent toys, games, movies, and television shows? And what of the status that comes with being more daring, flirting with death and basking in the attention this brings, first vicariously in the video game, or the action movie, later in reality through drug abuse, gang association, daredevil stunts, or crime? To gain leverage against many enticements of violence will certainly require innovations in education, legislation and marketing.

In the long campaign against domestic violence, much ground was lost with the early separation of child and animal protection efforts, which virtually began as one movement during the late nineteenth century. The causes, related in many ways, diverged until each became nearly oblivious of the other. Ask a caseworker from family services if she or he discusses with children, during interviews, their interactions with the family pet, and you might get a puzzled look in response. But pursue the topic a little further, and many will agree there is a logical connection between how the children, and how the pets, are treated. They may recall cases which exemplify the connection. A child may tell of the time daddy shot the cat as punishment for something the child had done, or threatened to kill the pet if the child revealed "their little secret." (as in sexual abuse)

There is no question that social workers, whose job is to investigate reports of abuse or neglect within families, have one of the most demanding and dangerous of careers. Rare is the caseworker who feels caught up on their caseload. They are overwhelmed with complaints to follow up, and agonize over decisions - whether or not to allow the child to remain with the family. Many do not relish the thought of adding one more environmental factor to assess.

Interestingly, the same could be said about animal cruelty investigators - overwhelmed, with no time for other social dysfunctions they often encounter. Responding to countless reports of cruel neglect, and less frequent cases of deliberate abuse of dogs, cats, and other domestic animals, they often come face to face with alcoholism, filth inside the home, and parental intimidation of the children. Animal abuse and other domestic violence are virtually inseparable.

This epidemic of violence is raging out of control in the United States, clogging our courts and prisons, bankrupting our local economies, and victimizing individuals in virtually every sector of society. The promise of breaking this cycle at the childhood level, by applying the animal connection, is that the earlier in life one receives treatment, the better chance that treatment has of succeeding, since the individual's personality is still developing. A second reason is that, as we have seen, children at-risk of becoming violent adults often target animals, the only family members more vulnerable than themselves, as their first victims.

By this time, some children may already begin to believe, from what has been drilled into them by their parents, that they themselves are "bad," and start to behave in ways they believe are expected of them.

The ability of the system to intervene early enough, when the child is first manifesting signs of living in a dysfunctional family, can be blocked by the very confidentiality designed to protect the child's reputation. Even when treatment is prescribed, a stigma comes with it, akin to the court-ordered sentences meant to correct the anti-social behavior of the adult offender. But to downplay early cruelty in the name of confidentiality, or forsake treatment, is not doing the young offender any favors.

Not anymore The criminal justice system in most states views cruelty to animals as a misdemeanor, and rarely results in sentences which reflect the violent nature of the crime or help to deter it. The grouping of misdemeanor convictions apart from more serious crimes makes it difficult to track individuals' patterns of violence over time.

In what at first glance appears to be one cause, there are actually two separate battles going on. One campaign is fighting violent crime and waging war against the criminal, who is viewed as bad through and through, and always having been so – like the burglar in the security alarm commercials. It is a fight against the stereotypical, violent adult male, personified.

The other campaign is being waged against violence itself. This campaign is not focused on a class of "bad people," but on a social sickness, passed on from generation to generation. It asks the question: What are the causes, characteristics and patterns of anti-social behavior? The solution lies within the answers.

To say that animals do not deserve our attention as long as we have so many human problems and human victims to deal with, is to limit the search for those answers. With greater attention to how and why animals figure in as victims, future human victims can be spared their suffering. Many of those human victims are children growing up in an emotional vacuum, afraid of touch, afraid to love for the pain that awaits them, out of touch with the cycle of nature - disconnected.

In the Sonoma County program, some of the children would not eat a bean, until they grew their own, then they relished them. Lisa Carreno, Director of the Sonoma County YMCA Battered Women's Shelter, which brings the children to the Humane Society's garden project, describes the changes she has seen in the children from week-to-week. They are afraid of touch and worried about their very survival in an uncertain world, moving from one setting to the next, and enduring frequent periods of real hunger. They blossom as their garden does. They begin to feel a sense of team work. They begin to ask questions, where they would not have before. They want contact. Their trust is coming back, in nature and in people.

The Y's mission is "to empower women and children," so they can, as these children are doing, take what they learn and influence those around them, becoming valued for their contributions.

The People and Animals Learning (PAL) program, at the Wisconsin Humane Society in Milwaukee, in 1993 paired small, manageable numbers of at-risk children with dogs turned into the shelter for behavioral problems. The children were taught how to obedience train the dogs. In this intensive, three-week pilot program, the pride of accomplishment worked its magic on the children, and the effects of their bond, both with the dogs and with each other, was carefully documented.

A very similar goal is attained each year in the City Kids and Calves program in Tacoma, Washington, where sexually-abused teenage girls are empowered, and infused with a sense of pride and teamwork, by raising dairy calves.

These local programs are combining the power of the human-animal companion bond with the knowledge that our behavior toward animals and each other are bound together. They are using this marriage to stop the violence cycle, and sending out waves of positive energy – the power of compassion.

We have seen AAT help individuals who are handicapped, elderly, or emotionally troubled. As this field continues to flourish and become recognized by the masses, it would seem the next step in the application of the bond, is to provide virtually all children with opportunities to gain a sense of empowerment, connection and self-worth.

But realistically, we cannot do that without first recognizing that atrocities toward animals, committed by children, are inextricably linked to their own treatment, and to continuing violence later in their lives. The pattern is numbing in its inevitability, at least when early intervention does not occur.

You can see the childhood fear still lurking just behind their vacant eyes, in photos that accompany the stories of their lives and crimes. The photos tell the story. These are the deadly results of a society that glorifies violence, condones child abuse at some level, and is just beginning to see the implications of animal abuse as one of the earliest symptoms.

What are we saying? That the issue is not animals, but cruelty itself. This is about the use of fear and the exploitation of vulnerability, versus the use of compassion and the promotion of self-worth – getting and maintaining control by force, versus being

119

comfortable with who you are, and accepting others. That is another reason why attempting to prevent violent crime with merely a greater show of force and punishment (i.e. incarceration) will not by itself succeed. Examine instead the source, pattern and direction of violence itself, while, at the same time, actively promoting kindness. Work at the roots, as early humane movement leaders put it.

These roots go deep, into sacred territory. Aside from the argument over genetic versus environmental influence, these roots have a definite masculine shape to them, even if there are a few female victims of abuse who become perpetrators, and even though each child, male, or female, starts out life in innocence.

How far back do we have to go, to reach all the roots? Back to where the father was given unquestioned dominion over all his "possessions," including his family (wife/wives, children, dependents), and his animals (livestock, work animals). Violence for the ages has been generated mainly by the male, and particularly by the father. Barbara Walker, in her book, The Crone, states,

> *"It is said children must have the fear of God put into them, usually by punishment, or they will grow up to be criminals and worse.*
>
> *Ignored are the findings of modern psychology that fear is the basis of violence, rather than its antagonist...The ability to intimidate is [men's] definition of power...Instead of trying to understand how others feel and react, they become bullies by using methods they know would work on themselves.*
>
> *Such men feel contempt for creatures who cannot offer them any physical harm in retaliation. Hence their contempt for women...Their cruelty is triggered by an appearance of vulnerability."*

Ultimately, men will have to overwhelmingly support and encourage the movement to make violent behavior a weak and powerless subculture, unacceptable at any age, scorned in any sport, entertainment, or social fad. Men have more to gain by allowing themselves to feel a broader range of emotions and be touched by others. Physical strength is not the only type of power, in any free society.

At this point, we have to work with the knowledge that even some decision-makers do not want to include a review of all violence in efforts toward its prevention. It is up to those of us who believe in the universal bond to show the folly in this stand. To say there is not enough evidence to prove a connection between cruelty to animals and cruelty to people, is to deny our childhood realization of the bond. There is no arguing it. Violence is violence.

The resistance of some adults to accepting the abuse link, is based on more than just the desire for more scientific proof, or the rush to stem the flood of strictly human problems. It is tinged with prejudice – an attitude learned and ingrained from centuries of repetition, an attitude that says, I am not related to them, I am above them. This prejudice is not far removed from another belief, just reversed in the last century – the belief that women and children had no rights. And so, even today, abused children go from looking at companion animals as equals, to feeling they are both equally worthless. Child-rearing must change, so that as adults, we still feel the power and magic of animals.

The word "animal" comes from the ancient Latin word, "anima," meaning soul, the life energy, that which breathes, and moves on its own. Ancient peoples understood the common connection, appreciating animals not just for what they provided, but also for their many unique characteristics and abilities – their beauty, grace, swiftness, keen vision, strength, subtle intuition, musical voices, nurturing manners, and even their ability to make people smile and laugh. They emulated their behavior as standards by which to live their own lives.

As I record these notes on tape, Lil, a floppy-looking terrier, and my working companion of twelve years, is sitting here beside me. We are driving to work down a beautiful, rural highway, past fields covered with frost, through alternating patches of mist and brilliant sunlight. Normally sleeping during the forty-five minute commute, she is up now to hear what I have to say, looking at me with this relaxing, alert, intelligent, adoring glow in her eyes, enjoying the moment with me, but in so doing, vastly enriching the moment for me.

Those of us fortunate enough to have animals as companions, see those animals' lives played out while still young enough to learn from them. We can apply what we have learned to our own lives. We learn to understand life and death, and appreciate the joy of simply being. The healing bond we have with companion animals is a means to regaining a sense of connection, and turning the epidemic of human violence around.

While some people, hardened by the sheer magnitude of this epidemic, remain complacent or worse, others take steps to bring change, and help the scars of the past to become less visible.

The affirmation of life can be measured by individual triumph and tragedies. The location of the 1989 attack on the Tacoma boy echoes now with the sound of children's laughter. The dense, wooded area near the Mansfield's home has been opened up and turned into a children's park. Typically far too late, the life destroying chain of violence that led to Earl Shimer has come to an end. He is serving a life sentence, with no chance for parole. The young boy's on-going physical and psychological recovery is being aided by a trust fund set up from donations received.

Dick Mansfield talks excitedly about a role-playing system he has developed, for enabling third grade students to resolve conflicts without violence, by acknowledging one another's uniqueness, and validating one another's feelings. Candy is planning to start an in-home pet care business, once their new daughter, Emily, gets a little older. In spite of all that has happened, she still remembers where her beloved "Marbles" was laid to rest, beneath the newly planted grass, right there next to the swings.

References: (- cited)*

Ascione, Frank R. (1993). Child Abuse and Animal Abuse in the Cycle of Violence. Presentation at Spokane, Washington for SpokAnimal C.A.R.E., (Children and Animals Research Project, Department of Psychology, Utah State University, Logan, Utah, 84322-2810).

Pearl Salotto

Budge, E.A. Wallis, (translation of) (1967). The Egyptian Book of the Dead (The Papyrus of Ani) (194). Dover.*

Deviney, Dickert, J., & Lockwood, R. (1983). The Care of Pets Within Child Abusing Families. International Journal for the Study of Animal Problems 4(4).

Farrow, Richard G. (1972, September). Violence. National Humane Review, pp. 12-13.*

Felthous, A.R., & Bernard, H. (1979). Enuresis, firesetting and cruelty to animals: The significance of two-thirds of this triad. Journal of Forensic Science, 240-246.

Felthous, A.R. & Kellert, S.R. Childhood Cruelty towards Animals among Criminals and Noncriminals. Human Relations, 38(12), 1113-1129.

Hellman, D. and Blackman, N. (1966). Enuresis, firesetting and cruelty to animals: A triad prediction of adult crime. American Journal of Psychiatry. 122, 1431-1435.

Locke, John, (1705). Some Thoughts Concerning Education.*

Lockewood, R., & Hodge G.R. (1986, Summer). The Tangled Web of Animal Abuse: The Links Between Cruelty to Animals and Human Violence. The Humane Society News.*

Melson, Gail, F. (1990, Fall). Fostering Interconnectedness with Animals and Nature: The Developmental Benefits for Children (Part 2). People, Animals, Environment.*

Protecting Children and Animals: Agenda for a Non-Violent Future (1992, September). American Humane Association Conference Summary. *

Ressler, R.K, Burgess, A.W., & Douglas, J.E. (1988). Sexual Homicide: Patterns and Motives. Lexington Books.

Robin, M., ten Bensel, R., Quigley, J., & Anderson, R. (1983). A study of the relationship between childhood pet animals and the psycho-social development of adolescents. In A.H. Katcher and A. Beck (Eds.), New Perspectives on our Lives with Companion Animals. Philadelphia: University of Pennsylvania Press.

Tapia, F., Children who are cruel to animals (1971). Child Psychiatry and Human Development, 2, 70-77.

Walker, Barbara, G. (1985). The Crone: Woman of Age, Wisdom, and Power (9). Harper and Row.*

CHAPTER 4

PET ASSISTED THERAPY IN EDUCATION

' 80 s

Section 1:
CHILDREN: THE FUTURE IS NOW

John Symynkywicz has over 25 years of professional experience in family and child services, mental health, and child welfare fields. He holds an MA in Counseling from Rhode Island College. He was Executive Director, Woonsocket Family and Child Services from 1970-1985. He also served as President of the Rhode Island Chapter, National Committee for Prevention of Child Abuse from 1978-1985 and on the NCPCA National Board of Directors from 1982-1986. He currently is the President/CEO of DAWN for Children, Inc., a volunteer state-wide child advocacy organization in Rhode Island.

Here's a news flash for those of us who would like to be a success in life. A recent survey of Fortune 500 Chief Executive Officers determined that 94% of those responding had a pet dog or cat as a child. Approximately 75% still had a pet as adults. This compares to 53% of United States households who own a pet.

Before you rush out and buy that expensive Pekinese or exotic Siamese cat, you might want to explore the relationship between companion animals, children and human development.

Children are widely understood as a wonderful and precious resource – a true celebration of life. Children are the future. Our whole future as a people and as a society depends upon the generation of children we are raising today. It is the children of today that will inherit, protect, and build upon what their parents and adults have been able to accomplish and achieve.

As Abraham Lincoln once said:

"A child is a person who is going to carry on what you have started. He/she is going to sit where you are sitting and when you are gone, attend to those things which you think are important. You may adopt all the policies you please, but how they are carried out depends on him and her. He and she will assume control of your cities, states, and nations. He/she is going to serve in and take over your churches, schools, universities, and corporations...the fate of humanity is in their hands."

No

Most children grow up with a relatively good, healthy place to live. They have caring parents, secure families, good health care and nutrition; safe sanitary housing; a decent standard of living; and a local community and educational system that works well for them and offers them a bright future as productive adults. Experiences with companion animals and nature for these children can only enhance their opportunities for nurturing, caring experiences that can enhance their lives.

For far too many children the world is not such a safe, healthy place full of hope and promise. For far too many children, the world is far more uninviting, harsh, dangerous, and unhealthy. Too many children are growing up each day economically deprived, often with bleak and uncertain futures. Poverty and unemployment, inadequate housing and homelessness, the decline of neighborhood and family life, drug abuse and child abuse, all threaten to harm and hurt children and youth growing up in today's society. These social and economic conditions continue to haunt the future of these children and the future of everyone.

It was into this world of fear and danger that Eric Dunphy entered. On August 20, 1994, police in the small suburban community of Woonsocket, Rhode Island, discovered the badly decomposed body of Eric Dunphy, three days short of his third birthday. Police determined that Eric had been brutally murdered approximately two weeks previously, having been stuffed into a cardboard Christmas ornament box and buried in a closet in a low income tenement. Shortly after the discovery, police arrested Eric's biological father, Timothy Dunphy, who allegedly confessed to the murder. Subsequent investigation indicated that the father had had a long history of personal and drug related problems, a criminal record, apparently had severely abused children previously, and had his parental rights previously terminated with another child, a daughter, due to allegations of severe child abuse. It also soon became apparent that two year old Eric had been removed from a safe, nurturing foster home where he had lived since birth, and placed by the Rhode Island public welfare agency in mid July 1994, with the father who allegedly murdered him within a month of his return. The response of the media, the general public, and child advocates was anger and outrage. Four months later, the Rhode Island Office of the Child Advocate was to conclude in its investigation of the case that: "the death of Eric could have been prevented...and is inexcusable."

Further investigation of the murder of Eric also quickly uncovered a troubling, but illuminating connection between animal abuse and Eric's violent death. Apparently, Timothy Dunphy, the father, had had a long and well known history of animal abuse. According to his younger brother, "his one pleasure in life seemed to be killing animals...he liked to shoot chipmunks, squirrels and birds in the woods, not as a hunter, but for kicks. A year ago, he dug a hole in the ground and put fifteen snakes in it. Then, he threw in toads and frogs into the pit so he could watch the serpents feast."

This tragic case illustrates both the need to better understand the link between animal cruelty and violence and the important therapeutic dynamic that Pet Assisted Therapy Facilitation can provide on behalf of children.

It is apparent that, despite the best efforts of parents, many children need the care and nurturing of more and more concerned adults and professional helpers. Children are, after all, dependent and vulnerable, too often the innocent victims of family and social circumstances that put them "at risk" to healthy development.

While all children are unique and individual, they do have much in common. There is a growing consensus regarding what children need in order to grow up into happy and productive adults. These factors include a safe, secure family and community environment characterized by stable relationships with caregivers they can learn to trust and depend upon. Children also need to develop a positive sense of self, characterized by a sense of direction, structure, self discipline and self esteem. Children who develop in a healthy manner also acquire a set of personal values, a strong sense of belonging, and usually have experienced an opportunity to care for and nurture others. From an early age (actually at birth), children begin to formulate a picture within themselves of how the world looks and how they fit into that world around them. If the child sees the world (and the people who populate it), as dangerous, uncaring, discouraging, and harmful, he/she will act on that perception throughout their childhood and adult life. On the other hand, if the world is perceived as a relatively safe place where one can be successful, feel competent, and live cooperatively, then the child is most likely to act in ways that reinforce and validate this world view throughout life.

This is exactly why families as a social institution are so important in our culture. The "family" is the first group into which the child is born. It is here that he/she begins the lessons of life and begins to put together the unique mosaic pattern of their future. It is here, within the family, that the child also typically needs to begin to develop a certain form of discipline – actually self discipline which is the essence of responsibility – the ability to discern and act upon what is good for himself/herself and the people around them (all at the same time). Some people refer to this as "character." The roles and responsibilities of parents and early caregivers and educators in this process are therefore extremely crucial. If the family and the community is not nurturing and caring, if it is discouraging and destructive, the children will suffer.

If parents and family have been unable to provide these nurturing characteristics, then the important task of child development must be taken up by educators, professionals and concerned citizens.

There are many ways that PAT can help achieve these goals and meet the needs for children and ourselves. The programs and approaches in the following pages are so practical, so basic, so human, that their positive impact on children might be underestimated. Yet, the truth is the exact opposite. These programs can have a most fundamental impact on the lives of the children participating in them. Here children learn the most basic, most important things about life – respect for self, respect for each other, respect for animals and nature, caring and nurturing, cooperation and working together for a common goal, in school, in the home, and in the community.

Section 2:
IS HOLLY WORKING TODAY?

Where?

__Barbara J. Wood__, Ph.D., A.C.S.W., L.I.S.W., is an Associate Professor of Social Work. She started work with her pet d̲o̲g̲,̲ ̲H̲o̲l̲l̲y̲, as a therapeutic b̲r̲i̲d̲g̲e̲ with inner-city children w̲i̲t̲h̲ ̲e̲m̲o̲t̲i̲o̲n̲a̲l̲ ̲d̲i̲f̲f̲i̲c̲u̲l̲t̲i̲e̲s̲ over ten years ago. She lives with her husband, pet dog Holly, two cats, and a Quarter Horse mare, in C̲o̲l̲u̲m̲b̲u̲s̲,̲ ̲O̲h̲i̲o̲.

For Holly and me it started with a stray kitten. Of course, the benefits to people of having animal companions were known at least as long ago as the earliest written histories. In ancient Egypt dog-headed Anubis was the physician and apothecary to the gods. The dog was the sacred emblem of the Sumerian goddess-physician Gula. Dogs were kept at the shrine of Asklepios in Greece, and the healing power of their licking wounds was renowned. The Gaulish Goddess Sequane recommended holding puppies to one's body to absorb the ills.

In the eighteenth century, it was reported from the York Retreat in England, that patients benefited from caring for rabbits and poultry. By 1867, in Bethel, Germany, epileptics were seen to improve with horseback riding and the association of companion animals. Germans developed guide dogs for blind veterans after World War I. Horses, dogs, and farm animals served in rehabilitation programs at the U.S. Army Air Force Convalescent Center in Pawling, New York, after World War II. In 1966 Erling Stordahl, the blind director of the rehabilitation center in Bertostoln, Norway, began employing dogs and horses with the blind and physically handicapped. In 1969, Dr. Boris Levinson, the first child psychologist in the United States to use and promote pet-facilitated therapy, wrote of his experiences with his co-therapist Jingles in his book *Pet-Oriented Child Psychology*. But the possibilities for my own professional work were not brought home to me until an abandoned kitten was found huddled in the winter weather on the front steps of the elementary school for emotionally disturbed children where I provide therapy three days a week.

The principal brought the homeless kitten to my office until other arrangements could be made. The children who came to my office while the kitten was there immediately brightened and chatted easily. Moved by the childrens' positive transformation, I wrote a proposal to the school authorities and received permission for my dog Holly to accompany me during counseling sessions.

I knew Holly, a seven-year old spayed female of mixed parentage who tips the scales at nineteen pounds, would be perfect for the job. After all, this was the dog who allowed the new kitten to chew on her ears. She is tolerant, gregarious, excellent on a leash, and in general, I thought well behaved. Although she was not reared with children, Holly has had ample exposure to them, so sticky fingers in her short brown fur would not come as a shock. She loves to ride in the car, an essential trait if she was to accompany me to the school on a regular basis. She had additional qualifications in knowing the standard commands "sit," "shake," "lie down," "come," and "speak" in English and in Spanish.

Preparations were made at the school. The children made signs for my office doors: "Holly is happy to be here." I installed a dog bed and bowls for dry dog chow and water. Holly has always enjoyed an open bowl policy at home, and the same seemed appropriate for her at work. I also secured a supply of doggy treats (the cereal-based multicolored ones) in case all went wrong and I was reduced to bribery. Holly and I were both going to be on trial.

My supervisor had made her lack of enthusiasm for the "experiment" quite clear with her curt questions: "What if 'it' bit one of the children?" "What if 'it' had an 'accident'?" I had submitted a ten-page proposal, which included a veterinarian's certification that Holly was free from disease or parasites and a testament to her even temperament, and all I could think of during this inquisition (but did not say) was, "What if one of those emotionally disturbed children bites Holly?" "Can Holly get a disease from a child?" Fortunately the other administrators, especially the principal, were supportive, and Holly and I were scheduled to begin.

I don't know if Holly knew we were embarking on a new life, but I did. I had thought I had enough worries even before my supervisor made it abundantly clear that any problems whatsoever resulting from the "dog experiment" would reflect on me. I bought Holly a new leash and collar, gave her a bath, shined her name, rabies and license tags, and we were off.

Holly was excited. She had never before been invited to get in the car when I was going to work. With purse, briefcase, lunch, and case notes, I didn't seem to have a free hand for her leash, but despite her harried mistress, Holly made a bright entrance at school. All went well until we reached the tile floor in the hall.

Holly has never liked linoleum, preferring carpeting like that at home, which gives her better footing. While she slipped and slid her way beside me down the hall, quivering but dutiful, it dawned on me that for all the preparations I had made, I had overlooked the most important one – of Holly herself. I had reviewed the literature on pet-facilitated therapy. I had cleared the idea with the teaching staff and the teachers' union and assured the janitor that Holly was house trained and would cause him no extra work. I had discussed Holly's arrival with my little counselees' and checked for allergies. Citing our rodent predecessors (many classrooms already harbored hamsters, guinea pigs, and gerbils), I had gained administrative support and official approval. The only one I had not consulted was Holly.

Half an hour remained before the children arrived. An announcement over the public address system alerted us there would be a fire drill that day. I gave Holly a treat; I could have used one myself, thinking of all the things there are in an institutional school setting for a house dog to adjust to: long stretches of tile floors, bells, the public address system, one hundred and twenty children changing classes, school buses roaring up, children yelling and shouting in the gym just down the hall, and the smells of disinfectant and strangers. And now the fire drill. I knew I should have brought Holly for a site visit over the weekend to familiarize her with the building at least, the largest she had ever seen.

My first counselee of the day knocked on the door. Holly barked as she does at home for the mail carrier, which is to say loudly and with conviction. I would have to talk to Holly about that – greeting insecure children with aggressive barking was, to say the least, therapeutically counterproductive.

I opened the door. A small boy entered, and he and Holly stared at each other warily. He asked, "Does that dog bite?" I suggested he might like to give Holly a treat.

He could pick any color he liked. He chose red. Holly has always been very careful and gentle in taking food from someone's hand. She has a soft mouth. As the boy stretched out his hand rather uncertainly, Holly neatly and gently took the treat, swallowed it, and licked his other hand. The crucial moment passed; they were friends. The meaning of the term "companion animal" became clear to me. "Companion "comes from the Latin, *com*, meaning "with," and *panis*, meaning "bread." A companion is someone you share food with. I saw this bond, so important throughout human history, at work before my eyes: the boy realizing Holly's teeth were no threat, that she would not bite, that she appreciated the treat, licking his other hand and looking for more. Her tongue and wagging tail said to the boy she accepted him. For some of the children at the school, Holly's would be the first unconditional acceptance they had ever experienced.

After a succession of little visitors came to our door at the sound of the bell, Holly realized that bells and boys (there are very few girls in this school) meant treats. She had found a gravy train. She soaked up the attention. She had never been petted or treated so much in her life. Then came the fire drill.

The first bell is intended to be loud, both piercing, and alarming. Its maker would be pleased to know that this school's bell probably exceeds the requirements. I thought the sound would be bad enough, but Holly would also have to traverse the slippery tile floors, smelling so strongly of disinfectant, and go down a flight of metal stairs booming and echoing with the footsteps of hurrying children and staff. All timed by a stop watch. No one likes fire drills, especially in winter, and it was now winter. An unsuccessful fire drill had to be reported and repeated under fire department supervision. It leaves a mark on the record. If there were any problems, Holly could be branded a fire hazard.

The alarm went off. Holly's ears went straight up, an appreciable feat for a floppy-eared dog. I grabbed her leash, snapped it on the stunned dog, put my other arm around the counselee and told both in my most authoritative voice to *Come*. I turned off the lights behind us and closed the door, as the fire code requires. We started down the hall wet from snow tramped in from afternoon recess. Holly needed more than four feet to stay upright on her own, but the crowd pushed her close to me. The stairs thundered. Holly went rigid. "COME NOW!" That or be trampled. Holly, who is a smallish dog, took the stairs in three leaps, dragging the boy and me behind her. We made it outside and in line just under the wire. We would not have to repeat the drill. There would be no black mark against the school. Holly has never grown happy with fire drills, but the wild eyes, heaving sides and terror have subsided with time. That first day was quite literally a trial by fire, but we passed.

On the following days, Holly willingly got in the car to go to work. She improved her greeting behavior until she became irresistible. She learned not to bark at a knock on the office door. I trimmed her nails short so her pads get more traction on the tile floors. I found a large piece of carpeting for my office so she can be more comfortable there, and now the children can sit on the floor to pet, brush, play with, talk to, and confide in her. She licks them all; adults may be inclined to wash off dog saliva, but to the kids it's liquid gold.

Holly has developed her own fan club. The counselees adore her, and the other children cluster at our office door in the morning to pet her and say hi. The same happens in reverse in the afternoon before the kids go home. Holly also makes class visits and has helped many a class reach a behavioral goal. Teachers come in for "pet therapy" as well. A short pat is restorative after a long day.

Holly

When a new student comes to school, a "veteran" student gives the child a guided tour. Holly is the first stop. Parents report how the "shrink dog" is talked about at home. When one class began a pen pal project with an out-of-state school, Holly was the subject of letters. Before Holly started at the school, some students tried to bribe me by offering me fifty cents to get them counseling during the time for their English or math test. Now Holly is offered a dollar.

I have become invisible at the other end of the leash. I didn't know how much so until I caught strep throat from one of my "huggers" (an occupational hazard when working with children) and missed two days of work. When I called in sick the first day, I was asked if that meant Holly would be staying home too. The second day I was asked if I could at least send Holly to work in a cab. It was not an unserious question, "Is Holly working today?"

Holly does work! Three months into the project, nine-year-old LeMar, a third grader who had been one of Holly's regulars, was shot and killed. A "boyfriend" apparently went "mad" and shot LeMar's mother four times. When, hearing his mother's screams, LeMar came out of his bedroom, and was shot dead. From their school bus, the other children saw the police and ambulance and the coroner taking LeMar's body away. By the time the children arrived at school, they were thoroughly frightened and in tears.

Holly and I went down to LeMar's classroom. LeMar's teacher, a woman in her early twenties, said with tears streaming down her face that her educational degree had not prepared her to handle a situation like this. One of the local television station's remote satellite vans was circling the building, no doubt hoping for pictures of sobbing children to increase their ratings. The children were crying for LeMar and because their teacher was crying and because they feared the same fate themselves. Their lives were just as precarious as LeMar's in a world where men and guns rule.

Nothing prepares you for a situation like this. But we were in it. First we talked about how crying was perfectly okay for adults and children alike, especially over something like the senseless killing of a nine-year-old boy in his pajamas. Being scared was okay too. Gunshots in the dark are something to be scared of. Intense feelings are normal – being able to feel is the essence of being human. The children calmed as we talked about missing LeMar. We wrote letters to LeMar's mother in the hospital (she survived the shooting), telling our sorrow about LeMar's death. It was when the crying had subsided somewhat that I realized what Holly had been doing.

Holly had worked her way around the room, going from child to child (and to the teacher), putting her front paws on their laps, stretching up and licking the tears from their faces. Many embraced her, running their fingers through her fur with an intensity that would have left her bald if it had continued all day. With her touch and tongue, Holly consoled each child on a deeper level than could ever be possible with words coming from an adult associated with the terrifying world. Through the dark day, and later at the funeral, and through the lingering sadness, Holly provided more comfort than anyone or anything else. It was draining work for her. She fell asleep on the back seat of the car before we even left the parking lot that day.

Holly does hard physical work as well. When the good weather began, each counselee wanted to take Holly for a walk. We would walk around the block and romp on the grassy area of the playground. The brief respite from the structure of school made for relaxed counseling. Holly soon trained each child how to go for a sniff around the neighborhood. Holly became quite a child trainer. In her own self-defense, lest the children run her ragged doing tricks hour after hour, she convinced them that she did not know how to "sit," "speak," "lie down," or "shake hands." She now taught them to follow her on the leash as she checked out an interesting smell here or a fascinating odor there. When playing chase, she knew just how fast to go to stay out of reach, while staying close enough to keep the game interesting. She knows the border of the playground, so no one gets too close to the street. On really active days, Holly also falls asleep on the back seat of the car on the way home. Some days I could join her. Maybe we could both use a cab.

Holly's fame spread. The school newsletter featured her in a full-page article. The newsletter editor alerted neighborhood newspapers, the city newspaper, and television news departments. But fame and success do not always bring appreciation. My supervisor "discovered" that end-of-the-year paperwork would take an extra day a week in the office to complete. One of Holly's days was cut. It seemed that if the "canine counselor" got any more publicity, we might face further cuts. Holly already whimpered on the two days she had to stay home when I went to work. I was disappointed, Holly pined, and the kids were depressed.

Evaluation of the counselees indicated that the "dog experiment" had made a positive difference. There were 10.3 percent fewer absences, and disruptive behaviors were less extreme.

These are children who could not function in a regular class setting, the "throwaways" of our disposable society. These children, on their own, got together a petition about Holly. It was badly typed, miserably spelled - and wonderful. Children who could hardly get along on a one-to-one basis and were disastrous in a group, cooperated in this effort, assigned their best (and only) typist, worked out the wording of their demands, and collected signatures. I only got wind of it when they asked me for the name of the program supervisor. I gave it to them.

Their petition was ignored, which was worse even than its being rejected. But I was not fired, and Holly was not branded a health or fire hazard. The kids learned that spelling, writing, and the other hated English lessons could have meaning outside of the classroom and, even more important, that they could work together without hitting and kicking. Of course, it would have been better if the petition had been taken seriously, but Holly and I are still there, and lobbying for the project's permanence and expansion.

I work with human emotions. I am trained in helping people reach and maintain emotional well-being. I am paid for this work. Holly does the same work: like most companion animals, she attends to the emotional well-being of people. She is not paid, though the work she is doing in a professional setting at school is well beyond her responsibilities as a private house dog. I do not know how to recompense her for this additional labor, and probably most people would consider even the idea of compensation ridiculous. I was already giving her a kind and loving home with good food and regular medical care, and I have not been able to think of any improvements or extras that she might enjoy.

I am concerned about the ethics of my turning Holly into a "professional" dog. I am scrupulously careful that Holly is not abused by the children although that has been easy so far, since no child has to date ever attempted to harm her. Only on one occasion have I asked her to go to school when she may not have wanted to. Freezing rain was coming down, monsoon-fashion, when she went out in the morning to do her business. She came back in and went back to bed. It was an intelligent assessment of the day. If I had had the choice, I would have gone back to bed too. But when I called Holly to get into the car, she came, so off to work we went. I felt guilty, however. When I am ill, I call in sick. Can Holly call in sick? Does she have an obligation as a professional to continue, regardless of her feelings and needs, with what she has taken on?

Holly responds eagerly when I ask, "Do you want to go school today?" She has become more assured and self-assertive than she was before. She takes less guff of the cats at home and now deals easily with the slippery floors and metal stairs at school. She handles the children with confidence and sensitivity. Her unconditional acceptance of the kids reduces their tension and anxiety and consequently makes counseling less stressful for all concerned. She makes my job easier and more enjoyable. She looks like she is enjoying herself.

So the answer to the question "Is Holly working today?" is "Yes, as long as she seems to want to." May the Dog Deities of ancient times smile upon her and her work.

Section 3:
THERAPY PETS AS ROLE MODELS IN THE CLASSROOM
(Pearl Salotto)

This article was published previously, in part, by the Latham Foundation.

The D. J. "Respect for Living Things" Program, in which a loving therapy pet works with a professional Pet Assisted Therapy Facilitator/Educator, who cares deeply about the children as well as the pet, can have a significant and life-changing impact on children.

Who would ever think that discussions based on reactions to a friendly and loving white dog can lead to character building, values development and reverberating good feelings about oneself, others, animals, and the environment that can last a lifetime?

- The children in the D. J. program have enhanced self-esteem, are empowered in their confidence that they can make a positive difference in their world, are able to get along with youngsters from a variety of backgrounds, are speaking up on behalf of children who are rejected or teased, are more considerate of family members including their pets, and appear to be serving not only as peacemakers, but as advocates for themselves, others, animals and the environment!

- The fact that D. J., a friendly, innocent, and yet fragile creature, has shared herself trustingly with the children, has perhaps opened "a window of awareness" in the youngsters of the fragility of all living things, that all living things have feelings and needs, and that, not only is it our responsibility to return love that we receive, but that it feels good as well!

- The children who have gone through this program are more prepared to make the right choices as they move along life's path and have the understanding and inner strength which leads to empathy and advocacy to help build a better world for all of our futures.

In today's world, sadly, where many, if not most families, are very stressed, where dys-functionalism and abuse too frequently replace quality family time, where substance abuse, early pregnancy, and domestic violence all too often interfere with healthy family communication and caring, how could we expect that children will come to school "ready to learn.' In addition, instead of schools being 'caring communities' as we would like them to be, frequently the school 'climate' is often filled with metal detectors, violence, teasing and harassment, to such a degree that some children have even been driven to suicide, as heartwrenchingly described on the Oprah and Maury Povich shows.

Leaders in society are beginning to take notice. The media has featured several school districts who are teaching character education programs. On the CNN program,

Pearl Salotto

Both Sides, Acting Deputy Secretary of Education Marshall Smith stated that teaching respect is among the critical needs that our schools must address. Another participant on *Both Sides* was the author of *Savage Inequalities* Jonathan Kozol, who stated that the notion of respect is one thing he has heard over and over as he talks to school children around the country, respect from each other, and respect from teachers. He added that young people need to go into a building where they feel respected, because they can not work very hard without respect.

So the question becomes what is the best way to teach respect so that it can be effective and long lasting?

Perhaps a clue lies in a statement issued as far back as 1933, by the National PTA Congress:

"Children trained to extend justice, kindness, and mercy to animals become more just, kind, and considerate in their relations with each other. Character training along these lines will result in men and women of broader sympathies, more humane, more law abiding - in every respect more valuable citizens. Humane education is teaching in the schools and colleges of the nations, the principals of justice, good will, and humanity toward all life. The cultivation of the spirit of kindness to animals is but the starting point toward that larger humanity which include ones fellow of every race and clime. A generation of people trained in these principles will solve their international difficulties as neighbors and not as enemies."

Similar statements were made by several leaders in the field, Edith Latham, George Angell, Leo Bustad, and others. In addition, therapy pets have long been recognized (via the profession of Pet Assisted Therapy) for their ability to comfort those in nursing homes, motivate those in need of rehabilitation to attempt to walk or speak, and to change angry and depressed prisoners into cooperative and, therefore, responsible individuals, who have a much better chance of fitting into society upon release. It is not an unreasonable assertion to say that the loving impact of therapy pets can have a positive effect on school children as well.

Perhaps the time is right to combine the need to teach respect in our schools with the much accepted concept of the therapeutic benefits of pets.

- Could it be that society now recognizes that there is a big gap in the education of our children?

- Could it be that teaching respect in addition to academics could help fulfill the original vision of our founding fathers, who initiated the concept of public education, in order to educate good citizens of society?
  ↘ workers

- Could it be that teaching respect as part of the school day could help make the difference between a violent or a peaceful world?

The effect of Pet-Inspired Values Development programs can be very powerful in reaching the whole child, mind and heart and body. Through a multi-sensory approach, combining interacting with the dog, discussions about respect of other people, ourselves, animals and the environment, as well as essay writing, reading, singing and

134

drawing, a child discovers a new sense of his own identity and a new view of the world around him/her, in which he/she feels responsible for his/her choices and behaviors toward all living things.

The D. J. "Respect for Living Things" Program, the original Pet-Inspired Values Development model, is a curriculum of several one hour sessions, designed for school children of all ages, preferably starting in the primary grades. In this curriculum my dog D. J. motivates and inspires children. The goal of the program is to help children enjoy positive experiences regarding the human companion animal bond leading to their making constructive choices. All of our children need such experiences, which are healthy and wholesome.

Touchingly, the benefits of the HCAB seem to know no limit. Through loving interaction with D. J or other therapy pets and by the childrens' observation of these pets' unconditional love to all, youngsters of all ages and in a variety of settings have learned a number of positive values.

Maj-En carries on D.J.'s tradition, here with Ricardo, Veterans School Central Falls. Photo credit: Jo Ann Diggle.

In a brief interaction with D.J., a child's world was changed. For example:

- *in which a paw was lovingly extended, as a huge white dog leaned gently against a child's legs (as he/she sat at a wooden class-room desk)*

Pearl Salotto

- *as this Dog of Joy appealingly and invitingly rolled over to be tickled, wrapping her strong but gentle paw around a child's arm.*

A child's world was changed.

These experiences, combined with a discussion in which every child gets to share and express herself/himself, can lead to everlasting memories, which would help preclude future involvement in abuse or violence against animals and people.

An example of such a response to this program is found in an essay by an eight year old girl: "I felt good when I petted D. J. She made me and my whole class feel good and she gave us feelings for other people. So if we have feelings, we can make our world a better place to live in."

Can a therapy pet lead to the internalization of not only lasting values, but also a truly passionate commitment to help the world improve. We find the answer to this question beautifully described by another young lady in the program: "We can learn to be gentle to living things. We can also learn to not be discriminators. D. J. does not go around and only play with white or black people. She's always happy, smiling, and calm. We could learn from her example. We can be kind to people who have disabilities. We can learn to be kind and gentle. These are all things we can do to help. That's what we can learn from D. J."

Many other unspoken lessons are learned as a therapy pet, like D. J., walks up and down the aisles of children with outstretched hands in classrooms or rotates around a circle of eager young ones, sitting amidst beautiful pine trees or on the YMCA'S gymnasium floors, warmed through caring interaction. I have found that D.J.'s presence – with her own unique personality – with her enthusiasm for life, with her spontaneous initiation of friendship with everyone – creates a lasting realization of her "aliveness" and her goodness.

Through such interactions, D. J. teaches the curriculum's first goal. Are animals living things? on her own, simply by being herself. Our discussion proceeds from children stating that D. J. makes them feel loved, to their recognizing that they have a responsibility to give love back to animals and to people from whom they receive it. Children readily recognize that love is caring and sharing, listening and cooperating, rather than the receiving of material things. The children find it easy to describe ways we can give love and respect back to animals and people. Touching responses include, for example, that, "You don't leave animals out in a snowstorm or a rainstorm," "I didn't know that people couldn't wake up their pets when they are asleep," "when friends come over you teach them the rules about how to treat the family pet," and "therapy dogs make older people happy – and they deserve to be happy too." These youngsters comprehend that we all deserve love and respect, and that we all have feelings and needs. Children who perhaps have never talked about feelings before are comfortable opening up in such a "sharing and caring" environment – which has been set up by D. J. and the childrens' spontaneous gentle responses to her.

I find that the childrens' comments invariably lead into the concepts I am trying to convey. Some child will, undoubtedly, mention how special D. J. is. This gives me a wonderful opportunity to let the children know that each one of them is special and unique, and that there is no one else in the world just like each one of them. As I ask the children to think about what makes them special and unique and as the realization gradually dawns on them, this awareness of their own special identity has a powerful and possibly life-changing impact. The children have had the opportunity to realize the meaning of their own uniqueness through getting to know D. J. and experiencing and talking about her uniqueness, as well as being gently led, one child at a time, to making the connection to themselves. Once all the children have internalized this idea of uniqueness, it is not a big step to help them begin the lifelong challenge of applauding their strengths and accepting their limitations. Whether a youngster doesn't have 20/20 vision or isn't the best on the baseball team, he/she still has the awesome awareness of his/her uniqueness, with its special balance of positives and negatives.

This program with D. J., as the teacher, inspiration, and motivator to the children, as well as to myself, is special, in so many ways. There is something strikingly touching about D. J.'s entering a gym, greeting, and being greeted, by about a dozen youngsters. Almost without any words, D. J. and I sort of "melt" to the floor with the children taking their places around us. Many hands are gently and rhythmically petting D. J. without any arguing, pushing, and hollering. The bond of love between D. J. and myself serves not only as a model of love and respect, but the LIVING of it, which to me, is just doing what comes naturally.

Laura, Veronica, Elizabeth, D.J., Jennifer, and Gina - D.J. - lovingly encircled in peace and harmony. Courtesy of the Woonsocket Call.

Pearl Salotto

On one occasion, when I did not bring D. J. to school, because the roads and walks were too icy, the children and I spent the session in an unforgettable lesson on ethics. By the end of the hour, each child, despite missing D. J., agreed that I had made the right choice. This reaction revealed to me that the power of love that these children had built up with D.J. over several years allowed them to see beyond their own needs, expectations and desires and feel for the needs of others.

I give the children, also, the same regard, respect, and concern as I do D. J. – again, doing what comes naturally. Working with children in Pet-Inspired Values Development programs, where the pet is the model, the facilitator must echo the same regard for the children, sincerely, spontaneously, and honestly.

Not only are these attitudes observed by the children, but they become contagious. Each child internalizes not only an intellectual respect, but a deep and sincere emotional respect for the therapy pet and all the people present. These ethical principles, which are the foundation of the PAT profession, that D. J. and I are helping the children discover and embrace, by example, through discussions, writings, and behaviors, will hopefully stay with them, as they become the caring professionals of tomorrow.

The effect of my relationship with D. J. on the children is evidenced through a youngster's own words: "D. J. is a good dog and never gets yelled at. Pearl treats D. J. with lots of love. Pearl asks D. J. if she wants to go to work or not. If not, Pearl does not force her. Pearl and D. J. love their job because they are always with someone who needs a friend."

D. J.'s trust and gentleness has provided for the children a glimpse into the wonder of it all, into the fragility of life, into the joy of giving and receiving love. These powerful emotional experiences of gentleness and intimacy with a living creature, perhaps never before experienced, combined with an understanding of our responsibilities to all living things, can pave the way for childrens' future choices.

- Will the children channel their love for D. J. into respect for family, teachers, friends, and animals?

- Will they channel their memory of D. J. into advocacy for people and animals in need including individuals in nursing homes, individuals who are mentally challenged, animals who are endangered, animals in zoos, and homeless or abandoned pets or children?

- Will the feeling of specialness, uniqueness and esteem that D. J.'s friendship and subsequent connections have planted in children, grow and bloom, creating caring adults who are committed and compassionate?

- Will the childrens' desire to follow D. J.'s example of unconditional love to one and all, lead them to respect others regardless of race, religion, age, health or economic status?

- Will the childrens' recognition that they are unique, help them respect their own mind, body, and heart?

As the youngsters have recognized, in the program thus far, that D. J. loves everyone, I then speak about what it means to be a Pet Assisted Therapy Dog and how D. J., through unconditional love, enhances the quality of life of individuals in such places as nursing homes and hospitals. I have developed several true stories into childrens' booklets which enable the children to appreciate D. J.'s impact on the lives of so many individuals who are elderly or ill.

D. J. and Vera
(see cover)

Vera is beautiful
Vera lives in a nursing home and is very lonely.
Vera misses her family, her home and her job.
Vera doesn't feel well
and she can't see or hear or walk very well either.
One day D. J. comes to visit Vera!
Can D. J. bring back Vera's health or home?
No, but at least now – Vera is smiling!

A second booklet that has tremendous meaning to children reflects another program theme: *Commitment to animals and people*:

D. J. "A Member of the Family"   ✝

D. J. has been a beloved member of our family for eight years.
D. J. has a job. She's a pet therapy dog.
D. J. went to school. It is good to go to school and learn.
D. J. loves her job. Her job is to make people happy.
She feels good when she makes people happy.
She doesn't care what race or religion you are or how well you walk or talk.
As you come up to D. J., she will wag her tail and give you her paw.
She will make you realize that you are unique and special.
D. J. is loved and special too.
After a day's work she comes home and relaxes, looking out the window from
her favorite spot on the couch
At night she sleeps in a warm bed with me.
D. J. always gets love and care from me even if I'm busy, tired or sick.
I respect D. J.'s feelings and she respects mine. It will always be that way
for D. J. and me.

Another booklet that I have recently written, printed with love by my granddaughter Stacey is called "Can We Follow Her Example and Build a Better World?", consists of simple questions and heartwarming pictures. (See Chapter 9, Section 4)

The effect of these little booklets on the children can be seen in the essays that their teachers often have them write following the program. One girl wrote: "When a child is born, the parents of that child have to make a commitment that they will love, take care, and respect their child. They must get up in the middle of the night to feed the child. But the first thing a parent must do is think, Do I have a good enough career to support my child? Do I have the time to take care of the baby and love my baby when he/she sick? Will I be able to teach my child to love and respect his/her body, others, animals, and other people's property/belongings? But most of all do I have the time to love this baby?" Another child wrote: "If I get a dog I will love him and always walk my dog and feed him and let him go on the couch and let him sleep with me. I will teach him to do tricks. I will give him a treat every day. I will always love him even if I die or he dies, but if he does I will cry. I will let him make people happy like D. J."

Other resources I have developed, in addition to booklets, include songs. "The Children's D. J. Song: Can We Follow Her Example And Build A Better World?" is a joy for children to sing, and encompasses all the program themes as well.

✝ **"The Children's D. J. Song:**
Can We Follow Her Example And Build A Better World?"
(this can be sung to the tune of the Battle Hymn of the Republic)

From all around the world, we are kids from far and near,
With friends and family by our side, we come to greet you here,
To stay in school, treat everyone right, respect ourselves as well,
We will follow all our dreams!

Our mascot is a special dog who's name is Dog of Joy,
In nursing homes and schools she works wherever there's a need,
Extended paw and wagging tail she always brings a smile,
She brightens up our world!

We all love this Dog of Joy, because she makes us feel special,
She teaches us to trust and care, she makes us feel so proud,
With gentle voice and gentle touch, we all gather round,
Oh, we respect D. J.!

Oh, D. J. loves each one of us, she loves us one and all,
She cares not if we're rich or poor, or if we're short or tall,
She cares not if we're old or young, or where we may come from,
She loves us one and all!

Can we follow her example, can we build a better world,
Can we treat each other kindly in all our words and deeds,
Can we welcome friends and neighbors from all around the globe,
The world is for one and all!

We will care for planet Earth, you see, it's the only one we have,
We need to keep it clean, oh, we need to keep it green,
Respecting animals in our homes and in the wilderness,
We will care for all living things!

We're all special and unique and have talents of our own,
We each have skills to share and something more to learn,
We write or draw or swim or sing, we'll build the world together,
We'll build it one and all!

We greet each day with lots of cheer and full of hopes and dreams,
We grow and learn in every way, so much we want to know,
Please join us in this magic song, we'll all work together,
We will build a better world

We will build a better world!

The joy of working in this field, which has inspired me to develop these booklets and songs (for example "Oh - We Respect," listed in Chapter 9, Section 4) undoubtedly will inspire others to develop their own multisensory materials.

Not surprisingly, this D. J. "Respect for Living Things" Program, affectionately dubbed *The D. J. Program*, by children, parents, school administrators and public officials alike, brings about emotional, behavioral and cognitive changes. As a result of childrens' overflowing need to express themselves, within a validating and empowering environment, along with their deep appreciation and amazement at the opportunity to give and receive love from a companion animal friend, as part of school, no less, they see the world anew. These mesh together in a manner which allows the children to develop a new view of the world and of their potential role in it. As the children sit quietly around D. J., offering her a cup of water when she is thirsty, holding a paw when she extends it, letting her sleep when she is tired, a wonderful sense of giving to another creature fills their minds, hearts, and souls with the awareness of just how good it feels – to "give" to another.

D. J, who has been described as a 'magnet', not only draws people to her, but allows people to get in touch with the 'best' within themselves, as well. In the 'joy of the moment' when a child's mind, body and heart are in perfect harmony – real learning takes place. D. J.'s gentleness allows children to get in control immediately of their own behavior, her trust encourages them to 'share' and her needs allow them to be respectful. D. J. has literally 'invited' us into her world of gentleness, with all of our senses. This world of connectedness to all living things feels so right, that we just might want to hold on to it, forever.

Is it possible that children of different races and religions, different intellects, and different health status, can sit in a classroom together, sharing D. J.'s love and discussing the values she models (calmness, sharing, friendship, unconditional love) and all of a sudden their own differences fade, in a common experience of fun, learning, and a vision of a better world, in which each one of them recognizes that he/she has a significant place? Does indeed empathy for all living things and an appreciation of each other's humanity result from singing, talking, listening, reading, and experiencing this shared love for D. J.?

Thus one can see that, with a child's enthusiasm for the therapy pet, it is easy for the Pet Assisted Therapy Facilitator or their teacher, after the program is over, to direct that passion and energy toward kindness and compassion through words and deeds, for all living things. This gives children a chance to develop social skills and a source of inner strength that leads them away from joining gangs, from discrimination, from teasing, abuse, and other forms of cruelty.

A teacher recently asked her third grade class, after I had presented The D. J. Program twice in her room, whether they would like to take the D.J. Challenge – of treating each other – as D.J. had treated them. This particular class had had a problem of teasing and isolating youngsters whose academic skills were low. As they discussed and charted their behavior, connecting it to the values of the D. J. program, over the next six weeks, they found within themselves, a new awareness of the feelings of their fellow students. They made a beautiful chart, which now hangs outside the principal's office with pictures of themselves with D. J. and picture captions documenting their new found respect for each other.

I overheard another teacher saying recently, from about twenty feet down the hall, as D. J. and I were waiting outside our designated classroom, "Can you children stand and wait quietly for your drink of water, as D. J. is waiting calmly and patiently to enter her class room?"

Dogs as role models? Why not?

D. J.'s simple message of love for all and the bond which children share with her, as well as the bond that I share with her and with them, touches them and inspires them to internalize deepened values and reverence for all of life.

Can programs, such as these, which focus on the children respecting animals, others, and themselves, give them a new sense of self-respect leading them to make the right choices even in difficult situations? Pet-Inspired Values Development programs can help children recognize appropriate and inappropriate behavior on the part of others toward them, their friends, pets, and all creatures. In an environment like this, where children feel it is safe to share, I have heard comments - sometimes tragic comments – such as the young girl who told me that her older sister, who takes care of her when her mother is working, hits the dog and hits her too. As this child's teacher and I exchanged horrified glances, and the teacher quietly informed me that she would make a social service referral, the child also realized, in that instant, following our thirty minute discussion of respect, that all of our talk about respect applied to her as an individual also. In that moment of internalization of the concepts of respect, love, and gentleness she realized that something was wrong with what she and her pet had been experiencing and that she and her pet did not deserve abusive treatment. At some point in her life she might have realized this anyway, but in a program which tied it all together, she was suddenly able to realize that she did not need to keep her awful secret any more.

Another potential benefit of this type of program can be helping children who have lost their trust in people through divorce, abuse or abandonment. Perhaps programs like this, emphasizing caring and sharing, can help these children take the first step toward finding their way back to trusting people again.

When teachers easily bond with D. J., children have a totally unexpected, but truly life changing opportunity to view teachers as "people" and to experience moments of intimacy. I remember a group of four year olds who 'slid' closer and closer from their spot on the floor with such smiles, that I realized that they had never seen such a moment of closeness before between the human and canine species or perhaps at all as their teacher lovingly held a paper cup of cold water, from which D. J. eagerly lapped. Following D. J.'s drink of water, she gave her paw, one and then the other, repeatedly, to the teacher. As the children gazed in wonder, feeling joy in the moment, it is clear that they were experiencing a moment of peace, respect, gentleness, calm, and caring that would forever alter their view of their teacher, as well as their view of the world. As my dear friend, Human Companion Animal Bond Specialist Dr. Dick Dillman says, "It is indeed the simple things, that lead to everlasting impressions."

When I work with the little ones, of course, adaptations to the program have to be made. I usually gather about three or four children at a time around the dog, and little hands can then learn the rich rewards of gentle touch in a manner comfortable and peaceful, for dog and children, alike. Conversation with very young children can be limited to an awareness that the pet is a living thing, through the childrens' own observations that D.J. is walking, breathing, has needs for hygiene, nourishment and most of all, a home, respect, and love.

These little ones dictate the most heart warming stories to their teachers such as the little one who said: "D. J. is white. D. J. is awesome. I love D. J. D. J. has feelings."

On one occasion a teacher asked D. J. and I to wait inside the classroom as her children would soon be returning from recess. As the children filed into the room, each one was greeted with an exuberant energetic Dog of Joy. It was hard to see who was more ecstatic – the dog or the kids. There was no pushing, but rather, spontaneous good manners – each waiting their turn and not crowding D. J. As five to ten minutes passed, the teacher said, "Let's hurry to our seats, kids. We have a program to start." I explained to the teacher that the program had already started. In fact, the momentary greeting between each child and the big white dog would be the foundation of the discussion that was going to come in the next hour. When children have made that initial 'connection' with D. J., they are ready to listen, ready to learn, ready to share.

In the program, I do not tell the children to respect animals or people. Instead I ask them questions that allow their minds and their hearts to recognize and acknowledge their responsibilities on their own. I might ask them how they show respect to their pets at home, what they think I would do if D. J. has to go out in the middle of the night, what they should do if they see children throwing rocks at an animal, why they think a cat should have a litter box or possibly even a harness or leash, how they can show respect to parents, siblings, a new friend in the neighborhood, perhaps a new child who has come into the classroom in a wheelchair? 'Learning,' therefore, goes from D. J. or another therapy pet to the children's understanding of their world and then back again through their own role in it, as the children realize that their choices and behaviors will improve the world for all living things.

From such moments of closeness and caring, and an opportunity to express oneself in a validating environment, can come our vision of our own role in the world. As an example, my daughter, Ruthie's, vision of her world and her place in it, was shaped, by an unforgettable few minutes she had, when she was eleven years old, on a day when she accompanied me to my substitute teaching job at the School for Children with Cerebral Palsy in NY. During music therapy, she lifted an eager youngster from his wheelchair, cradling him in her arms, and dancing with him. The emotional impact of that brief moment in time set her on a course so clear, so strong, that despite many obstacles, she is today, twenty years later, a leader in the movement for inclusion of children with special needs and an advocate and friend to the many youngsters she teaches.

Similarly, will the young lady who wrote the following essay, look back twenty years from now and see the interaction with D. J. as a turning point in her life? Listen to her words: "Everyone can remember D. J. Some people might remember her as a white fluffy dog, but I remember her as a nice and friendly pet. Last year I thought she was just a nice dog coming to visit, but now I see what she was really doing - bringing happiness. It's only two words, but explains a lot. If you don't know what I mean, let me explain. Last year, when I was in third grade, I was introduced to D. J. and the program. I liked it a lot. The program built up character in me – my esteem and respect for others. I heard about D. J. going to nursing homes. I was told she made people happy. I sure believed it. Last year, the second she walked through the classroom door, I loved her. I will always remember that day, when D. J. came to school, to teach us to be nice."

Will the power of a moment in time with D. J. or with another beloved therapy pet to whom children have bonded, set them on a course of caring and compassion? Will this course help them to avoid drugs, premature pregnancy, violence, and school drop-out? Could this help to assure their role in relationships, which are based on respect and commitment, all initiated in the first place, by the extended paw, of a big white dog, named D. J.?

Section 4:
BENEFITS OF PET ASSISTED THERAPY TO THE SCHOOL MILIEU

Alberta Elaine Severs, an Associate Professor in Nursing at the Community College of Rhode Island, has worked with pediatric and adult clients in both the acute care and rehabilitation settings for the past thirty-two years. The desire to expand nursing students' concepts of collaborative therapies has involved her in Pet Assisted Therapy. She, her husband and children have always had pets as an integral part of the family life. At present, Ziggy (a black four year old part Chow and Neufie) is involved as a Pet Assisted Therapy dog at a local nursing home and rehabilitation center. Alberta's goal, as an educator, is to promote experiences for health professionals to explore Pet Assisted Therapy as a goal directed therapeutic intervention that can be adapted to a variety of settings with children and adults of all ages. Pets create MAGIC during human-animal interactions if given the chance. Severs has completed The D. J. PAT University Certificate Program.

Introduction

Pet Assisted Therapy is a program by which individuals or groups can experience the unconditional love and interaction with a pet who has been temperament tested and the pet's facilitator, usually the owner. Interaction with a pet, "who is spontaneous, alert, friendly and responsive," provides opportunities for individuals or groups to receive a positive relationship with a giving pet. No student is forced to interact. Some individuals like to watch the pet's activities; some like to talk about their own experiences with their own pets or other animals; some individuals like to more actively be involved in touching, stroking, offering treats and toys (supplied); and some other individuals even talk to the animal (One of my favorite activities. Pets are so attentive, nonjudgmental and are fantastic listeners.).

Rationale

The literature has presented the importance of the Human-Animal Companion Bond for centuries, documented "as far back as 1790 at York Retreat in England when Pets were first used as Facilitators". Many different kinds of pets can be used as facilitators. Each pet has a distinct personality and temperament. For the purposes of this program, Ziggy (my 4 1/2 year old Chow-Neufie mix-the mush) and Trevor (my 11 year old Ally Cat-the belly rub king) will be the Pet Assisted Therapy Companions with myself (a Pediatric nurse and educator, as well as a PAT intern) as the PAT Facilitator. The site for the visits will vary according to the pet's personality and the needs and interactive capabilities of the individuals to be visited. There is a difference between pet visitations and therapeutic interventions with a trained PAT animal. Both have value. Visitations allow the pet and facilitator to visit with different individuals or groups to stimulate discussion; decrease anxiety; promote a more relaxed atmosphere; and encourage touching, hugging and reciprocal interactions. Therapeutic interventions, with a PAT pet and educated facilitator, have specified goals (both short and long term) that are individualized for each student or group. The same pet, facilitator and students have regularly scheduled classes. Interactions in the classroom are also documented according to the established short and long term goals. The goals vary according to the special needs, concerns and abilities of the student who is interacting with the pet and facilitator. "We all need to feel the power and Magic of animals. One needs to personally experience the effects of Pet Assisted Therapy at work." (Quotes taken from this book.) The PAT companion and the PAT facilitator will act as role models of a positive human-animal bond relationship, assuming responsibilities and respect for others, as well as, themselves.

Benefits

There are many benefits to the Pet Assisted Therapy Programs. The classroom teachers, ancillary staff, students, PAT Pet Companion and PAT facilitator all benefit from a PAT Program and its therapeutic activities and interactions. I prefer the goal-oriented type of program. The classroom setting, with the same student population from week to week, provides for long term continuity and also allows for better planning and attaining of established goals. My background, as a pediatric nurse, will enhance the assessment, individualized planning, implementation and evaluation of the effect of the PAT Program on the student population. Children come from a variety of backgrounds, experiences and have special physical and psychosocial needs and concerns. The PAT pet companion can meet these needs and concerns in a nonjudgmental, spontaneous, loving, attentive manner. The following represent the expected benefits to be experienced by those involved in the PAT program:

The PAT Pet:

Is temperament tested for adaptability and personality traits.
Attains a training certificate.
Is trained to react in the best way to different people; to increase socialization skills and responsiveness; to respond positively to guidance and cues.
Gets the opportunity to express love, responsiveness and perform (on his own terms).
Receives stroking, gentle handling, affection and positive praise and communication from the facilitator, all the individual students and other professionals involved.
Gets to go for rides and investigate new settings.
Gets to exercise and have additional play times.
Gets to spend quality time with his owner.
Gets to be groomed and primped more often.

The PAT Facilitator:

Spends quality time with pet.
Meets and interacts with professionals, as well as, individual students.
Gains knowledge of methods of interaction, problem-solving and manage-

ment skills with a variety of students in various settings.

Gets positive feedback from pet and students, as well as, the school personnel where the program is presented.

Is given the opportunity to be altruistic with others.

Can gain pride, appreciation and satisfaction from pet's performance and elicited responses resulting from the student's participation.

Can promote the worth of a valuable profession, Pet Assisted Therapy.

Can experience satisfaction in providing a service to both animals and mankind.

Can attain an academic certificate as a PAT Facilitator.

Can create opportunities for modeling positive behavior, respect for all living things, and taking responsibility for self and those you love.

The Student:

Gets diversional activity.

Gets goal oriented activities to improve quality of life and functioning.

Increases socialization opportunities and skills.

Gets a time to remember and relate memorable experiences with pets and other animals.

Gets time to explore and express feelings, fears and concerns with a good listener.

Receives unconditional love from a spontaneous, active pet.

Can touch, feel, stroke, cuddle, play with or observe a pet interacting with other people and toys.

Gets to have something to look forward to that is positive.

Gets to have some experiences (PAT) that can later be shared with others.

Has opportunities to feel relaxed and decrease feelings of anxiety or concerns.

The Principal, Teachers and other Staff Members of the School:

Observe their students' interactions with the PAT pet, facilitator, staff members and other students.

Share and develop goals (both short and long term) with the facilitator for each student involved.

Get to interact with different professionals and share ideas and goals.

Get to interact with the PAT Companion and receive the positive results (touch, decreased anxiety, increased relaxation, unconditional love and attention) in return for interactions and reaching out to the pet.

Get some diversion from routine job responsibilities.

Get opportunities to be creative in interactions with their students/parents.

Get to create situations to increase meeting established goals for self and the students.

Pearl Salotto

The School:

> Gets the opportunity to offer a valuable form of therapy to its students.
> Provides ongoing educational opportunities to its staff.
> Meets a need to provide a setting for a PAT Program for a PAT.

Companion and PAT Facilitator:

> Expands their multidisciplinary approach to providing care, comfort, therapeutic interventions and diversional activities for the students.
> Utilizes creative approaches for activities that will meet the individualized goals of their students and staff members.
> — Can document the PAT Program as part of their credentialing process for a therapeutic intervention when reapplying for their own licensure and mandated educational requirements.
> Promotes use of various rooms, etc. for socialization and education for their students, etc.
> Gets good PR & can serve as a role model for other agencies, etc.

All participants benefit in a variety of ways from the PAT Companion Programs. The opportunities for positive interactions and achievement of established goals are not on a time frame. Each individual involved will progress at their own pace and in their own unique way. I call this a guided, spontaneous opportunity. The facilitator chooses a setting that is safe and conducive to positive interactions and provides guidance and cues for the PAT companion pet to be alert, spontaneous, reflective and responsive to the participating students. Just observe the changes in the individual students that invariably result. MAGIC tends to happen. Role modeling can effect the future interactions of the students in later life with their improved self-concept, positive interactions with peers and authority figures, as well as, potential parenting skills for our future children.

Ethics

> The Facilitator shall take responsibility for the care and physical and psychological welfare of the Pet.
> The Facilitator shall provide proper training, temperament testing, immunizations and health care for the Pet.
> The Facilitator shall involve only a Pet that has a temperament and training that is conducive to positive interactions with students.
> The Facilitator shall ensure that the Pet is provided a safe environment and one free of communicable diseases.
> The Facilitator, the School Personnel and the Student are to provide positive interactions for the Pet and the Student.
> The Facilitator, School Personnel or Student shall discontinue the Pet's participation in a session if the Pet or the Student becomes distressed or

148

either of them demonstrate behavior that is inappropriate.

The Facilitator shall not allow an ill Pet to participate in a classroom program.

The Facilitator and School Personnel shall develop a program that fosters the personal growth, self-worth and humane treatment of both the Pet and the Student.

The School Personnel shall support the goals and objectives of the program.

The Facilitator and the School Personnel shall maintain a commitment to pursue and adapt the objectives of the program to the individual Student and Pet's needs.

The Facilitator and School Personnel shall have an ongoing communication and evaluation of the program.

The Facilitator and the School Personnel shall demonstrate a non-biased selection of Students to participate in the program. The facilitator and school personnel will screen for allergies.

The School Personnel shall not knowingly fail to disclose any risk factors in the environment or the student population that could be harmful or distress the Pet.

The Facilitator and the School Personnel shall not knowingly misrepresent the program and benefits to the Student.

The Facilitator shall maintain the confidentiality of the Student's privileged information.

The Facilitator and the School Personnel shall improve the public's understanding of the role of the Pet Assisted Therapy Program.

This code of ethics can be implemented in a variety of settings and with a diversified group of students. This code of ethics is appropriate for this classroom setting, its staff and its students.

Guidelines

The Pet Assisted Therapy Companion Will Be:

Healthy and well groomed prior to each visit.

A temperament tested pet.

In an environment that is safe, comfortable, and free from any harm during each PAT session.

The initiator of the interaction.

Able to rest when necessary.

Accompanied and supervised, at all times, by the facilitator.

Approached by students who are free of animal-transmitted diseases.

Approached with the permission of the facilitator.

Given treats, food and toys only when advanced approval for these have been given by the facilitator.

Handled gently at all times.

Handled by one person at a time with the facilitator's guidance.

Behaviorally appropriate and gentle in his/her interactions with everyone present during the sessions.

Allowed to discontinue an interaction if his/her feels stressed, anxious or threatened in any way.

Able to be spontaneous in his/her interactions with individuals during the classroom activities.

The PAT Facilitator Will:

Complete a pre-visit prior to bringing in the PAT Companion.

Complete a pre-visit with the PAT Companion prior to the therapeutic interventions with the students.

Complete an in-service meeting with the staff members of the school prior to the established student classroom presentation.

Have reviewed, accepted and will plan to adhere to the policies of the school in which the classroom sessions will be scheduled.

Communicate with the appropriate liaison person, from the school, concerning student selection; student special needs and goals; changes in setting; time frame for the classes; and will identify what additional personnel are required for each class.

Be properly educated and prepared as a PAT Facilitator (or an intern working under a mentor who is an experienced facilitator).

Present proper health records for pet.

Present proper insurance certification coverage for the pet and the facilitator.

Maintain confidentiality of the students' school records, and the specialized needs and behaviors exhibited during the classroom sessions.

Establish long and short term goals with the appointed liaison person and staff members while acting as a part of the multidisciplinary team.

Document goals, observations, assessments and evaluations of the student's participation in each class with the liaison person or the staff members involved with students on a regular basis.

Establish a time frame for each classroom session based on the needs of the PAT Companion and the individuals or group involved in the scheduled sessions. (Times may vary but would be prearranged and potentially 40-90 minutes, depending on the age of the students and their attention span.)

Complete an ongoing evaluation of the PAT Program.

Keep liaison person informed of this ongoing evaluation process.

Establish a focus and lesson plan for each classroom presentation.

Provide activities that are age appropriate during each presentation.

The School Administration and Liaison Person Will:

Review school policies with the PAT Facilitator.

Keep credentials of the PAT Pet Companion and PAT Facilitator on file at the school.

Appoint a Liaison Person as the contact person to communicate with the PAT facilitator.

Cooperate with any in-service program the PAT facilitator deems necessary prior to and ongoing with the staff members of the school.

Identify potential setting(s) for the PAT Program sessions.

Identify, along with the facilitator, who will select the students to participate in the classes.

Obtain the necessary forms completed by the students, families or whoever is responsible for the student legally.

Identify how the PAT facilitator will be kept informed of changes in student and school status prior to each planned class.

Participate in the ongoing evaluation of the PAT Program.

Continually keep PAT facilitator informed of the ongoing status of the PAT program and its evaluation.

Suggest recommendations to the PAT facilitator, through the Liaison person, when the program needs to be adapted to the changing needs and concerns of the student and the school.

Promote Pet Assisted Therapy as a helping and therapeutic profession.

Methodology

This Pet Assisted Therapy Program is developed for the purpose of creating a relaxed atmosphere conducive to attaining the following goals:

decreasing anxiety

promoting communication skills

increasing positive interactions

observing positive role modeling behavior between the PAT Companion and the PAT Facilitator

exploring feelings and concerns about animal and human experiences

creating activities to foster independent thinking and self-expression

producing a personalized student Scrapbook containing the student-PAT experiences.

These identified goals would involve a multidisciplinary team approach according to the individualized special needs, concerns and behaviors of the students participating in the PAT Program. The professionals providing the interactions in the classroom may vary from one session to another. The PAT Facilitator would be an active part of these therapeutic interactions with the PAT Companion acting as the mediator during the individual classes. The PAT Companion potentiates and creates the oppor-tunities for the interactions that occur with the selected students.

The goal of this PAT facilitator is to create a Scrapbook with each individual stu-dent selected to participate. This personalized Scrapbook will include photos of the individual (if approval is obtained), the PAT companion, the PAT facilitator, teachers, staff and any other persons involved in the classes. Some creative activities will be incorporated into this Scrapbook {example: collages of pets; their activities; stories about PAT pets and student's pet and animal experiences (previously, as well as, those experiences, feelings, behaviors occurring during the scheduled classes.).

The PAT facilitator and the appointed liaison person will establish a schedule to provide for continuity of students to be followed. Documentation will occur on the student's school and teacher's records according to established policies agreed upon.

The Scrapbook will be reviewed with the student , at the beginning of each class, to provide clarity and understanding of the results of the classes and will be a carryover from one class to another. This will enhance the meeting of established goals (both short and long term) and encourage active participation and decision making by the student.

At the end of the last scheduled class, the Scrapbook will be discussed and given to the student as a memento of the therapeutic activities that were experienced.

This student can then share these experiences with others, friends and family, etc. at home and in other settings. This Scrapbook will also include the stated short and long term goals for this student and how these were met.

✓ *The Steps Implemented to Complete this Methodology would be the Following:*

Establish contact with the administrative personnel of the school chosen, to gain approval for the PAT Program.

Obtain the appointment of a Liaison person from the school.

Arrange and complete a visit to the setting to be utilized for the classes.

Identify the length of the classes and the actual dates for the classroom presentations.

Identify the selection process for the individual students to be chosen to participate.

Send permission slips to the parents of the children to be included in the program with the list of classroom schedule attached and the goals of the program. (The PAT Facilitator could meet with the parents at a sched-uled time to convey this information and answer their questions about the program and their child's participation in it.).

Attain permission for Photographs (for the Scrapbook) from the legal guard-ians of the participating children (Separations and Divorces, Foster and Adoptive children may pose special issues for legal approval for participa-tion and photos.)

Obtain a list of allergies and information concerning any positive or nega-tive pet or animal experiences from the children and their parents. (The latter part of this information could be obtained by means of the child or parent writing a story about these previous experiences.)

Provide proper documentation of the approval obtained, according to the agreed upon process and policies (examples: allergies documented, photo releases, any restrictions, etc.).

Prepare short and long term goals for each student based on school records, student history and special needs and student concerns. This will be accomplished in conjunction with the liaison person and other staff members as deemed necessary.

Create an evaluation tool(s) to measure the success and adaptation needs of the PAT Program being presented.

The PAT Companion will complete a visit, prior to the first scheduled class presentation, to become acclimated to the setting.

The staff in-service will have been completed by the PAT Facilitator prior to the first scheduled classroom presentation. This in-service will include an explanation of the guidelines and goals of the PAT Program and the roles of those involved.

Blank Scrapbooks will be created, by the PAT Facilitator, for each student prior to the first class. (Each week things will be added to this Scrapbook.)

An established focus will be identified and a poster created for all the scheduled classes (1st to last) and the activities will be the following:

FIRST CLASS:

Meet with the children (and any parent), either individually or as a small group.

Talk about the scheduled classes.

Talk about the long term goal of creating a Scrapbook that will be theirs at the end of the PAT Program.

Explain how this Scrapbook will be used by them from week to week.

Bring pictures of Ziggy and Trevor and talk about them and their part in the PAT Program.

Explain to the students how they can interact with Ziggy & Trevor.

Make a request for each student to bring in 2 pictures of their pet(s) or of a favorite animal (from a magazine) for next week's class.

SECOND CLASS:

Ziggy comes today and time to interact with him is provided.

The Scrapbook pages from last week's class will be reviewed.

Discuss what we learned last week.

Each student will write a little story about the pictures

brought in and why these were chosen.

Near the end of class talk about Ziggy's first visit and how he must have felt.

Discuss how the students felt about Ziggy's first visit and create a poster about Ziggy.

THIRD CLASS:

Trevor's first classroom visit. Allow time for the students to interact with Trevor and ask questions about him.

Discuss Trevor's and students' feelings about Trevor being in class. Compare to Ziggy's first day (Likenesses and Differences).

Create a poster about Trevor in class.

Tell the students that both Ziggy and Trevor will come to the remainder of the classes.

Review Scrapbook.

Share pet and animal stories written last week.

Tell students to cut out different pet and wild animal pictures from magazines, etc., as well as, photographs and bring to next class.

FOURTH CLASS:

Review Scrapbook and what we learned last week.

Ziggy and Trevor present.

Create a Collage from the pictures and photographs. Describe differences and likenesses. Group according to a pet or wild animal. The animals would be discussed from the point of view of qualities-soft, pretty alert, etc. (The students would make a list of these qualities. The benefits of the qualities would be explained through small discussion groups or as a class (depends if I have other helpers like high school students or student nurses).

Discuss how Ziggy and Trevor get along.

FIFTH CLASS:

Review Scrapbook and what we learned last week.

Ziggy and Trevor present in class.

Make a list of the physical needs of the PAT Companions. Ask the student if the needs are different if the PAT Companion is a different kind of animal. (put information on a poster)

Discuss what physical needs a human has. Are human physical needs the same or different than pet or animal needs?

154

SIXTH CLASS:

Review Scrapbook and what we learned last week.

Ziggy and Trevor present in class.

Make a list of the psychosocial needs of the PAT Companions.

Ask if these vary by type of animal. Compare to humans.

Have the students describe what the PAT Companion gets from coming to our class etc.

SEVENTH CLASS:

Review Scrapbook and what we learned last week.

Ziggy and Trevor present in class.

Make a list of benefits students get from coming to this class.

Each student will write a little story of how they feel when they touch Ziggy or Trevor. They will also state how they feel when they talk to the PAT Companions. Should they talk to them and why. What do the pets and the student get out of touch and talking to pets?

The students will share their individual stories with their classmates, one at a time. (If a student doesn't want to read or talk about the story, the PAT facilitator could do this for the student.)

The written story will be added to the Scrapbook.

EIGHTH CLASS:

Review Scrapbook and what we learned last week.

Ziggy and Trevor present in class.

Make a list of the important things we must think about when choosing a pet of our very own. (Review the Posters we made in weeks 2 and 3. The chosen pictures of pets and animals the students brought in to class. The collage created etc.)

If we go to a shelter to choose our pet, how do we feel about the animals we left behind and have no home to go to? (May want to relate this to foster and adoptive children if the age group is appropriate. Stress finding a home and the positive aspects, not the rejection aspect.)

How can students help the pet adjust when he/she comes to his/her new home. (Again might make correlation to foster and adoptive children or to new students who come to this school. How can we help them to adjust?)

Poster would emphasize feelings and steps to choose a

pet, as well as, how we can help make pet (or New
Student) adjust to new home or new environment.

NINTH CLASS:
Review Scrapbook and what we learned last week.
Ziggy and Trevor present in class.
Discuss and make a list of how Ziggy and Trevor made
friends with the students and personnel in the classroom. What did they do to make this friendship happen? Were there days when they didn't want to do things
with the students? Describe their behaviors and discuss how the students' felt about that. (Could again
make a correlation to what it means to have a friend
and be a friend.)
Develop the Poster based on these behaviors and feelings
about having a friend and being a friend.

TENTH CLASS:
Review Scrapbook and what we learned last week.
Ziggy and Trevor present in class.
Good Health of Animals
Discuss what we do for Ziggy and Trevor so they don't get
sick.
Discuss how we would know that Ziggy or Trevor was sick.
Discuss what happens to Ziggy and Trevor when they go to
the Vet's for their check up and health care.
Discuss what would happen if Ziggy and Trevor went to
the Vet's because they had an accident or were sick.
Review the important points for Ziggy and Trevor's over
night stay at the Vet's and how they would feel.
Poster would again represent these discussions.

ELEVENTH CLASS:
Review Scrapbook and what we learned in the last class.
Ziggy and Trevor present in class.
Discuss how we would know we are sick.
Discuss what our Mom or Dad or a grownup does when
this happens.
Discuss what happens in the doctor's office versus when
you are in the hospital. (May have student nurses here
today.)
Bring equipment and things used in both settings for stu-
dents to handle and talk about.
PAT Facilitator will tell a story about the doctor's office
and the hospital (Explain different hospital areas —
ER, x-ray, etc. and show the book "Randy's Hospital Story" about the hospital experience).

Discuss how you feel when Mom or Dad or a Sibling, etc. goes to the hospital and what we can do for them.

Poster will reflect these discussions.

Ask students to write down their birth date and those of any of their pets and bring to class next week.

TWELFTH CLASS:

Review Scrapbook and what we learned last week.

Ziggy and Trevor present in class.

Discuss how we know that Ziggy and Trevor are Healthy & Happy.

Discuss how we can help them to continue to be healthy and happy.

Discuss how we feel when we are healthy and happy.

Discuss how we feel when those around us are healthy and happy.

A collage could be made from pictures of healthy and happy animals and people. (The poster for today.)

Have each student draw a happy pet and a picture of themself when they are happy directly in their Scrapbook.

This would create the final pages of their personalized Scrapbook. The last activity would be to celebrate all the students' and pets' Birth dates with a Birth day Party. The Personalized Scrapbook would be reviewed with each student individually during this last class.

The Scrapbooks would be a going away present from Ziggy, Trevor and the PAT Facilitator (myself).

The students would have a living record of their PAT Program experiences with the help of their personalized Scrapbook. The multiple Posters (that were created during each class and displayed weekly in the classroom) would present discussion potential and review of the memorable experiences the students shared together with Ziggy, Trevor, the PAT Facilitator and their classmates. These would all help with the adjustment to the ending of their PAT Program and breaking their ties to the PAT Team.

I feel this PAT Program could be established with elementary school students. I feel this program would have the most beneficial outcomes with this age group due to the activity design.

I realize this is a very ambitious program and would involve not only the time for the classroom preparation, but much additional preparation time to set up classes; complete the Scrapbooks (on an ongoing basis from week to week) for a number of children; complete the evaluation forms for the PAT Program; evaluate the established long and short term goals for each student; to share the experiences, evaluations (program and students) with the liaison person and PAT Mentor. All of these facets must be accomplished in order for the PAT Program to be successful.

157

Pearl Salotto

My goal is to not only create an interesting and beneficial PAT Program for these children but also to leave them with improved socialization skills, positive interactive experiences, positive self concept and potentially with a feeling of respect for animals and the people around them. Maintaining the children's attention and enthusiasm will be a real challenge. Ziggy, Trevor and Myself (as the PAT Facilitator) have our work cut out for us!

Deuce (family therapy pet of PPATF Alberta Severs) and the children - enjoying each other's company at the Brown University Fox Point Educational Center.

Evaluation

Several evaluation tools would be designed: one for PAT facilitator, mentor, liaison person, administrative and other staff members; one for the students; and one for the parent(s). These evaluation tools would depend on policies, setting, as well as, the student population chosen for the PAT Program.

The evaluation tools would give a summary statement of the classes presented and the activities the children completed. The setting and the time frame for the individual class presentations and the number of classes would be reviewed. The use of the personalized Scrapbook and the displayed posters, as well as, the classroom process of reviewing previous classes and learning would also be included in the evaluation. The actual topics or focus for each weekly class would be listed for the children and they would be asked to pick out the class they liked the best and to state why. This would also be done for the class they least liked and again state why. Their Scrapbook and posters would help with this recall of the individual classes. The children would be asked if they liked having Ziggy and Trevor in their classes with them and why.

Part of the teacher, staff and parent evaluations might to be to have an open-ended section on what the student talked about (concerning the PAT Program sessions) with them and also to state any changes in behavior they may have noticed since the PAT Program began.

The interval evaluations, to be completed by appointed staff or the liaison person and the PAT facilitator, would be during weeks 4, 8 and 12. The children and the parent(s) will complete the evaluation forms during weeks 6 and 12. The results would be documented and shared with these individuals, as well as, the PAT facilitator's Mentor and the administrative personnel of the school setting.

The liaison person and the PAT facilitator will communicate on an ongoing basis weekly and incorporate changes in the PAT Program that are deemed necessary and agreed upon by the PAT facilitator and the PAT mentor. The results of these adaptations implemented would also be evaluated and shared.

The key to any successful PAT Program is to create the opportunities for positive interactions for the PAT Companion, the PAT facilitator and the student population. A positive atmosphere allows for more relaxation and decreased feeling of anxiety in a confined setting (classroom) that usually has a set of rules and expected behaviors. Children need to know they can freely express themselves in an environment in order for learning to occur. Learning about relationships, caring, touching, feelings, responsibilities, sharing and coping behaviors are very sophisticated concepts for children to integrate. The method of positive role modeling behavior (PAT facilitator and PAT Companion, as well as, staff interaction with the PAT team) has a definite impact on the expectations for student interactive behavior. The student interactions with the PAT Companion, the PAT facilitator, the staff and other peers create a powerful influence on the children's future interactions in society , as well as, future adult employees, employers, family members and parents of our future children. PAT Programs have proven to have a positive impact on all these areas. The spontaneity and unconditional love of the PAT Companion and the guidance and teaching of the PAT facilitator can make this all become a reality. MAGIC happens when positive interaction and reinforcement are experienced. We all want to be loved and accepted. Each of us has a strong desire to express our uniqueness. That's what makes us valuable to ourselves and to others. We are all irreplaceable. We all walk to the beat of a different drummer and make our unique mark on this world.

Section 5:
INTRODUCTION OF PET ASSISTED THERAPY INTO SERVICE LEARNING AT FEINSTEIN SCHOOL

Linda Passarelli Jones is currently teaching a class entitled Service-Learning. Mrs. Jones received a Bachelors Degree (1971) in Secondary English from Mount Saint Joseph's College in Wakefield, Rhode Island. She received her Masters Degree (1976) in Reading (K-12) from Rhode Island College. For twenty years she worked as a Reading Specialist at Camden Avenue Elementary School in Providence, Rhode Island. At Camden Avenue School she served as a Volunteer Coordinator liaison for the Adopt-a-School Program with the Providence Marriott and was introduced to the Service-Learning Concept through Providence College. In September 1994 she began teaching at Feinstein High School. Mrs. Jones is married to a Providence attorney, Paul Jones, and has two children: Paul, 19, a sophomore a UMass-Amherst, and Keith, 11, a sixth grader at Holy Ghost School in Providence. For more information you can visit us at our Web site: www.feinsteinhs.com The school is located at 544 Elmwood Avenue, Rhode Island 02907 — (401) 456-1706.

Feinstein High School for Public Service was established in September 1994. The school was initiated through a gift from Alan Shawn Feinstein and developed cooperatively by the Public Education Fund and the Providence School Department. The school's curriculum focuses on Service-Learning. Service-Learning is an educational process which engages students in challenging activities, solving problems, and planning projects as a real part of the academic curriculum. The school day consists of three ninety-minute blocks and one thirty-minute advisory period. Every other Wednesday Issues and Ethics classes are conducted or Town Meetings are held for the entire school. Students are assigned to community service as part of the school day/curriculum. Students move through the school's three stages – Explorer, Apprentice, and Scholar according to carefully monitored academic standards and based on the demonstration of increased responsibility, skills and personal growth. FHS features a state-of-the-art computer lab and a fully equipped high-tech library.

The Alan Shawn Feinstein High School for Public Service in Providence, Rhode Island, is a school whose curriculum is integrated with each student's community service. The school offers a trimester course entitled Service-Learning which prepares the students for community service. During this preparation the students are encouraged to explore many types of volunteer opportunities. Our expectations were surpassed, in 1996, when, the Pet Assisted Therapy (PAT) pilot program, presented by Pearl Salotto, and her therapy pets, ten year-old D. J. and one year old Maj-En, proved to be both a unique and meaningful experience for the students.

The PAT program was offered within the Service-Learning class and as part of the Issues and Ethics curriculum taught in every class bi-weekly. Five ninety-minute sessions (now expanded to seven) were devoted to PAT. The training, designated as Level 1 PAT, focused on issues that directly affected many of our students, such as depression, loneliness, fear of animals, respect for all living things, respect for each other, caring for the sick and elderly, violence, and the responsibility of society to all living

160

things. The students made a real connection to the positive way animals could and should fit into one's life.

High School student Ruth with Pitou (family therapy of PPATF Claire Senecal) - Photo credit: Carol Terranova

As part of the Service-Learning class the students are required to maintain a journal where they can *reflect* on what has been covered each time the class meets. I would like to share *reflections* from the four different groups of students who have had this program in the last two years.

"PAT is a program that explores the bond between a person (a child, an invalid or elderly person, a prisoner, etc.) and his/her pet. It gives people a way to relieve stress, sometimes related to violence, a feeling of companionship, and most importantly someone to love." Marissa Snead- Grade 11.

"In nursing homes and hospitals pets give the patients a positive attitude about life. It is something for individuals who are sick or disabled to look forward to." Michael Davis- Grade 10.

"PAT made me change my mind about animals. I was afraid of dogs. I have learned that pets that are treated badly can be bad, but pets that are treated with love and respect will treat people with love and respect, like DJ." Felipe Mercedes- Grade 9.

"Pets are the best medicine for people of all ages. In schools a PAT program could give children more self-esteem. In turn their attendance and grades can improve." Sam Hector- Grade 10

"PAT can help with non-violence. The prisoners convicted of violent crimes in the movie, on Lorton Prison, spent their time caring for pets rather than getting in trouble. They said pets helped them feel happier, healthier, and safer. It made them realize what a better life they could have. This would be a good program for teens at risk." Patricia Garcia- Grade 9

"My thoughts about the video are sad because little kids can't talk and can't see. But when I saw that they had a dog and the dog was smart and helpful it made me feel more relief. Now that I know they have a pet dog to help them do things they will be able to learn, like us, even though they can't walk or talk. I wish I could go see them and thank the dog for giving the children back part of their life." (referring to therapy dog Cheer in a program called, *A Classroom Canine Companion: Opening Doors to Learning* developed by Sally Brockett) "My thoughts about the video, on Bumper the Bull, were sad at the beginning because he was raised without a mother or a family. I thought that a bull could never be a pet. I thought wrong. It also was nice of the children to take care of him and raise money to save him. I was happy when he didn't get slaughtered. I wish I could see Bumper the Bull because he looks cute and friendly (referring to Dick Dillman's Companion Animal Dropout Prevention Program.) Linda Pron - Grade 10

At FHS second, third and fourth year students are required to do an Exhibition at the end of the school year. An exhibition is a presentation by the student describing his/her community service using all academic subjects to do so. Those students who did not have a successful experience at community service (these were students who had been identified as 'at risk') were forced to return to my Service-Learning class for the remainder of the school year. As a result, they could not do an Exhibition.

This year as part of the Service-Learning class, the students were able to plan and teach a course entitled, *Respect for Living Things*. Fifty fourth grade students from Camden Elementary School in Providence participated. The FHS students spent time planning two ninety minute sessions. This process enabled the students to work in teams, setting objectives and goals, and developing strategies to successfully teach 'respect for living things.' It gave the students an opportunity to further research PAT using the Internet as a resource.

At the first session the students from Camden arrived at FHS and were assigned to groups and introduced to D. J. High school and elementary youngsters sat on the floor, relaxed and petted D. J. while brainstorming about pets and self-esteem. Soon the children were engaged in small groups sharing ideas on how we 'respect all living things.' One young girl stated that there was nothing special about her. The FHS students were quick to respond and through questioning helped her understand that we are all special because we are all unique, and we all add something to make this world a beautiful place! In the young girl's reflection she wrote about some of the things that she now realized made her special.

The second session was, also, carefully planned, this time with Maj-En assisting. Each team of high school students selected a topic and short video to present. One of the most powerful discussions was about people with disabilities and the role of pets in their lives. The FHS students had the children role play to understand some of the disabilities. The message also included how to respect and treat people with different disabilities, as well as how to respect the feelings and needs of the hearing ear and service dogs, who help them.

It was so good to see our high school students, who were so empowered by D. J. and Maj-En and what they learned in PAT, that they were eager, willing, and able to pass this on to the next generation. As the hour drew to a close and the bus with the fourth graders left the parking lot, the student/tutor, Michael Davis, overheard their joyful cries – "I love you, Maj-En." This initial curriculum was so successful, that a year later it is being expanded, and will be brought directly into Camden School, with our students working under the supervision of a professional PAT.

Another wonderful component of the PAT program was Jeanne Davis' guest lectures, with her therapy cat Skeeter and therapy rabbit Tulip. Jeanne, a leading spokesperson for volunteer PAT, who has also completed a university PAT program, touched the youngsters with her plea for spay/neutering and the heart wrenching plight of homeless pets. Jeanne climaxed her talk by describing how her cats had comforted her during a painful experience last winter. In the course of a brutal winter storm, she had feared that one of her favorite trees would be torn asunder. Walking back to the house, from her porch, in despair and sadness, she glanced around the room, noticing how her cats were curled up, sleeping peacefully on the sofa. She felt, once again, that all would be right with the world. Several months later these students visited a nursing home with Jeanne and Tulip. The students took turns accompanying Jeanne to the individual rooms where they engaged in conversation with the patients. They were amazed at how receptive everyone was. They were able to see how it gave the patients an opportunity to reminisce about their childhood, about pets they may have had, or just have someone to talk with or the comfort of a warm, cuddly pet! The students commented about the presence of the pet and how it 'opened the door' for them to visit and spend a little time with each resident.

With the inception of this program I have found that FHS has found a new and creative way of dealing with some very real and serious subjects. In addition, this program has appealed to many of our 'at risk' students. It has given them incentive for attending school and for finding a community service in which they have taken owner-ship. It has given students the opportunity to participate in a variety of special experi-ences including a newspaper interview and showcasing PAT as part of career day. Pet Assisted Therapy was included in a school-wide assembly, that acknowledged stu-dents for excellence in courses, activities, or community service.

This program also gave a few selected students the opportunity to be responsible for D. J. or Maj-En on a few occasions, when Pearl had to briefly leave the room. Those of us who know Pearl, know what a high compliment that was.

This program has also given our youngsters an opportunity for fun, joy and smiles – such as I have never seen before. Many precious and heartwarming comments have been made during these fun-filled and educational classes. On an occasion when Pearl was querying the students on the meaning of the human-companion animal bond, one young lady said that the unconditional love that pets give us without asking for or wanting anything back is sort of like the community service that we at Feinstein lov-ingly give to people in our community. On another occasion, a young lady explained, as she was saying goodbye to the therapy pets, "and to think that I thought that I was going to hate this class." Another student showed Pearl a picture of his dog and when she smiled and thanked him and tried to return it, he said, "this is my gift to you."

The Level 1 PAT program was so successful that in the Fall of 1997 we expanded the program by developing Level 2 PAT, as well. Many of the students who had ex-tremely positive reactions have continued into this second level and can now go out into the community. They are now working at a local shelter and at a nursing home around the corner from the school (see page 359). Some of these students, who choose the nursing home placement, are assisting a university student, with his therapy pet, who is on staff. These students go twice a week throughout the school year and receive service learning credit.

The phenomenal effect of this program on students is heard in Ashley O'Neil's comment, on the very first day of Level 2 PAT at St. Elizabeth's Home: "That was cool. I loved it. She was satisfied. She was happy. Now I can see the real meaning of every-thing we learned last year." Ashley made this comment during reflection time after the residents had left the solarium.

I was also very pleased with the students' reactions to the therapy pets, as well as to learning about PAT. Our students, during the course of this year, had the unique opportunity of watching Pearl Salotto's puppy Maj-En, (one year four months old when the program started last fall) change and grow. Always loving and energetic Maj-En no longer barks every twenty minutes, wanting to go outside and run around the school. In fact, on our last day of school this year, we witnessed Maj-En, calm and in control, as he sat for an hour while one of our students presented PAT to his teachers and administrators.

Our students observed many of life's important lessons through D. J. and Maj - En and the way that Pearl interacted with them. They clearly saw the different personalities of Pearl's two therapy dogs - both 'love dogs.' Our students never favored one or the other, but gave the same unconditional love to whomever Pearl brought in. In heartwarming words, one student said "D. J. makes me feel like relaxing and Maj-En makes me feel like running around the school."

It is clear that the lessons go far beyond PAT. Perhaps our students will be more respectful of the different personalities of their friends, relatives, and colleagues. Perhaps someday, when they are parents themselves, they will be able to appreciate their children's varying developmental stages, as they did with D. J. and Maj-En.

The way that Pearl treated both dogs, loving and appreciating them, and not expecting them to do anything they did not want to do, was as powerful a lifelong lesson as her teaching of PAT. Whether the dogs wanted to stroll up the aisle or sleep, whether they wanted to play with the toy or put paws up on a students' shoulder, Pearl's acceptance of both dogs for who they are will surely have a lasting impact on our students.

This impact on students can be seen, for example, in one of our students telling our state senator that, "pets, as well as people, are **individuals**." Ashley O'Neil, found himself telling the senator about the unconditional love of the therapy pets. This same student won a national award for his community service work in Level 2 PAT.

The words of Katherine Hernandez, who has been active in the program for two years, says it all: "I have had a wonderful experience working in the Pet Therapy program and The D. J. 'Respect for Living Things' Program. I have had the opportunity to work with the elderly and children. I have always liked to help people and work with kids; it is special to work with kids. Working with kids gives me the opportunity to make a positive impact in their lives. The D. J. 'Respect for Living Things' Program gave me the opportunity to do that. The special thing about working with children is that to make them understand what you want to teach them you have to combine what they like to hear with what you would like them to hear. I know that in teaching them how to respect living things, I have taught them something they will carry with them for the rest of their lives.

"By working with Pet Therapy and The D.J. Respect for Living Things Program I have learned many things myself. I have learned to appreciate the lives of others. Giving unconditional love is one of the most beautiful parts of this program because to teach others how to give unconditional love I had to understand myself, how important unconditional love is; loving and understanding the pain and the sadness of a person I didn't even know. Working with the elderly, at St. Elizabeth's Home, has been a beautiful experience for me. Making those people feel special makes me feel special and good about myself. Especially when I see the improvement in the person's life after the program. Every reaction of the person, any word, any movement, is a great accomplishment for me.I not only feel good about myself, it's more then that, more than a grade. It is making a difference."

I was pleased by the way teachers and administrators have been moved, excited and inspired by having the therapy dogs and the PAT curriculum in our school. For example, D. J. posed for our art students, a teacher has a picture of D. J. on her desk and other staff have talked to me about including readings and lessons on PAT in their curriculum. PAT was also included in our career day, our parents' night program, and our awards program. We have taken our Level 1 PAT students on field trips and they have had a major role in planning and participating in annual D.J. "Respect for Living Things" Days.

As an educator, I have already begun to speak with teachers in other high schools about the PAT program and how successful it has been at FHS. It gives high school students a new approach to solving problems in the community. The program could connect with any academic subject. Many schools are beginning to offer classes in Issues and Ethics, as at Feinstein, in which PAT would fit perfectly. Some of the topics that would tie into PAT would be drugs, violence, homelessness, animal abuse, dealing with stress, loneliness, short and long-term illnesses, along with many more. We at FHS plan to continue to offer this class and highly recommend it to other high schools. The students were motivated, challenged, and ready to incorporate PAT into their community service.

My personal reflection – The program is a great success. Pearl has a very special way of connecting with each student in the class. The students at FHS come from many different backgrounds. Many of them are from homes where little or no English is spoken. PAT is a program in which there is no language barrier. Each student is very excited about sharing what they have experienced with others. They feel 'very special' about being given the opportunity to learn about PAT with their new best friends, D. J. and the puppy…Maj-En!

As Alan Shawn Feinstein says "the greatest achievement of all is helping to better the lives of others." Our students realize and appreciate how well pets and Pet Assisted Therapy live up to this beautiful mission.

High School students Richelle and Gladys with Peanuts (family therapy pet of PPATF Gail Richardson). Photo credit: Carol Terranova

Section 6:
THE ELEMENTARY SCHOOL COUNSELOR AND THE HCAB

Linda Nebbe lives with her husband and three children on twenty two acres of reestablished prairie and hard wood timber near Waterloo, Iowa. She graduated from Iowa State University with a BS in Child Development and Elementary Education. After teaching for a number of years she received her MS from Iowa State University in Guidance and Counseling. Currently she is employed by the Cedar Falls School System as an elementary counselor. Wildlife Rehabilitation and Animal Assisted Activities/Therapy are a lifestyle for Linda and her family. Their home has offered a haven for a multitude of animals and children (foster) through the years. Currently living with a variety of domestic animals, the Nebbe's are licensed wildlife rehabilitators and yearly take in over 150 orphaned or injured wild animals. Linda was on the founding board of the Iowa Wildlife Rehabilitator's Association and is currently President. She has also helped organize a group of local volunteers that help with rehabilitation - the Black Hawk Wildlife Rehabilitation Project. In addition, eleven years ago Linda helped found P.E.T. P.A.L.S., the local Animal Assisted Activities/Therapy program that is affiliated with the Black Hawk Humane Society. She has served as both coordinator and advisor for that group. Animals are also incorporated into her job as an elementary counselor. Linda does frequent educational presentations and speeches on Animal Assisted Activities/ Therapy, Wildlife Rehabilitation, and the environment. Nature as a Guide is a book written by Linda about the application of animals, plants, and nature in Counseling, Therapy, and Education.

Reprinted with permission of author and publisher – Elementary School Counselor

During the last decade, the significance of human-animal relationships has become evident. With this recognition, scholars have sought to document the phenomenon through research. The data is still sparse, although there is enough to give credibility to the importance of the human-animal bond. The research also encourages a new aspect of the helping profession, animal-assisted therapy - or in a broader sense, nature therapy.

Some of the early research on the human-animal relationship focused on the elderly. Pet ownership has been correlated with a positive attitude toward self and others and an enhanced social life (Cusak & Smith, 1984). Heart disease patients who owned pets were discovered to live longer than those who did not (Beck & Katcher, 1983). In a classic study, the physiological effects of pets were noted as a person's measured blood pressure significantly decreased when the person was interacting with his or her pet (Cusak & Smith, 1984).

As the importance of pets in the lives of the elderly has come to light, the relationship between children and animals has also drawn attention from both practitioners and researchers. One study reported that a pet is an important part of the child's environment. Levine and Bohn (1986) reported that in families with pets there is less incidence of thumb sucking. They concluded that this indicates a more emotionally secure environment. Levine and Bohn also observed that a pet helps to teach important skills to children, including patience and control of temper (Levine & Bohn, 1986), as well as greater empathy for other human beings (Bryant, 1986; Malcarne, 1986). This is true, however, only in families in which the animal is perceived as a family member (Soares, 1986).

A poll of Fortune 500 chief executive officers determined that 94% of the respondents had had a dog or cat as a child. Approximately 75% of those respondents still have a pet. This figure compares with 53% of U.S. households that own a pet. These executives reported feeling that their pet was significant to them during development. The executives said they learned responsibility, empathy, sharing, and companionship from their pets. Many noted that the pet was someone to talk to ("Business Bulletin," 1984).

Montagner reported that in cases of severely disabled or mentally handicapped children, animals are able to induce desirable behavior patterns not otherwise appearing (Montagner, 1986).

Displaced children and those in long-term foster placements in which dogs were part of therapeutic treatment seemed to progress faster than children in therapeutic treatment without dogs. The dogs provided the children with a sense of constancy and, in some cases, control in an erratic, tumultuous, and unpredictable environment (Gonski, 1986).

In an interview with adolescent juvenile offenders entering a resident facility, the interviewer included her dog in ten to twenty interviews. In every case with the dog present, the interviewer found the young men responded with increased openness and less hostility than in the interviews without the dog present. Interviews with the dog present logged 280 interviewee responses as compared with 40 interviewee responses in the interviews without the animals present (Gonski, Peacock & Ruckert, 1986).

McAdams (1988) had graduate student observers rate counseling sessions involving a sighted counselor and client, a nonsighted counselor and client, a sighted counselor with a dog and client and a nonsighted counselor with a dog and client. A script was followed so that the variables were the presence of the dog and sight of the counselor. Thomas, Cash, and Salzbach rating scales used included the Confidence for Counseling Outcomes Expectancy Scale, the Continuation of Counseling Scale, and the Counselor Traits Scale. Ratings for the sighted counselor with a dog were significantly higher than the other ratings. The sighted counselor without a dog was second highest. The nonsighted counselor with a dog received the third highest rating. The lowest rating was that of the nonsighted counselor.

Institutionalized adolescents given a rabbit to care for over a six-week period demonstrated less aggressive behavior than adolescents in another activity program or the control group (Davis, 1986).

Researchers have discovered a link between animal abuse and human violence (Sussman, 1985). A study titled *Childhood Cruelty Toward Animals Among Criminals and Noncriminals* (Moulton, 1987) reported that childhood animal cruelty occurred to a significantly greater degree in the population of aggressive criminals. It is hypothesized that as children, these persons learned from "models" in their environment to be abusive to animals. As they grew, the abuse transferred to people (Moulton, 1987). Evidence indicates, although no research to date supports it, that this trend can be reversed through education and strong role models while the persons in question are still children (Sussman, 1985).

Pearl Salotto

Davis observed that emotionally disturbed children become involved more readily with animals than with people or tasks (Davis, 1986). Levinson (1969), a child psychologist, said that when the child (client) relationship begins to transfer from the animal to the therapist, the child is "getting well."

Another study by Davis (1969) indicated that children who stutter were more effectively motivated toward spontaneous speech when in therapy with a dog. Speech students in therapy with a dog showed significant improvement in areas of self concept, advanced language structure, and more appropriate and efficient use of speech.

The positive effects of an animal's presence with adults depends on the adult's early experiences and feelings for animals, but animals seem almost universally to provide a beneficial and positive influence on children. (Beck & Katcher, 1983).

Why There Is "Magic"

There is little doubt about the seemingly "magical" quality that exists between animals and people. The "why," however, is only theoretical at best.

Levinson (1969) stated that pets help to prevent or overcome a sense of alienation from nature that is frequently experienced by many individuals. He contended that the connection with our "natural" environment is necessary for positive mental health and for normal mental development. Pets in many cases can provide this connection.

Beck and Katcher (1983) wrote that animals are a tie with our beginnings. Personal peace and tranquillity are inspired by cues from our natural environment that can act as the stimulus to promote feelings of peace and tranquillity. Pets, providing this connection, can also provide the cues to promote such feelings of peace and tranquillity in people.

Swan (1977) maintained that there is an important exchange of life energy among all living things. This exchange of energy is necessary for a quality of life. Humans have surrounded themselves with a constructed or artificial environment. Pets brought into human homes provide one means for this necessary energy exchange.

Some clue to understanding this bond comes from examination of child development theories. Pearce (1977) had developed a theory that closely follows Erikson's eight stages of development. Pearce named each stage a "matrix." Every person experiences an ever broadening matrix as growth occurs. Each new matrix needs to be a successful experience if optimal development is expected. The child's first matrix is the womb. This is followed by the matrix of the mother. The third matrix is the earth matrix, which is generally in place by the age of seven. Pearce stated that the child's interaction with and exploration of natural elements are essential before he or she can move on to matrixes including the physical body, the abstract thought processes, and mind-brain with other mind-brains. The earth matrix would coincide with Erikson's Sense of the Intuitive.

A child seems to perceive animals as peers or as objects. This can be understood by examination of Piaget's (Maier, 1965) stages of cognitive understanding coupled with examination of the role models the child observes and with what the child is taught. Our culture promotes the personification of animals to young children; thus, the majority of children will perceive animals as peers. Similar to a child's perception of fairy tales, with maturation his or her concepts of animals will become more complex as he or she thinks in more abstract ways. With this in mind, it is understandable why a child will be able to empathize more easily with animals exhibiting simple and obvious behavior, as opposed to the more complex behavior another person exhibits.

Theory is only our best guess. What we do know and can observe is the simplicity of the human-animal relationship. It is an easy and safe relationship. It is low risk. An animal is accepting, openly affectionate, honest, loyal, and consistent. All these wonderful qualities fulfill a person's basic need to feel loved and worthwhile.

Incorporating The Human-Animal Bond In A Guidance and Counseling Program

I have found a variety of ways to incorporate animals into my work as an elementary school counselor.

First, and probably the most important, the animals help me establish rapport with the children I work with. The children's trust and respect for me seem to be enhanced because of this special interest. A bond seems to exist between us because of our relationship with the animals. Even children with fears or allergies are curious and interested. As long as I accept and respect the positions of these children, the animals do not seem to interfere with my relationship with the child.

Case Example: Brice was a 12-year-old fifth grader. He was big for his age and prided himself on being "tough." In the middle of fifth grade, he was transferred to my school to become part of a learning disability class. Brice found his new placement undesirable, and his transition was extremely rough. The teacher asked me to visit with him. On his first visit Brice was silent. Tears welled up in his eyes several times. Finally, he told me he didn't need to see "no counselor." I asked him to come one more time. The second time he did not come. When I went to get him he tried to avoid me. The session was completely unproductive. I told him he didn't need to come any more. Then the teacher and I scheduled an "animal" guidance presentation in her classroom. Our hope was that the animals and the enthusiasm of the other children would make me less intimidating to Brice. My dog, Peter, was my helper during the planned guidance class. Brice was withdrawn, but as class continued he became part of the group and an active participant. We had no direct contact. Although our appointment had been canceled, the following week Brice was at my door at the time his appointment had previously been scheduled. When I greeted him, he responded with, "Is your dog here today?" With Peter's help, Brice and I have become good friends. In fact, on a recent survey of what he liked and did not like about school, my animals were his number one favorite!

In the counseling office I find a warm, soft, furry friend to be irresistible to almost every child. The animal's warmth, acceptance, and uninhibited response easily convince a child he or she is a lovable person. The honesty and simplicity of the animal's behavior is less threatening than that of a human. I have observed that children who find it difficult to trust me will relax and "talk" to my dog or cat. Later, because I "belong" to the animal, the children begin to trust me. It would be ideal if such a companion could always be with me when I work, but when that is not practical, an occasional visit by the animal is beneficial and seems to have continuing influence even when my pet is not present.

Case Example: Rodney was a second grader. It was impossible to define the trigger that sent him into a closed world of his own, refusing to speak to anyone, to do anything, to move! After one of these "spells" the day was lost. It seemed impossible for him to recover. When this behavior occurred the teacher would move him to the office. He would remain there, unresponding, for hours. No one, including me, seemed to be able to enter his world. One day Peter, my dog, was at school with me. The principal informed me Rodney was in the office again. Peter and I went in to see him. Rodney was sitting at a table with his head buried in his folded arms. Peter nosed Rodney's elbow. There was a pause. Then Rodney slid off his chair onto the floor beside Peter. His folded arms slid around his neck and he buried his head into Peter's coat and sobbed. I waited and Peter waited, sharing an occasional nose or lick with Rodney. Nearly ten minutes passed before Rodney withdrew and looked up at me and smiled. I asked, "Can Peter walk back to class with you?" He nodded. The teacher reported the rest of the day went well. We were able to build on the positive experience to restructure Rodney's behavior in the future.

A friendly puppy, kitten, or dog gives the child with low self-esteem a boost. The aggressive child can experience being gentle with a nonthreatening and accepting recipient. These skills can be transferred. Social skills can be taught and accepted with a friendly animal. Touch is easily accepted and given, even by children who have little experience with people-touch or who find touching people threatening. A child can experience control while walking a dog or having him/her do special tricks. Trust can be demonstrated by giving a child responsibilities, such as feeding the fish or staying with the dog. Feelings and fears are easily projected to an animal as a person identifies with the perceived feelings of the animal. Role-playing with an animal or observation of the child's behavior with an animal often gives insights into a child's personality. The list of possibilities is endless.

Case Example: Chad was a second grader. He was built very slightly and so quiet he could almost be considered nonverbal. Chad was usually alone. On a sociogram of the classroom he had not been chosen. He was labeled learning disabled and assigned to a resource room. I was hoping to help him socialize by encouraging verbalization skills and finding ways to enhance his extremely low self-image. Talking to me was next to impossible for Chad. During the third visit, I was on the phone when he arrived, so he pulled up a chair in front of my aquarium and began a conversation with the fish. During that session and in many more to follow, he talked to the fish and through the fish. Soon I gave him the important job of feeding the fish on the days I was at another school. This job turned out to have a lot of prestige, and other children were begging him to choose them to help. Problems at home and with his brother were revealed through his conversations with the fish and with parents' help those problems were remedied. By the middle of his third-grade year, Chad was chosen by all the third-grade boys on another classroom sociogram.

I find animals a valuable aid in teaching classroom guidance. The simplicity of the animal behavior and the honesty of response demonstrate feelings, cause and effect behavior, and evidence of the results of love and kindness (or the opposite). The presence of an animal can enhance an atmosphere of trust and respect, as well as one of concern. When these values are learned in respect to animals, they can be carried over to interactions with human beings. Lessons that seem natural involving skills (reading unspoken language in animals and people), manners, peer relationships (how we act affects the feelings and behavior of others), feelings (use of animal feelings shown in pictures like one available through the Humane Society of the United States *Kindness Magazine*), and many more.

Case Example: Mrs. Sullivan had 25 sixth graders who could all be labeled _high risk_ children. In most of their families there were multiples of the following character-istics: single parents, unemployment, parents in prison, drug abuse, alcohol use, and child abuse. Overt and aggressive behavior in the classroom had followed this class throughout elementary school. Multiple daily incidents were normal. Interventions seemed to have no effect. Mrs. Sullivan found two orphan kittens whose mother had been killed and brought them to school. The difference in the classroom was immedi-ate and dramatic. The children could remain quiet and stay in their seats so the kittens wouldn't be frightened. They took turns caring for the orphans. Gentle behavior was acceptable with the kittens around. As the kittens grew, the children observed their behavior and drew analogies to their own behavior and social interactions. One little girl from an extremely dysfunctional family wrote in her journal, "I can hardly wait for school because Fluffy is there. She is so warm and soft. I love her and she loves me."

Case Example: Tim seemed troubled. His teacher was concerned and asked the counselor to talk with him. There was no obvious problem. Then Peter, my dog, and I visited the classroom. I told Peter's story. The children asked many questions. Tim asked if there was anything Peter was afraid of. I said Peter didn't like to be left alone. He would cry and whine if I put him into a room and closed the door to keep him in. Later that afternoon Tim came to my door.

"I have to tell you something," he said. "I have that thing Peter has."

"You feel like Peter?" I asked, a little confused.

"Yes, you know, when he is alone and stuff," Tim responded.

As I eventually learned, Tim, an only child of eight years, spent every afternoon and night after school home alone. He was so frightened and lonely he would hide under the table and sometimes even sleep there. He had never told anyone of his fear and loneliness.

Other residents in my office include a tank of huge, hungry fish. They provide a distinct point of interest and help me to establish an interesting discussion about possi-bilities and opportunities for "responsibility" tasks.

Case Example: Amy, a fourth grader, came in the first day of school crying. It seemed her beloved parakeet had been "accidentally" released outdoors by her brother during the summer. The parakeet was special because her "only" friend who had moved away in first grade had given it to her. Now, back at school, her poor social situation reminded her of the loss. To make matters worse, she had gotten a new parakeet, Pop-corn, who was "mean." That morning her dad had threatened that if Popcorn bit him one more time he would squeeze him to death! I tried to explain to Amy what she needed to do to work with Popcorn. We read books. Amy reported no success. Finally, we decided that Amy would bring Popcorn to school on days I was there, and we would work together on teaching him to be nice. We did eventually win Popcorn's trust. Amy received much peer recognition for her task (thanks to the classroom teacher) and frequently brought "friends" in to help. Popcorn became a school hero and an example of making changes, and Amy and I made great strides in understanding and working through her family relationships.

I am just like children. Working with animals makes me feel good too. A friendly face, a wagging tail, or a lick on my hand can melt away any frustrations of a normal day. I have a friend.

Guidelines For An Animal In The Office or Classroom

Laws and Rules

Federal Law: It is a federal law that any person working with wild animals that are endangered or migratory must have a Federal Education Permit from the Department of Natural resources.

State Law: in most states:
* There are laws covering service animals that accompany handicapped persons.
* Animals are not allowed in food preparation or food service areas.
* Animal bites must be reported to the Public Health Department.
* There are also laws governing animals in public institutions and public places.
* To find out what your state laws are, contact a state congress representative, the local library information service, or the Humane Society.

Institutional Rules:
It is important if you are planning to take an animal into an institution or public place to first find out the rules and policies and to obtain permission.

Most school policy's state that the animal must be safe, under control or in a proper container, and have permission to be in that institution.

Here is the policy of one school system about visiting pets or animals.
* The animal must be safe.
* The animal must be under control or in an appropriate container or enclosure.
* The person bringing the animal must have permission to do so.
* The animal is a "visitor" and will stay only as agreed upon or short amount of time unless other arrangements have been made and approved.

It is important to be sensitive to the visiting animal. If the animal is unduly stressed and uncomfortable, the visit needs to end.

Guidelines:

1. It is important that you are established and effective in your counseling or teaching role before incorporating pets into the office or classroom.

2. You must *feel comfortable* and confident with the animal and the situation. You must always be aware of what is going on and always be in control.

3. The *administration needs to be aware* of what is being done and approve the activity. This is why it is important for you to be knowledgeable about animals and animal assisted therapy, and be prepared to convey the information to the administration.

4. You are *liable*. Check with your insurance agent for information. If you feel the response has been inadequate, continue checking with other companies.

Insurance companies have different ideas about coverage in this area. If a personal pet is involved, the personal liability coverage may be included as part of your homeowners or home renters policies. Again, it is a good idea to clarify this with your insurance agent.

5.   The *temperament and health of the animal* is important. A commitment to the animal's health is imperative. Dogs and cats should have current shots and health-check ups, as well as "just be feeling good.' Be prepared to visit a veterinarian if the need arises. Even when fish are sick, they need to be cared for in the most humane way possible.

6.   You are the *role model*. What others learn is what they see you doing. You are teaching about caring for others, animals, and people. If an error is made, *error on the side of too much care. You can not teach too much compassion.*

7.   A *proper environment* for the animal is essential. The animal needs an environment where he/she can be comfortable, remain healthy and meet its needs. Choosing that environment and helping others to understand why you chose him/her is a tremendous opportunity for teaching empathy, as well as scientific knowledge.

8.   If *death* occurs, treat it as any loss. Be as honest as possible. Model appropriate feelings. Follow the needs of the group. Talk about the death. Allow for grieving. If some individuals are more traumatized than others, work with them alone. There is a place for humor, but not disrespect. Stop disrespect immediately. "Doing something" appropriate with the body may be important. Even "flushing" (the fish) is OK if handled appropriately! A full blown traditional funeral may not be appropriate and under most circumstances, creative alternatives may be found. (The book *The Tenth Good Thing About Barney* by Judith Viorst is an excellent resource.)

9.   *Humane treatment* and respect for the animal is essential. A scared or uncomfortable animal needs to be relieved of the stress immediately.

10.   Never speak harshly to an animal, *discipline* the animal harshly or strike the animal. You are a role model. If the animal needs such discipline, the animal is not appropriate for the situation.

11.   If the animal is *not suitable* for the office or classroom, change the situation or the animal. For example, if a hamster is a biter, and continues to be one, something is wrong. Talk with the children about why the animal bites. Draw up new rules with the help of the children so the animal will not be in the position to bite. Perhaps simply not handling the animal is the solution. ***If an animal is dangerous, it does not belong in an office or classroom.*** Working to find the best alternative is imperative. Be honest about the situation. There will be concern about where the animal will go and what will happen to it. This is an

opportunity to stress the responsibility of careful selection, responsible and knowledgeable rearing and commitment to the animal.

12. Never assume an individual knows how to *interact* with or handle an animal. Affinity between animals and children is natural, but often children need direction or information about what to do and how to do it. Also, you never know who else has "modeled" human-animal interaction for the individual.

13. You are ultimately *responsible* for the animal. Before you leave, check the animal, the food, and the equipment.

14. If you cannot be there, make arrangements with some other adult to check for you. Sending a classroom or office pet (the typical caged rodent or bird) to different homes on the weekends is not always a good idea. This can be very stressful for the animal. If arrangements can be made for a custodian to feed and care for him/her on *weekends or short vacations*, leaving the animal in the office may be best.

15. If *sending the animal home with children* is the only alternative, make up a guidebook of care and handling. Leave your name and number or the name and number of another responsible person if problems arise. Many positive things can come from this if it is handled carefully.

16. Be aware of the *problems* you may encounter and prepare for them in a preventative manner. The way you handle problems is very important. Don't become overly excited. Always remember you are a role model.

17. It is illegal in most states to keep a wild animal in captivity, but at times wild animals (snakes, turtles, and so forth) end up in a classroom. Do not allow anyone to touch or handle a wild animal. Unknown disease or wounds can be avoided this way. The wild animal will be stressed by handling.

18. If any abuse occurs to any animal in the office or classroom, deal with it immediately and in a demonstrative manner. Abuse cannot be accepted. The animal may be taken from the room for a period of time and new rules established to emphasize the importance of kind and gentle care.

In The Beginning - The First Week:

When an animal is introduced into a classroom or office, the introduction and first few days will set the tone for the entire experience. Here are some suggestions on what to do with those first few days. It takes a conscious effort to really "make it work.'

* Introduce the animal right away. He/she is not an "object," but a vital part of that space. In a classroom, this can be done with the group. In an office, introductions need to be made individually. Treat the animal much

the way a new student would be treated by the classroom.

* Be very clear about the initial expectations! It is fair to ask that the animal not be handled at first, until everyone gets to know everyone or until the animal feels comfortable in the new surroundings. Write expectations down, as well as talk about them.
* Talk about how the animal feels:
    * being in a new place
    * being so small with so many strange giants around
* Ask if they have ever felt that way
* Decide what you can do to make the animal more comfortable
    * move slowly and calmly
    * talk when approaching
    * refrain from grabbing or handling at first
* Name the animal and refer to the animal by that name. Naming animals give them an air of respect, as well as taking away from the "object" image.
* Do some research on the animal. Read a book to the class or have the book available in the office. Have individuals look up information about the animal and share with his class or with you. (In an office, a poster could be made about one facet of the animal's natural history or care.)
* Model the attitude and interaction you want others to have.
* Share little stories about what you have observed the animal doing. This will model observation behavior and be one way you can share about the animal.

Evaluation

The best evaluation is feedback from the children. Do you like what you are seeing and hearing? Do the children interact with the animal in a responsible and caring manner? Do you feel good about it? If so, it is working. If not, pinpoint why and try again or end the experience.

Insensitive handling can undo all the positive contributions of a beautiful and meaningful experience.

Conclusion

Although using (working with) animals is not practical or possible for many counselors, a knowledge and understanding of the human-animal bond is important and essential. This field is growing rapidly. Information is available from the Delta Society, a nonprofit organization for professionals working with and supporting the human-animal-natural environment bond. Delta's files maintain current research in the field and its membership offers a network of professionals all over the world. The Latham Foundation and CENSHARE are additional resources.

Section 7:
PLAY HARD AND LEARN

Dr. Dick Dillman, *D.V.M., was a small animal veterinarian in the Miami, Florida area for twenty-six years. In 1986, he retired from clinical medicine to become involved in dropout prevention programs for disadvantaged inner-city children. He received the Outstanding Volunteer of the Year Award from the Dade County Public Schools in 1988 and 1989. Additionally, in 1997 the Florida State Education Department awarded him Volunteer of the Year. He was author and Program Director of a three-year grant from the W.K. Kellogg Foundation that was administered through the Miami-Dade Community College. Through the funding of this grant, he has organized Companion Animal Programs - an organization dedicated to initiating animal programs for disadvantaged children. His program concepts are to initiate pleasant interaction between children, animals, and caring adults. This format is intended to provide positive reinforcement, improve self-esteem, and promote good moral values. He is author of the photo-essay book, First, Let Them Be Children. He is a strong advocate of improving school curriculums so that they can better address the needs of children as children, and vigorously emphasize the teaching of good moral values to the children in the classroom. Companion-Animal Programs are dedicated to this task. Dick presented his program at the 1995 "Web of Hope" conference in Rhode Island out of which the Windwalker coalition was formed.*

It has been said that nothing is certain except death and taxes. The fascination children have for animals is also a certainty. Children may show their fascination in different ways. Generally, there is a strong desire of the child to interact with the animals in their lives in a way that is stimulating and fulfilling. Usually, we know what to expect when a child can handle or play with a puppy, kitten, baby duck, or any other cuddly creature. Joy, laughter, and curiosity will prevail. Granted, some association with animals may illicit fear, intimidation or anxiety in a child. However, these learned attitudes could readily be overcome by appealing to the intrinsic fascination of animals that is in each person. Opportunities provided for the child to interact with animals in a pleasant, non-threatening manner, can nurture the feelings of fear or intimidation into respect and love. This simple concept, combined with the appreciation that children must be children first, allows us to develop programs that can be tremendously educational and therapeutic.

The varieties of responses that children exhibit to animals are largely due to learned experiences in childhood and to instinctive fascination. The child that naturally loves to cuddle a bunny or a puppy, also may believe that all snakes are horrible and should be feared. He learned about snakes as a child from parents who hate them or the movies that depict their aggressive attitude or "old wives tales," or all of the above. Persons raised in the city who never visited a farm would likely be intimidated by a horse, bull or even a goat. In working with inner-city elementary school children in a Dade County, Florida Public School farm program, such was the case. However, almost without exception, the students would ultimately succumb to their natural fascination when they were allowed to interact with the animals in a relaxed manner. "Bumper" is a Brahma mix steer that was orphaned and bottle fed as a calf by school children. He became bonded to children and is as sweet as a kitten. However, "Bumper" weighs one thousand eight hundred and eighty pounds. This alone might be intimidating to a seventy pound fourth grader. Students that would not even approach him at the start of the school year eventually competed for the opportunity to brush him, comb his tail, pick sand-burrs from his feet and wash away tears that occasionally stain his face.

Bumper – the icon of the original Bumper's Buddies Companion Animal Programs.

A small child must learn that little critters like lizards, toads, frogs, butterflies, beetles and others are significant in our lives. Teaching this in the classroom or on nature walks, can provide an exercise in personal compassion. Linking this with other lessons in human-animal interactions, children will ultimately develop a respect and sensitivity for living creatures that reflect their association with people.

Working with animals in the classroom, in the outdoors, or in farm programs has proven to be a great (modality) in developing motivational programs for all kinds of students. Though these programs have been very successful, most of them have originated through private organizations or individual teachers that were very innovative. The beauty of this approach to education is that all students may benefit from this concept - from the gifted to the learning disabled.

Nancy is a good friend of mine and the trainer and moderator of the Exotic Animal Show at Miami Metro Zoo. The animals in the show are raised and handled much the way a child would be raised in a loving family. This is done so that the critters will not be stressed when presented to the audience. Nancy had three baby clouded leopards at her house, going through the bonding process, and my wife and I were invited to come over and visit with the kittens. I didn't know what to expect when the bathroom door was opened to allow the little guys to come into the bedroom. It immediately became evident that four month old baby leopards do not have a serious thought in their heads. They jumped on the bed, climbed up on the dresser top, scaled up to the handlebars of an exercise bike, and proceeded to do flying leaps all around the room. The human torso was not exempt from their playful attacks. A wadded sock tied to a string on the end of a fishing pole was used as a lure to get these characters to play "predator". Even a fuzzy teddy bear was not safe from the kittens claws and teeth. After the better part of an hour of uninhibited play, the kittens stopped play, laid down and fell asleep in our lap or crook of the arm.

Pearl Salotto

Nancy explained to me that clouded leopards are arboreal and nocturnal. They hunt at night in trees in search of smaller predators. When the prey is located, the leopard will leap through the tree limbs to subdue their meal - often falling to the ground. She further explained that everything the youngsters did this evening was a lesson in survival and socialization. They were playing hard to learn!

In some respects our childrens' needs are analogous to the needs of the leopard kitten to play and learn. It is generally accepted that pre-kindergarten and kindergarten youngsters need much play in their school curriculum; however, as the students progress in elementary school levels, play is rapidly replaced by structured disciplines. Too often, the teaching process deviates from the normal tendencies of child behavior to the stress of personal restraint. It is not natural for small children to sit still and rigidly adhere to rules that inhibit their normal impulses for a whole school day. Rules of conduct can easily be enforced even if the youngsters are allowed to act just like kids.

The disadvantaged children involved in our Companion Animal Farm Program cannot control their most basic impulses when they interact with animals on the farm. All of them laugh and giggle. Most of them pet and cuddle. Some are reluctant to handle the animals. An occasional child may be aggressive or mean to an animal, and this is not tolerated. Moral values of respect, responsibility, trust and sensitivity are continuously emphasized in the program and any deviation from these values elicits discipline. However, two things must be considered when taking disciplinary action. One is that reference to the incident with the child must be directed toward the reasons why such action was bad rather than that the child was a bad person. The other consideration is that it is essential that the incident be viewed as an opportunity to teach the child rather than belittle. A change in facial and voice mannerisms, expression of concern for the animal and an appeal to the child's intrinsic sensitivity, almost always changes an aggressive act into a learned lesson in respect.

The word "play" is defined in Webster's Dictionary as: "to amuse oneself, as by taking part in a game or sport; engage in recreation." Play can be very active, such as running, throwing and catching a ball or climbing a tree. Play can also be subtle, such as a leisure walk, admiring butterflies flitting among the flowers or sitting and cuddling a rabbit. All these things are amusing and recreational. Incorporating play into a child's school curriculum will encourage student participation and enjoyment; hence, the prime requisite for learning.

Of course, all forms of play are not suitable for classroom activities. Thirty children, all playing tag together may be a bit overwhelming for most teachers; however, a leisure walk around the schoolyard, meadow, or woods can provide endless opportunities to teach many facts of science. Granted, it is logical to assume that the children will not all walk in a straight line or be quiet. The will run, pick up sticks, chase butterflies, step in mud puddles, laugh, scream and do other kid things. But, this is good! Now they are participating in school. That is what the kids are going to do, so what must the teacher and aides do to organize chaos into a learning experience? Two things are essential in this concept of education. First, the teacher must make the children understand the rules necessary to allow this activity to be provided and be consistent in enforcing the rules. Secondly, the adults should actively interact with the children in the capacity of a teacher, companion, friend, and protector. There is no doubt that this scenario of education will require creative and innovative input by the teachers, but it is this kind of attitude that symbolizes teaching professionalism at its greatest level.

The Animal Companion Science Program organized at Amelia Earhart Park Farm in Miami, Florida is a magnificent example of utilizing play in classroom lessons for fourth and fifth graders. An example of this starts when the students are escorted by the teachers and aides from the bus into the classroom. This is a time for adult-child interaction. Pleasant greetings, conversation, "high-fives" and the occasional hug are exchanged. In the classroom, the children will engage in activities that teach about science and animals, and will be allowed to associate with the resident rabbit, gerbil, cockatiel or snake. They are then oriented to the rules and values that are expected of them as they participate in the activities outdoors. The children proceed to the barnyard for some people-pet bonding with an assortment of farm animals. Structured academics are put on hold while we groom, pet or converse with the animals. When the students get the chance to witness a calf, lamb or baby goat being born, a lesson in reproduction and birth is initiated right there in the barn. A mother hen and her chicks represent a great lesson in responsible parenting. Overcoming the fear of a horse or bull will provide a real personal accomplishment for a child that opens the door for adults to congratulate and offer positive reinforcement.

After the barnyard experience, the children may be taken on a nature walk in the nearby woods. Rolling over a dead log to expose beetles, centipedes, scorpions and ants elicits a basic course in entomology. The enthusiasm and appreciation by the adults of the natural things that are seen soon generates similar enthusiasm in the youngsters. The children are not allowed to hurt any of the living creatures or damage any of the plant life. These value lessons in respect and sensitivity will carry over in their association with each other.

Not all teachers would feel comfortable with barnyard activities or nature walks, but it is the attitude of spontaneous teaching and personal interaction that I am emphasizing. The staff and facilities at the Amelia Earhart Farm are available to eighteen elementary schools on a regular basis throughout the school year. This allows teachers from these schools to coordinate with the science teacher at the Farm. The experiences that the students have at the Farm are a great nucleus on which to build supplemental lesson plans back at the school. For instance, the kids in our program loved to play classroom bingo – "Farm-O" as we called it. Instead of numbers, vocabulary words to which they had been introduced were used. The children would strain their little minds to identify a new word in order to win a prize. One session may follow repeated trips to the barnyard and words like stallion, mare, ewe, gander or steer are used. After our gardening season, the children are challenged with words like cotyledon, stamen, pistil, cultivate or harvest.

The kids in the Animal Companion Science Program are "at risk" students. They are involved in our program because they were bored or overwhelmed with routine classroom curriculum. Almost without exception, these little troopers would enthusiastically participate in all the games and activities that we provided. Discipline is not a major concern with these children. Their enjoyment and eagerness to be involved made it easy for them to want to follow the rules and values that control the program.

Play can continue back in the classroom. In music class, kids can make up or sing songs about farm animals. Great things can be done with "Old MacDonald Had a

Pearl Salotto

Farm" because the kids know all there is to know about farm animals. Arts and Craft class can take advantage of all this enthusiasm. The math teacher can create relevant problems for the students to solve. A mother hen had eight chicks and half were males. A fox ate two chicks – one male and one female. If all remaining females grew up and had six chicks of their own, how many new baby chicks would there be? This could be fun. Play a game with this. Pick teams and let the kids do some collective reasoning. Let the teacher interact right in the middle of this contest and do not forget the positive reinforcement when the opportunity is presented.

A great game that we play at the Farm is called "The Food Chain." It mainly is a lesson in who eats who or what in the world of nature. Each child is assigned to be an animal or a plant – a fox, mouse, butterfly, bumblebee, flower, or other natural thing. Essentially, the idea of the game is for each child to chase and catch whatever thing they need to survive. The fox eats the mouse. The butterfly needs the flower; however the fox does not chase the flower or the butterfly does not catch the fox. All plants have to get whoever is water. All things must watch out for "natural disaster" – fire, hurricane, tornado, disease, etc. It can catch everything else. The children all run around chasing each other, laughing screaming, panting – all with great confusion; but, they love this game of organized chaos. What a great game for physical education class! Beats kickball! The students can have relevant classroom lessons before the game and learn about things like prey, predator, scavenger, survival and ecological balance.

Do not forget subtle play – especially when needing to address the personal needs of a child having a bad day. A child that comes to school after being abused or humiliated will not be ready to learn. As a matter of fact, classroom tension may further depress the youngster. Providing special attention for this child may be all that is necessary to reverse a feeling of despair into happiness. One way this can be accomplished is to let the child interact with an animal that will give unconditional love. Allow the youngster to cuddle a rabbit, or help clean and care for the gerbils, or attempt to teach the parrot some new words and you will have a child that forgets her or his problems. When the mood changes, it is the ideal time to provide as much positive reinforcement as possible.

One good way for school to provide these opportunities would be to have a well organized animal room with specially selected animals that will enjoy the interaction with kids. The care and cleaning of the animals can be delegated to the students – they will love it. A comfortable lounge area will allow a child to relax with an animal, and the area would be a great place for mentoring or counseling. Selection of special animals and veterinary care can readily be solicited from local veterinarians who would be pleased to help the kids out.

I have had the privilege of working with disadvantaged children in need of special attention, and my enthusiasm continues to increase as I see what a beautiful effect this concept of education has on the children. It is obvious that educational reform is long overdue in this country. Let us hope that all of those contributing to the plan realize that all of society must be involved in the welfare of our children. The concern utmost in my mind is that the basic natural needs of the children are the greatest influential factors in determining an approach to educational reform. All children of this world are born with the same innocence and basic needs. As they grow from infancy, their lives are changed by parental attention or lack thereof, cultural differences, prejudices, health, economic status, and other social influences. For those children that do not have the love and respect that they need to develop as a person, other people in the child's life must compassionately assume responsibility of nurturing them very early in their development. These basic needs are not complicated and are easily identifiable – unconditional love, respect and guidance. If a child has these factors in their lives, they will mature into compassionate adults. If they do not have these factors, then compassionate adults must intervene and help provide guidance. As adults, we must remember what it was to be a child and realize that children act the way they do for a good reason. It is absolutely necessary for us to realize that children must be children first, before they can become functioning adults. We must love the children, teach the children, guide the children and always remember: First, let them be children!

Section 8:
STEPPING INTO ANOTHER'S PAWS

__Karen Pagano__ has a MA in the education of children with emotional needs and has been teaching for twenty years. She has been a therapeutic tutor, diagnostic prescriptive teacher, special education teacher, school adjustment counselor, inclusion facilitator and socialization trainer. She has taught courses at North Adams State College entitled, "The Psychology of Children with Special Needs" and "Peace in the Classroom." She is an advocate of proactive and interactive education and incorporates the principles of conflict resolution and peer mediation into her teaching. Most recently, Karen became involved in developing a curriculum in building character, confidence, and socialization skills. She may soon be teaching at the college level a course entitled "Peace, Pride, and Pets in the Classroom." Karen is always willing to look at new ways of thinking and constructing safe and nurturing learning environments with the help of her students. Her years of working with children has taught her that the miracle of teaching only happens when a student feels safe and involved enough to take the risk to listen, trust, practice, try out a newly presented idea, and learn. Over the last several years, Karen has been privileged to work with PAT's Denise and John DeSanty and therapy pet, Jessie.

Karen and her dog, Ditto, visiting their favorite place - the ocean.

My class has been privileged to take part in the pet therapy program offered by John and Denise Desanty and their dog, Jessie. I originally signed up to take part in the program with the hope that the activity would afford my special needs class the opportunity to have an 'up close and personal' experience with a trained animal. That has happened and more. The changes that I have seen in my group since we have begun the program are wide ranging and truly therapeutic.

Because of the integrity and honesty with which the program is offered, what I witness as happening for the kids is that they now can find a way to open up, communicate, and trust their own perceptions and ideas as well as those of the therapeutic team John, Denise, and Jessie. Because of that trust and the honoring of truthfulness and respect, we can begin to change our perceptions and beliefs.

Some examples of the effectiveness and carry over of the program follow: We have begun to use and demonstrate an understanding of many new feelings and the words that represent them (trust, pride, confusion, loneliness, fear, excitement, temptation, connection, relaxation, safety). We are learning how to be empathetic, step into another's shoes (or paws) and try to understand the feelings and experiences of others. We are practicing self control in order to be more like Jessie in her ability to recognize temptation and trouble. We can now talk about and practice patience because of the way that Jessie shows us it can be done. We are learning about safety and personal space and we try to reflect on the behaviors that Jessie demonstrates to show her needs and abilities in nonthreatening ways. Notice that I say 'we' as I describe the attributes that we are learning. I, as well, as my students, are learning new ways for us to be together as we spend important learning time with Jessie and her trainers. It is so wonderful to watch the process of change as it happens naturally and productively through a program such as this. I would like to see this program continue for my kids for countless reasons: the most important being that they will (and are already) benefiting from interacting so closely with Jessie. My students have been identified with and demonstrate severe social and behavioral difficulties and I believe that they need to be helped and taught how to get along in the world in as many ways possible. They need the time and opportunity to process. Because of their relationships with Jessie, they can start to expand and practice what they are learning in that world. Jessie, John, and Denise give us a much needed tool for growth and success.

My students and I talk often about the lessons that we are learning from Jessie as we struggle through the social challenges of each day and we all realize the importance that she now has in our lives. I asked them recently why Jessie is so special to us and these are a few of the comments that they made."

Family: Denise, John, Jessie, and Jody.

◊ Talking about our problems helps us learn.
◊ Jessie is teaching me to be gentle.
◊ It's okay to cry in front of Jessie.
◊ We like her to sing to us and we like singing to her.
◊ Jessie won't tease us.
◊ Because Jessie barked and protected us when someone came to the door – that means she cares about us.
◊ She knows us because we talk to her and now she knows our voices.
◊ I don't want to hurt her feelings and she won't hurt mine. I think she loves me.

I know of no way as powerful as listening to the honest thoughts of the children to describe and determine the magnitude and importance of our experience with Jessie. I hope that we can continue to work together with Jessie to become safer, gentler, more understanding and successful in our relationships with family, teachers, and friends. This program is one of the special things about our inclusive educational offerings at Plunkett Elementary School. I am grateful for the opportunity to share the time with Jessie, John, and Denise.

Section 9:
WILDLIFE REHABILITATION

Linda Nebbe lives with her husband and three children on twenty two acres of reestablished prairie and hard wood timber near Waterloo, Iowa. She graduated from Iowa State University with a BS in Child Development and Elementary Education. After teaching for a number of years she received her MS from Iowa State University in Guidance and Counseling. Currently she is employed by the Cedar Falls School System as an elementary counselor. Wildlife Rehabilitation and Animal Assisted Activities/Therapy are a lifestyle for Linda and her family. Their home has offered a haven for a multitude of animals and children (foster) through the years. Currently living with a variety of domestic animals, the Nebbes are licensed wildlife rehabilitators and yearly take in over 150 orphaned or injured wild animals. Linda was on the founding board of the Iowa Wildlife Rehabilitators Association and is currently President. She has also helped organize a group of local volunteers that help with rehabilitation - the Black Hawk Wildlife Rehabilitation Project. In addition, eleven years ago Linda helped found P.E.T. P.A.L.S., the local Animal Assisted Activities/Therapy program that is affiliated with the Black Hawk Humane Society. She has served as both coordinator and advisor for that group. Animals are also incorporated into her job as an elementary counselor. Linda does frequent educational presentations and speeches on Animal Assisted Activities/Therapy, Wildlife Rehabilitation, and the environment. Nature as a Guide is a book written by Linda about the application of animals, plants, and nature in Counseling, Therapy, and Education.

Wildlife Rehabilitation is the care of orphaned, injured or ill wild animals until they are ready for release back into their wild environment. Although individuals have always cared for injured and orphaned wild animals, wildlife rehabilitation as a field is new. Care for oiled sea birds and beached whales has been a concern for a number of years, but focus on other wild animals has developed over the last twenty years.

All wildlife rehabilitators must be licensed by the federal government if they work with raptors, migratory animals or animals listed by the federal government as endangered. States have different licensing requirements that cover animals native to that state.

Most wildlife rehabilitators belong to the large group of volunteer, backyard rehabilitators. These individuals take the orphaned or injured wild animal to their home, caring for him/her with sometimes rudimentary facilities, until it is time for release. A few rehabilitation centers exist in the United States and other countries. Some of the individuals working at the rehabilitation centers are employed, but often rehabilitation centers depend on volunteer help to make up the difference between the small number of paid staff and the many hours of animal care needed to aid an individual animal.

Facilities, expertise, philosophy, and release options often influence the methods of rehabilitation. In most circumstances, the rehabilitator does the best they can under the circumstances; ideally focusing on what is best for the animals physically and behaviorally.

Networking among rehabilitators is essential. Because of the vast number of species and the variations in requirements for each species, rehabilitators often do not have appropriate facilities or knowledge to aid every animal and need to know where to turn for another placement for an animal or for information on treatment for the animal. The rehabilitator can obtain information from either of the two national organizations for rehabilitators, the National Wildlife Rehabilitators Association and the International Wildlife Rehabilitation Council. Both organizations have developed valuable libraries of information on rehabilitation, as well as an extensive list of members.

Why do rehabilitators rehabilitate? They often are reminded that the animals they release make very little difference in species populations. Rehabilitation consumes major amounts of time, it is confining, and it can be very expensive. Naturalists advise "If you really care for the animal, then leave it alone in its natural environment. The more humans interfere, the worse it is for the animals." (Rehabilitators believe this also.) Rehabilitators are motivated by several reasons.

Rehabilitators believe that it is time to "mess" with our wild friends who need help. If we do not do it now it may soon be too late. Unfortunately, humans have already interfered with the environment. In addition, Rehabilitators estimate that over 95% of the animals they aid come to them because of human intervention, kidnapping, habitat destruction, man-made obstacles (wires and cars), and hunting and trapping accidents. Rehabilitation is an effort to even the score a bit, to give something back to our wild heritage that humans have already taken away.

Helping the individual animal is the primary motivation of most wildlife rehabilitators. Although many rehabilitators specialize in specific species, others work with a variety of animals.

A rehabilitator working with "common" animals is often challenged about why they care for such an abundant species, particularly those animals other humans may consider a nuisance. Responses to this challenge vary. Rehabilitators recognize that all animals are an important part of the ecosystem in their natural state. All species of animals are important to know about and understand. Perhaps there are too many raccoons now, but at one time there were billions of passenger pigeons, too. What a rehabilitator may learn caring for a bunny may be the skill needed another time to aid a black-footed ferret. No one knows what the future will be or what animals or knowledge will be important tomorrow.

Another motivation encouraging the rehabilitator is learning about the behavior and biology of the animals they work with. There are so many species of wild animals, and there is still so much to learn about our wild friends. Very few humans have the opportunity to really "know" a wild animal. Living, as rehabilitators do, in an intimate proximity with the animal, they have the opportunity to observe behavior that few other humans have seen. Only those like Hope Ryden, Farley Mowett, and Jane Goodall, who have gone to live intimately with the wild ones in the animal's own environment, have experienced the intimacy the rehabilitator experiences.

Educating others about animals and the environment is another motivation of the wildlife rehabilitator. Alone, rehabilitators know they cannot change anything. Sharing what they have learned with others to enhance their awareness and understanding of the earth and its inhabitants is the only way there can be a difference. Education through sharing is an important goal of a rehabilitator.

Helping people is another motivation of the rehabilitator. Many people care, and when they see an animal in need, want to help, but find it difficult. It is illegal for them to keep the wild animal, even if they are helping him/her. It is difficult for them to care for the wild animal, and correct information is hard to find. Often the animal suffers and dies even with the best of intentions. Rehabilitation offers them an option, a way to help the animal.

Particularly important are children who want to help animals. Childhood is the time when the human develops empathy and altruistic attitudes. Helping a child help an animal is a step toward these objectives. As the child matures, it is believed that the kind behaviors will generalize to all living things, including other humans. (Levine, 1986; Bryant, 1986; Malcarne, 1986)

Linda Nebbe with Whitney (student client) releasing an orphaned bird that Whitney had helped rehabilitate.

Another way people are aided by the rehabilitator is when they and an animal are not compatible in the same space, but the humans do not wish to harm the animal. Frequently the rehabilitator can offer reasonable suggestions to either make cohabitation easier or induce the animal to find a new home.

Wildlife rehabilitation can help people in another way. Research has substantiated that the human-animal bond can have a powerful influence on the mental health and well-being of an individual. This field is referred to as Animal Assisted Activities/Therapy. Although Animal Assisted Activities/Therapy is usually associated with domestic animals, particularly dogs and cats, this is primarily due to the legal restrictions on possession of wild animals and the accessibility to the wild animals. There are, however, many possibilities for incorporating Animal Assisted Activities/Therapy with wildlife rehabilitation. Following is an overview of Animal Assisted Activities/Therapy outcomes with examples of how wildlife rehabilitation can help individuals reach those outcomes.

Pearl Salotto

The *Delta Society* has defined Animal Assisted Activities (AAA) as providing opportunities for motivational, educational, and/or recreational benefits to enhance the quality of human life. According to *Delta*, AAA are delivered in a variety of environments by a specially trained professional, paraprofessional, and/or volunteer in association with animals that meet specific criteria. According to *Delta*, the AAA provider might include individuals who are activity directors, animal health technicians, animal shelter workers, camp counselors, nursing assistants/aids, occupational therapy assistants, physical therapy assistants, recreation therapy aids, dog trainers, educators, licensed practical nurses, licensed vocational nurses, nature counselors, riding instructors, student nurses, trained volunteers, visiting pet specialists, and 4-H leaders. Wildlife rehabilitator is not included in this list, but when one examines the professions included, it appears that wildlife rehabilitator could be added to this list.

Animal Assisted Therapy (AAT), according to the Delta Society, is a goal-directed intervention in which an animal, meeting specific criteria, is an integral part of the treatment process. AAT is delivered and/or directed by a health/human service provider working within the scope of her/his profession. AAT is designed to promote improvement in human physical, social, emotional, and/or cognitive functioning, in a variety of settings and may be group or individual in nature. The process is documented and evaluated. The professional who delivers and/or directs AAT is a health/human service provider with expertise in incorporating animals as a treatment modality and is knowledgeable about animals. The AAT specialist is licensed and/or recognized by a separate professional discipline. This individual complies with the legal and ethical requirements of his/her profession, as well as local, state, and federal laws relating to this work. This may include individuals as licensed counselors, occupational therapists, recreational therapists, social workers, physicians, psychotherapists, vocational rehabilitation counselors and others. If a licensed professional prescribed a client to work with a wildlife rehabilitator or in some way involved wildlife rehabilitation in their treatment plan, this would be AAT. (Delta Society, 1992)

Giving

Probably the most obvious outcome of AAA/T is the opportunity for an individual to help another. Being socially conscientious and able to "give" to others is a characteristic of a mentally healthy person. One of Alfred Adler's therapeutic tasks is for the client to "give" (Corsini, 1979). For a person with low self-esteem, giving can be threatening and difficult. It is easier to give to an animal than to a person. Just the act of giving can make a person feel better, more worthwhile.

There are many ways an individual can help a wild animal. If one finds an orphaned or injured wild animal, he/she can help that animal by taking him/her to a wildlife rehabilitator. The satisfaction is knowing he/she did something; he/she helped. Many wildlife rehabilitators will allow the individual to follow the animal through the rehabilitation process, giving information on the animal's progress and eventual release.

Wildlife rehabilitation offers many opportunities for individuals to help. In almost all cases, wildlife rehabilitators are volunteers and if organizations exist, they are nonprofit. Wildlife rehabilitation is expensive and time-consuming. If one cannot do volunteer work, gifts to the rehabilitator or organization can help greatly. There are many gifts that any individual can afford to give, like gathering acorns (natural food for many animals), old towels or T-shirts (for bedding), etc. are great gifts.

Example

Help Out Wildlife, HOW, was a project for one elementary school each spring. Children were asked to bring something from a long list of items that would help the local rehabilitator. Items included simple and easy-to-find objects like an egg (for food), plastic ice cream buckets, corn, unused dog houses and cages, and old T-shirts and towels. If no items were available and the child was willing to give up a candy bar, then twenty-five cents may be all it costs to help wildlife. (Parents were asked not to do this project for the child.)

Case Study

John was a fourth grader who had many difficulties at home and at school. Because of his inappropriate behavior, John was not well liked by the other students. Frequently, angry outbursts got in John's way of successful classroom work. One day on John's way to school, he found a baby squirrel. The squirrel looked dead at first; it was at the foot of a tree, cold and still. A dog was nearby. John picked the squirrel up and was immediately surrounded by other children, curious about what he had. When he discovered he/she was alive, John decided that he/she needed to go to a rehabilitator he had heard speak. He took him/her to his counselor at school and asked for help in calling the rehabilitator. At lunch, the counselor took John and the squirrel to the rehabilitator. The counselor was able to keep John informed of the squirrel's progress. When release time finally arrived, the counselor planned an occasion with John and the other children who were there when he first found the squirrel. They visited the rehab center and had a party to celebrate the release. This experience was instrumental in enhancing the positive regard the other children had for John. John felt very good about the contribution he had made.

Instruction

When lack of knowledge leaves a person feeling afraid or insecure, instruction can be therapeutic. Teaching an individual about wild animals empowers that person through enhanced knowledge. The person no longer needs to feel afraid or insecure in situations involving a wild animal.

If a wildlife rehabilitation presentation is done well, it can be an inspiring and empowering personal experience for the members of the audience. Not all wildlife rehabilitators personalize their presentations, but teachers and counselors can build on the rehabilitators presentation with their client by their follow up.

Example

An example of such a presentation would be one on bats. Often at the beginning of the presentation, people will express many negative comments about bats. After hearing about this beneficial and harmless animal, the audience's fear is reduced and replaced with awe. Further instruction on how simple it is to cope with a bat intruder in their home gives the audience members confidence. If the audience has the further opportunity to "meet" a live bat, to see how small it actually is, the presentation can be even more powerful. Simple instruction erases fears and misconceptions and can be empowering.

Presence

Simply being in the presence of a wild animal can be renewing and revitalizing. Studies support the fact that the presence of animals in a safe setting or even pictures of animals that appear safe and serene can be relaxing (Ulrich, 1991). The intensely beautiful owl, the awesomely cute baby raccoon, the amazing bat can all be inspiring when viewed intimately.

Example
In a presentation to some junior high school age students who were mentally challenged, the presenter, was accompanied by a live owl. After the presentation, the instructor asked if the owl could be brought closer to Mike, a legally blind student who could not see the owl from where he sat. Mike was allowed to come as close as possible to the owl. He did not touch the owl, but made an outline of the owl's body with his hand several inches from the owl. The room was silent. As a tear rolled down his cheek, Mike said, "I've never seen an owl before."

Five years later in a classroom assignment to write about a very special experience, Mike reported that his special experience was "the day he 'saw' the owl."

Example
A similar presentation was given to a group of physically challenged individuals. After the presentation, the group wrote thank you letters. One girl wrote, "When I heard a one-winged owl was coming to our school, I thought it wouldn't be good for much. Well, I was wrong. Seeing that owl sit up there so beautiful, I knew he was good for something. He was teaching us."

Feeling and Expression

Everyone likes to talk about his or her favorite things, especially when someone is really listening! Almost everyone has an animal tale to tell. A wildlife rehabilitation presentation or a bird feeder can be a catalyst for numerous stories and memories to be recalled and shared.

Traditional therapy is represented by clients talking about their feelings, experiences, and problems. The listener is usually the therapist or counselor. However, just talking to someone, or even to no one, can also help an individual to clarify thoughts and express feelings. The accepting and confidential ears of animals, wild or domestic, can be therapeutic (Ruckert, J., 1987).

Traditional approaches to feeling therapy involve intellectual expression of feelings, and Animal-Assisted Therapy through wildlife rehabilitation provides a variety of ways to illicit such expression. The client can identify or empathize with the feelings of the wild animal, transfer their feelings to the wild animal, or talk about feelings in respect to the natural stimulus.

Death/loss

Loss is change. All that lives will change and die in the natural process. Loss can be traumatic and to some debilitating. By experiencing some losses and changes, individuals learn that loss is all right, that the hurt eventually subsides, and that life continues. Animal Assisted Activities/Therapy, through wildlife rehabilitation, allows for loss to be experienced and for an opportunity to express grief. It also teaches about the continuing and connected cycle of life. Experiencing loss and talking about loss in various ways aids clients as they deal with personal losses or search for their own identity and their views of mortality.

Example
Wildlife rehabilitation offers a way to experience and talk about life and death. Sometimes this comes about in indirect ways. After listening to a wildlife rehabilitator and learning that often fresh road kill feeds hungry carnivores, children who normally would look at a freshly killed squirrel in the road and see something gross, now see something that is food, something that will bring life to another animal.

Children or adults who bring an orphaned or injured animal to a rehabilitator may find the animal cannot be helped. The animal may die or need to be euthanized. Both give the people who helped an opportunity to touch death, to become familiar with death, to talk about death. At such a time they may also have the opportunity to see death as a friend.

At-Risk Youth

A special group of young people (and sometimes adults) who can benefit greatly from Animal Assisted Therapy, through wildlife rehabilitation, are those we refer to as "at risk." Often from dysfunctional or even abusive families, many of these children themselves are abusive to animals. Individuals in abusive families often abuse animals. Sometimes children raised in abusive families are abusive to animals because it is what they see modeled; others vent their anger on the animals. Over 70% of aggressive, incarcerated criminals were reported as being abusive to animals as children (Advocate, 1987) (Sussman, 1985). These children have not seen another choice modeled for them within their life experiences. Opportunities to work with Animal Assisted Activities/Therapy and to observe the rehabilitator as a strong role model, will give the children choices.

Sometimes individuals are abusive because of the lack of nurturance and personal need fulfillment. Children deprived of nurturance are often unable to nurture others. According to Aaron Katcher, (Katcher, 1992), the measured brain waves are the same for an individual being nurtured as an individual nurturing. Thus, to nurture is to be nurtured. Teaching an individual to care for a small, helpless animal teaches nurturing and in turn is nurturing to the individual.

Example
A wildlife rehabilitation presentation was given to a group of sixth graders at a school were many of the students in the group were notorious for various acts of vio-

lence and aggression, often toward animals. Two of the boys were currently on probation for vandalism. One of the boys often bragged about setting cats on fire. Although none of the students commented or responded to the presentation, they did listen.

It was some time later when the two boys came to the rehabilitator. Something was tucked under one of the boys' shirt. Tears were in the other boy's eyes. The first boy handed her a baby squirrel. They had found it clinging to its mother who had just been killed by a car. "Here, we don't know if you can help it or not, but we thought you could try," one boy said as he gently gave the baby to the rehabilitator.

The wildlife presentation had brought the boys a role model they had never known existed, one that was kind, compassionate, and demonstrated a reverence for life. Now the boys had a choice. Not all individuals will make the compassionate choice, but some might.

Developmental Needs

According to Erik Erikson, during the developmental stages of infancy and initiative, the exploration of the earth and interaction with other living things is a very important component. These experiences lead to an understanding of one's relationship with all life on earth crystallized later during the period of identity. Interaction with animals (and nature) is an essential component of a child's development (Maier, H., 1965).

Piaget's theory of cognition implies that young children see animals as peers. (Our culture also supports this view in the presentation of animals dressed up in clothing, talking, etc.) Thus, teaching children to be kind to animals, wild and domestic, and to treat animals with respect, is teaching them to also be kind to and respect other people (Maier, H., 1965).

Empathy

Studies report that children who live in homes where there is a pet (which is considered a member of the family) are more empathetic than children in homes where there is not such a pet (Levine, 1986; Bryant, 1986, Malcarne, 1986).

Because children see animals as peers, teaching them to be empathetic with an animal is easier than with a human. With animals, "what you see is what you get." Humans play games. Feeling with animals is easier than feeling with humans because of the animal's simplistic behavior. Empathy will transfer from experience with animals to experiences with humans as the child becomes older. Although studies have been carried out only with domestic animals, wild animals may also offer opportunities for empathy development and transfer.

Case Study

Carol had just been removed from her home by the court and placed in a foster home. She had come to the counseling office to talk. The wildlife rehabilitator had just finished a presentation to Carol's class and had shared with the class a peek at week old baby raccoons in her care. While the rehabilitator finished her conversation with the counselor, Carol sat down beside the orphan baby raccoons. "I know how you feel," she said. "I bet you are really scared. I am. But you will be OK. I know she will take care of you."

Control

Control is a nebulous concept which can refer to internal, or self control, and external control. Marked control problems and manipulation tactics are characteristic of a psychopathic individual. Victims, on the other hand, are people who perceive that they have no control. People with strong self-esteem have self-control. Animal Assisted Activities/Therapy offers a realistic basis for control therapy. With wildlife, one must respect the self control of the animal. And yet, there is opportunity for exhibiting control in subtle ways like putting food out at a feeder or helping an orphan baby get the help it needs to survive.

Animals (and nature) aid in bringing individuals out of themselves

Individuals who are mentally ill or even just have low self esteem focus on themselves. Animals draw these individuals out of themselves. Rather than thinking and talking about themselves and their problems, they watch and talk to and about the animals.

Studies show that in classrooms with pets (not as an object, but part of the room), the students spend more time on task (Katcher, 1992). Wild animals brought into a classroom for a presentation appear to have a similar effect.

Case Example
One counselor works with several special classrooms. One classroom has a "classroom" cat. In each classroom, when the counselor enters, the children gather around her and tell her about their problems. In the classroom with the cat, the children gather, but talk about the cat's antics. Similar behavior exists after the wildlife rehabilitation program in all classrooms. The children want to talk about the animals.

Fulfillment of Psychological Needs

There are several theories naming the basic needs that living beings have. All of the basic needs theories agree that people do have basic needs, and to experience well-being, these needs must be met. Feeling loved, respected, and useful; being needed, accepted, trusted, and important to someone are inherent needs of a mentally healthy person. Caring for a dog or cat can mean the difference between a lonely existence and a fulfilled life. These basic needs can be fulfilled also by caring for wild animal friends. The individuals must perceive they are contributing something important to another's life, whether it is food at a bird feeding station in winter or contributions of service to a wildlife care clinic.

Physical Contact-Touch

Much has been written about the importance of touch for living things. Persons lacking this important physical contact can actually die from the lack of touch (Montagu, 1986). Often, for people, touch from another person is not acceptable, but the warm furry touch of a dog or cat is!

Touch itself is not practical (or often, safe) between human individuals and wildlife. Even wildlife animals selected and involved in education are very much wild animals and may be dangerous for a human to touch. Touch, however, in its metaphorical sense, can occur. Standing close to a large owl, looking into his/her eyes, one does not need to come into physical contact with him/her to be touched by the experience.

For individuals involved as volunteers with wildlife rehabilitation, touch in appropriate ways with the wildlife they are caring for may be an important component for filling this human need.

Wildlife Rehabilitation Release

Wildlife Rehabilitation releases can also be a source of Animal Assisted Activities/Therapy. Song birds, squirrels, ducks, and other appropriate animals can be released near nursing homes, schools, and with private individuals. There are many feelings associated with reestablishing the animal's natural life. "Keeping" an eye on the released individual provides a sense of nurturing. The released animal can become a source of focus for individuals who might not otherwise take note. The entire event can create an awareness of life and wonder.

The above examples of the benefits of Wildlife Rehabilitation as Animal Assisted Activities/Therapy are only a few. Individuals relate to each animal and each story in their own way. The interaction is intensely personal. All animals are important. Even an insect can be a vehicle for Animal Assisted Activities/Therapy. When individuals perceive they have done something to help, to give life or to make life easier for someone else, their own life is enhanced.

A person need not be a wildlife rehabilitator in order to work with the Animal Assisted Activities/Therapy aspects of Wildlife Rehabilitation. A wildlife rehabilitator may give a presentation at a school, and the counselor or teacher can follow up. Counselors in private practice can link up with a rehabilitation project and find ways their client may benefit from interaction with the project. This can be done by a group or an individual doing a project like collecting acorns from a tree on the playground or near the counselor's practice. If a client brings to school an orphaned baby bird, he/she found, the teacher or counselor can contact the wildlife rehabilitator and transfer the animal to them for help. Likewise, counselors in private practice can refer their clients to the rehabilitation center.

Even if a counselor cannot work directly with a rehabilitator or rehabilitation center, knowledge of the importance of the human/animal/nature connection is essential. Likewise, a rehabilitator may not be involved in Animal Assisted Activities/Therapy, but knowledge of the power of the impact of the human-animal relationship is essential.

If you wish for information on wildlife rehabilitation in your area contact your State Department of Natural Resources or write to :

National Wildlife Rehabilitators Association
14 North 7 Ave.
St. Cloud, MN 56303
(612) 259-4086

International Wildlife Rehabilitation Council
4437 Central Place, Suite B-4
Suisun, CA 94585

* If you wish more information about Animal Assisted Activities/Therapy contact:

The Delta Society
321 Burnett Avenue South
Renton, Washington 98055
(206) 226-7357

**Reverence for other living beings enhances ones reverence for ones own life.
Thus, self esteem is enhanced.**

References:

Childhood Cruelty Toward Animals Among Criminals and Noncriminals. (1987, Winter). *Advocate.* American Humane Association.

Bryant, B.K. (1986). The Relevance of Family and Neighborhood Animals to Social Emotional Development in Middle Childhood. University of California, Davis, CA 95616.

Corsini, R.J. & Contributors (1979). Current Psychotherapies (2nd Ed.). Itasca, Ill.: F.E. Peacock Publishers.

Delta Society (1992). Handbook for Animal-Assisted Activities and Animal Assisted Therapy. South Renton, WA.: 321 Burnett Ave. 98055: Author.

Katcher, A. (1992, April). Delta Society Pet Partner Instructor Training. Renton, WA: Delta Society.

Levine, M.M. & Bohn, S. (1986). Development of Social Skills as a Function of Being Reared with Pets. Living Together: People, Animals and the environment. Boston: Delta Society International Conference.

Maier, H. (1965). Three Theories of Child Development. New York: Harper & Row.

Malcarne, V. (1986). Impact of Childhood Experience with Companion Animals on Concern for Humans and Other Animals. Living Together: People, Animals and the Environment: Boston: Delta Society International Conference.

Montagu, Ashley (1986). Touching: The Human Significance of the Skin (3rd Ed.). New York: Harper & Row.

Ruckert, J. (1987). The Four-footed Therapist. Berkeley, CA: Ten Speed Press.

Sussman, M.B. (Ed.). (1985). Pets and the Family, New York: Hayworth Press.

Ulrich, Roger S. (1991, October). The Power of Natural Settings. People, Animals and Nature: Delta Society Tenth Annual Conference, Portland, OR: Delta Society.

Section 10:
SWANS ON THE POND

__Jared DeAlmo__ is a student at Holliman School in Warwick, RI. He is an avid soccer, baseball and basketball player. He lives with his family [mother, father, brother, two dogs, three cats and assorted fish] on a small pond close to a major thoroughfare in the City of Warwick. Jared has been "buddy pals" with his dog, Skippy, since he was 14 months old, We are a family of animal lovers, at times rescuing all sorts of strays, injured birds, rabbits and even a Canadian goose. How lucky we are to have such dear friends who give us their unconditional love and attention and ask so little in return. We are fortunate to be able to look out our window and for a while forget the noise of a busy city and truly enjoy the beautiful creatures who visit our pond.

After a long, cold New England winter we are all anxious for the first signs of spring – those first crocuses, new buds on the trees. But living on a pond I listen for that first shout of, "Mom, the swans are back!" It surely must be spring!

I look out the window and there he is, a beautiful swan. I can tell he is a swan because he is larger than the geese that live on the pond all year long, and his neck is longer. I rush downstairs, grab some bread, and then head for the dock and call, "Come here, swanny, swanny." This year I named him Alfred. I usually jump up and down until I get his attention. Then when he spots me and swims over, I tear up the bread and throw it in the water so he can eat it. I don't touch him because he is a wild animal, and sometimes he hisses at me or my cat, who usually follows me down.

One year the swans stayed all summer and surprised us with babies. They would sometimes leave the pond and walk into the street. To get them safely back in the pond I had to herd them back with pieces of bread. I wondered where they were going. I had a lot of fun that year watching them grow from fuzzy little "swanlings" into big swans.

I wish kids didn't throw rocks at the swans because they scare them away and they could hurt them. Maybe this is why they haven't come back to stay for the summer. I enjoy the swans and I hope I will look out my window next year and see them again.

I am excited, yet somewhat disappointed each spring with the arrival of the swans, only to have them stay for a day or two or sometimes a week or more and then discover that they have left our little pond once again, for what I think must be quieter waters.

The summer we watched our little baby swans grow into beautiful, graceful birds was an exciting time for the whole neighborhood. We all watched over them like they were our children. There were many lessons to be learned from these wild creatures; how caring they are for their young.

Each spring when I hear Jared call, "Mom, the swans are back," I hope this will be the year that once again they will make our pond their home. Maybe next spring!

Jared with the swan.

Section 11:
CHARLIE'S "LOVE FOR ALL" LITERACY PROGRAM

Deborah C. Terilli *of West Greenwich, RI is an R.N., married with two children and has worked seventeen years at Kent County Memorial Hospital on a surgical ortho-pedic unit. She is a graduate of The D.J. University Certificate Program in Pet Assisted Therapy. She now works at Steere House and Rehab Center as a head nurse and brings her big and beautiful golden retriever, Charlie, to work with her. Thus, she continues to provide PAT in conjunction with her nursing job.*

Program Description

Through this program Charlie assists the teacher and the Pet Assisted Therapy Facilitator in helping non-English speaking Rhode Island residents learn to speak and write English, take care of basic medical needs, and learn about important health is-sues. Each session takes approximately forty-five (45) minutes and will be spread out for separate visits. We will use visual aides, photos, paints, crayons, cameras, and a blackboard to help Charlie help others.

The foundation of this program is Charlie's presence and how he helps make learning English fun and enjoyable. Charlie shows each student complete acceptance and in turn gains acceptance from each student. Charlie provides the bridge between teacher and student…and giving each student something to look forward to with each PAT visit

Introduction

Visit I

- Charlie and I introduce ourselves to the class. Each student then introduces him/herself by name. We all state our ages in ENGLISH and write them all on the blackboard along with our names.

- I bring in signs with pictures showing commands for Charlie to do. They include: sit, shake, and down.

- We go through each command with Charlie demonstrating. Then every student comes up to Charlie, gives him a command in English, and then every student can reward Charlie with a treat.

Visit II

- Review *Visit I* commands: sit, shake, down

- ONE NOSE
  TWO EYES

FOUR LEG
Compare with their own parts.

- COLORS: YELLOW FUR – BROWN EYES – BLACK NOSE – PINK TONGUE — with comparisons to their own.

Visit III

- Review previous visits.

- With crayons, have each student color in an outlined picture of Charlie using all correct colors and labeling the correct body part in English (i.e. black nose, brown nose, yellow fur).

Visit IV

- Prepositions – in/out, over/under, through: with Charlie demonstrating.

- Students draw their family tree (with the help of the Feinstein PAT students).

Visit V

- Review prepositions and colors.

- Each student receives an outlined hand. Each student paints in non-toxic paint their own skin color and then they sign their drawing. The kids really enjoy this lesson.

Visit VI

- The pet facilitator verbalizes in plain terms: doctor visits, medications, and reading labels. We include Charlie by discussing his vet visits, preventative care, and animal medications.

- We discuss the advantage of exercise, and how it effects the body. I then listen to everyone's hearts and document each pre and post exercise. Then each student listens to their own, Charlie's, and my heart rate.

- We document all heart rates pre and post exercise on a graph. Show below…

Visit VII

- Students make a Charlie out of play-doe. Making parts, such as eyes, ears, nose, and teeth.

Visit VIII (Last)

- For our last visit we collect copies of all the materials presented at class and make booklets. With a Polaroid camera each student takes a picture with Charlie to put on the front cover of their own booklet.

Outcomes

The students will walk away from this experience with a new knowledge and verbalization of the English language. In addition, we are optimistic they will walk away knowing they are truly accepted for who they are. They can be proud of all they have accomplished.

Charlie and I are fortunate for the opportunity to meet them.

Section 12:
4TH GRADE SCIENCE FAIR REPORT - WHAT IS PET ASSISTED THERAPY?

<u>Stacey Salotto</u> is currently in <u>high school</u> in Norton, Massachusetts. She plays on the high school JV soccer team, as well as for an indoor soccer team. She also plays flute for the high school band. She enjoys reading and writing her own stories. She also enjoys her involvement in youth theater, as a former member of various casts and currently as a stagehand. She lives with her parents and a younger brother, Ross. With her brother, she <u>participated in The D. J. "Respect for Living Things" Program.</u> She now shares her life with a family pet, her black lab, Midnight.

In second grade Stacey wrote an essay which the author, her grandmother, thinks sums up the meaning of this book – <u>D. J. the Dog:</u>

D. J. is white. D. J. goes to nursing homes. D. J. is friendly and beautiful. D. J. gives me her paw. When D. J. goes to nursing homes she makes the people happy. I love D. J. a lot.

Stacey, here years later.

TABLE OF CONTENTS

Purpose: I wrote my Science Fair report on PAT: Pet Assisted Therapy Facilitation because I wanted to learn more about what my grandma does for a job. I thought it was interesting when I learned that animals can help people in many ways. I hope that when people read this report, they will understand what PAT is and will tell other people about it. Maybe some kids who read this report will grow up and become PAT's.

Introduction: The Human Animal Companion Bond is the relationship between people and animals. HCAB has been around for about 12,000 years.

The relationship between animals and people has four stages:

(1) Fear
(2) Worship
(3) Tamed and Controlled
(4) Equals

The first program with animals as Facilitators took place at the York Retreat in England in 1790.

In 1867, another program that helped people took place in Bielefeld, Germany.

An organization called the SPCA, that wanted to protect animals, first started in England in 1822. Then in 1866, it started in the U.S.A. George Angell, in 1868, started the Massachusetts SPCA in Boston. He believed that people had to be taught to treat animals with respect.

In 1918, Edith and Milton Latham, brother and sister, wanted to teach children to be kind to all living things, so they started the Latham Foundation.

Animals helped soldiers after WWII, at the Army Air Corps Convalescent Hospital in Pawling, NY In the 1960s, psychologist, Dr. Boris Levinson, and Drs. Elizabeth and Sam Corson found that people would talk to them more when there was an animal around.

In the 1960s, veterinarian Bill McCulloch found that veterinarians could help people by helping the pets in their lives.

In 1987, the National Institute of Health wanted people to study about how animals help people.

Dr. Leo Bustad taught a course called "Reverence for Life" and set up PAT in schools, prisons, and nursing homes.

Dr. Aaron Katcher and others found out that if you have a pet your blood pressure goes down.

The very first, and at the time the only, college program was at Mercy College in NY in the 1980s, taught by Dr. Stephen Daniel. My grandma, Pearl Salotto, graduated from this program.

Benefits to People: PAT is when companion animals help people with special needs – such as the elderly, children, people who have mental, physical and social problems, and people in hospitals and prisons.

A 1986 survey of doctors found that some of them prescribe animals for people when they are lonely, depressed, inactive, blind, deaf or have high blood pressure, or when people are addicted to drugs.

Pets provide many benefits: Physical, Mental, and Social.

Physical Benefits: Pets help you live longer. A 1977 survey of ninety-two men showed that the men lived longer after one year if they had a pet when they came home from the hospital after having a heart attack or chest pain.

	Had Pets	No Pets	Total
Living	50	28	78
Dead	3	11	14
Total	53	39	92

Researchers think pets helped the men because the pet's owner wants to be healthy and take care of his pet. The men get exercise, which keeps their hearts healthy. Exercise helps because pets need to be walked, brushed, played with and petted. Pets also lower a person's blood pressure.

Mental Benefits: PAT helps people feel less anxious. Pets in hospitals, nursing homes, and other places, help people feel comfortable without their family around.

A study at a dental school showed that when people are nervous and they see fish, they feel better.

Another study showed that children were less nervous, during a reading experiment, when there was a dog around. You can tell if the children are nervous if their blood pressure is high and their heart is beating fast. So when the dog was around, their blood pressure was low and their heart was not beating as fast.

Pets give unconditional love which means that animals love anybody even if they are rich or poor, short or tall, or old or young (see page 140) – they will still love you. Odean Cusak says that "our relationships with our fellow humans may be deep and fulfilling, but they are subject to whims, moods, other obligations, and pressure of everyday life. The pet, however, is always loving, and always willing both to give and to accept affection."

PAT will teach children to trust others because they can trust animals. Animals can teach children confidence in themselves that they can do things.

Social Benefits: Pets can teach children to have responsibility for themselves and to other people. Pets also teach children to respect others.

A study showed that if you saw strangers it would be easier to talk to them if they had a pet. When Robert Andrysco rode in an elevator for ten weeks nobody talked to him. Then he brought his dog with him, for another ten weeks, and people liked the dog and then began to talk to him. Then he went in the elevator alone for ten more weeks. The people continued to talk to him because they made friends when the dog was around.

PAT also helps people in prisons by teaching prisoners to respect life and cooperate with other prisoners and guards. David Lee of Lima State Prison did a study of two groups of twenty-eight prisoners. One group took care of pets and one group didn't. After one year he checked on the behavior of the two groups. The group that didn't have to take care of pets had twelve fights and three suicide attempts. The group that took care of pets had only one fight and no suicide attempts.

Benefits to Therapy Animals: Besides benefiting people, PAT also benefits animals. If puppies are around people for a long time they will get used to them. If that puppy has company the puppy will not be scared, but if you train a dog with a lot of people, like at an institution, the puppy will get to know a lot of people.

Pets who live in an institution get a home and receive care, love and safety, if the program is based on respect for animals.

Seven Benefits to Therapy Animals:

1. They have something fun to do.
2. They feel special and proud.
3. They have something to look forward to. ?
4. They make new friends.
5. They get lots of love.
6. They get to go places with their owners.
7. They get to be with their owner everyday.

PAT Programs: *Companion Birds* – This program was started by Marilyn Larkins in 1985 in Florida. She started this program because she wanted individuals who are elderly to have a friend when they are lonely. She also works with children or adults that are sick or depressed. She works with Cockatiels. She works with Cockatiels because they are sweet, devoted, affectionate, not expensive and live a long time.

The following are comments that people in the program have said about the program:

"What a joy it is to wake up in the morning and have someone to love and be loved by, waiting for you."
"Pretty Boy keeps me from crying a lot of times. I taught him a lot of cute little tricks, as well as to talk. I love that little guy and he loves me."
"Something to look forward to – a reason to get up sometimes. I can't thank you enough for the happiness you've given me: happiness' name is Buddy."

Early Intervention (EI): Kathy Dunn works with her dog, Jetta, at Early Intervention in Fall River, MA. EI helps children who have special needs. Jetta's job is to provide these children with love and opportunity for relationships with animals. Jetta helps these children by helping them with their language and motor skills. These children learn to get along with others. They learn to feel important.
Is Holly Working Today?: Barbara Wood was a counselor at Beatty Elementary School for children with emotional problems, in Ohio. She wrote a proposal to bring her dog, Holly, in as an experiment to see if Holly could help her children. According to Mrs. Woods, the experiment worked. Mrs. Woods found that the children had less absences and had less bad behavior.
Companion Animal Dropout Prevention Program: Dr. Dick Dillman started a program for inner-city elementary school children in Dade County, Florida. He believed "It is not natural for small children to sit still…for a whole day. Rules of conduct can easily be enforced even if the youngsters are allowed to act just like kids." Fourth and Fifth grade kids come to this program because they are bored or can't handle a regular classroom. Even though they aren't in a regular classroom, they still learn everything I do.

Pearl Salotto

<u>Gym</u> – nature hikes, animal tag

<u>Science</u> – nature, animals

<u>Art and Music</u> – projects and songs about animals

<u>Math</u> – make up problems about farm animals. For example: A mother hen had eight chicks and half were male. A fox ate two chicks – one male and one female. If all remaining females grew up and had six chicks of there own, how many baby chicks would there be?

Humane Education teaches children and adults to be kind to animals. In 1933 the National PTA wrote this statement in support of humane education – "Children trained to extend justice, kindness, and mercy to animals become more just, kind, and considerate in their relations with each other. Character training along these lines will result in men and women of broader sympathies, more humane, more law-abiding - in every respect, more valuable citizens."

The D. J. "Respect for Living Things" Program: My grandma, Pearl Salotto, continues the tradition of working with children. She had developed a program where she and her therapy dog, D. J., work with children. This program lets kids, be just kids, where they can have fun and learn too.

<u>Five Results of this program</u>:
1. Kids learn respect, self control, kindness and responsibility.
2. Kids learn that education is important.
3. Kids' self-esteem and self-respect grow and become stronger.
4. Kids learn to take care of their mind, body, and heart.
5. Kids learn that <u>commitment</u> is important in all relationships.

Pearl Salotto developed a four session program.

<u>Session One</u>: *All living things deserve respect.* She gives the kids an assignment to write and illustrate a story about someone they love and how you show love back.

<u>Session Two</u>: *Gifts of a therapy dog.* The kids' assignment is to write an essay on what we can learn from D. J.

<u>Session Three and Four</u>: *Life values – respecting others, yourself, animals and the environment.* Their assignment is to write an essay on what you want to do when you grow up and how you will reach your goal.

After the kids are done with the program they can join the Kids Kindness Club, where they can put their ideas, concerns, and values into action.

<u>Conclusion</u>: I learned that PAT has benefits to people and animals. I learned how long animals have been around to help us. The three main benefits for people are physical, mental and social. There are many benefits to animals also. I also learned about programs that help children and adults.

It is not a common job, but I hope it will be a common job someday because it will help more people.

Bibliography:

1. Arkow, Phil (1992). <u>Pet Therapy: A Study and Resource Guide for the Use of Companion Animals in Selected Therapies</u>. Colorado Springs, CO: Humane Society of Pikes Peak Region.

2. Cusak, Odean (1988). <u>Pets and Mental Health</u>. New York: Hayworth Press.

3. Dillman, Dick, Dr. (pending publication). Play Hard and Learn. In Pearl Salotto, <u>Pet Assisted Therapy: A Loving Intervention and an Emerging Profession</u>.

4. Dunn, Kathy (pending publication). Making Children Happy. In Pearl Salotto, <u>Pet Assisted Therapy: A Loving Intervention and an Emerging Profession</u>.

5. Katcher, Aaron, Dr., et.al (pending publication). Social Interaction and blood pressure Influence of Animal Companions. In Pearl Salotto, <u>Pet Assisted Therapy: A Loving Intervention and an Emerging Profession</u>.

6. Larkins, Marilyn (pending publication). Companion Birds. In Pearl Salotto, <u>Pet Assisted Therapy: A Loving Intervention and an Emerging Profession</u>.

7. Salotto, Pearl (pending publication). <u>Pet Assisted Therapy: A Loving Intervention and an Emerging Profession</u>.

8. Wood, Barbara (pending publication). Is Holly Working Today. In Pearl Salotto, <u>Pet Assisted Therapy: A Loving Intervention and an Emerging Profession</u>.

Section 13:
QUADRAPED CONQUERS CULTURE

Barbara J. Wood, Ph.D., A.C.S.W., L.I.S.W., is an Associate Professor of Social Work. She started work with her pet dog, Holly, as a therapeutic bridge with emotionally disturbed, inner-city children, over ten years ago. She lives with her husband, pet dog Holly, two cats and a Quarter Horse mare, in Columbus, Ohio.

Aiko had been in my social work class the previous semester, and had enrolled in my subsequent, elective course on Animal Assisted Therapy and still she rarely said a word. Aiko came to the U.S. to study innovative, adjunctive therapies to augment her BA Degree she had just completed in Japan. She was a model student, she taped lectures to study later, her written material was extensively documented, well written and accurate. She was ideal, except in one respect. In the American university system, a student is encouraged to participate, ask questions, and contribute to class discussion. However, Aiko never spoke. In addition to the Japanese expectation that students are quietly respectful in class, Aiko seemed to be personally, quite shy. The double factors of culture and personality seemed impenetrable.

She was an excellent student in the Art Therapy course and dedicated to the theory, research, reading and written assignments in my Animal Assisted Therapy course. However, she had difficulty with the field visits. She was apprehensive of a gentle therapy dog that had been comforting troubled school children for years, she avoided the resident cat that sat quietly in patients' laps at the nursing home, and she was extremely anxious when the goat at the Lima prison visit came near her. When the class went to observe a therapeutic riding program, Aiko could barely walk down the aisle of stabled horses. These horses had been carefully selected to work with physically and developmentally handicapped children. Aiko could barely put theory into practice, and the final course assignment was for the students to go horseback riding at the stable where I kept my Quarter Horse.

It was not clear how to help her. My husband and I had her over for dinner, but our dog and three cats only made her visibly uncomfortable. How could the gap be bridged? My life had been enriched by animals. After all, I had gotten my first pony as a child. I had worked with my own dog in therapy with emotionally disturbed children and I had witnessed the pupils' positive transformations in behavior and school attendance. As a therapeutic horseback riding instructor, I had watched children emotionally absorb the horse's strength which helped heal their damaged self-esteem along with improving their physical well-being. Aiko's aversion to animals, especially horses, was as foreign to me as no doubt, my integration of animals into my life personally and professionally was to Aiko. Yet, she stoically endured it all without complaint, until the horseback riding assignment.

Aiko asked to speak to me before the trip to the stable. She never before initiated a conference with me. In a halting conversation, Aiko explained she had never had a pet. In Japan, living space is limited and the closest she had been to even a dog was her neighbor's Pekinese. Horses were particularly overwhelming. In Japan, open land is scarce and she had never even been near an animal bigger than she was. She asked to be excused from the horseback riding trip. It must have taken a great deal of personal courage for Aiko to request an exemption, something such a conscientious student would normally never consider.

If social work clinicians were going to make referrals to treatment facilities that used Animal Assisted Therapies and if they were contemplating using Animal Assisted Therapy in their own practice, they should personally experience its effects. However, I assured Aiko that no one would force her to ride a horse or even make her touch one, but she should accompany the class to the stable. She reluctantly agreed.

Aiko wordlessly joined her classmates in the van to the stable. Aiko stayed with me near the stalls. As I saddled Merry, the quietest and gentlest horse in the barn, Aiko stretched out a tentative hand and petted her. Since there were more students than horses, they were taking turns. I made sure that the least experienced rode the most reliable mounts and the students were obviously enjoying the experience. When her classmates suggested that Aiko take a turn, she demurred. I promised Aiko that if she would just sit on the horse, that I would not leave her and would hold the horse the entire time. A combination of peer pressure and professional persuasion influenced her reluctant acquiescence. She followed me to the mounting block and with much encouragement, got on Merry.

We stood motionless, until Aiko was breathing easily again. Then I suggested that we could walk around the ring, with me leading the docile mare. Aiko nodded yes. Merry had assured many an unsteady rider and walked like she was carrying fragile glass. With every step of Merry's steady stride, Aiko's tenseness lessened. Soon a miraculous transformation I had seen before, began to overtake Aiko. Her chin lifted, her shoulders softened, her rigid back relaxed. After a few laps, I asked Aiko if she would like to try a turn around the ring on her own. She said yes. From then on, Aiko was on Merry's capable back and the two of them soon trotted off into a new world of self confidence.

The Animal Assisted Therapy reading and research findings came to life before our very eyes. Aiko did not want to get off Merry. She had been enjoying her so much she did not realize the class was over and it was time to return to the university. In the van on the way back, Aiko chatted about Merry. She asked if it was possible to ride again. How could it be arranged on a regular basis? When could she start? Would the stable let her come frequently? Aiko, who had rarely said a word in two semesters, was talking up a storm. She dominated the conversation all the way back to the dorms. I immediately signed her up for Beginning Horseback Riding class offered through the Physical Education Department. Merry had conquered culture.

Aiko was transformed. Her classmates reported that she socialized more and other professors commented that she now asked questions and joined in course discussions. Before Aiko returned to Japan, she told me although it would probably be impossible for her to have a horse, she was going to get a dog when she got home. Merry, a wise, gentle mare had shown us all how to put theory into practice.

CHAPTER 5

ANIMALS HELPING US EXPAND OUR HORIZONS AND
REACH OUR POTENTIAL

Section 1:
A CAT - MAN'S BEST FRIEND

__Ruth E. Gallucci__ lives in Warwick, Rhode Island with her husband Frank, daughter Francesca, son Joseph, a cat, Mima, and a dog, Pashi. She has her Masters Degree in Special Education and is currently working on her Certificate of Advanced Graduate Studies in Special Education Administration. Ruth has been a Special Education Teacher since 1988. She advocates for the rights of all people and animals. Ruth respects diversities in humanity and hopes to teach Francesca and Joseph the same. She wishes to thank her mother, Pearl Salotto, for her guidance in becoming the person she is today. Ruth strives to give Francesca and Joseph everything her mother has given to her.

Thinking back on my childhood and on the many "happy times," my thoughts take me back to our family dog. Dutchess, who we lovingly nicknamed "Mutley," came to us when I was about five years old. She brought more happiness and love to our family than we could have imagined. She knew what unconditional love meant. We learned from her how to give it back.

My roommate and I read the ad in the paper, "long haired kittens – free to a good home." The next day we went to pick out our new pets. Arriving at the house we were amazed to see a hundred or so cats of various colors and sizes. Inside the house the owner had multiple kittens of multiple litters. "Take any one you want, except this one," she said, pointing to a tiny and frail multi-colored kitten with swollen eyes. "She's not doing very well." As I glanced over at her she looked up at me. I saw much love, so much hope. She needed a chance – don't we all! My roommate picked a pretty white kitten with orange and black patches. Her eyes were also swollen. My decision had been made. I took home the black and brown kitten with the white chest, nose and paws, who at the time looked so sick.

My roommate named her kitten Willobie. I would call mine Mima. After numerous visits to the veterinarian and many mornings wrestling with the kittens to allow me to apply their medications, their eyes finally healed We learned weeks later that they were taken from their mother too early. We had to teach them and be patient. They did not always clean themselves. My roommate became an expert at bathing kittens. They also did not know how to use the litter basket. It took quite some time to master that feat. Mima came to look at me as her mother. She would sleep on my head at night. She would roll over to have her stomach rubbed and then thank me by licking my face like a loyal dog! This was the beginning of our friendship.

Mima proved to be my greatest entertainment and my very loyal friend. She has initiated many games which take place routinely in our home. My husband and I have found endless hours of enjoyment watching and playing with her. She enjoys interacting with us in games of hide-and-seek and tag. She seems to enjoy having us chase her around the house. She loves hiding on the steps and peeking her head up just enough to get a quick glimpse. she meows loudly when she wants the water turned on for a drink, a door opened, or her stomach rubbed. One of her favorite times is dinner time. She sits next to me in "her chair" and gently pats my arm for a piece of chicken. My husband gets the same treatment while eating strawberry yogurt. When we go out she waits in the window only to greet us at the door upon our return. She loves to be picked up, to wrap her paws around my neck and to kiss my face or to sit on my shoulders and purr. She has never been known to sleep on our bed unless my husband is out of town, when she sleeps next to me all night.

The love I have for Mima can only be understood by someone who feels the same way about a pet. I often think of my wedding day. My grandparents were in Rhode Island from out of town, staying at a local hotel. The night before the wedding my grandmother had a stroke. Needless to say this was an awful experience. My grandmother insisted that we go ahead with the wedding and honeymoon. While away on our honeymoon, with my new husband, my grandfather stayed in my home to be close to my grandmother, who needed further hospitalization. Along with being worried about my grandmother, I worried about Mima. Would she accidentally get out the door as my grandfather left and returned? Would she be there when I returned from my trip? Anyway, my fears turned out to be unfounded. My grandmother recovered in many ways and Mima was fine. She had never been known to like people, besides my husband and I and a "chosen few." Miraculously, "Pa" and Mima had built a nice relationship. She would sit on his shoulders while he ate breakfast and sit on the bed as he fell asleep at night. She gave him the love he needed during that very difficult time and he gave her the company to ease her loneliness.

Joseph, born four years later, is also loved by Jemima..

The stories of Mima and the endless pleasure she has given to us are numerous. I could not possibly state them all. Instead, I will end with our most recent situation. As mentioned earlier, Mima has never been friendly with other people, especially children. She has been known to bat her paw or hiss at children in our home. We were terribly concerned that she would be a danger to our new baby. My husband and I spent many hours discussing Mima's behavior, "what ifs," and possible options. The day we brought our daughter home was the happiest day of my life and yet the saddest. I cried all night, believing we would have to find a new home for Mima. To our astonishment a miracle took place. Mima never hissed or batted at the baby. In the beginning she would look at her with curiosity and smell her feet and hands. As days passed she seemed to care more and more for the baby's well-being. She would run to her when she cried. Recently she has been licking the baby's hands and head.

Did Mima somehow understand that the baby was staying? Did she know she only had one chance? Does she actually care for the baby, as she does us? Whatever the reason, what a wonderful gift she gave to our family.

In a world so filled with sadness, who would think a small cat could be such a good friend.

Frankie and Jemima - Best Friends!

Section 2:
"HEALTHY" BABIES ARE BROUGHT UP BY "HEALTHY" PARENTS
(Pearl Salotto)

As my daughter, the previous author, stated, "In a world so filled with sadness, who would think a small cat could be such a good friend," one might also ask, in a world so filled with challenges and dangers in bringing up children, who would ever think that parents modeling respect for animals might go a long way toward enhancing the possibility of their children making the right choices as they move through life.

Healthy parents need to not only feed and clothe their children, and see that they receive appropriate medical care, but also need to model and LIVE values for life.

Among the values we must model for our children are honesty, respect, fairness, kindness, ability to be calm, to listen, to share, and to trust. A very important value that we must model for our children, one not frequently talked about or even thought about – is – respect for living things.

When children are brought up to see parents being tender with anything that expresses life – whether is be a ladybug crawling along a window sill, a neighbor's dog lonely and starving, tied to a stake in the backyard, a woman who is elderly who needs a seat on a bus or a youngster in a wheelchair munching on french fries with his family at McDonalds – they will have taken a giant and powerful step toward raising their children to becoming compassionate and empathic human beings.

Ruthie, Frankie, and D.J. – A parent living good values.

Pearl Salotto

Whether or not parents like animals is completely irrelevant. Whether they treat animals with respect and appreciate them for who they are is very relevant and sends a powerful message to their children as to the meaning of life, of feelings, of responsibility, of nurturing. They will also be giving their children the opportunity to know the joy and comfort of interacting with all living beings. My grandson Ross' tears were turned into smiles and laughter as D.J. got up from the floor spontaneously and comforted him after he slammed his finger in a cabinet door. Luckily for Ross, he had grown up in a family where pets were allowed to be themselves, providing the comfort only they can give.

Parents who recognize this, through intuition or through education, will be raising children who will give respect back to them in decades to come, who will be more content within themselves, and who will be more likely to become the responsible committed fathers and mothers and pet owners of the future, thus making our society a healthier, friendlier, and more peaceful place.

Joseph and Paschie - Best Friends!

OUTLINE OF IDEAS FOR PARENT WORKSHOPS

I.   **Introductory Concepts:** All benefits of a companion animal to children are contingent on the fact that the pet is considered a member of the family.

II. **Benefits to children** — Opportunities for:

Responsibility	Unconditional Love
Companionship	Enhanced Self-Esteem
Exercise	Opportunity to Nurture
Humor	Someone to Talk to,
Commitment	Someone to Trust
Expression of Joy	
Enhanced Appreciation of Living Things	
Internalization of Life-long Values	

III. **Important Considerations:** Before a pet comes into the family —

   a)   Have the puppy or older dog evaluated for temperament.

   b)   Make sure that each and every member of the family understand that:

   1. A pet is a living thing.
   2. A pet has needs and feelings and deserves love and respect.
   3. A pet can bring boundless joy, but also requires sacrifices.
   4. A pet is a 15+ year commitment.

IV. **Research** has shown that when pets in the family are considered members of the family, then children will develop:

   a) more self-esteem
   b) more sensitivity and empathy

V.   **Parental Responsibilities:** It is important that parents —

   a)   supervise children when interacting with the pet.
   b)   serve as role models of love, care, and protection for the pet.
   c)   praise demonstrations of care and respect for the pet.
   d)   help children realize that the pet has feelings just as they do (i.e. happiness, sadness, pride, jealousy, embarrassment, stress, etc.).
   e)   help children realize that they are unique and special, as is the pet.

f) help children realize rules are made for the pet's safety, just as for the children's.

g) help children realize if a pet makes a mistake, we still love him/her, just as we do with a child.

h) help the child realize that pets deserve to have their love returned, just as people do.

i) help children realize that commitment and sacrifice are necessary in all relationships in order to receive the rewards of said relationships.

j) help children realize that pets thrive better, as we do, in calm, peaceful environments.

k) help children realize that we need to take care of ourselves in order to take care of our pets and others.

l) help children realize that, just as companion pets give unconditional regard to all, regardless of race, religion, health, or economic status, that this is a good example for us all.

m) help children realize that pets need education (training), just as they do.

VI. **Final Thoughts:** Pets in families where there is appropriate supervision, modeling, and communication can lead to internalization of values and a commitment to attitudes and behaviors of kindness and respect toward all living things, for a lifetime, including self, others, animals and the environment.

All Love Is A Gift allowing the recipient to display KINDNESS
A Companion Animal in the family is one such Magnificent Gift

Midnight keeps Anthony company.

214

Section 3:
CHRISTMAS ANGEL

__Jan Hindley__ recently received her Master's Degree in Social Work and is currently employed as a Substance Abuse Counselor at CODAC Treatment Agency. Having spent much of her life working towards the humane treatment of animals, she is a firm believer in the power of the human-animal bond to improve conditions for all living creatures, and plans to incorporate this belief in her social work career.

Although I have shared many joyful and sad experiences with the animals that have entered my life, I chose to tell about a particular feline who greatly changed another's life, and as a result, impacted on the lives of many other people.

During Christmas season several years back, an elderly couple was busy preparing for the holidays. Although in their eighties, they were quite self-sufficient, and the woman was well-known for her strong opinions and rather domineering ways. She made the decisions in the family and her husband carried them out. This had been their manner of life together and it had carried them through more than fifty Christmas seasons successfully. During this season, however, things would not go as planned. The elderly gentleman was suddenly hospitalized because of a blood clot in his leg. His wife refused to spend the holidays at any of her children's homes, saying she was quite capable of doing for herself.

On the day before Christmas, I received a phone call from this woman, saying that she had a skinny stray cat at her door, and would I take her in? Having six cats at the time, I declined the offer, but suggested that I could bring over cat food, a litter box and litter. The woman agreed to give it a try and a marvelous relationship was born. The cat became her Christmas "Angel" and worked her magic that Christmas. The woman began to experience taking care of someone else's needs. Reluctantly, she began to get up at 5:30 a.m. to let the cat out, and to do the same at 6:00 a.m. to let her back in!

Sharing her life with this "Angel" has allowed tenderness, humor, and caring, buried in this woman, to surface. This change had helped her to reach out to those around her, and has made it possible for those who viewed her as unapproachable to reach out to her. The presence of this "skinny stray" transformed this woman's life from one of preoccupation with her own comforts to one of concern about the comforts of others.

What a wonderful gift "Angel" brought for Christmas!

Section 4:
THE TELLINGTON TTOUCH

Linda Tellington-Jones *is the internationally recognized expert who created "The Tellington TTouch," a technique that promotes healing, training, and communicating with animals. She is the author of several books, and videos on horse training and is founder of TTEAM, the Tellington-Jones Equine Awareness Method. She lives in Santa Fe, New Mexico.*

Sibyl Taylor *is the author of several non-fiction books. She lives in New York City.*

> Linda Tellington-Jones' work over many years has enhanced the well-being of animals of all sizes and descriptions. Through her ability to communicate with animals who are sick, injured, angry, depressed, or bored, and through her ability to teach her pioneering methods of therapeutic touch to others, she has tremendously enhanced the quality of life, not only of the animals with whom she has worked, but the people who care about these animals, as well. Her heartwarming story of Joyce is presented here with her permission from her book, The Tellington Ttouch, to acquaint our readers with her visionary and transforming method.

^ *Joyce*

One of the most affecting moments in my life with animals was the recognition expressed to me by a Burmese python named Joyce. Joyce is eleven feet long and about the circumference of an average man's upper arm. She's very beautiful, with her light and dark brown body designed like a camouflage jacket and her diamond-like head. I met Joyce at the San Diego Wild Animal Park Zookeepers Conference. At the invitation of Art Goodrich, historian of the American Association of Zookeepers and longtime keeper at the San Diego Zoo, I was to work on a number of animals, among them a reptile, a bird, and an exotic cat. The cat turned out to be Speedy, the hyperactive serval we met in Chapter Three. The reptile was Joyce.

I had already had the experience of working with an injured python at the Los Angeles Zoo and with many other snakes in various zoos around the world, and I was looking forward to learning more. I was told the snake was owned by people who had kept her as a pet until she grew too big to keep at home. Now she was on loan, one of the animals starring daily in the Park's educational Critter Encounters show.

Joyce was just fine for the show, I was told, but apparently, every year at some point she suddenly grew sluggish and miserable. Also, she suffered from a recurrent respiratory ailment.

The Critter show was headquartered in the midst of the park's lushly landscaped eighteen-hundred-acre spread. I waited to meet Joyce in the training area, a cement apron about twelve by sixty feet. A show was in progress down the hill from the training compound and I could hear the magnified voice of the lecturer-trainer echoing over the loudspeakers.

When Joyce was first brought out to me, she was placed on top of one of those round stools on which elephants balance their feet. She raised her head inquisitively.

Since the python was having respiratory problems at the time, my intention was to demonstrate how to work on her to prevent recurrence and to help relieve the congestion.

Gently, using a Raccoon TTouch no heavier than a three, I placed my hands on the smooth scales of her body in the area about three or four feet behind her head. Even this light contact, however, made Joyce very twitchy. And when I decreased the pressure to a one she still continued to twitch her skin. Like people with congestion and inflammation of the lungs, she may have had a sore back.

Switching to the flat-handed and tranquilizing comfort of the Lying Leopard TTouch, I slowed my breathing and kept up very light circles. As I concentrated on the snake, all verbal mental chatter vanished and the world became centered in my listening hands and the connection between us. Intuitively, my fingers moved to a position under her.

I picked her up and released her very gently at one-inch intervals using the rhythmic six-second hold-and-release pattern of the Belly Lift, a TTouch we usually employ on any animal in shock or with a digestive problem.

After a few minutes of work Joyce began to slide down from her perch on the stool. She moved in slow undulations, like a rope uncoiling, until she lay in the center of the encircling group of keepers, her body forming a shape like two joined Ss. Then, as we watched, she stretched out completely, straight as a stick, to her full eleven feet.

The keepers were amazed. Joyce lived in a small enclosure and was taken out once a day. I began to get an inkling of what might be causing the respiratory problem. A snake's lungs [pythons have two but some other species have one] are not limited just to the upper part of the body but run half its entire length. When a snake doesn't have a chance to exercise or can't stretch out fully, the effect is somewhat like what happens to a human who is encased in a corset all day long.

Joyce's lungs were probably in need of a good workout. So several assistants and I stood side by side and formed a line the length of Joyce's body. Like a human wave, one after another, we gently and slowly picked up and released her body in the Belly Lift and then repeated the action, though this time we very slowly moved the skin up just a quarter of an inch and then released it in what we now call the Python Lift, in honor of Joyce.

After that we stood back to see what Joyce would do next. She raised her head, looked around at us, and then went slowly off for a luxurious slither.

As I watched her gliding across the unyielding cement, I suddenly recalled a video I had seen of a python swimming in the Amazon River, and soon we were all giving Joyce a bath. She loved it, and reached her head up as we splashed refreshing water all over her body.

Afterward, we formed our snake-treatment conga line again, each of us working on a different part of her with Lying Leopard circles. This awakened her torpid respiratory system and allowed her to sense her entire body, all eleven feet from head to tail.

So far we had worked with Joyce forty minutes. I decided it was time to try the TTouch again on what had been the sensitive and especially twitchy area a few feet behind her head. This time she was perfectly quiet and didn't twitch at all.

As I moved over her in the Raccoon position, she curved her body and brought her nose around to my hands to observe the entire proceedings, hovering there with such obvious and intelligent curiosity that all we humans were fascinated.

Afterward, I sat back on my heels in front of Joyce and continued lightly working her head while we discussed her case. As I talked she began to slide gradually up my body until she reached my right shoulder, where she paused for a moment before moving very slowly and gracefully across my left shoulder. From here she rose in a fluid motion until she came to rest with the side of her head against me just above my left ear.

I will never forget the sensation of her careful gentleness, the soft way she moved, barely stirring my hair before she pressed her head against mine with a pressure as light as a soap bubble. She hovered there, head to head, for what seemed like a full minute, sending a clear and unmistakable feeling of thanks and acknowledgment. Nothing like that had ever happened to me. I was absolutely astonished, but there was more to come.

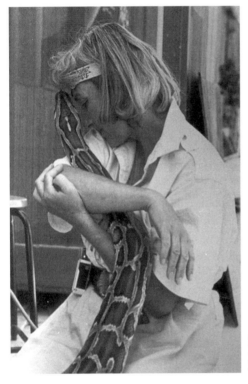

Joyce thanking Linda Tellingon-Jones. Courtsey of TTEAM

Two days later I was out on stage, demonstrating the TTouch to the approximately one hundred members of the conference who sat facing me in chairs arranged beside a small artificial lake. Joyce was brought out. As soon as she was released from her carrying case she headed straight to where I waited in a kneeling position. When she arrived in front of me, she rose up before me like an Indian fakir's snake rising from a basket. She hovered for a moment at eye level, and then flicked her tongue against my forehead in a salute so light it was like the graze of a snowflake. It felt exactly like a gesture of greeting. Having done that, she slid back down across my lap to wait quietly for me to begin my demonstration.

Section 5:
OVERVIEW OF THE JINGLES AWARD

<u>Bill Ballaban</u> found a second, albeit unpaid, career in the Human-Animal Bond, upon retirement from a career that began in the days of live television. His interests range from veterinary education and practice to the goal of <u>getting more assistance animals into service</u>. Among his activities, he has involved himself at the School of Veterinary Medicine, University of California, Davis; The Center for Animals in Society at the Vet School; the Delta Society, Assistance Dogs International; and he serves on two committees of the California Veterinary Medical Association.

[According to the author, Pearl Salotto] Attending Bill Ballaban's presentations of the Jingles Awards at Delta Society conferences from 1987 to 1992 and getting to know the people-pet teams personally, has not only been among the highlights of my career, but has taught me the power of the Human Companion Animal Bond in ways that no textbook could do.

The Beginning

When I attended my first Delta Society conference in Texas I made a presentation to the Board of Directors for a program that was then called RX Pet (Prescription Pet). Some of the board members viewed me as a little crazy and others sought me out to discuss the project further. I have no idea what deliberations were made by the board, but several years later at the International Conference in Boston in 1986 the first Assistance Animal Awards were presented.

The selection process for the awards consisted of letters of nomination, supporting letters by health care professionals, people who observed the benefits of partnership with the animal, and a veterinarian's certification of good health and proper care. Newspaper articles and other publicity and awards the animal might have recieved were usually included. This material was then sent to a panel of judges around the country with evaluation sheets, consisting of ten areas to be rated on a one to ten basis, plus an overall one to ten rating. These sheets were then collated and composite scores calculated with the highest score being the winner in their category. The animal with the highest number of points became the overall winner.

For the first two years I served as a judge as well as Emcee of the event. It was a very emotionally draining experience. It took a great deal of reading and rereading of the material submitted before one could even start to make a judgment. I think that the entry that evoked the largest lump in my throat scored highest on my evaluation sheet. I finally decided that I could no longer judge and then have to write an introduction for the winner, when I knew that first and second might have been as close as a point or two. I salute all of the others who have acted as judges. It was not an easy task, but an enriching experience.

The first step after the winners were selected was to telephone them to introduce myself as the Master of Ceremonies for the presentation of the awards and attempt to get a feel for their individuality, to elicit some information that may not have been in the judging material, and possibly to answer any questions and ease any apprehensions they might have. From my experience in live television, I have found that you can never prepare too much for such an event. My final task, in the later years, was to edit the video tape of the winner at work that had been submitted and write introductions that, hopefully, would evoke both tears and laughter - to make the audience remember what they had seen and heard. When I heard that someone on the way to the event told a friend, "..it is a two handkerchief affair," I knew that I had achieved my goal.

As no one was assigned to shepherd the winners when they arrived at the conference, I took on the obligation to make certain that they enjoyed all that the conference had to offer and that they felt like the very special teams that they were. By doing this, I was able to learn more about the relationships that they enjoyed with their animals, although I rarely changed my introduction. In order to maximize the effect of the presentations I would dine with the winners the night before the luncheon to brief the recipients on what type of response I thought might be appropriate, give them a copy of my introduction to make certain that there was nothing that would offend them, and again answer any questions that might arise. The order of introduction was based on what I hoped would make the most impact on the audience and in no way reflected on the importance of any of the winners.

Prior to the award luncheon we would seat the winners convenient to their access to the stage and rehearse the Guide Dog winner so that the animal would know where to go and his partner would know where to find the microphone. I feel that all of these preparations were well worth the time and contributed to the success of the event.

Retrospective

Although the awards were presented to the animals, it is impossible not to think of the winner without considering the human partner. I have never seen a stronger bonding or more love and devotion than I was privileged to witness at close range with the winners. There was not a team that did not have a wonderful story to tell. These are memories that fuel my efforts on behalf of the whole field of assistance animals and the human-animal bond. It would be impossible for me to select any one of the thirty-five winners and their people as being a favorite or most outstanding during the seven year period that I was associated with the Jingles Awards. The one that I was with was my favorite at that time. I cannot even come to terms with the idea that there were any nominees who were not winners. True, some of the teams do stand out in my memory more than others, but that is for reasons unrelated to the performance of the animal alone. Let me share some reminisces of the winning teams.

Abdul

No narrative of assistance animals can be made without the inclusion of Abdul. Not only was he the first Service Dog, but he was the pioneer who proved that it could be done. And Kerri, his person, bright, articulate, and an eloquent spokesperson for Service Dogs and individuals with disabilities, was a delight. Much was to be learned from this young woman. The one story that she told and I have repeated scores of times - was about the time when after a few years of service she felt that Abdul was entitled to a vacation. She went to a farm in Oregon where Abdul could romp and play dog and her mother could take care of her needs. Upon arrival she released Abdul and told him to go play. He did. For about an hour he explored his new surroundings and then returned to Kerri's side, which he did not leave again. I have used this story to let people know that the animals love their person and love their work and are not exploited as some would have you believe.

Odin

Odin taught me about the ability of an assistance animal to learn additional behaviors on his own. Odin was trained for William who is both blind and deaf. It took the program over a year just to find the right dog and about the same to train him. The first meeting with Odin and William was at lunch in Los Angeles. As there was no way for me to communicate with him except through his instructor, we met at the Braille Institute. The foremost thing that I found remarkable was what a happy young man William was. He was delighted to talk about Odin, whom he referred to so many times in his acceptance as, "my best friend." He was not afraid to go anywhere. He had such confidence in his Black Labrador. Among the amazing stories that he told was that during the big earthquake in Los Angeles, Odin came and took William's hand in his mouth and led him into the backyard to safety. When Odin first came home and was hungry, he just picked up his bowl and brought it to William. Of course he understood some sign language and learned more.

Shantih

Shantih was the first Akbash dog I had ever met. Jean, the woman he brought, is one tough lady. As the director of a program there is not much she cannot do from her chair with Shantih at her side. But when Shantih threw his body in the way of Jean's chair as it was sliding backward and was severely injured, and with a long recuperative period, Jean could only think of the day that "Shan" would be healed and out of pain. Nothing was too good for Shantih, and there was nothing that Shantih would not do if Jean should ask.

Blaze

I learned about dedication and devotion to a dog from Dan who, when he lost his sight knew that he wanted a Guide Dog, but health problems prevented his going into training at the time. When he regained his health Dan started training with Blaze. Again his health failed and he was hospitalized, but not before he promised Blaze he would return. And return he did. After a kidney transplant, he and Blaze finished their schooling and graduated, right into the ranks of the winners. As an aside to this love affair, Dan, a college student, is teaching Blaze Russian.

Pearl Salotto

Kosmic

As a former Producer/Director I always considered the planning of a production as most important. When I worked in TV there were two things that I never wanted in a show – Children and Animals – a directors nightmare. So when Kosmic became Service Dog of the Year, young Travis came with him. A bright juvenile with the charm and personality that usually takes many years to develop. I had no idea what Travis was like before he partnered with Kosmic, but I am fairly certain that the fame that came with Kosmic was a major factor in his development. When I discussed with Travis how he would be most comfortable making his remarks and offered several options he replied with a statement that I translated as meaning, "Don't worry about me old man, I'll take care of everything." And take care of everything he did. I could not have staged his entrance nor put words into his mouth, half as appropriate as what Travis presented with the assurance of a veteran performer.

Of Tears Of Joy

Very few of us are ever in a position where we have to acknowledge an individual recognition given to our animals. One would imagine that pride would be the driving sentiment. Some of our people obviously held a much deeper and stronger emotion than pride when making their acceptance. I restrained myself from asking what went through their minds as the tears poured forth lest I tarnish their memory of the moment.

Rerun

A most moving occasion was when Rerun was being honored. His partner Robert was a hearing impaired dairy farm manager, who, until Rerun came into his life, had been withdrawn from society. With the arrival of Rerun into his life, Robert's attitude of life and his impairment changed, particularly when Rerun pushed him off of the road as a car was bearing down on him. Robert was eloquent as he told of his experiences with his canine partner until his voice broke and a flood of tears prevented him from continuing. One could feel the effect that this had on the audience and the support and understanding that they gave to Robert.

Brandy

When Sandy accepted for the Therapy Horse winner Brandy, the outpouring of feeling was understandable. The horse who had aided her physical rehabilitation had died prior to the presentation and most naturally she was overcome by emotion. Several years later I viewed a different sentiment from Sandy as she smiled and told us that the prize money that Brandy had won provided a successor horse who had just arrived at the program.

Dixie

In 1988 the Guide Dog and Overall Winner was Dixie. Doreen was very eloquent on behalf of her partner and made a fine response to the honor that had been accorded Dixie. That is until the very end when emotion took over and with tears streaming down her face she appealed to the audience from many disciplines present to "keep on doing what you are doing". I don't doubt that the those present had their energies renewed.

Oscar Ray Leonard And Laddie

Perhaps the most perplexing of the tearful acceptances were by Pam, who represented Oscar Ray Leonard, the feline winner as Social Animal and Mary, speaking on behalf of Laddie, the Therapy Animal of the Year. Mary is a therapist who deals with children on a daily basis.

One would tend to think that she would be accustomed to the role that Laddie played in her therapy sessions and that recalling them would be rather routine by now. It restored my faith in the humanity of the scientific community.

Pam runs the Animal Control Department for a Texas town. After dealing with day-to-day operations of that type of facility, conventional wisdom would seem to be that one becomes hardened to the abuse and waste of animal life, as a defense. But Pam too showed an emotional involvement that belied the stereotype of animal control workers. As she stroked Oscar, who quietly rested on a table in front of her, her speech was interrupted from time-to-time as she caught control of her emotions and wiped the tears from her eyes. Once again the audience showed patience and understanding while Pam regained her composure.

Nemo

The awards presentations were not without humor. Almost every one of the recipients injected some amusing anecdote. One that sticks in my memory was told by Mary. Nemo had won the Guide Dog honors and Mary recounted her experience of getting accustomed to being guided and putting her trust in her new partner. As she was walking down the sidewalk one day, Nemo stopped, obviously there was some obstruction ahead or above. Mary checked and could detect nothing that would be a danger to her so she commanded "forward". After several repetitions Nemo failed to respond. More insistently, Mary urged Nemo on and on he went. Mary walked through a lawn sprinkler. She had learned to put her faith in her new partner the hard way.

Jake

When Micky accepted for Jake she did so with great enthusiasm. Her wonderful Bull Mastiff Therapy dog looked so bored. There seems to be something intrinsically humorous in watching such a large dog exhibit such gentle and anthropomorphic attitudes while being lauded for his good works.

Pearl Salotto

Little Irish Maggie

Another side benefit of the awards was to inspire new or additional careers. Little Irish Maggie inspired Ann to take on the task of being an advocate for all Hearing Dogs and the program who trained her. Ann serves on the board of the program and gives her time to any effort to further the acceptance of hearing dogs.

Booker

Booker, a handsome Golden Retriever, who was there for Carol in so many ways, brought her to the awards, where she learned about the work of the Delta Society. Being around the conference for just a few days influenced Carol to become an activist for individuals with disabilities. She started a consulting business and never missed an opportunity to speak to a group to inform them of what was going on in the world in which she lives. And then there was the story of the additional duty that Booker took upon himself. Because of Carol's disability she was unable to go upstairs to check on how her sons were keeping their room. Not to worry, Booker would go upstairs and if there were socks on the floor he would bring them to Carol, who would then know that it was time to remind the boys to clean up their room.

Dawn

One of the educational surprises that we had came in the first year. Dawn, a rescued Doberman who won as the Guide Dog of the Year worked for a husband and wife team. Norman and Cindy would alternate days that Dawn would take them to their respective jobs. As Norman was rather tall and Cindy short, Dawn had two harnesses. Of course she would guide them both when required, with Cindy on Norman's arm and Dawn piloting them both.

Echo

Six years later Echo, the Hearing Dog winner, alerted both Jean and Bill to all of the standard sounds for which she had been trained. Again the intelligence of assistance animals was highlighted in that Echo knew that she did not have to alert the Case children.

Nugget

Larry came with Nugget whom I considered the most educated Hearing, if not any, Dog. Larry was in grammar school when he was teamed with Nugget, and they were together when Larry graduated from college. So I always felt that Nugget had attended more classes than any dog in history and should have picked up something. Larry wrote a beautiful tribute to Nugget after he had made the decision to give Nugget the "good sleep". It helped me when I had to make the same decision years later.

Emily

One of those events that as they say, knocks your socks off, was another marvelous surprise for me and the audience. A wonderful Otter Hound named Emily brought Debbie to the awards. Debbie was married with two children and working part-time while studying for a degree.

Cerebral Palsy did not hold Debbie back, and with the arrival of Emily in her life she was living at an unbelievable pace. Debbie told me that she had a surprise, would it be O.K.? I could do nothing but approve. (If only these people realized what they were doing to my digestion.) After Emily and Debbie had been introduced, Debbie presented a plaque that she had laboriously carved, thanking Emily's trainer, then she read a poem that she had written conveying the freedom that Emily had given her. Saying that it was a poignant moment is like saying the Taj Mahal is a nice little building. How I was able to continue is a mystery to me.

Kim

That there are people and institutions who resist giving assistance animals their place in the sun is beyond belief. Kim and Randy faced that problem when they went to college, and of all places at a college for the deaf. A landlord would have no animals. For a time they had to live in Randy's car and endure a physical attack which injured Kim as she tried to protect her charge. Now, as the Hearing Dog of the Year, Kim seemed slightly bored and nonchalantly sat at Randy's feet as he spoke and signed of what they had toughed out and how "Animals are God's handiwork" and of the unconditional love that Kim gives him, that "Animals are like flowers popping up between the cracks in the sidewalk...animals can be stepped on too. " The audience was absorbed in his words, as he was telling them how the work they do on behalf of animals is so important. Again more fuel to fire the efforts of those in attendance.

Children

Having had a career in the entertainment industry I remember an old motion picture proverb; put a child and an animal at risk and you will have a hit. Our animals certainly did not put the children at risk, rather they helped the at-risk children. We only had a couple of minutes of videotape to show the animals at work, but in combination with the history of the Therapy Animals presented by their people, their work would soften the hardest of hearts.

Cheer

A picture I retain is that of Cheer, who worked in a Connecticut classroom with Betty, leading special needs children through a maze of obstacles and then through a tunnel that they would refuse to enter on their own, but eagerly followed Cheer.

Laddie

Laddie who worked with Mary in therapy sessions. Unknown to the children he would be controlled by Mary to make them speak or whatever the occasion called for. Who could resist his appealing face and eagerness?

Lemonade and Gandolf

It was impossible to bring the equine winners to the event but I always had the desire to visit them. I most remember the accomplishments of Lemonade and Gandolf.

It would be impossible to truly separate what the horse achieved without mention of the owners. When judging Lemonade, the most outstanding memory I have is that of four Vietnam Veterans who are physically challenged and how they became rodeo champions. The fact that Lemonade's owner Mary was an Occupational Therapist at Fitzsimmons Army Hospital, was quite fortuitous for these veterans. But it was the training and gentle nature of the horse that allowed these challenged equestrians to gain the confidence to compete.

One of the times that made me frantic was when, at the briefing dinner the night before the awards were to be presented, Donna, who was to receive the award for her Therapy Horse Gandolf, told me that she didn't know that she was counted on to make a talk. Since her accident had impaired her speech she had not spoken in public. Without showing my panic I said that of course it was expected. The next day Donna delivered an acceptance that should have made Gandolf proud. Another example of how pride in their animal made a person rise to the occasion.

Some People

Thinking back on the history of the Assistance Animal Awards it was an opportunity for me to meet some great people. I have written of some of them with their animals yet there are two that I admire and regard in a special way. They are among the people who work so hard training and fund-raising and trying their very best to put more teams together.

The first is Sheila, who directs a program that was a three-time winner of awards. She was the first to recognize the value of an award dinner for her own program, with their winner being automatically nominated for the Assistance Animal Award. She made me feel a bit more useful.

One of the few people I have met through this all who understood my sense of humor, is P.J. She was kind enough to let me know the value of the publicity that was generated in her area when Emily won her award. Again, she was one of the few who took full advantage of the basic idea.

Final Thoughts

Of the many remarks directed to me over the years, the one that gives me the warmest feelings were made by a much admired scientist who had been a skeptic of the value of the Jingles Awards. He came to me and said that over the years he had felt that presenting these stories was an exploitation of people and animals, but, that he had now changed his view. I had learned that the scientific types do not like their emotions involved, but I hold that what we presented showed the absolute results of all of their studies. All of the scientific investigation is of less value unless it is put to a practical application.

Judging from the observations that were made on conference evaluation forms and the many comments that have been made to me, I can only conclude that the opportunity to hear the comments people will make about their animal in a friendly and understanding venue brings forth the real emotional value of assistance animals and enables those who have only companion animals to truly appreciate what unexpected benefits we receive from our partners. Although the scientists admit that anecdotal evidence is far from scientific study, the large segment of the population (without the background to understand scientific data) know in our hearts that what we do to provide and promote the benefits of animals for individuals with disabilities is not only valid, but genuinely enriches the lives of both people and animals.

Bill Ballaban with friends, Babe (left) and Commander (right).

Another benefit to me, because of my participation in the awards, was an education about individuals with disabilities. At first, in my ignorance, I was somewhat timid in the way I would deal with the human partners. But through the years I was taught by some, and learned from others, that sensitivity to a disability does not mean that you cannot say, "next time you see me . . ." to a visually impaired person. I would not speak as rapidly, as I tend to do, when a conversation is being signed to a hearing impaired person. Look people in the eye because they are people first, albeit with a disability that they can deal with. The question seems to be, "Can we?"

If I gained nothing more from the experience with this group of people and their animals, it was humility. I will miss the annual event that always revived any flagging resolve to put forth the effort to prepare for the occasion, and some of the other work that I do. To be able to observe the reciprocal love and interdependence between man and animal that gives independence and purpose to life is something that has given me a new appreciation of how my companion animals have enriched my life. These are memories that I will carry with me to the end of my days.

Pearl Salotto *Universality of connections w/ animals*

✓ TULIP THE RABBIT – HELPING ME FIND MY HUMANITY

***Maria Lariviere** is an animal loving native of Rhode Island. She is the companion of two dogs, Sam and Ben, a cat, Sarah, and a cockatiel, Hank. She is a student at the Community College of Rhode Island in the Occupational Therapy Assistant Program. She is a former student in Pearl Salotto's, D.J. Pet Assisted Therapy Certificate Program, during which she wrote this impression of a field trip.*

I had the opportunity to attend two site visits this semester, St. Joseph Hospital and Meeting Street Center. Meeting Street Center is renowned for the education of children with developmental challenges. Each visit was a valuable experience, but of the two, I feel I was awestruck by the visit to Meeting Street. While the session at St. Joseph was interesting and we did see the facilitator and therapy animal in action, I think what I received most was a more in-depth view and understanding of the clinical/administrative facet.

When I first arrived at Meeting Street Center, I was actually a bit nervous and perhaps a bit apprehensive as well. I was not sure what to expect. I knew of the school and its basic mission, but I had never been there before and really didn't know the scope of the population. When Jeanne Davis (a leader of the volunteer initiative in PAT in New England) and I walked into the first classroom, I saw all the children sitting in a group. My first reaction was so pained I tried very quickly and unobtrusively to immediately pull myself together. I have never in my life felt such sadness, sympathy, and anger. I felt sad that these children (most of them anyway) would never know a "normal" childhood. They would never go to roller skating party, ride a bike or even run around a playground. I wished so much that I could do something to help. Then, I felt angry, how could these things happen to an innocent child?

Once Jeanne allowed me to hold Tulip, the therapy rabbit, and participate in the therapy, I was so thankful, that I didn't feel so sad. I was actually laughing with the children and appreciating them in a new light. They didn't need sympathy, nor were they angry. Each and every one of them is their own person with their own unique attributes, just like you and I. When all my emotions had settled and I felt more comfortable I totally enjoyed myself. I opened my mind and my heart and allowed myself to openly bask in this experience. I watched Jeanne as she moved through her routines. I observed how caring and attentive (not to mention compassionate and patient) the staff was. But especially, I watched the children. Their expressions – especially in their eyes – spoke volumes. Many of them didn't have very good motor control, but their eyes said everything. They were happy and excited – they felt good.

Jeanne is an amazing woman. She and I spoke after the therapy sessions and I have immense respect and admiration for her – and for the things she taught me and the experience she shared with me. I truly am grateful.

I drove away from Meeting Street School a different person from when I had arrived. I learned life is what you make it, don't be afraid to care and show your feelings, and most especially to count your blessings. In seeing these children smile and pet Tulip, while their eyes shone, I felt blessed to have been afforded such a soul searching experience.

PART III

ETHICS

CHAPTER 6

ETHICAL ISSUES IN PET ASSISTED THERAPY

Section 1:
A SELF-IMPOSED HANDICAP

__Dr. James Harris__, a Companion Animal Practitioner, graduated Michigan State University in 1958. He has been the owner and director of Mount Claire Veterinary Hospital in Oakland, CA. for thirty-five years. He was the winner of the Bustad Award in 1989. He is certified as a Grief and Bereavement Counselor. Dr. Harris has also chaired ethics and peer review committees for the Veterinary Society for over twenty-five years.

Webster's Dictionary defines ethics as "moral principles, quality or practice; a system of moral principle, as, social ethics, medical ethics, professional ethics forbids him; the morals of individual action or practice."[1] If the reader considers him/herself a professional the following would apply. In the case of my profession, veterinary medicine, Jerold Tannenbaum writes:

> "Veterinarians are members of one of the few learned professions. Essential to the legal definition of these professions is a commitment to fundamental ethical principles that are imposed upon members by the professions themselves. Theses principles in turn, serve as a major source of legal obligations applied to the respective professions by courts, legislatures, and regulatory bodies. Indeed, the law considers ethical behavior — in personal, as well as professional life — so important to veterinary medicine that in most states the license to practice can be denied to those who lack good moral character."[2]

Ethics are embodied in the Golden Rule: Do unto others as you would have others do unto you. This is a personal ethic. In the case of professionals the whole group is involved in defining, revising and updating, and complying with their set of ethics. Ethics might be defined as a set of moral handicaps voluntarily accepted and self imposed upon a professional group. This then becomes the accepted proper conduct expected by the group.

As mentioned earlier, where government has jurisdiction through licensure and regulation, ethics and legal requirements develop and are intertwined. Where does ethics come into play in the case of Animal Assisted Activity (AAA) and Animal Assisted Therapy (AAT)? Granted that many individuals involved in this field are members of professions that are licensed and have codes of professional ethics, but AAA and AAT are not fields currently licensed or organized into a professional organization, as are human medicine, veterinary medicine, dentistry or social work. In

---

[1] Webster's New International Dictionary (2nd ed.) (1951) Springfield, MA.
[2] Tannenbaum, Jerrold, MA, J. D.(1993, September). Ethics: The Why and Wherefore of Veterinary Law. The Veterinary Clinics of North America: Small Animal Practice. 23(5). Pennsylvania: W.B. Saunders.

spite of this, AAA and AAT are conducted in a professional manner by people with professional demeanor. Just because there is an absence of government control does not mean that there is no need for ethical conduct or that unethical conduct can be ignored, accepted or tolerated. In fact, the lack of formal government control should encourage us to self regulate, to establish a code of ethics and to be self disciplined.

The principles of professional ethics of other professions would certainly apply to AAA and AAT. Of all the professions, the ethical principles of veterinary medicine come close to fitting the needs of this field. This is so because both activities have a triad of interactions:

1) Ethical treatment and care of animals who are working in pet therapy programs.
2) Ethical behavior towards the recipients of the program.
3) Ethical relationships with colleagues, volunteers and other professionals that interface with the activities of AAA and AAT.

The Delta Society's Handbook for Animal Assisted Activities and Animal Assisted Therapy includes a "code of ethics." This code states:

"Code of Ethics for Personnel in Animal Assisted Activities and Animal Assisted Therapy: 1) treat people, animals and nature with respect, dignity and sensitivity; 2) promote quality of life in their work; 3) abide by the professional ethics of their respective professions and/or organizations; 4) perform duties commensurate with their training and position and 5) comply with all applicable Delta Society policies and local, state and federal laws relating to their work."[3]

Ethics and Animals

Working with animals demands the highest standard of ethical conduct. Whereas our fellow humans can and should respond to poor treatment or care and inappropriate interactions, the animals cannot. We must serve as advocates for them. The animals must be in good health and condition. They must not be unduly stressed or excessively handled. While involved in visits or working with clients the animals must be constantly observed for signs of overheating, fatigue and the like. This is especially so with small mammals such as rabbits, guinea pigs and rats. Working with multiple small animals with lengthy rest periods prevents overheating and stress.

Animals must be protected from physical abuse at all costs. There must be continuous supervision by the handlers. Animals can be inadvertently dropped by frail clients. Children, in their eagerness, can over handle an animal and animals should not be exposed to violent individuals unless safeguards are in place and there is no chance

---

[3] Fredrickson, M. (1992). Handbook for Animal-Assisted Activities and Animal-Assisted Therapy. Renton, WA: Delta Society.

that the animal can be injured or abused.

Ethics and Recipients

Regardless of physical or mental condition or appearance, clients must be treated with respect at all times. Some situations and visits may be difficult and require great control and understanding on our part. Confidentiality must be maintained regardless of the circumstances. Although discussions might be appropriate during the post-visit debriefing with the supervisor, conversations after this are akin to gossip and are not acceptable. The privacy and dignity of clients must always be maintained, during visits, as well as before and after visits.

Ethics and Colleagues

Practice the "Golden Rule." Do so at all times. Never waiver from this position.

If one is privy to observations and insights regarding clients, give the information to the appropriate person. Make ethical referrals to colleagues when necessary. Know the colleagues you are referring to, contact them, and give them the benefit of a history and any other pertinent information that might be useful to the managing of that case. If you are referred a case, acknowledge it and follow-up with a written progress report.

As the field continues to grow, I hope that practitioners will form professional organizations and that there will be ethics and peer review committees within these organizations. The functions of these committees are to remind the members of the profession of the body of ethics, to review the ethics and make changes as society and the particular profession changes, and if appropriate, to interpret the ethical code and act as a mediation service when there is an intra-professional or extra-professional complaint or question. Ethics committees should be composed of a representative membership with a required number of years working in the field. A peer review manual will need to be developed for use by ethics committees. One such manual is the Peer Review Manual of the California Veterinary Medical Association.[4]

Dr. James Harris with Toes.

[4] Peer Review Manual. Sacramento, CA: California Veterinary Medical Association.

Section 2:
A GREAT JOY AND AN AWESOME RESPONSIBILITY
The Therapy Pet Calls the Shots
(Pearl Salotto)

Wherever the true Human Companion Animal bond takes place — including Pet Assisted Therapy programs — it is required that the needs and well being of both parties are met. The beauty of the Human Animal Companion Bond is that each party of the bond freely gives "gifts" of his/her love, trust, and uniqueness to the relationship. It is each ones' intuitive spontaneity and warmth that allows the relationship to be meaningful.

This Human Animal Companion Bond, which in many cases allows our pets to be our "best friends," is also the basis of an emerging health profession called Pet Assisted Therapy. In PAT our pets and clients interact on an ongoing and mutually beneficial basis. Research has documented the wide range of benefits that individuals can reap when they enjoy and look forward to the company of that special therapy pet. Those of us who have brought "our most special friends" into contact with individuals, who bond with them, are well aware of the **joy** that these therapy pets receive back from their work. Perhaps it is not as well documented, but those of us who work in Pet Assisted Therapy can attest to the indescribable joy and enhanced quality of life, that the therapy animals receive from the sharing of their gifts (not unlike how we feel when we help others). Would that we should all be so eager to go to "work" as DJ, as evidenced by her running around the house after me when I've told her we are going to PT (Pet Assisted Therapy), her squeals of joy as the car approaches the familiar facility and her eagerness and delight, as she gives her paw time and again, to her "friends" in nursing homes, hospitals, and schools.

We must always keep in mind, then, that PAT does not involve the "use" of animals, but rather a relationship between two parties who wish to interact.

PAT requires Codes of Ethics as does any other field, although it is the love of the PATF for the pet that ultimately protects the pet in this profession.

Sample Code of Ethics

We, as professional Pet Assisted Therapy Facilitators, affirm that:

1. All interactions will only take place if they are safe, healthy, and comfortable for both parties to the bond.
2. All interactions that take place will be guided by a philosophy of mutual respect and dignity for both parties.
3. All interactions will provide for the willing participation and free choice of both parties.
4. All interactions will be structured in a manner that protects both parties from hazards, disease, harm, stress, and fatigue.
5. Everything in our power will be done to maintain the **BOND** that is formed between the two parties.

237

6. All of our actions and deeds will reflect advocacy for this profession, therapy pets and clients, and other professionals.
7. All interactions will be individually planned, goal-oriented and treatment-based, when in a medical setting.
8. We will always use language that is respectful and uplifting and reflective of the BOND, which would preclude such expressions as "use of animals" or "animals as tools."
9. We, as Pet Assisted Therapy Facilitators, and our family therapy pets, will be properly educated. We will strive to work toward professional credentialing and/or licensure.

In these happy, healthy and meaningful relationships, grounded in such Code of Ethics, PAT "shines" at its best.

It goes without saying that individuals, working with D. J., care deeply for her, respect and appreciate her, as she does them. Their care for her is demonstrated in so many touching ways, where her needs become more important than theirs. (If she is tired, they let her sleep. If she has to go to the bathroom, they are willing to forgo some of their time with her.)

Problems can arise, however, when PAT programs take place with individuals who, for whatever reason, are not able to "understand" and/or "appreciate" the therapy pet's aliveness. Therefore, it is the responsibility of the Pet Assisted Therapy Facilitator to design programs that acknowledge the rights of the therapy pet, as well as the client.

Sample Rights of Therapy Pets

1. The therapy pet has the right to a quiet private place to rest for approximately twenty minutes out of every hour. (Break time needs to be flexible depending on environmental conditions and the therapy pet's own needs.)
2. The therapy pet has the right to a place to exercise and to eliminate, as well as access to water, as desired.
3. The therapy pet has the right to be accompanied at all times by a Pet Assisted Therapy Facilitator or staff the PATF deems responsible.
4. The therapy pet has the right to be approached by only one person at a time.
5. The therapy pet has the right to be approached by clients free of any possible transmittable disease.
6. The therapy pet has the right to be approached by clients free of emotional or cognitive problems that could be potentially harmful. (If there is any possibility of harm, a plan might be able to be set up providing for enough staff support and rigid guidelines. Alternative techniques such as hand-over-hand, hug-over-hug, or a designated staff person preventing erratic movement of a individual's limb, might allow for participation that would not otherwise be safe.)
7. The therapy pet has the right to be protected from potential hazards, such as medication on someone's hands, medicine on the floor or loose

on a table or shelf, and cleaning chemicals that might be left unattended. Pet Assisted Therapy Liaison is to check for hazards prior to therapy pet entering client's room or activity room.

8. The therapy pet should not be offered food by anyone, without prior permission of the Pet Assisted Therapy Facilitator.

Sample Rights of Clients

1. Client shall have a right to have Pet Assisted Therapy as a form of treatment.
2. Clients should have choice of whether or not they wish to participate in Pet Assisted Therapy treatment.
3. Clients shall have the right to be asked if they wish to participate that day.
4. As long as medical referral is on file, client shall have the right to structure visit as they choose, per Pet Assisted Therapy guidelines. The client shall decide if they wish to just look at therapy pet, have the pet sit near them, have the pet sit on their lap, on bed, have photo taken, etc.
5. Client shall have a right to attend an alternate program with Pet Assisted Therapy Facilitator, if pet is too tired to interact, if at all possible. (pictures, discussion, etc.)
6. In the case of two clients sharing a room, the program will not take place there unless both patients are agreeable to having the therapy pet in the room.
7. Client has the right to see medical and temperament test records on therapy pet.
8. Client has the right to participate in their goal setting for Pet Assisted Therapy.
9. Client has the right to participate in evaluating the Pet Assisted Therapy program.
10. Client has the right to have family informed about Pet Assisted Therapy.
11. Client has the right to have Pet Assisted Therapy coordinated with other therapies. (via Treatment Team)
12. Client has the right to be screened for allergies (i.e. medical referral) and if they are allergic, they have the right not to be in proximity of the pet.
13. Client has the right to have bond with the therapy pet, maintained, if at all possible.

If the program is not going to serve the needs of the individuals (i.e. if he/she is allergic or doesn't want interaction), then of course the interaction would not take place. Similarly if the interaction is "uncomfortable" or unsafe for the therapy pet, then the interaction should not take place either. It is the responsibility of the Facilitator to assure that programs take into account both parties' needs.

As the therapy animals are the ones who make this profession work, it is our responsibility to hold their well-being uppermost in our minds, always. Part of that responsibility is recognizing that Pet Assisted Therapy is not for everyone. If, for whatever reason, an individual's movements are uncontrollable or their behavior erratic, then PAT is not appropriate. However, the Facilitator does have the responsibility of making every effort to attempt to structure situations so that as many individuals as possible can participate. One effective way of doing this is to have one-on-one staffing. Another extremely effective way of allowing individuals to participate without compromising the therapy pet's safety is hand-over-hand assistance. Precautions such as assessing an individual's health, behavior and functioning level is also necessary to determine whether individuals are appropriate for PAT. We must then determine how the interaction will be structured. If a client's reactions are unpredictable and their level of awareness is limited, then we must use our judgment and our love to assure our therapy pet's safety or programs will not take place.

As it is our pets who share their lives with us, and together with us, help people in need, it is our awesome responsibility to protect their well-being. As in any other relationship, when one gives love, one deserves to receive love in return. It is hard to imagine any greater love than that which our therapy pets give. They, therefore, deserve no less in return.

When the well-being of people and animals is the foundation of all interactions, then, not only is this emerging profession living up to its ethical responsibilities, but the lives of both people and animals are truly enhanced.

It is not enough, however, that I protect D. J. and keep her safe. In addition, she needs to be able to demonstrate her enthusiasm and her spontaneity and to share her gifts, in her own way and when she wants to. When I work in the field with D. J., she calls the shots and that's the way it should be. Because, despite all the guidelines that I or anyone else have or will develop, it is **only** the way we actually work in the field, with our beloved pets and the clients, that really counts.

As a practicing PATF, I have learned many things. I also have much to learn. But one thing I do know — with a heartfelt and profound conviction — is that in PAT at its best, and actually in the only way PAT should be run, the therapy pet has to be allowed to be himself/herself and to enjoy himself/herself. If D. J or another therapy pet barks unexpectedly at the thunder while in a Rehab Center or if she jumps on a couch in an administrator's office or if she moves out of a circle of children to take a nap, to return when she feels like it, this is just fine and just the way it should be.

With a deep and abiding appreciation for D. J.'s gifts and for her (as a living creature) just as she is, I find myself laughing when she barked totally unexpectedly (she had never barked in a facility in eight years) and when she jumped on a couch unexpectedly at an interview, thinking she was about to do Pet Assisted Therapy with a client. I appreciated her spontaneity and enthusiasm. **We need to laugh with our pets; to appreciate them; to find humor in unexpected events, as long as no one, of course, is hurt.**

There is no reason, therefore, to be embarrassed in these situations. We do not expect everyone to love our pets. If we happen to come across an administrator or staff person who is more concerned about a minuscule piece of dog biscuit under a mat, than he/she is impressed by all the good treatment that is going on, it is not the end of the world. We need to keep our priorities straight, even if others, on occasion, do not.

In PAT, therefore, you need a sense of humor. You need faith in your therapy pet. You need to let her/him call the shots, just as I do with D. J. D. J. deserves it. She has been giving of herself to others for years. I would not dream of telling her to relate to someone — when she wants to rest. Neither would it be good for the client.

Thus, in my view, PAT is willing participation on both the part of the client and the therapy pet. We would not dream of asking a client to relate if he/she did not want to. Why should we expect the therapy pet to, either.

To have any other attitude would be to presume that the therapy pet is simply a tool at our service. This attitude has no place in our beautiful profession of love and reverence for life — as eloquently laid down by Albert Schweitzer, Leo Bustad, Edith Latham, and others. A client who would want to relate to the therapy pet when he/she would rather be sleeping, is not the right client to be in the program, in the first place.

When my childrens' group recently enjoyed loving interaction with D. J. for a half hour (with giving of paws, kisses, petting, and talking), after a while D. J. moved away from the circle and lay down about fifteen feet away and fell sound asleep. The understanding glances between the children and myself, without a word from me, told me that the children had internalized the most important of life's values — respect for all living things. Our discussion continued while D. J. slept and after fifteen minutes or so, D. J. on her own, awoke and eagerly came back to sit with the youngsters in the circle.

All felt right with the world!

D.J.

Pearl Salotto

Section 3:
ETHICS IN ANIMAL ASSISTED THERAPY

__Ann Ashenfelder-Littel__ currently resides in Illinois with her husband and a family dog. Ann took an intensive workshop in PAT from Pearl and was a student at the University of Illinois with Linda Case, an author in this chapter. She has attended international conferences on the HCAB and is an advocate for this profession.

Is Animal Assisted Therapy an ethical practice? Most of the emphasis of AAT is placed on the benefit to the client. But does this benefit come at some cost to the animals involved? Is the animal being used or abused or is the animal also benefiting from the interaction?

Before we can consider the specific issue of AAT, we must agree that animals in general should have their interests considered. Jeremy Bentham used a good argument to show that animals do have interests that matter. Bentham (1948) wrote: "The question is not, Can they reason? Nor Can they talk? But, Can they suffer?" While people are still undecided about whether or not animals can reason, and we know they cannot talk (at least not the same way we do), most people who have had experience with animals will agree that they do have the capacity to suffer or experience enjoyment or happiness. If we agree that animals can suffer, then we must begin to consider their interest in not suffering. According to Gabriel Moran (1987), the director of the graduate program of religious education at New York University, "As we should not unnecessarily inflict pain upon a human being, so a dog or a cow or a deer merits our concern not to impose pain on the basis of human whim." Moran (1987) also wrote: "an ethic centered on possession, use and consumption is inadequate for today. We need a moral language in which relations other than usefulness are able to be perceived and appreciated." Leo Bustad and Linda Hines (1986) stated: "as we reflect on our interdependence with the animal world, we can see that the idea of dominance over animals must be converted to one of responsible, compassionate stewardship."

While these people argue that we must treat animals ethically, they do not state that it is wrong to have companion animals. However, some animal rights individuals believe that even keeping pets is wrong (Hearne, 1991) and that "using" them in AAT is also wrong. Other people interested in animals such as Edward S. Duvin also have reservations about AAT. Duvin (1990) stated that "some programs exploit the animals; second, many programs inadvertently reinforce an anthropocentric view of animals as tools to meet human needs."

Being ethical and careful of the animal's interests in AAT programs with children is not only therapeutic for them, but it also teaches them ethics and the humane treatment of animals. Hopefully, in addition to the possible therapeutic benefits, we are training a new generation to be more ethical and more humane in general. Also, some people feel that animals also benefit from their interactions with us. Vicki Hearne (1991), an animal trainer, stated that "the wild is not a suffering-free zone or all that frolicsome a location." She went on to say:

242

"There is something more to animals, a capacity for satisfactions that come from work in the fullest sense — what is known in philosophy and in this country's Declaration of Independence as 'happiness.' This is a sense of personal achievement, like satisfaction felt by a good wood-carver or a dancer or a poet or an accomplished dressage horse. It is a happiness that, like the artist's, must come from something within the animal, something the trainers call 'talent.' Hence, it cannot be imposed on the animal."

I really liked Vicki Hearne's way of defining the possessive words used when talking about a pet. She stated that "the important detail about the kind of possessive pronoun that I have in mind is reciprocity: If I have a friend, she has a friend. If I have a daughter, she has a mother. The possessive does not bind one of us while freeing the other; it cannot do that. … In these bindings, nearly inextricable, are found the origin of our rights. They imply a possessiveness, but also recognizes an acknowledgment by each side of the other's existence." (Hearne, 1991) This describes a relationship with companion animals that goes beyond ownership. Just as parents are responsible for the welfare of their children, we should be responsible for the welfare of the companion animals in our lives.

This leads us to the difference in ethics that is suggested by using the term Pet Assisted Therapy instead of Animal Assisted Therapy. I do not mean to imply in any way that AAT programs are not necessarily as ethical as PAT programs, but when therapists are working with an animal to whom they are bonded, they tend to feel more responsible for the well-being of their animals and would not be as likely to put the animal at risk. Animal Assisted Therapy is a much broader term and encompasses animals that we do not tend to think of as pets, such as farm animals. Since farm animals are typically regarded as production animals, their interests are not usually given as much thought as the animals we keep as pets. An example of this is that, in our society, it is acceptable to eat meat from a cow, but the majority of people would not consider eating a dog or cat. Therefore, if we intend to work with animals that are not pets, we must be careful to make sure that we are giving the animal the consideration that he/she deserves and not basing our feelings on the species of animal involved.

Why should we practice Animal Assisted Therapy? I think that the answer lies in the many possible benefits of AAT. These are the benefits that Michael J. McCulloch (1986) noted:

Psychological Benefits

1. Positive affective state (elation)
2. Affiliation (i.e., the need to be in physical proximity to other living things)
3. Humor
4. Play
5. Self-esteem
6. Need to be needed
7. Independence (as in the case of seeing eye and hearing dogs)
8. Increased motivation

9. Education
10. Sense of achievement

Social Benefits

1. Catalyst effect — *neighborhood dog walkers*
2. Social cohesion
3. Cooperative play (sports, relay races in therapeutic riding)
4. Increased cooperation with caregivers

Physical Benefits

1. Recovery from illness
2. Coping with illness
3. Neuromuscular rehabilitation (especially evident in therapeutic riding)
4. Life expectancy (requires further investigation)

Any or all of these benefits can make a person's life better and more rewarding. The benefits that can result from AAT can go on to influence the rest of the person's life and can help them to be happier, healthier people.

What are the possible benefits to the animals? Animals receive companionship and the ability to interact with many humans. Also, some of the animals working in AAT are rescued from animals shelters where they might have been euthanized. The animals are given a "job" where they are welcomed and usually adored by humans with whom they have contact. Most dogs and some cats, as well as members of other species seem to derive a great deal of pleasure from their interactions with humans. In fact, dogs, otherwise, exhibit a variety of unwanted behaviors due to boredom and loneliness such as chewing, digging, and barking when separated from their owner(s) or the person/people to whom they are closely bonded. If an animal does not seem to benefit from the AAT then that animal is not appropriate for AAT.

What animals are appropriate? This depends a great deal on the humans involved. An active, playful dog may be good for a child or for visiting an elderly person, but may not be the best choice for a pet for an elderly individual living alone. Some dogs, such as poodles or other species may be the right choice for someone with allergies. A cat may be better for someone with diminished physical abilities who would not be able to walk a dog. Horses may be the best choice for individuals who are physically disabled. For the most part, I do not feel that exotic animals are appropriate to work with in AAT. However, some people like Ken and Marilyn McCort (1990) have had a great deal of success working with exotic animals and seem to be very aware of the special concerns one must deal with when working with these unusual animals. Zoonotic diseases must also be considered when choosing an AAT animal. For example, we should not work with turtles since they could possibly spread salmonellosis. Some birds may carry psittacosis and should, therefore, be treated with special food with antibiotics in it before being included in AAT. All animals must have an appropriate temperament (friendly, outgoing, not aggressive, willing to participate, etc.), must be properly trained, and must be free of any known zoonotic diseases and parasites. The type of program must also be considered. A visiting dog may not need the advanced training that a dog working in a specific therapy setting might be required to have, such as walking off leash or responding to individuals with limited communication skills. Dogs that are permanent residents in a facility may be required to learn to stay out of certain areas or to learn other specific commands that a visiting dog would not need to know. Also, just because the animal is appropriate for a certain type of program and at a certain age does not mean that the animal will be the best animal for a different type of program or will always be appropriate.

What people are appropriate? This must also take into account the type of program that is being considered. An individual who would not be able to take care of a pet of their own might still benefit from a visiting animal program. An individual who is violent, especially one who is known to have abused animals, would not be appropriate. A person with erratic, uncontrollable movements is probably also not appropriate. It would not be appropriate to work with animals for whom people have a deep hatred or deep fear. However, AAT programs may help some people overcome their fear of certain animals if done carefully so as not to cause undue stress to the person or harm to the animal. Dorothy Dengel (1988) brought up the idea that care must be taken before working with individuals with schizophrenia. She worries that individuals who are released from an institution may decide to adopt a pet as a result of an AAT program during the stay in the institution. This in itself is not a problem, but if these individuals are allowed to adopt a pet, another person, preferably someone living at the same residence, must agree to assume responsibility for the animal in case of a relapse. Some individuals who would not be appropriate under certain conditions may still benefit from AAT under more controlled conditions. Staff support is an important consideration when determining the appropriateness of a client. A person with uncontrollable movements who enjoys animals may be appropriate when there are enough staff members to help control the person's movement and use a technique, such as hand-over-hand assistance to assist the individual in interacting with the animal.

Whenever we interact with animals we must consider the animal's interests, as well as our own. This is very important in AAT programs since a program that lacks ethical considerations is not beneficial to the humans involved and may even cause harm. For example, an animal whose temperament is not appropriate for AAT may not create the bond with the client that is necessary for the greatest benefit, or the animal may even bite or harm the client in another manner. Also, a client who is not appropriate for AAT may not benefit from the interaction and may purposely injure or kill the animal. Therefore, it is important to take ethical considerations into account when designing and implementing any AAT program. The Animal Assisted Therapist must be aware of the safety and interests of both the clients and the animals. Pearl Salotto (1991) wrote a professional code of ethics for Pet Assisted Therapists that takes into account the interests of both the humans and the animals. All ATT programs should have a code of ethics similar to this one to protect all of the individuals involved, both human and animal.

In order to make sure that AAT programs are being conducted ethically, it is important to set some national, and hopefully international, standards for training and certifying animal assisted therapists and therapy animals. To my knowledge, there are very few certificate programs at the college level for training animal assisted therapists

Pearl Salotto

in this country. The Delta Society has started a Pet Partners program for testing and registering individuals and their therapy animals. Several of these programs are working on setting standards in the field, but more needs to be done. Dr. John New (1990) talked about the issue of standards and why they are needed, but he also brought up a very important point. He said:

> "There is an important thing that standards will not do. That is to relieve a person of personal responsibility. If standards are used only as a checklist and not a guide for personal responsibility, they will ultimately do little to protect the benefits of AAT. If the person in charge of the animal is not personally responsible for the health, safety, appropriateness and welfare of the animal, no set of standards will fill the gap."

Animal Assisted Therapy can be very beneficial for the client and the animals and can be very rewarding for the therapist as well. When AAT programs are conducted ethically the chance for harm is lessened and the possibility for benefits is enhanced. We should realize that no matter how careful we are there is always a chance for accidental harm to be done to a person or an animal, but through carefully designed and implemented programs we should be able to significantly reduce the number and severity of these occurrences. An example of an accident that was not really preventable was given by Treva Lind (1990). She told the story of Jake, a bull mastiff, (with Mickey Niego) whose ear was pinched badly by a resident with a spastic disorder. Because the dog was well temperament tested he was able to remain still and wait for his owner to remove the woman's fingers. This was a situation that could have become much worse. This story shows how an appropriate animal, handler, and client can make even the inevitable accidents relatively minor. Laura Vear (1988) stated that "as facilitators, we must protect the animal from stress or injury, and, at the same time, provide the client an opportunity to connect with the animal."

Is Animal Assisted Therapy an ethical practice? In many cases, it is. Sometimes the emphasis is on ethics for the humans, and in other cases, it is for the animals. Is it sometimes unethical? Unfortunately, yes. Guidelines and standards need to be established and followed. Many people and organizations are working toward these goals.

I think veterinarian Dr. John New (from an editorial written by Linda Hines in 1990) summed up the idea of why we need ethics, when he said, "Many pet therapy programs fail because of a lack of appreciation for the animals' needs. These are not bottles of medicine that can be placed on a shelf only to be taken down three or four times a day."

References:

Albright, Jack L. (1986). Animal Welfare and Animals Rights. National Forum, 66(1), 34-37.
Arkow, Phil (1990). Pet Therapy: A Study and Resource Guide for the Use of Companion Animals in Selected Therapies. Colorado Springs, Colo.: The Humane Society of the Pikes Peak Region.
Behling, Robert J. (1990). The Need for Standards in Animal-Assisted Therapy and Visitation Programs: Program Standards. People Animals, Environment, 8(2), 16-17.

Bentham, Jeremy (1948). <u>Introduction to the Principles of Morals and Legislation,</u> New York: Haffner.

Bustad, Leo K., & Hines, Linda M. (1986). Compassion for Animals. <u>National Forum.</u> 66(1), 2-3.

Dengel, Dorothy (1998). Letter. <u>InterActions,</u> 3(1), 5+.

Dillman, Dick (1994, December 3). Telephone conversation.

Hearne, Vicki (1991, September). What's Wrong with Animal Rights: Of Hounds, Horses, and Jeffersonian Happiness. <u>Harper's Magazine,</u> 59-64.

Hines, Linda M. (1990). Letter. <u>People, Animals, Environment.</u> 8(2), 6.

Hines, Linda M., & Bustad, Leo K. (1990). Historical Perspectives on Human-Animal Interactions. <u>National Forum.</u> 66(1), 4-6.

Hines, Linda M, & Duvin, Edward S. (1990). Letters. <u>People, Animals, Environment.</u> 8(2), 5.

Iannuzzi, Dorothea, & Rowan, Andrew N. (1991). Ethical Issues in Animal-Assisted Therapy Programs. <u>Anthrozoos.</u> 4, 154-163.

Jainchill, Nancy, (1993, November 8). A Special Bond. <u>Newsweek,</u> 10.

Lind, Treva (1990). Why A Wag Of The Tail Isn't Enough. <u>People, Animals, Environment,</u> 8(2), 9-11.

Mangan, Dennis (1991, December). Arthur Schopenhauer: Philosopher of Compassion (1788-1860). <u>The Animal's Agenda,</u> 22-23.

McCort, Marilyn & Ken (1990). Letter. <u>People, Animals, Environment,</u> 8(2), 6-7.

McCulloch, Michael, J.(1986). Animal-Facilitated Therapy: Overview and Future Direction. <u>National Forum.</u> 66(1), 19-24.

McCulloch, Michael, J., McCulloch, Lynne A., & Anderson, Robert K.(1990). Perspectives on Public Health Issues in Human-Animal Interaction. <u>National Forum.</u> 66(1), 38-40.

Moran, Gabriel (1987, December 4). Dominion Over The Earth: Does Ethics Include all Creatures? <u>Commonweal,</u> 697-701.

New, John (1990). The Need for Standards in Animal-Assisted Therapy and Visitation Programs: Animal Standards. <u>People, Animals, Environment.</u> 8(2), 17-18.

Regan, Tom (1983). <u>The Case for Animal Rights.</u> Berkeley: University of California Press.

Rowan, Andrew, & Tannenbaum, J. (1990). Animal Rights. <u>National Forum.</u> 66(1), 30-33.

Salotto, Pearl (1992). <u>Professional Code of Ethics.</u> Class handouts. New York. SUNY Brockport.

Salotto, Pearl (1994, December 3). Telephone conversation.

Serpell, James (1986). <u>In the Company of Animals: A Study of Human-Animal Relationships.</u> Oxford: Basil Blackwell.

Singer, Peter (1990). <u>Animal Liberation.</u> New York: The New York Review of Books.

Tebay, Jean (1990). The Need for Standards in Animal-Assisted Therapy and Visitation Programs: Overview. <u>People, Animals, Environment.</u> 8(2), 15-16.

Tester, Keith (1991). <u>Animals & Society: The Humanity of Animal Rights.</u> London: Routledge.

Zoo Animals Provide Therapy Too. (1988, September). <u>People, Animals, Environment.</u> 6(1), 11-12.

Section 4:
ADDRESSING THE NEEDS OF ANIMALS IN AAA AND AAT

__Linda Case, M.S.__ teaches Companion Animal Science in the Animal Sciences Department at the University of Illinois and is the Coordinator of the AAA program, Paw-to-Paw, at the BroMenn Life Care Center. She and her husband train and show Golden Retrievers in Obedience Trials and tracking tests and also own and operate Autumn Gold Dog Training Center in Mahoment, Illinois.

One of the direct results of the acceptance of knowledge about human-animal interactions and increased understanding of the importance that animals have in our lives is the proliferation of Animal Assisted Therapy (AAT) and Animal Assisted Activities (AAA) programs in health care settings. The psychological and emotional benefits that companion animals provide are well documented. Indeed, it is the personal experience of these benefits that usually stimulates volunteers and therapists to become involved in AAT or AAA programs in the first place. Scientific research has merely proven what pet owners have known all along — that animals are good for both our health and our happiness. It is therefore not surprising that people who experience the joy of sharing their life with a loving pet wish to share these feelings with others. One of the ways that they are able to do this is through established AAT and AAA programs. Populations that are often targeted are those which tend to be socially isolated and have little or no opportunity for positive interactions with animals. Depending upon the program, these may include individuals with medical illnesses, physical disabilities, mental and or emotional disabilities or those socially isolated.

Well structured AAA/AAT programs include procedures for volunteer/therapist orientation and training (or certification), animal health and temperament screening, infectious disease control, staff briefing, and client selection. All animals attending these programs must be well-mannered, clean and well groomed, and possess a temperament that is both appropriate for the setting and compatible with the individual clients with whom they are matched. Because the bond between animals and people is the primary reason that the AAA/AAT team is present in the health care setting, it goes without saying that the companion animal is an enormously important component of this team. The pet comprises one third of the patient-volunteer/therapist-animal triangle. In this role, the pet may facilitate human/human interaction, provide unconditional affection and love, stimulate reminiscing and feelings of affection, or provide tactile stimulation and physical rehabilitation. These functions are well documented and many benefits can result from the development of a positive and strong relationship between client and pet. The companion animal also has the potential to benefit from these interactions and relationships. Increased social interactions with people and other animals, regular and controlled play periods, mastery of new obedience commands or tricks, the tactile stimulation associated with petting, and the health benefits of regular brushing and grooming can all be considered benefits to a companion animal that is participating in an AAA/AAT program. In addition, companion animals that are properly suited for AAA/AAT enjoy their roles as animal companions and appear to experience an increased meaning and purpose of life. As enthusiasm for

AAA/AAT programs expands, and an increasing number of companion animals are included, it is important that the focus of attention of program directors and institutions includes the needs of the animals and the impact that the program will have on their lives, as well as on the needs of the clients who are being served.

Why must AAA/AAT programs address issues of animal welfare and needs?

It is often assumed that anyone who is involved in AAA/AAT must love animals and therefore, will naturally be aware of the needs of the pet that is under his/her care. However, it is remiss to assume that this motivation alone is adequate to assure proper animal care. People participate in AAA/AAT programs for different reasons and they possess varying levels of knowledge about animal care and behavior. While some have been involved in animal-related activities all their lives and may even have professional training, others become involved in AAA/AAT because they are generally active in community programs and would like to help the specific institution at which the program is conducted, or work in a health care setting and wish to incorporate AAT into their professional duties. As a result the term "needs of the animal" may mean different things to different people. The responsibility of both defining animal needs and welfare, and training volunteers and therapists to identify and respect these needs falls to the program's director and designated staff personnel. Issues of animal welfare and care must also be thoroughly addressed in all written program protocols.

The basis of AAA/AAT programs and the benefits that clients in these programs receive revolves around the relationship that volunteers and therapists have with their companion animals. It is the sharing of this relationship that allows individual clients to benefit from the presence of the pet. The companion animal is an active and important participant in the development of these bonds. Just as two humans can never develop a positive relationship without mutual consent, neither will an animal be able to interact positively if he or she is not willing. Therefore, from the perspective of program success, the physical and emotional needs of the animals must be considered because the goals and objectives that are set up for clients cannot be met if the pet is not a willing partner in the interactions that are set up for them.

While the impact upon program success is certainly important, attending to animal needs within AAA/AAT programs is more directly vital because of the basic responsibilities that all humans have to their companion animals. When man domesticated the dog and the cat, selective breeding practices over many generations resulted in the loss of the ability to live independently in these species. Today, dogs and cats are dependent upon their human caretakers for food, shelter, health care, and the provision of love and affection. Companion animals live in very close association with man and provide companionship, affection, unconditional acceptance, and love to their human caretakers. In return, humans must accept the responsibility of caring for and respecting the animals with whom they share their lives. This goes beyond merely providing food, water and health care. It is also a responsibility to provide a quality life and to make decisions about the animal's life that are in his or her own best interest. When a decision is made to include a pet in an AAA/AAT program, the impact that this involvement will have on the animal's life must always be evaluated. In the course of determining the potential benefits for the client, the potential benefits for the pet must simultaneously be identified. The possibility that repeated interactions and long-term involvement in the program may induce reactions of stress or anxiety in the animal must also be evaluated. One of the assumptions that is commonly made is that because a person's pet is happy to be in the company of that person, or that person's family, that the pet will also enjoy being in the presence of the clients that are selected within the AAA/AAT program. Although a pet may pass all temperament tests and health screening, this does not necessarily mean that every interaction that the pet will have from that day onward will be enjoyable and positive. Attention to animal welfare and the needs of each individual animal within the program is an ongoing process that must be a central component of every AAA/AAT program.

What are the responsibilities of the institution to the animal?

All clients who are involved in an AAA/AAT program should be screened for inclusion in the program prior to meeting any animals. Clients who have the potential for harming animals in any way should not be included in these programs. The institution that is involved must be aware of the importance of properly screening clients and matching them to appropriate pets. Clients are expected to interact gently and appropriately with all animals. Inappropriate behavior or intent to do harm to any animal must never be tolerated in an AAA/AAT program. Animal Assisted Therapy is an adjunct therapy that can often complement and support other forms of more conventional therapy. It will not be successful in all cases and is not appropriate for use with all clients. If there is any danger to the pet involved, AAA or AAT should not be used. It is the responsibility of the health care institution to work with the program director to ensure that the clients who are selected for the program have the potential to benefit and present no known risk to the animals involved.

Are animals the "tools" of AAA/AAT Programs?

When caught up in the enthusiasm of AAA and AAT programs and when convinced of the potential good that can arise from involvement in these new programs, it is easy to lose sight of the fact that AAA and AAT are very unique modalities. Unlike other forms of therapy or recreational activity, AAA and AAT, by their definition, involve the inclusion of another living, sentient being. While the inanimate objects of conventional types of recreational or occupational therapy can all act as tools, animals that are involved in AAA and AAT programs should never be looked upon as tools or implements to be used in the therapeutic process. Rather, the animal must be accepted as an active participant in all interactions, whose needs and feelings receive the same degree of respect and consideration as do those of the client or patient. The potential to provide a client with physiological or emotional benefits must always be weighed against the impact that the interactions with the client will have upon the chosen animal. Successful AAA or AAT programs include matches between clients, handlers, and pets that prove to be beneficial to all involved. Sessions can then result in the development of long-term and productive bonds between clients and animals. These bonds are necessary for the attainment of the goals and objectives that have been set for clients and can also contribute to the quality of life of the companion animal. Animal Assisted Therapy and Activity programs should never be viewed as an adjunct therapy in which volunteers and therapists are "using" animals to provide benefit to people. To do so is an abuse of the devotion, unconditional acceptance and trust that companion animals give to their human caretakers. Rather, participation in AAA/AAT must be viewed as the sharing of a relationship. At its finest, AAA/AAT results in the extension of many of the benefits of that relationship to other people with whom the pet readily and willingly bonds.

Section 5:
RESPECTING THE ANIMALS WITH WHOM WE WORK

__Emmanuel M. Bernstein__ has been an animal welfare activist, on-and-off for the past 61 years, beginning at the age of three with a refusal to eat meat when he found out where it came from. He began to work ardently for animal welfare at the age of 14, when he founded the Adirondack Animal Welfare Society in 1944 in his home town, and later returned to help found the Tri-Lakes Humane Society in 1973. Dr. Bernstein has been a psychologist in private practice, for the past two decades, high in the Adirondack Mountains of Upstate New York. He has been President of Psychologists for the Ethical Treatment of Animals (PSYeta) for the past decade. For the past ten years he has also served as a consultant for several institutions for individuals with developmental disabilities, where he observed Pet Assisted Therapy both work and fail. For the past eight years he has been the editor of Humane Innovations and Alternatives, a publication designed to disseminate ways to make life better for animals in practical ways.

In the early 1970's when I first went into practice as a psychotherapist, my dog, Twiggy, whose mother was a boxer and father a basset hound, soon joined me as a co-therapist. I had not realized she would make such a fine co-therapist until she attended a group therapy session. There, she picked the most distressed individuals and went over to them, one-by-one, putting her head on their laps, her huge, soulful eyes meeting theirs with perfect eye-contact. My patients and Twiggy both loved the experience. Both felt better afterwards.

It was not long before people knew that when they came to me for therapy, they would also be greeted by Twiggy, who took great delight in putting in a full work day with me. Twiggy could simply bark to leave the room at any time, but she chose to be in my office all day and often all evening.

After Twiggy died, our cat, Pierre, quickly took over, and was a constant presence in my office, which again was his choice, usually staying for an eight hour work day. After Pierre, at the time of this writing, my four year-old cat, Aurora, has been putting in the same long hours, by her choice!

Although the cats were more selective about whom they honored with their attention (favorites tended to be those allergic to cats or with a cat phobia) I quickly realized that companion animals were often helpful to people in psychotherapy. Having the dog or cat present helped most humans feel more comfortable, be able to express themselves more fully, and/or have a warm experience holding and caressing a fellow-being with whom they could relate intimately, to name a few benefits.

My patients loved animal assisted therapy, and my animals loved it too. For more than a decade I only heard of one or two therapists who worked with their companion animals in this way, and I often thought it such a good idea that it deserved to be promoted. I even thought of writing a paper to encourage it. About a decade later I noticed that animal involvement in therapy was becoming popular, as it is today. I was pleased.

It was a long time before any ethical issues came to my attention. My first suspicions were aroused when I noticed some animal welfare groups were promoting animal use, as if it were always good for the animals as well as the people involved. Slowly, I began to think in terms of, "What does the animal get out of this? and "Can this sometimes be a form of animal exploitation or abuse? Soon I found that some animals WERE ABUSED in animal assisted activities and therapy.

My second thoughts came in the 1980's, when I was asked to comment on monkeys who were helping paraplegics. I had seen articles where the human primate and slave non-human primate were depicted as mutually enjoying life together in rich companionship. I read more, and found that electric shock was used in the training, and that the shock device was also given to the animal-assisted human. It occurred to me that there would obviously be extreme differences between humans administering shock to their animal assistants. There would be those empathetic, kind, gentle and non-punitive humans who would have a positive, warm relationship with their monkeys, and rarely shock them — and others who would relate in demanding, angry, negative ways with their monkeys. Thus, I suggested that there be a monitoring device put on the shockers to see how many times each human shocked their assistant. I noticed that the trainers and groups promoting this brand of animal assisted activity were assuring the public that it was rare, if ever, the shock was used. The reality remained untested, with no data to back up these claims, as far I know. Later, another issue came to light — the monkey's teeth were routinely extracted.

Then I began to notice situations where individuals with mental illness and mental disabilities interacted with animals. I observed that, on occasion, animals were abused. It was rare, but an occasional child or adult would squeeze the puppy too hard, poke a kitten in the eyes, hit a rabbit, kick a dog, or pull long soft hair that resulted in suffering. The dynamics that led to abuse were many. Sometimes the animals were harmed because the person simply did not know the kitten had feelings, and /or she/he mistook a real rabbit for a toy one, and/or hurting another being made him/her feel good, and/or adults who care about animals were not there at the moment, or the caretaking adult did not realize the animal was being traumatized.

These days, danger-alert flags appear in my mind whenever I hear promotions of pet-assisted therapy or pet-assisted activities. I want to IMMEDIATELY hear about HOW the welfare of the animals will be implemented. I want to know if the welfare and sensitivity to animal welfare is balanced with the concern for the human welfare involved. I have a great many questions that worry me. I expect them to be answered WITHOUT HAVING TO ASK whoever is promoting the activity. Otherwise, I assume that the welfare of the animals involved is being negated.

I saw people drop off their rabbits at an institution, not knowing who would work with them or exactly in what manner. I found that these people assumed their rabbits would be humanely treated, assumed they would be treated with respect and gentleness, and assumed they would not be abused. But after they left, I observed animals being poked, squeezed, stepped on by mistake, kept too hot, kept too cold, unwatered, teased with no harm intended, and placed in situations that resulted in pain, upset, and/ or suffering. It was usually innocent. Staff were just not quite attentive enough, or aware enough of the suffering. Most humans hurt animals unintentionally, sometimes never having learned how other beings can suffer from their behavior. I find that animals need continual protection from unintentional abuse.

I believe that GUIDELINES which assure the well-being of the animals involved must be EMPHASIZED with pet-assisted activity programs, as well as highlighted in any literature or articles. Otherwise, there is bound to be animal abuse, despite the well-meaning helping professionals and participants involved.

I will now list some of the issues involved, and try to communicate a sense of the kind of questions and wording that might go into effective guidelines:

1. **What is the personality of each animal involved?** Is she/he gregarious, and does she/he enjoy being with all kinds of people? Does this individual feel comfortable being with children, petted by lots of hands? *Possible guideline*: IF YOUR INDIVIDUAL HAS NEVER EXPERIENCED THIS KIND OF AUDIENCE, WATCH HIM OR HER CAREFULLY, AND IF THERE IS UPSET, REMOVE HIM/HER IMMEDIATELY FROM THE PERSON(S) INVOLVED. FOR EXAMPLES, WATCH FOR ESCAPE ATTEMPTS, FEAR AS SHOWN BY EXPRESSIONS INCLUDING EYES, AND AGITATED VOCALIZATIONS.

2. **Who will be in charge of the individual animals?** Will this person ever leave them in charge of anyone else? Will they ever be left alone with clients, spectators, or others whose attitudes toward animals are unknown? Where will they be when they are not working in the activity? How sensitive to the animals' needs is the person in charge? *Possible guideline*: MAKE CERTAIN THAT THE PERSON IN CHARGE OF THE ANIMAL(S) IS ONE WHO IS PROTECTIVE OF ANIMALS AND SENSITIVE TO THEIR NEEDS. REQUIRE THERE BE PROTECTED PLACES FOR THEM WHEN THEY ARE NOT BEING SUPERVISED. MAKE SURE THAT NO UNKNOWN STAFF ARE GIVEN CUSTODY TO WORK WITH THE ANIMALS.

3. **Who will find and consider the individual animal's fatigue threshold?** For example, Lassie could be stressed in less than one-half hour, whereas, Rufus could be content to stay a large part of a whole day's worth of receiving and exchanging affection, with only a few nice play breaks.

4. **How will bonding and losses be handled?** Both human and animal suffer loss if a bond has been cemented and then broken. Where there is an opportunity for a single human and non-human animal to become bonded, consider the loss reaction if this relationship cannot become a permanent significant-other relationship. Would there be too much risk of loss reaction with one party, or another, or both? Could the bond be allowed to continue?

5. **Exactly how will we work with the animals?** Will individuals be taken out and GIVEN to people to hold? HOW do they PLAN to tell when an individual is in distress? What are the guidelines for the person in charge to look for when deciding how and when an animal needs to be taken away from an individual or a group? HOW is a situation to be handled where an individual is traumatized by a human participant? *Possible guideline*: PLAN HOW TO HANDLE SITUATIONS WHERE AN ANIMAL IS TRAUMATIZED BY A HUMAN PARTICIPANT: For example, you might take the human away or take the animal away immediately, or model gentle behavior and allow one and only one more chance to be gentle.

6. **What are the signs of agitation, trauma, or pain IN THIS SPECIES AND WITH THIS INDIVIDUAL?** Anyone who knows a species can come up with ways that particular species can show upset, but just as important are the INDIVIDUAL RESPONSES within that species. Often there are particular communications of dis-

tress by the individual that are NOT that common with the species as a whole. Some animal individuals fear males, females, children, or other kinds of beings. This is similar to human fears, for example when a person has been traumatized earlier by a certain kind of group or individual.

7. **What are the purposes of each pet facilitated session, and is there an animal welfare element there?** Do all others who will work with these animals know the goals? Ideally all those working with the animals should get together and talk about goals. Because most non-human animals cannot speak for themselves, in order to be ethical, the following are the kinds of goals that need to be implemented wherever there is animal assisted therapy: Some goals I find important are:

* NO ANIMAL HURT, HARMED OR STRESSED
* A SUCCESSFUL EXPERIENCE FOR THE HUMAN
 (which might first require modeling gentleness and perhaps some verbal teaching of loving, empathic handling and relating —then hands-on help with proper handling — followed perhaps by solo relating with and handling of an animal)
* AN ENJOYABLE EXPERIENCE FOR THE ANIMAL
* A HUMAN WHO WILL BE MORE SENSITIVE TO NON-HUMAN ANIMAL NEEDS AFTERWARDS.
* AN EXPERIENCE IN GIVING AND RECEIVING, NURTURING , LOVING, CARING, AND CLOSENESS.

I have often found that staff goals are too general, partially because of low expectations. They do not realize the experience can be meaningful. For example, I have found staff that simply expect the experience will bring a smile or laugh or be a happy moment for the client. This, too, is an important goal, but if we add to that learning some empathy and/or how to have a gentle, positive relationship with another, or evaluating whether or not the client is capable of having more experiences with companion animals, powerful new dynamics are harnessed. These new focuses by staff members and clients can generate a kind of progress that is otherwise lost.

8. **What will the animal(s) gain from this?** There is an element of "fairness" in ethics. Perhaps a dog who loves affection will enjoy all the petting and relating to others. But what if the activity is more of an ORDEAL for another animal? Should not that individual be spared the ordeal, or at least be rewarded with an extra something that the individual loves best, such as a long play time outdoors or other favorite activity?

9. **How will species-specific, as well as individual needs, be taken care of ?** CAREFULLY study the species being put in contact with humans. For example, screen out undesirable stimuli that could be upsetting to the species, as in the case of mice, who have an incredibly sensitive auditory apparatus, so that loud noises can be painful for them. THEN carefully study the individual with whom you are working, because I have discovered that variations among individuals WITHIN a species can be as great as variation BETWEEN species! For example, some individuals enjoy being held and/ or petted, whereas, it quickly becomes stressful for other individuals within the same species.

Pearl Salotto

All in all, it seems to me that when dealing with living, sentient beings, we must ethically consider their treatment as seriously as we would a human in the same situation. When we work with animals in a way that can lead to unpredictable harm and trauma (presenting them to strangers we know little about), we must find ways to protect them from unforeseeable sufferings, and to make certain that ALL involved in ANY pet assisted activity or therapy always keep in mind the question, "How would I like it?" We need to make certain that safeguards for nonhuman animals are specific, clear, and are firmly in place.

Section 6:
RETURNING THE FAVOR

<u>Nina Natelson</u> *founded Concern for Helping Animals in Israel (CHAI) in 1984, and has been its Director since that time. She has been a vegetarian and active in <u>animal rights issues</u> since 1980, and has been a vegan since 1982. She lives in Annandale, VA with her husband, Murry Cohen, MD., a psychiatrist and Co-Chair of the Medical Research Modernization Committee (MRMC) and their two dogs (including Patterson) and five cats.*

For as long as I can remember, animals have given me love and support, through good times and bad. The love we have shared has been the one constant that has sustained me, no matter how bumpy the road.

Patterson, the best dog in the whole world, who inspired all of Nina's good work.

My very first memory is of meeting the cat that raised me. I was sitting on the steps outside our house in Rockford, Illinois, when a long-haired gray cat with green eyes walked right up to me and let me pet her. I was about four years old at the time. My father admired her high intelligence and mousing ability, and chauvinistically named her Grayman, although she was a female.

Realizing that the cat must belong to someone, my parents placed a notice in the newspaper. By the time the woman who was Grayman's real human showed up to claim her, Grayman and I had bonded for all time and no one, but no one, was going to take her away from me. One look at me fiercely clutching the cat, tears streaming down my cheeks, and the woman promptly announced that there must have been some mistake after all, the cat was clearly too big to be the one she had lost. Bless that woman for her understanding and wisdom.

Whenever the practical jokes of my three older siblings got to be too much for me or when anything in life wasn't going well, I sought refuge with Grayman. After a while, my father started calling her Dr. Grayman, since she seemed to be able to cure whatever was troubling me, physically and emotionally.

In those days, people didn't show love toward one another outwardly the way they feel free to do today. Grayman was the repository for all the love from every member of the family. It radiated to her and out from her, and she sustained us all. When she finally died shortly after I went away to college, my father wrote a beautiful eulogy about how she had raised four children and now that her task was complete, she could go. More than thirty years later, he still carries her picture in his wallet.

I have lived with and loved many other animals since Grayman's departure. All were special to me, and all were my teachers. Nim Teng, a Siamese who came to me as a stray in terrible condition and who died last year at the age of about sixteen, taught me the tremendous power of love to transform all. My dog, Patterson, taught me not to be afraid of dogs, and by extension, of all other animals with whom I had not yet come into contact.

Pearl Salotto

Patterson is a large husky/shepherd/border collie/lab and whatever-else-you-might-imagine mix, black with gold markings. He and I first met at a mental hospital where I had gone to visit a friend who was a patient there. The nurses had found him as a stray next to a building called "the Patterson building" and decided to "use" him for "pet therapy."

He was kept outside in a tiny cage, without proper food, water, or exercise. If I drove up in winter, I found him shivering in the cold. Only his thick fur kept him from freezing to death overnight. In summer, I found him panting, obviously suffering from the heat, with no shade except inside the blistering hot excuse for a dog house — a few boards peppered with holes. Unsupervised mental patients were allowed to spend time with him, and I saw one beating him, the patient's version of "training." Sometimes Patterson's water bowl was broken, and he had nothing to drink. Sometimes the patients would shove peaches, donuts, mashed potatoes and other food from the cafeteria into his cage, not knowing any better. The food would eventually rot and become covered with flies. Excrement wasn't cleaned out of the cage very often either, so Patterson had virtually no clean place to sit.

No amount of letter writing, phone calls or offers of a free dog house and food would change the attitude of the hospital staff. He was their "property", they insisted, like a table or some other inanimate object, and if they wanted him to have a proper dog house or anything else, they would take the money from the canteen. Anyone who has tried to put an end to such situations legally knows that our laws regarding animals are still in the Dark Ages. "Adequate shelter" can be the overhang of a roof or a metal drum, and "adequate space" is barely enough room to stand up, turn around, and sit down.

Conditions like those Patterson endured are the reason I oppose "pet therapy," except under the most carefully supervised conditions. Pet Therapy can all too easily turn to animal abuse. When that happens, the animals become nothing more than tools for human use. Those who run programs where this is the case don't realize that the program can only work properly when the needs of both animals and humans are met and respect for the needs of both are shown.

Patterson was finally freed thanks to a helping hand from Dr. Michael Fox of the Humane Society of the U. S., who wrote a letter threatening to sue the hospital if they didn't either spend a lot of money to improve the care and condition of the dog, or release him to a good home. When I learned that they had agreed to release Patterson, I was certain that just out of spite, they would never consider giving him to me, but I was wrong.

The tiny townhouse in which I lived at the time was much too small for a huge dog and four cats, so we moved farther away from the city to a house with a large back yard. I spent weeks looking at Patterson and worrying what to do with him and for him. Cats sleep or wander outside if the neighborhood is safe and away from traffic, or play with each other or by themselves. But dogs? What exactly do you do with a dog after you've fed and walked him, I wondered. Besides that, I realized I was still a little afraid of dogs. The fear had been passed down to my mother and then to me by my grandmother, who had a chunk taken out of her leg by a dog when she was trying to escape the persecution of Jews in Eastern Europe. It was common in those times for people to sic dogs on Jews to control them or stop them from escaping.

Little by little, Patterson taught me not to be afraid of dogs. He knew I loved cats and became so careful of them, he would walk out into the street to avoid disturbing a cat sitting on the sidewalk, looking at me the whole time to make sure he was doing the right thing. In every way, he was a gentleman's gentleman. Soon, Patterson began to accompany me everywhere I went, and I do mean everywhere. He loved riding in the car. Truckers honked and said obscene things when I kissed his velvet ears or hugged him while we stopped at a red light. Others watched and smiled, especially people with dogs in their cars.

Today, the only remnants of Patterson's hospital stay are a touch of arthritis and fear of thunderstorms from being left out in the cold and wet, and a refusal to eliminate anywhere near his home. He insists on getting a walk a good distance away from the house. He bears no bitterness or resentment toward anyone, and has greeted patients and staff at the hospital warmly when we've gone back for a visit. Humans have a lot to learn about forgiveness from animals!

In 1984 I founded Concern for Helping Animals in Israel (CHAI), after witnessing the terrible conditions for animals in that country while on a visit to relatives. During its first decade, CHAI has promoted animal protection legislation, initiated humane education in the schools, given direct support to the few, small animal shelters, stopped the mass strychnine poisonings of animals at municipal pounds around the country, and much more.

Following a March 1994 highly successful conference co-sponsored with Israel's Ministry of Education, "Preventing Violence in Society Through Education," highlighting and discussing the link between violence toward humans and violence toward animals, CHAI and the Ministry are cooperating on humane education programs, including a special program to bring together Jewish and Arab children at the SPCA in Israel in Tel Aviv to learn about animals and to participate in hands-on projects to help them.

Sometimes people ask why I help animals when I could be helping people. The answer is that animals have given me so much over my lifetime that I could never repay the debt of gratitude and love I owe them. Animals never criticize or judge or demand anything more of us than that we meet their basic necessities of life. They demonstrate what unconditional love and real friendship are all about. What an incredible gift to the world!

People who cannot appreciate animals or communicate with them are not fully alive. Like children deprived of language or music when they were young — who have difficulty speaking or appreciating the beauty of a melody; people who haven't shared the love of an animal are missing out on the very best of what life has to offer.

The work of conservationists who teach people to appreciate nature is at long last becoming valued and understood. The work of those who strive to instill a humane ethic deserves equal respect and appreciation. I can't think of anything else I would rather do with my life's energy than work to relieve animal suffering and raise consciousness about the respect and care animals need and deserve, and thereby perhaps give back a tiny fraction of the help and love given to me by animals who have added so much joy and light to my world.

Section 7:
LIVING MY ETHICS

__Roberta Preziosi__ is a lifetime animal lover and advocate living a vegan lifestyle. She writes educational poetry and prose relating to animals and the environment. Roberta is currently working with legislators toward passing laws that extend waiting periods for animals awaiting adoption and banning the gas chamber at city and private shelters. She works as a Pet-Assisted Therapy Facilitator along with her therapy pets, Mindy and Golden Girl. Her current project is designing a custom home that is animal-friendly and safe, including sprinkler fire alarms, separate cat and dog quarters, cat walks, outdoor cat runs and double fences for dogs, heated floors, sunspaces, and vestibules to protect pets from accidentally getting out when doors are opened.

Roberta with Mindie and Scottie - playing love games in the backyard.

Nearly two years prior to my enrollment into Pearl Salotto's university Pet-Assisted Therapy (PAT) course, I began seeking formal coursework offerings on the topic. It took me that long to locate a course, finally stumbling upon Pearl's certificate program through referral by a coworker. This book is a long-overdue, necessary tool for use in colleges across the country as more PAT programs are developed in every state to meet the demand for education as the field continues to expand.

My background in animal rescue work complemented my personal interest in PAT. From rescuing a stray, injured dog found on a Texas vacation and flying her home to Rhode Island for medical care and adoption to capturing, domesticating, and adopting out feral cats, PAT became an additional channel for animal advocacy. My primary interest in PAT, however, was on behalf of my pets' anticipated enjoyment in having the opportunity to get out and about visiting friendly people. One of my Scottish Terriers, Mindy, absolutely loves meeting people and exploring new places. She is very outgoing and has a pleasant, tender personality. I thought PAT would be a confidence booster for her because she gets so proud and excited in receiving praise and strokes from gentle human friends. Pets should be given the opportunity to communicate their approval or disapproval of external exposure from their home environment. Indulging in safe exposures, they can expand their personalities, gain memories and learning experiences, exercise their mind and body, or simply try something new. These exposures can include walks in the park, visits to extended family members, good behavior or agility classes, strolls at the beach, or in our case – PAT work. Mindy's brother, Scotti, has no interest in meeting new people and enjoys staying within the safe confines of his home and fenced-in yard. Golden Girl, the family feline, gets pleasure from meeting people, does not fear car rides, is tranquil and personable.

All this talk about my own pets brings me to my primary ethic – A good pet-assisted therapy facilitator (PATF) does not force a pet to do something she shows reluctance in doing. For example, forcefully transporting a pet in a vehicle knowing it will be stressful is cruel. If you have only taken your pet for rides to the veterinarian, if she gets car sick, or just does not like car rides, can you blame her for showing reluctance? Using force or overpowering an animal is not acceptable, unless intervention is for their safety such as physically pulling a dog from a dangerous situation. Because my Mother brought her children up to love and respect 4-legged animals and all other precious creatures, I was lucky to have grown up around cats, dogs, fish, turtles, gerbils, and truly feel in tune to sensing what most pets do and do not enjoy. Since I never played with dolls but instead always had a stuffed animal in tow – my imprint to serve animals has continually presented itself throughout my life. My family knows how much I've loved dogs particularly, in childhood and adulthood, so helping animals is intertwined into my heartbeat to this day. Ethical PAT simply means acting lovingly, safely, and respectfully toward a pet who has shown initiative in meeting new people and visiting new places without any fear. That includes no fear of car rides and your commitment to safe travel, keeping PAT visits close to home. A long ride to and from a PAT site after a 30-60 minute visit can be very stressful overall even to the most youthful, assertive pet.

When Pearl asked us to write a code of ethics for her class assignment, I was nervous at first, thinking the ethics I had in mind would be too extreme or shocking because I felt pets should be the absolute priority of anyone who assumed a PATF role. To my surprise, Pearl appreciated my respect and dedication to the ways in which I thought PAT sessions should be handled. She encouraged me to submit my ethics to The Latham Letter, and they proudly published my words in 1997. That was the beginning of earning my reputation as the ethics woman, an animal advocate still spreading her wings to protect four-legged creatures.

Throughout my 100-hour internship and my four-year professional PAT career, I have assured that any facility we work with reads, understands, and complies with the fact that my ethics will be adhered to fully. Each facility cooperates with the manner in which our program prioritizes the pet's needs, meaning that each session actually evolves based upon how my pets feel on a particular day. For example, if Golden Girl is tired, we let her rest and my backup plan for not focussing so much on her includes reading animal stories, quietly singing happy songs, or drawing animal pictures. A quality PATF has alternative activities planned for her audience, just in case a pet is not in the mood to interact. If a lack of desire to interact continues, the PATF must consider the fact that this particular pet may no longer enjoy PAT work and is trying to say "Please let me be a home pet – I really don't enjoy this any longer." Reading your pets' body language and communicating with him or her is imperative in order to have a working relationship, beyond the home environment.

A PATF must be sensitive to when her pet is not in the mood to work so no actions are forced upon the pet. There have been days when Golden Girl indicated that she did not want to go to work and there were days when the weather was not pleasant (heavy rain, icy roads, extreme cold or heat), so she stayed home. These unpredictable situations are built into my contract and when they occur, I call the facility to reschedule, visit with Mindy, or visit independently without a pet, depending upon the situation at hand. I have done PAT without either of my therapy pets because the weather was harsh or roads were too icy to take any pet out in a vehicle. Arriving without a pet turned heads of initially disappointed seniors, but once I explained the reasons and described what we were going to do instead, they all agreed that it was better not to take any chances with a pet riding in a vehicle on an icy day. So I read pet stories and assured they had fun in other ways while turning the session into an educational opportunity on why pets must be protected and cared for like human infants, in that we have to make decisions that have their best interest in mind — even if it slightly disappointed the people. Again, my pets are the priority in every situation. I was pleasantly surprised to learn that the clients enjoyed me — even without precious Goldie — so this was assuring when the situation to visit alone presented itself in future situations.

Another example of quality ethics is insisting that each facility respect the pet as an equal partner to the PATF, not as a tool, entertainment, or treatment mechanism. For example, one facility insisted that I work with Mindy in a hobby craft room because it had ceramic floors should Mindy have a toilet accident, which had actually happened once. The other rooms had thick carpets and would be difficult to clean if another accident occurred. I thought this was fairly reasonable but in the winter I mentioned taking blankets to lay on the floor for her. I also requested the floor be cleaned prior to each PAT session so no remnants of craft work would remain, posing a danger to Mindy, such as glitter, glue, or thumb tacks. My contract requires each facility to maintain a pet-friendly environment. Because they continually left pins, glitter, and spots of sticky glue on the floor, I severed the professional relationship because it was not safe for Mindy. Either party should be able to break a PAT contract without penalty should ethics or other professional issues come into conflict.

I would not put my pets in a situation under which we could loose control. For example, Golden Girl is not accustomed to being around children. During one PAT session, three small boys were visiting their Grandmother and the boys were quite loud, irritating Goldie. They wanted to play with her but I would not allow them to approach because I could not predict her reaction nor did I wish to directly expose her to these children, who were frightening her. I invited Goldie into her cat carrier, where she could be safe and alone, then asked the boys to quiet down after explaining why. It was a learning experience for the children in showing consideration for Goldie. Then I read to the seniors while Goldie took a reprieve. I do not consider PAT work as entertainment and never apologize for my pets doing something that comes naturally such as barking, being tired, getting scared, or not being very social on any particular day. I do apologize if Mindy has a toilet accident, which can be a bit embarrassing, but I explain that she is simply excited to see everyone and lost control for a moment. Such situations are natural byproducts of working with pets and are expected to occur from time to time. Perfection and predictability do not coincide with the term living being.

Living my ethics takes no conscious effort because it all comes naturally from within, through my love and respect for animals and the PAT profession. You don't have to work by my ethics to be a reputable, ethical PATF but you need to possess a similar ethical base of love and respect for your particular pet while at work and at home. Ultimately, the pet is a respected, beloved family member first, then secondly may have the desire and potential to become an equal PAT partner. If your pets are not family members, then I personally see an ethical problem already. How can you ask your pet to give more of him or herself by working with you in the PAT field when you have not already given everything possible to your pet by incorporating her or him into your family as an equally-deserving, loved member?

Since writing my ethics four years ago, I have lectured to new students enrolled in that same university course I so enjoyed, people have requested reprint permission of my ethics, a variety of forums have entertained my ethics in debates, and I have written numerous articles on the topic of ethics. I will continue PAT work for as long as my pets wish to remain active, equal partners. It is my opinion that ethics apply when addressing all living beings. An emotional connection occurs when ethics are properly in place. When considering PAT, which involves non-human and human beings, wouldn't ethics surface as the one absolute, obvious necessity? It is an honor to be included in this book so that my words may influence students, perhaps future PATF professionals, to instill upon themselves a knowledge base that perpetuates an honest, true respect for pets that can lead to an ethical PAT career.

For Your Consideration:
A Pet Assisted Therapist Facilitator Code of Ethics

1. The therapy pet must be the Pet-Assisted Therapy Facilitator's (PATF) priority at all times, ensuring the animal's complete safety when working within the therapy field. The PATF must never put an animal into a potentially dangerous situation and some precautions to take include:

- *The therapy pet has the right to be approached in a safe, calm manner only by medically and psychologically stable clients. Mandate completion of physician consent forms to screen against pet phobias or allergies, communicable diseases, physical restrictions, or mental illness that could prevent a client from acting humanely toward a therapy animal. The PATF makes the final decision on whether or not a client participates in PAT sessions. The client cannot be capable of potential harm, have a tendency for violence, consciously or unconsciously, and must possess a consistent, demonstrated capacity for empathy and gentleness;*
- *Insisting that the animal is fully respected and accepted as a professional by clients and staff with equal rights amongst all therapy session participants;*
- *Making every effort with regard to pet safety by securing pets to a leash or harness, using a carrier (particularly with a cat, ferret, or rabbit), and allowing the pet to become accustomed to new encounters such as elevators, automatic doors, speaker systems, wheelchairs;*
- *Carrying adequate insurance because any work performed outside of the home is typically excluded from homeowner policies; insurance is necessary in order to carry the title of a professional PAT. People nor animals are completely predictable — accidents can happen — and facilities will be more likely to hire an insured professional than one who is uninsured;*
- *Screening pets against undesirable animal behavior, such as tendencies for bites, nips, or growls, then humanely training for correction by socializing and teaching — not punishing. Eliminating those traits so the pet can be more relaxed and personable is best for the pet. However, a pet with these tendencies should not be brought into the PAT profession. The pet will be a happier family member if such traits can be humanely dissipated;*

2. The therapy pet should never be forced to leave the home to go to work. A therapy pet should show desire and excitement to leave her home, ride in the car, and visit a therapy facility; otherwise, the PATF should cancel the session since forcing a pet is never acceptable behavior. Occasional cancellations are unavoidable but if a pet shows a frequent lack of motivation and illness or aging is not a factor, perhaps the companion animal is no longer interested in therapy work and prefers staying home with her family; the PATF must respect this desire.

3. The PATF will use language that is respectful, positive, and reflective of the bond that would preclude such expressions as "therapy animals are used." PATF is not a mere means to a therapeutic end but a mutually beneficial animal-human intervention. Allow interactions to occur in a manner consistent with the pet's natural behavior. For

example, if a pet is nervous, she could be sensing something volatile with a particular situation or person and forcing, except in her own best interest for safety, is disrespectful. It must be enjoyable for the pet – which is the PATF's responsibility. If Fido does not wish to sit for Mr. Jones to pet him, then walk about with Fido instead.

4. Know your animal extremely well and do not put a therapy companion animal in a situation where he or she is not comfortable. Some pets prefer one-on-one therapy work exclusively and it is the responsibility of the PATF to make this determination and use consistent good judgment. The therapy animal should initially be approached by one person at a time then move to group sessions gradually. For example, a pet not used to being around children should not be brought to visit an elementary school class with anxious hands and loud voices. This could very much frighten a pet and could result in an explosive, unsafe situation.

5. Adjust the animal to the therapy field gradually to avoid stressing her. This includes acclimating her to automobile travel beginning with very brief neighborhood rides. Strange surroundings, sounds, or smells can frighten an animal putting her into a defensive mode of behavior, which can be dangerous for the pet and clients. Avoid all stress during PAT work. Repeated stress will compromise a pet's immune system; therefore, brief, casual visits are recommended until the pet remains relaxed after spending 45-60 minutes at a facility. Visits should not surpass this amount of time. Stress signs to be aware of include pacing, thirst, panting, fast heartbeat, sudden urine or bowel movements, tail or ears down and stiff, crying out or barking excessively, or not cooperating. To dissolve a stressful situation, bring the pet out-of-doors or in a quiet, comfortable place. End the session if necessary. This is not indicative of bad pet behavior. She simply senses something that she does not like – accept that respectfully and if it continues, no longer visit that site or no longer perform PAT work with this particular pet. She is a family member first – therapy pet second.

6. Companion animals enjoy gentle playing, relaxing, and touching with human family members. Safe fun, unconditional love, and respect during human socialization will be the fundamental motivation necessary for a born therapy pet. A therapy pet cannot be made; the traits are within the pet or not. Some pets simply do not enjoy being away from their home or family members – their beloved pack. Others just blossom when interacting with other pets and people; they have the potential for therapy work.

7. The therapy animal should be given a quiet time period during each therapy session to rest or eliminate outside; this quiet time will vary depending upon the animal's age and overall health, climate, facility room temperature, and type of therapy session.

8. The PATF should never leave the therapy pet alone or out of visual range during a therapy session unless left with a person with whom the PATF has complete trust and the pet feels comfortable staying with for a short time.

9. The PATF must protect the health of the therapy animal by inspecting the premises in which the animal will visit to verify cleanliness, particularly the floors. An animal-friendly environment should be specified within the contract. Blankets can be taken to lie down for the animal's comfort and for sanitary purposes. Animals walking on medical facility floors, licking the hands or face of a client (although the PATF should discourage licking), can be exposed to medicinal or chemical residues when they lick their

paws. Pills can be dropped on the floor and quickly ingested by a pet. Human shoes collect, transfer and deposit a variety of viruses and bacteria onto floor surfaces where animals collect the same onto their paws, lick off, and then become susceptible to a variety of diseases (this is a primary means by which Parvo was spread). Animal booties can be purchased to protect the animal from chemicals, medicine residues, and viruses or to improve footing on slippery floors.

10. The PATF should not allow clients to share their food with a therapy pet. Only food/snacks brought by the PATF should be offered. Supplies brought to each session should include fresh water from home also.

11. A client should never be allowed to make contact with a pet if that client is diagnosed with an illness that could be transmitted to an animal. The PATF is responsible for screening each client's medical status and for checking with a veterinarian to understand which human illnesses are transmittable to their particular pet. Contracts should specify that clients use anti-bacterial agents to clean hands before and after petting a therapy pet or anti-bacterial liquid can be carried by the PATF and supplied to clients before interacting with the pet.

12. Therapeutic interactions will be consenting in nature, guided by a philosophy of mutual respect and dignity for all participants. Benefits should be continually evaluated to assure mutually-willing participation. Interactions should cease if either therapy animal or client become uncomfortable.

13. Local laws vary but at minimum, rabies inoculations are necessary. Traditional, holistic, or homeopathic options are available. It is not necessary to over inoculate simply because your pet will be interacting with the public. Adhere to required local inoculation laws and mandate that clients and facilities are clean.

14. Alternative therapy animals such as ferrets, rabbits, or horses have unique needs not addressed in these ethics. The PATF must take responsibility to see that these needs are fully met with regard to working within the PAT environment.

15. Because the therapy animal is a respected and valued life and work partner, her comfort, health, and safety rights are equal to that of the client and PATF.

16. The PATF abides by the humane principles of positive reinforcement and nonviolent corrective behavior modification during all pet interactions. Punishment or aversive techniques, verbal or physical is abusive and unacceptable.

17. An animal first aid kit should be a supply carried at all times. The PATF should maintain animal CPR certification, often available through local American Red Cross offices.

18. During extreme heat, the PATF should only transport a pet if the visiting facility and automobile are adequately air conditioned, particularly with overweight or older pets. The PAT contract can specify ideal temperatures for the pet and allow for discontinuing sessions if the facility is, for example, warmer than 70 F degrees.

19. An ethical PATF does not "use" a therapy animal as a medical tool or form of entertainment. An ethical PATF recognizes the traits of a born therapy animal then incorporates those traits into the therapy field by simply bringing along the pet to do what comes naturally to the animal. This includes enjoying the human voice, touch, and companionship, during which time the PATF consistently ensures this interaction takes place within a safe, healthy environment. Therapeutic healing and educating our

youth result from relaxed, honest, calm interactions. Performing trick
tivities are not important. Above all, if the necessary personality trait
within your pet's natural temperament, then forcing such an animal to wo
therapy field constitutes "use" or "abuse" of that precious life, which is
competence. In order for PATFs to succeed as professionals, we must de   ate
competence and respect for our animal friends and the humans with whom they interact. Following a good ethics foundation leads to a safe PAT career for all involved.

PART IV

THE FUTURE OF PET ASSISTED THERAPY

271of432

CHAPTER 7

PROFESSIONAL PET ASSISTED THERAPY LEADING TO A FRIENDLIER, HEALTHIER, AND MORE PEACEFUL WORLD

Pearl Salotto

Section 1:
THE IMPORTANCE OF ANIMALS TO THE WELL-BEING OF PEOPLE

Dr. Leo Bustad, *DVM, Ph.D., pioneered a new partnership between people, animals, and the environment. He is the Dean Emeritus of the Washington State University School of Veterinary Medicine and the first president of the Delta Society. He directs the People Pet Partnership in Washington state. He is an internationally known spokesperson for the relationship among people, animals and the environment. His compassion, dedication and energy have inspired many individuals to continue his ideas.*

reprinted with permission of author and publisher — Delta Society

> *This is a subject in which I have invested a great deal of effort and resources over the past 15 years. And I have committed the rest of my days to it. It has been a very rewarding 15 years, principally because of the many capable, wonderful people I have met who are devoted to contributing to the well-being of people, animals and the environment.*
>
> *I used an invitation from the American Animal Hospital Association to submit a manuscript on this subject to pay tribute to a very dear friend and associate in the Delta Society and in our Northwest Regional Program in Veterinary Medicine. Dr. Michael McCulloch was a remarkable human being whose contributions and influence nationally and internationally were nothing short of phenomenal. We are grateful for his life and work with us; we miss him terribly!*
>
> *This presentation is an abbreviated version of what was published in the American Animal Hospital Association's [AAHA] publication,* **Trends**, *[Bustad, 1985], and we appreciate AAHA's permission to include it in this book.*

It is with a heavy heart, but also with great hope, that I write this article chiefly because of the life and recent death of an uncommon man and dear friend, Dr. Michael McCulloch. This article is dedicated to him and his pioneering work. A few brief quotations from the Congressional Record of Thursday, July 18, 1985, entitled "Memorial for Dr. Michael McCulloch, " summarize well his life and his work. Senator Proxmire said:

> Mr. President, exceptional men deserve recognition. Particularly when their life's works enrich all of us...Dr. Michael McCulloch was an exceptional man.
>
> Friends, acquaintances, and relatives describe him as a devoted family man, deeply caring for his wife, his four children, and nephew who was welcomed to the family following the tragic loss of his parents.
>
> Colleagues and patients describe him as conscientious, professional, sensitive. "An able physician," a leader in psychiatry," a man whose "quiet

suggestions" made a real difference in the lives of those he touched.

His training in psychiatry gave him a special understanding of human behavior. His love of animals, beginning at an early age, made him keenly aware of the special affinities between people and animals. He believed, recalled his brother, Dr. William McCulloch, that through medicine he could help people, and through knowledge of people-animal relationships, he could improve the healing art....

To understand the human-companion animal bond, McCulloch called for a disciplined effort by scientists from several fields and initiated his own careful studies.

In 1977 he helped establish the Delta Society to study human/animal relationships and how they may be used to facilitate therapy. The society grew; its membership spread across the United States and drew from many disciplines. It became the leading professional organization conducting research on the effect of animals on human health; initiating companion animal programs for disturbed children, handicapped persons, prisoners, and patients in hospitals and nursing homes; and educating Americans about the benefits of human-animal interaction. The research and education activities of the Delta Society played a key role in securing passage of the pets in the elderly housing bill which I introduced in 1983.

This legislation prohibits discrimination against elderly or handicapped persons who wished to have a pet companion and who live in federally funded housing. It reflects recent research findings that pet ownership can significantly improve the physical and emotional health of older or handicapped people.

Those who heard Dr. McCulloch speak about the bonds that link humans and companion animals recognized him as an exceptional communicator. He marshaled his information about human psychology, medicine, and animal behavior carefully. He conveyed complex matter with professional clarity. He described the wondrous results of human/animal interactions with a quiet, but convincing passion. Both in his lectures and in his writing, Dr. McCulloch revealed himself as an uncommon teacher.

On the morning of Wednesday, June 26, Dr. McCulloch was shot to death in his office by a deranged, former patient.

He will be missed. The loss will be felt not only by his family, his friends and others who knew him. This exceptional man, who worked so hard to increase our understanding of the bonds which link all living creatures, and to use this knowledge to cure those who are ill and comfort those who cannot be cured, will be remembered by all of us.

I am deeply grateful for all he did to enrich my life, that of my family, our college, profession and our society.

A decade ago, I wrote an article entitled "Pets-For-People Therapy" in which I discussed the benefits of companion animals. I proposed their use in a number of situations, such as placement in local nursing and convalescent homes, a project we had already begun. I explained in this article that animals could improve the psychological well-being of countless people. In the intervening ten years, I have traveled exten-

Pearl Salotto

sively and learned of the experiences and studies of many people reported at a variety of meetings, including three international conferences. I am now even more convinced that animals, properly selected and maintained, can contribute to the health and well-being of many more people — not only psychologically, but physically and socially. More and more health professionals will be recommending that people obtain animals as companions or as helpers. In this regard, this past year, Tom Ferguson, MD, quoted me in his article "Medical Self Care:" I believe the day is coming when doctors will sometimes 'prescribe' pets instead of pills....What pill gives so much love, makes one feel safe, stimulates laughter, encourages regular exercise and makes a person feel needed?"

This day is already here! In this brief article I believe I can best express my feelings telling you what I would do if I was a dictator. A portion of the summary of the following is taken from the International Symposium on Human-Pet Relationships, honoring the 80th birthday of Nobel Laureate Konrad Lorenz in Vienna, Austria, in 1983, which I prepared with the help of Dr. Michael McCulloch and others:

"In jest I have often stated what I would do if I were a dictator. In concluding this meeting, I am, on the basis of what I have learned here these past two days as well as my experiences over the past decade, telling you what I would do relative to the human-animal bond if I were dictator:

Dr. Leo Bustad with Bridget. Courtesy of the Delta Society.

"1. The first thing I would do is to incorporate into the curriculum of all school systems including universities, courses on the human-animal bond. It would begin at a very early age; as a result, within one generation we could have responsible pet care as the "rule," rather than as the exception it is now in our society. The course offerings would be designed to improve the selection process for choosing companion animals, thereby remarkably improving the strength of the bond in a variety of situations. A course on "Reverence for Life" modeled after the one I teach at Washington State University would be required. This would hopefully raise the sensitivity level of future generations so they will not consider animals as "throw-away" items, but will take killing seriously.

"2. The second thing I would give special emphasis to as dictator is a subject I have already alluded to, and that is improved selection of animals. In our experience, the failure to experience a positive human-companion relationship, a healthy and re-warding bond, is the poor selection of animals [and recipient]. This, along with the ignorance on the part of the recipient, portend a disastrous relationship. As we progress we must develop a better selection criteria that may well include setting up special breeding programs for appropriate 'therapy animals.'

"3. As dictator I would have veterinarians assist in facilitating the proper selection and placement of pets and insuring the health and welfare of every animal. As impor-tant members of a team approach to animal-assisted therapy, veterinarians could con-tribute to development of a scientific profile and scoring system for dogs that would aid in their appropriate selection and placement. Such scoring could also be used in evaluating qualitatively and, hopefully, quantitatively the effect on the animal from its use in various situations with a variety of patients. From such dedicated effort could come immeasurable happiness and well-being for both animals and people.

"4. As dictator, I would install aquaria in all dental and medical offices, elemen-tary school classrooms and conference rooms and lunch rooms of all businesses, insti-tutions, prisons, schools and governmental offices. All interviewing rooms would have as residents one or more docile, friendly animals. Similar animals would also be ap-propriately housed in student dormitories, nursing and convalescent homes.

"5. Hospitals would have assigned wards where patients who required their ani-mals to accompany them when they go to the hospital would be accommodated. Hos-pices would have provisions for accepting terminal patients and their companion ani-mals, and terminal patients would have an animal available if they wished to have one. All hospital forms will be modified to include two additional questions: 'If you live alone, do you own a pet or pets?' and, 'Who should be called to care for them in emergencies?'"

"6. Appropriate guidelines would be established and respected for companion ani-mals in nursing and convalescent homes, retirement homes and all government hous-ing. Hopefully, they would be extended to privately owned housing as well.

"7. Animals programs would be implemented in all penal institutions. The objec-tives would be the education of the prisoners and their provision of useful service to the community. Service could include training specially selected animals to help people with handicaps, nursing injured or diseased wildlife back to health, and obedience training of selected animals for animal control centers so they would be better com-panion animals after adoption.

"8. Subsidized pet care programs, possibly government sponsored, would be es-tablished to provide health care for animals vital to the well-being of low-income people.

"9. Disaster plans that include provisions for evacuation and care of animals as well as people would be implemented.

"10. In most households, at least two companion animals of different ages would be recommended, especially in single person households and with the elderly and people with handicaps.

"11. Any new buildings would be constructed to accommodate not only the elderly and people with handicaps, but also companion animals. Park facilities would also be constructed so as to address the needs of companion animals and their owners.

"12. As dictator, I would establish a very generous research fund to support promising proposals on the human-animal bond. This addresses the most urgent need voiced by the Delta Society, i.e., careful investigations. This is the basic tenet not only of the Delta Society but, as I understand it, of all the official human-animal bond societies sponsoring this symposium including AFIRAC of France, IEMT of Austria, JACOPIS in Australia and SCAS of the UK.

"13. As dictator, I would establish animal care facilities in certain industries and business establishments. I've made this suggestion for several reasons. Many single people who live alone have one or more pets; often it's a single dog that has to be placed in a kennel every day or left home alone all day. It would be far better for the animal and its owner to be able to bring the dog to work every day. The dog could be visited during breaks and taken for a run at noon. Information sessions and dog obedience instruction could also be arranged for the noon hour or after work. Cooperative programs could be developed with children in day care centers at these establishments. Such programs could involve instruction of children on the care of, and interaction with dogs and other animals. Health benefits to children interacting with carefully selected pets have been shown. Provisions for grief therapy could also be provided for both employees and children [and animals]."

More and more people are recognizing the extent to which pets can facilitate therapy for an assortment of human problems. They provide security and comfort for older people, positive focus for those who are in prisons, and important therapy for those who have serious disabilities. Veterinarians should continue to work toward adopting laws that would permit the use of pets in institutions in each of our states rather than denying people who reside in institutions this remarkable source of comfort and help.

On the basis of experiences by many people and institutions in Australia, Europe, New Zealand and North America, companion animals must be recognized as vital to the physical, psychological and social well-being of people and as agents of therapy in a great number of conditions and situations. Almost everyone could benefit by contact with warm "fuzzies" [unless we are allergic], and our companion animals offer us security, succor, esteem, understanding, forgiveness, fun and laughter and, most importantly, abundant and unconditional love. Furthermore, they make no judgments, and we can be ourselves with them. They also need our help and make us feel important.

I close with a statement from Dr. Michael McCulloch's presentation on animal-assisted therapy at the International Conference on the human-animal bond at the University of Pennsylvania, October, 1981: "If pet therapy offers hope for relief of human suffering, it is our professional obligation to explore every available avenue for its use."

References:

Bustad, L.K. (1985, December). The Importance of Animals to the Well-Being of People. *Trends*, 54-57.

Institute for Interdisciplinary Research on the Human-Pet Relationships (Eds.) (1983). <u>The Human-Pet Relationship: International Symposium on the 80th Birthday of Nobel Prize Winner Prof. Dr. Konrad Lorenz</u>. Vienna, Austria.

Section 2:
REFLECTIONS: THERAPY PETS IN THE FIELD PAVING THE WAY FOR SOCIETIES' CHANGES
(Pearl Salotto)

Glancing up, as I ran with Majee at Pilgrim High School, I saw the smiling faces of several high school youngsters looking down from a second floor classroom window. In that instant my mind flashed back over the last twelve years, contemplating the thousands of smiling faces of folks of all ages whose hearts, minds, days, and lives have been brightened by my best friends — D. J., an eleven year old Samoyed, and Majee — a two and a half year old Samoyed, and more importantly, also a love dog.

Over the past dozen years — through the "love chain" of smiles — the world has become a softer, kinder place and in the process, society's vision of the helping professions has expanded to include PAT:

• from a statewide Commission trying to prevent violence, based on our knowledge of the link of abuse between pets and people.
• to our interaction with individuals in the Health Department, developing and disseminating guidelines on volunteer, as well as professional PAT.
• to sitting with the doctors, nurses, and social workers on the Infection Control Committee at a local hospital, developing PAT guidelines which led to the approval of the hiring of a professional PAT.
• to seeing young high school students, to whom I taught PAT last year, participate on the cutting edge of this educational and treatment based intervention, as they share their humanity, as well as their pets, at an area nursing home.
• to viewing a local school district's focus on nonviolence and respect for all living things, which included The D. J. "Respect for Livings" Program.
• to the college administrator eagerly responding to my overtures to talk about including PAT as part of expressive therapies or as a minor for human service professionals.
• to sitting at the RI statehouse proudly listening as high school students I have taught, tell the senator of their new found awareness of the unconditional love that D. J. and Majee have helped them discover, and of their recognition that just as D. J. and Majee are individuals, so too are they.

Nathan Arruda with D.J. - Dog of Joy.
"D.J. and The D.J. 'Respect for Living Things' Program have had a big effect on my life. I still, at age 15, have this picture of D.J. and me on my dresser, which was taken when I was nine."

- to my university students tenderly appreciating and connecting with my recently produced video, *D. J. — A Dog of All Seasons*, which I made as a gift to my grandchildren — to share with them my everlasting commitment to give D. J. all the best that life can offer (whether it be a Frosty Paw, turkey from the deli, a walk in the park or simply looking out the window from her favorite spot on the couch) with the beautiful voice of my grandson Ross singing "My Prayer for D. J."
- to sitting on the bedroom floor at 4:00 a.m. with a hot mug of coffee and a paw of each of my best friends lovingly placed in my hand — warming my soul.

I feel overwhelmed that life has given me the privilege of recognizing the impact of therapy pets in the field, through D. J. and Majee's love of participating with me in helping to pioneer this profession. The significance of PAT in society is being recognized more and more with each passing day as this "loving intervention" leads to bonds that create human beings more capable of helping to build a friendlier, healthier, and more peaceful world.

Given the changes that one pet therapy team (namely this author and two therapy pets) has seen over the past twelve years, the potential for the many possible benefits to people, animals, and society in general, with hundreds of professionally educated PATs is stunning, as suggested below.

- PAT is good for therapy pets because, among other things, it increases the bond between the PATF and his/her pet due to increased shared, mutually rewarding time together.
- PAT provides the therapy pet the opportunity, on a regular basis, to do something which he/she enjoys doing, that is, going to "work."
- PAT leads to an enhanced awareness on the part of professionals and the public as to the gifts that animals share.
- PAT is also good for animals in the long run, as the therapy pet's example of unconditional love is helping to raise the next generation of children to be committed in all their relationships, including their pets.
- PAT enhances quality of life and potential for treatment for individuals in hospitals, nursing homes, rehabilitation centers, shelters, hospice centers, or prisons.
- PAT enhances potential for schoolchildren to give and receive respect within their school environment, by elevating their awareness of their uniqueness and identity and their recognition of their responsibility to all living things — people, animals, the environment and themselves.
- PAT enhances the potential for children at all levels of education, through Service-Learning, to reach out and connect with people of other generations, as well as people facing unique challenges in life in a loving and mutually rewarding way, over not only the common bond with the pet, but through deeply caring for each other as individuals.
- PAT enhances the realization of parents that in order for their children to grow to be compassionate and empathetic, they must **live** respect for all living things, whether or not they like animals.

- PAT enhances potential for professionals to be creative in their view of treatment to include PAT as a motivator and stimulant for patients to meet countless treatment goals. (i.e. range of motion, socialization, language stimulation, among others.)
- The study of PAT is a great **leveling** experience which enhances all of our sensitivity to each other, due to the common shared love for the pet.
- PAT enhances potential for society's established organizations, whether they be violence prevention coalitions, Chambers of Commerce, empathy building task forces, PTAs, or other professional/community associations, to broaden their visions, understandings, goals, and actions.
- PAT enhances potential for university students in a myriad of disciplines, from human service to ethics, from philosophy to sociology, from psychology to medicine, from criminal justice to education, from human health to veterinary medicine, from counseling to social work, from history to science and human development, to be more effective in their work based on their understanding of the Human Companion Animal Bond and/or the link of abuse.
- PAT expands the potential for inter-generational programs.
- PAT enhances likelihood of youngsters, who care for animals and people, to graduate from high school and go to college, as they see a wider spectrum of career opportunities.
- PAT, as part of the curriculum, enhances ability of students at all levels (elementary, secondary, higher education) to become aware of each of their own opportunities to make a difference in their world, thereby raising their self-esteem and each of their ability to set and accomplish educational goals.
- PAT enhances the potential for universities across this land to fulfill their mission of educating students to be caring and productive members of society.

The following section gives further details on how universities could set up a PAT program.

Section 3:
INGREDIENTS OF A PROFESSION
(Pearl Salotto)

At a recent gathering of individuals who were concerned about the well-being of people and animals, I found myself explaining The D.J. Pet Assisted Therapy (PAT) Certificate Program that I developed and subsequently taught at the State University of New York, at Brockport from 1990-92, through their Continuing Education Department.

As I went on to talk about not only the first course, which was a basic introductory course covering history, benefits, model programs, ethics, safety and legal issues; the second course which was a "hands on — "paws on" understanding, appreciating, and training of therapy pets; and the third course which was a 200 hour internship with the student and the therapy pet working, if possible, under the supervision of a Pet Assisted Therapy Facilitator, a member of the group listening commented, "That's an extremely intensive program. You take this very seriously, don't you?" My spontaneous reply was, "I can't overstate how seriously I take this."

Indeed, working toward the development of PAT as a profession is a very serious and important endeavor.

Defining the Profession: *PAT is a mutual and loving intervention — between a client, who is allergy-free, is aware that the therapy pet is a living creature, and who wishes to relate — and a therapy pet who wishes to relate, has been medically prescribed, health checked and temperament tested, and is part of the overall treatment plan for that client — in which the interaction leads to feelings of giving and receiving love, choices over one's environment, therapeutic stimulation and reminiscing, and which paves the way for trusting and open relationships between the client and the therapy pet. This can, in turn, lead to motivation for sharing of feelings, increased quality of life, increased speech, range of motion, balance, exercise, independence, and overall improved physical and mental health. Pet Assisted Therapy is an individually planned, treatment based, ethically run program, in which the client and therapy pet both eagerly interact and benefit.*

Despite the fact that good hearted and caring volunteers have been bringing animals into nursing homes and agencies for years, leading to much joy, many smiles, and many medical benefits, as well, society needs to move Pet Assisted Therapy from volunteerism to professional status.

A Pet Assisted Therapy Facilitator is a professional working with an approved therapy pet in order to enhance quality of life and to accomplish specific treatment objectives based on individual needs, interests, strengths and functioning level, as part of the Interdisciplinary Treatment Team (ITT), and working within an ethical framework based on improving the well-being of the individual, the pet, and society. The facilitators will be responsible for planning, implementing, and evaluating PAT programs based on the human-companion animal bond. They will be an integral part of the Interdisciplinary Treatment Team and will serve as advocates for clients, therapy pets, and the Pet Assisted Therapy profession.

Therefore, A Pet Assisted Therapy Facilitator is a person, who has a deep and abiding respect for people and animals and who knows how to work effectively and creatively with his/her therapy pet to create a positive effect. This is someone who:

1. *innately cares about each and every human being, animal, and the environment.*
2. *is intuitive enough to sense pain and joy, strengths, and needs.*
3. *is empathetic, open and enthusiastic enough to develop a trusting friendship.*
4. *has enough knowledge of physical conditions, mental conditions, learning styles, and cognitive development to know what the client's needs are.*
5. *is able to detail a written treatment plan with long-term goals and short-term objectives.*
6. *is able to evaluate and document progress, as well as revise and update treatment goals.*
7. *has the necessary communication and cooperation skills to work on an inter-disciplinary treatment team.*
8. *is an enthusiastic advocate for the profession.*
9. *has enough love for his/her therapy pet to be ever aware of the therapy pet's eagerness/willingness to work, and who further understands and respects the therapy pet's joy, enthusiasm, and choices, as well as his/her signals of stress, fatigue, discomfort, etc.*

Those of us working toward building a solid, ethical, and effective foundation for this emerging and unique profession want the educational requirements and licensure safeguards that come with any profession. This is necessary for implementation and development of effective policies and guidelines, such as the draft below.

Sample Pet Therapy Policy for a Medical Setting:

1. *Pet Assisted Therapy Facilitator must have completed their education in PAT in a university program.*
2. *Medical and temperament records must be filed and regularly updated.*
3. *Contract and insurance policy must be on file.*
4. *Pet Assisted Therapy Facilitator will conduct staff in-service training on PAT.*
5. *Pet Assisted Therapy Facilitator will seek client, staff, and family input in program planning.*
6. *Pet Assisted Therapy Facilitator will be an integral part of treatment team.*
7. *PAT will secure a release form for minors with parent's signature.*
8. *Pet Assisted Therapy room will be designated, as well as appropriate entrances and areas for elimination.*
9. *Medical referrals for clients are required prior to entry into program.*
10. *Individual assessment and treatment objectives will be developed for each referred individual.*
11. *Therapy sessions will be regularly scheduled to maintain bond.*
12. *All interactions will be documented.*
13. *Rights of all patients will be respected.*

(Patients will have choice whether or not to interact with pet or have pet in their room, as well as choice whether they want pet on bed or lap.)

14. *Rights of all therapy pets will be respected.*
 (All interactions will be founded on the therapy pets' enthusiasm and free choice, as well as their eagerness to interact.)
15. *Pet Assisted Therapy Facilitator must remain with therapy pets at all times.*
16. *Pet Assisted Therapy Facilitator will be informed of environmental hazards or physical or emotional changes in client, that could present a hazard.*
17. *Therapy pets are not allowed in eating areas, medication stations, laundry or isolation areas.*
18. *Enough staff support must be provided for sate and effective interaction.*
19. *Photo releases are required prior to photographs being taken.*
20. *Evaluation procedure must be in place.*
21. *No one will feed therapy pet without permission.*
22. *No one will approach therapy pet without permission.*
23. *Therapy pet will be included in emergency evacuation plan.*

The benefits of PAT encompass all aspects of human existence including social, physical, and psychological. Pet Assisted Therapy interactions can have a tremendous impact on the health and well-being of individuals in nursing homes, hospitals, and treatment facilities for those who are developmentally and physically challenged, mentally ill, and for those (all too many among us) who have been battered and abused, and even for those in prisons.

But, as quickly as that statement is uttered, those of us working in Pet Assisted Therapy, are also aware of potential issues (i.e. allergies), potential concerns (i.e. whether the needs of the therapy pets, as well as clients are considered in program planning) and potential problems (differing standards, breaking of bonds that have been developed when programs cease, lack of overall accrediting bodies and differing means of documentation). The list is endless.

We, therefore, as responsible professionals, who know first hand how much PAT can mean to clients, animals, and society have the awesome responsibility of helping to professionalize this magical interaction between people and animals.

There is a need to develop Undergraduate or Continuing Education Programs in Pet Assisted Therapy. Undergraduate Programs could provide PAT as a "minor" to compliment a major in education, social work, occupational therapy or other human service fields. The Continuing Education Departments of Universities could develop PAT programs for health professionals and educators. These programs would provide an educational foundation for those who have an intuitive understanding of the human companion animal bond, as well as those individuals who are open to new ideas on how to better reach their clients/students.

Another outgrowth of university programs, would undoubtedly be the formation of professional organizations. These organizations would set professional, ethical, and educational standards, credentialing requirements, re-credentialing requirements and professional development opportunities, all of which would hopefully lead to certification or licensure in this profession.

Following the expansion of educational programs and the development of professional bodies, the decision-makers in our society would hopefully facilitate the opening of funding sources, so that clients receiving Medicare or Medicaid could receive reimbursement for Pet Assisted Therapy. This could also be the first step in convincing insurance companies to cover Pet Assisted Therapy treatment when physicians indicate that PAT be part of the client's treatment or discharge plan.

The following essay, which I wrote early in my career, demonstrates the power of pets in our homes, communities, and agencies and makes a plea for the professionalization of the field.

Frankie, D.J. and Stacey
- Cousins in love with
each other and D.J.

Can D. J. change your life? Can she make you smile even when you are sad? Can she make you laugh even when the day is gloomy? Can her reach of a paw or a messy kiss remind you that someone cares? Can her bouncy exuberance on a cool crisp fall day make you feel like running even before you have had your first cup of coffee? Can her exquisite softness give you a sense of well-being? Can her need for love make you sit on the floor and give back to her some of the love she is always giving to you — even when you have just gotten off the airplane, you have a suitcase to unpack and a class to teach at 8:00 the next morning? Can her gentle love give you the courage to face life's decisions? Can her "energy of life" make you want to come home even when no one else is there? Can her companionship allow you to be the best that you can be?

Are the gifts that D. J. and other therapy animals have, worth their weight in gold? More so!

Is it not true that the majestic appearance of these dogs — whether Samoyed, Dobbies, Labs, Cocker Spaniels, any other breed or the "Muts Are Best" variety — is surpassed only by their intuitive understanding and responsive nature? Is it not true that whether they bring tears to your eyes from laughter, as you watch their antics or whether the tears come from the joy and pride and amazement you feel as you watch these therapy dogs sit gently against the knees of a person who is crying or wait calmly while a teacher picks up a child who had difficulty walking and has just fallen on her. These animals do change behavior, attitudes, mood, health, and lives.

Is it so surprising that these special creatures have demonstrated that emotional and physical healing can be enhanced; speech, smiles, and participation can be renewed; behavior can be changed; trust can be developed and/or be redeveloped; blood pressure can be lowered; chances of survival from a heart attack can be increased and self esteem and independence and respect for all living things can be boosted?

NO — it is not surprising and the time is no longer in the distant future — but NOW — when health professionals and nonprofessionals, politicians, educators, counselors, and family members; caring and intelligent people of all walks of life — are realizing that pets and professional Pet Assisted Therapy programs should be available in nursing homes as well as families; that Pet Assisted Therapy Facilitators should be on staff (just a Recreation, Music, and Art Therapists, Social Workers, and other health professionals) in schools, hospitals, rehabilitation centers, alcohol and drug treatment facilities, mental health facilities, etc.; that individuals, whether they live in private homes or public housing, should have the right to choose whether or not they want a pet, and furthermore, the time is long overdue that college and graduate level courses in PAT be available across the country, so that our youngsters of today (who will run our country tomorrow) will be aware of the profession of Pet Assisted Therapy, either as a most important and rewarding career or as a body of knowledge to better serve their clients.

As these sentiments were true when I first wrote this essay (1989) and when Dr. Bustad wrote his essay which starts this chapter, these thoughts are ever more true today.

We, therefore, need to begin educating and certifying enough PATFs, with the compassion, understanding, and knowledge (see curriculum outcomes at the end of this article), to meet the needs of the institutions across the country. We need to begin educating all human service professionals in the psycho-social benefits of pets. They need to learn the impact of pets, both as prevention and intervention, throughout an individual's lifespan.

The goal is that in the near future each hospital, agency, and nursing home should have a full-time PATF on staff. Therefore, sick and lonely individuals who have had pets in their past, would again be able to have regular contact with friendly therapy pets. And those who have not enjoyed this special relationship, may find a new found lease on life, via a pet therapy friend.

Just as PATFs have to possess certain personality traits to be effective in this field, therapy pets also have to possess certain qualities to make him/her appropriate and effective. Whether a PAT facilitator is working with a dog, cat, bird, rabbit or other animal, these therapy pets must: enjoy interacting with everyone, be intuitive, responsive, confident, loving, and forgiving.

The following tribute to D. J., which poured out of me, spontaneously, one evening, has served well to allow my university students to understand the answer to their most frequently asked question: "How do I know if my pet would make a good therapy pet?"

Mary Ionata and D.J. - Long time friends.

D. J. — A Dog of All Seasons

D. J., tail up and wagging is eager to take on the world in a loving way. What more could one ask?

D. J. responds appropriately, if there is an accident, (i.e. someone falls on her) just as a person would, knowing that it was not intentional.

D. J. responds caringly if someone were in pain — just as, hopefully, humans would.

D. J. loves her work and goes bounding around the house when I tell her we are going to PT. (Would that people would love their work as much.)

D. J. understands when individuals walk with great difficulty and — believe it or not, in these situations, her intuitive understanding of peoples' needs and abilities even overcomes her "sled dog" instinct to pull.

D. J. loves everyone — young or old, rich or poor, well or ill or differently abled, individuals who do not know English or who cannot speak at all — D. J. always responds with her "famous" paw extended in friendship, eager to bring you back her dumbbell, sit against your leg or sleep across your feet — while you reminisce. D. J. loves to roll over to be tickled or just lie quietly, while many hands move rhythmically across her soft fur, with loving touches.

D. J. is completely trusting, as this Pet Assisted Therapy Facilitator with whom she works, has always placed top priority on her well-being and has seen to it that she never has been hurt.

D. J. has been on magazine covers and received certificates of merit, but her greatest reward is having a young child on her way to school stop to pet her, an elderly person at a nursing home talk lovingly to her, or the mailman stop and say "Hi, D. J." as he drops the mail in the box.

D. J. is "hooked" on people and that is what makes her a true therapy dog!

PAT professionals, with their beloved therapy pets, will set up, according to professional standards, a variety of programs to meet individual treatment needs and to enhance quality of life. In addition to working with appropriately evaluated and trained therapy pets, other projects, that clients select, could be developed. Bird feeders could be made. Dog biscuits could be baked. Relevant movies could be watched. Aquariums could be built. Field trips, depending on health and abilities of clients, could be taken. The list goes on and on.

A full-time PATF on staff would be part of the Care Plan team. He/she could develop objectives and methodology via PAT, as well as document interactions, write reports and evaluations, conduct staff in-services and work with families, as do other professionals.

As all these ideas come to fruition we will see that just as other professions have moved along a long, but worthwhile path from a Dream or Good Deed to a profession, which is accountable, PAT will gradually evolve from a volunteer effort to a duly licensed profession, with ethical, educational, and certification standards.

It is my most fervent hope that by the time my grandchildren Stacey (12), Ross (10), Francesca (4), and Joseph (newborn) enter the job market, in the next decade or two, that Pet Assisted Therapy will not only be the newest health profession, but one of the most effective, leading to great benefits for the individuals and pets involved.

EDUCATIONAL OUTCOMES OF
PAT UNIVERSITY PROGRAMS

Five *general* outcomes for programs are as follows:

1. Student will gain an awareness of the big picture of animals in our lives, of the benefits of the Human Companion Animal Bond, and an understanding and respect for this emerging profession.
2. Student will have the knowledge of key individuals, therapy pets, organizations, programs and research that have brought this profession from Boris Levinson's discovery with Jingles in 1953 to D. J.'s work in the 1990's.
3. Student will be able to plan, implement, and evaluate ethically-based, safe and effective PAT programs based on the Human Companion Animal Bond that benefit people, animals, and society.
4. Student will understand the needs and strengths of various populations, as well as the needs and gifts of therapy pets.
5. Student will develop a view of the world in which all living things are respected. (individuals who are elderly, individuals with challenges, animals of all shapes and descriptions)

The following is a list of competencies around which to build a university program in PAT.

Pearl Salotto

Program Administration: Student will be able to:

A₁ Select suitable facility — a facility where administrator has indicated that he/she wishes to employ you on a contractual basis as a Pet Assisted Therapy Facilitator, and where you have presented your credentials as a professional, temperament test and medical records on your therapy pet, and proof of professional insurance.

A₂ Establish communication with Pet Assisted Therapy liaison (appointed by the administrator) and with Infection Control, Risk Management, Quality Assurance committees and with other professionals on the Inter-disciplinary Treatment Team .

A₃ Develop Pet Assisted Therapy policy and procedures in conjunction with Administrator, Pet Assisted Therapy liaison, and Infection Control Committee.

A₄ Develop system of written documentation for Pet Assisted Therapy, consistent with documentation system in place in facility for Inter-disciplinary Treatment Team or for School Based Support Team.

A₅ Develop public relation plans, within institutional guidelines.

A₆ Serve as a representative of your facility for Pet Assisted Therapy in the community, state and nation.

A₇ Conduct in-service and staff training.

A₈ Conduct family awareness meetings on Pet Assisted Therapy.

A₉ Conduct meeting to inform residents about PAT and to gain their input.

A₁₀ Keep abreast of new developments in the profession.

A₁₁ Plan Pet Assisted Therapy services as part of an individual's treatment plan, based on a medical referral stating that the individual is free of allergies, and a patient or family sign-off stating that the patient chooses to participate.

A₁₂ Provide for "enough" staff support, based on abilities of the clients as indicated on clinical referrals and initial assessment, so as to protect the safety of your therapy pet. In facilities where clients are mentally ill or developmentally delayed, it is generally essential to have a 1:1 ratio — one client, one staff person, with you and the therapy pet in all sessions. In nursing homes it is likely that the Pet Assisted Therapy Facilitator might not require this extensive staff support. Staff support is always necessary, however, on an "on call" basis in order to assist and enhance the program, to give advice, to move the client, etc.

A₁₃ Set up and plan for a variety of types of Pet Assisted Therapy interventions (individual, group, drop-in services), related activities (when pet is tired), spin-off activities (between weekly visits), vocational or career related activities in schools.

A₁₄ Continually evaluate and upgrade program, as well as individual goals, in conjunction with administration, staff, clients, and families.

A₁₅ Schedule PAT treatment sessions, following receipt of referral, initial

assessment and approval of your PAT goal, objectives, and
methodology at Treatment Team meetings.

A_{16} Be an advocate for your profession of PAT, and for the therapeutic
benefits of the HCAB, as well as for people and animals in your
personal and professional life.

Patient Care:

B Provide for the safety of both the therapy pet and the client.

B^1 Provide an emergency plan.

B^2_3 Seek PAT referrals, with initial recommended goal and medical
sign-off that the client is free of allergies and phobias, and can
safely participate. The referral or social history should provide
information about the client's background, so that the PATF can
establish initial dialogue; enough about the individual's functional
abilities, so that PATF can plan appropriate programs and an indication whether or not client is aware that pet is a living thing, so
that appropriate staff support can be provided. PATF should also
be allowed to read client's chart or records.

B_4 Initial assessment by PATF, both with the pet and without, in order
to establish a baseline and seek client choice to participate.

B_5 Develop a caseload of PAT clients and provide for appropriate
scheduling.

B Develop a variety of treatment possibilities.

B^6 Develop individual treatment plan.

B^7 Coordinate with other therapies.

B^8 Treat client with PAT.

B^9 Document each interaction.

B^{10} Provide quarterly reports.

B^{11}_{12} Continually interpret and evaluate data and seek input on each
individual's progress in PAT, with objective and subjective data,
and client, staff, and family input, leading to maintaining or revising goal(s).

Skills To Work Creatively, Safely, and Effectively with Your Therapy Pet as Part of a Treatment/Educational Plan:

C_1 Be able to appreciate, evaluate, understand, and train your therapy
pet.

C_2 Be aware that you need to seek temperament testing of your pet,
by an impartial and competent evaluator.

C_3 Be aware that you are responsible for evaluating your pet's temperament on an on-going basis.

C_4 Be aware of medical and health protocol for Pet Assisted Therapy
and have an understanding of zoonotic diseases.

C_5 Provide appropriate medical documentation for your therapy pet
on a regular basis.

C[6]   Train PAT pets in skills necessary for safe and effective interaction, which would include obedience and PAT skills.

C[7]   Assure emotional and physical well-being of therapy pet at all times.

C[8]   Do not allow any interaction to take place unless it is good for the pet, as well as the client.

C[9]   Be aware that you need to be with the therapy pet at all times during client interaction, as well as when the pet is resting.

C[10]   Provide for the safety of the therapy pet in case of an emergency in the facility or an emergency with the PATF.

C[11]   PATF must have understanding and belief in the therapeutic benefits of the HCAB and respect and treasure their therapy pet as family.

Education/Advocacy/Professional Development:

D[1]   PATF must have the educational and experiential background, as well as the basic humanity, so as to be able to work effectively with individuals who are elderly, with children, with individuals with mental illness, developmental disabilities, or problems with chemical dependency, or those in need of rehabilitation, in a validating and empowering manner.

D[2]   PATF must have education in PAT, via an academic certificate through Continuing Education or through College Degree Programs.

D[3]   Be able to demonstrate oral and written skills necessary to work effectively as a treatment team member.

D[4]   Network with other Pet Assisted Therapy Facilitators.

D[5]   Continually upgrade skills and knowledge dealing with people and animals.

D[6]   Participate in conferences, workshops and organizations.

D[7]   Offer internships or field visits to PAT or other human service students.

D[8]   Consult with individuals, families, governmental bodies, health departments, school boards, libraries, police departments, insurance companies, professional groups, institutions or community groups — whoever is interested in the understanding of or support of or the practical applications of, the therapeutic benefits of the HCAB.

D[9]   PATF should be able to develop and participate in research projects following appropriate ethical and legal protocol.

D[10]   The PATF should be able to teach PAT in elementary schools, middle schools, high schools, and universities.

D[11]   The PATF should have leadership ability, good judgment, and professionalism, as well as an understanding of the big picture of the potential of animals in our lives and of this profession.

D[12]   The PATF, in addition to knowledge in the field, and compassion and respect for people and animals, should have the confidence and passion to be a spokesperson for this emerging profession.

Section 4:
FUTURE DIRECTIONS IN PET ASSISTED THERAPY
A DRUG PREVENTION MODEL

<u>**Marion Joachim**</u> *has been involved in human services for fifteen years. She is a licensed chemical dependency professional and a nationally certified counselor. She has a Master's degree in Agency Counseling from Rhode Island College and a certificate in PAT from the Community College of Rhode Island. She is currently a member of Windwalker Humane Coalition.*

Anyone exposed to Pet Assisted Therapy (PAT) intuitively feels that it is special, unique and therapeutic in a somewhat mystical and inexplicable way. The only half-way rational explanation is to attribute this phenomenon to the magic of the Human-Animal bond. We have an ethical and moral obligation to expose as many people as possible to the as-of-yet vastly unexplored benefits of PAT and to explore its full potential.

We must subject this approach to rigorous and systematic scientific study, without losing sight of our primary mission of healing and comforting our patients.

Aside from this enormous task, we also need to continue to develop a theoretical frame of reference so we have a sound foundation against which to interpret empirical outcomes. A theory needs to include some set of basic assumptions about the nature of human beings, animals, and their relationship with each other, speaks to the change process and theory of personality and provides a set of techniques for therapeutic intervention.

Discovery House began its foray into PAT by doing first and then figuring out what happened, which is very typical for our movement. My partner, Suzanne Sorois (who has been volunteering with her therapy pet, Nikita, for the past five years) and I did not just start a PAT program. We spent a lot of time preparing for this challenge and enrolled in a college-based PAT certificate program. First, there were two very work and time-intensive semesters at a local college with many site visits to existing PAT sites, guest speakers, readings, papers, etc. We then had to select an internship site, get our dogs temperament tested, and obtain health certificates. Next, we approached the Discovery House Board of Directors with a brief plan to assess the chances of approval. We then proceeded to write policies and procedures, guidelines and ethical codes and a job description, which were unanimously welcomed by the Discovery House Board of Directors. We then contacted the program's licensing body — the State of Rhode Island's Health Department; again, more approval and interest on the part of Facilities Licensing.

Equipped with all of this preparation and support we made our first PAT foray in a newly established, small out-patient methadone treatment program.

Our patients are adult, chronic, opiate-addicted men and women, some of whom have been hardened by a lifestyle marked by crime, mental illness, childhood abuse and institutionalization. To overcome their protective defenses and establish trust is not an easy feat. Patients had never seen animals in a treatment setting and seemed quite surprised to see us. Cautious observation gave way, inadvertently, to questions and superficial interactions with both the therapy animals and their human companions. Unexpectedly, patients were afraid that we had introduced drug-sniffing dogs into the program. This issue had to be resolved in week one.

After some time the patients made a point of bringing in their children and interacting jointly with the children and the animals. The subsequent week saw patients coming in early and spending quality petting time; gone was the pretense of visiting for the children's sake.

Another therapeutic breakthrough was scored when everyone anxiously inquired about the dogs who had to miss a Saturday due to training. We knew we were established when outwardly aloof patients began asking other staff members questions about the dogs and were reporting their experiences in their regular sessions with primary counselors. Patients tended to come in earlier and stay longer, playfully interacting with the dogs and obviously seeking the unconditional creature comfort of human-animal companionship. Patients also started to come in and share problems with the staff while they petted the animal. More self disclosure and emotional expression have been noted.

The presence of the animals has had a positive side effect on the work atmosphere. There appears to be more interaction between staff overall and in addition, a warmer and lighter feeling tone can be noted which underlies all clinic operations.

At some point, Suzanne Sorois and this writer plan to engage in preliminary surveys and actual research. We plan to facilitate a stress management group for patients whose blood pressure will be taken pre- and post group to see if PAT has an effect on physiological parameters; a control group will just have their blood pressure taken twice without intervention.

Another area of inquiry is the impact of an animal presence on work atmosphere and job satisfaction. Our hunch is that a therapy animal program on premise also contributes to lower self-reports of employee stress and higher job satisfaction ratings. We also plan to administer a brief questionnaire to see how patients rate the animals, therapists, and their response to both. When at work, without my dog, I experience significantly higher levels of stress and tension compared to days when I am in his soothing company. In fact, practicing PAT is a mere extension of my true and centered self as I act in congruency with my Real Self in a state of unself-conscious emotional comfort. I can truly be present for my patients and my psychological gates are open.

The patients at Discovery House are dealing with chemical dependency to heroin and other narcotics and they experience shame especially when new to the treatment. When this is the case it is challenging to build a rapport. Usually, the first theme when meeting a new patient revolves around their negatively charged drug use, with the therapist as the "expert" and an oftentimes defeated patient. Thus, inadvertently, there is the establishment of inequality and alienation as the patient experiences the things that separate rather that connect him or her with the human race. When working with the dog, therapeutic conversations generally develop around positively charged themes, such as the dog's name, how old he is, etc. This ripple effect sets the stage for more conversations around positives and strengths, rather than problems. Instead of talking about problems, we immediately move into solving them. Therapy occurs against the background of a healthy and supportive rapport between patient and therapist. As therapists, we sometimes get lost in our patients' problems and we do not attend to their need for comfort from their pain. Ethical guidelines of the counseling profession severely and rightfully curtail physical touch when that is sometimes just what a particular patient needs. All I can say is thank God for my dog, who can, and has the ability to provide unconditional positive regard and tactile comfort.

All of these cursory and superficial observations will hopefully be systematically studied in the near future.

We have observed that the ice breaks somewhat quicker when the dogs are around, and that patients seems to express more and deeper feelings as they talk about their problems. We have also noticed that everyone quickly adapts to the animals and misses them when a Saturday PAT session has to be rescheduled. PAT is used as adjunctive therapy in a multitude of settings, but is not yet practiced as a primary and independent modality. We are at the beginning of exploring its vast therapeutic potential.

Historically, every therapy movement has gone through a fairly predictable development process. A few committed visionaries co-create a vision and begin to educate groups which subscribe to the same basic beliefs and value system and which are open to learning new approaches to assist their patients. Initially, a confluence of diverse views and philosophies with a consensus building process takes place, which will unify the movement via basic professional standards and ethical guidelines. Now gaining in momentum and with increased awareness, the message spreads into the general public. In the next stage, the movement organizes to gain credibility and acceptance. Small schools and associations develop and more followers are recruited and trained. This next generation of practitioners advocates for inclusion in the professional community and access to colleges and professional organizations. This inevitably leads to exposure to the general public. Suddenly, the movement is elevated to exclusivity and becomes public domain.

The approaches' identity and vision is preserved by establishing internal and external controls of licensure, elaborate codes of ethics and professional conduct and commonly approved standards for clinical practice. It appears that PAT is at this critical juncture as a therapy movement. Future challenges will be to continue to develop a cognet theoretical framework with assumptions regarding human nature and the change process combined with a set of standardization and commonly accepted techniques and interventions. Any new theory has to withstand the rigors of systematic scientific inquiry. Basic research deals with the theory's underlying assumptions and applied research focuses on systematic manipulation of interventions and on maximizing treatment outcomes. PAT is put into practice first and is being introduced into diverse treatment settings to explore where its optimal applications are. Systematic research of PAT will be very complex because the unit of investigation is the therapeutic triad of animal, patient, and therapist, rather than the common patient-therapist dyad, and it can also be assumed that setting factors influence the players differently.

PAT is more than just another therapy approach; it is more akin to a world view. Its practice would; therefore, automatically bring with it a set of sociopolitical implications and a set of values. Does the practice of PAT, for example, require strict vegetarianism? Whose welfare is more important, the animal's or the patient's in a case of therapeutic mishap? Is there informed consent on the part of the animal? At what point is the animal exploited in the therapeutic situation? Is it ethical to charge a fee for exposing patients to the naturally occurring human-animal bond? And if so, is not every human being entitled to partake of its benefits free of charge? Major ethical dilemmas have still not been touched.

Our small state may play a leading role in establishing PAT as a credible therapeutic approach. Currently, there are established programs at several area hospitals, rehabilitation centers, nursing homes, agencies, and schools. It appears that the Health Department will lend its support, and it is hoped that they consider the inclusion of PAT into facility licensing regulations. Our Windwalker Humane Coalition has organized several state-wide seminars and a conference on the link between animal and child abuse. A fifteen member state commission, spearheaded by the Windwalker Humane Coalition under the leadership of State Senator Rhoda Perry, has been formed to study people-animal connections and to enact progressive legislation requiring law enforcement to inform child protective services, automatically, of animal abuse in case dependent children are in the same household and vice versa. This would constitute the nation's first cross-reporting law of its kind.

It appears that the PAT movement has to accomplish a number of challenges: Undergo scientific study, develop a cogent theoretical foundation and continue to address ethical issues. Dedicated and caring people will continue to give their energy and heart to see that PAT is established as a viable form of treatment.

PROFESSIONAL GUIDELINES

Standard PAT Operating Procedures:

Scope: To provide PAT-related patient services on-site as part of a college-based internship program consistent with internal, State and Federal regulations.

Purpose: To provide high quality PAT-related services at an agency for methadone treatment, consistent with all applicable health, safety and ethical standards.

Timeframe: Effective for the duration of the D. J. PAT Certificate Internship program.

Procedure:

1. Upon completion of the new employee orientation, the PAT intern will conduct a staff in-service training on PAT.
2. Clinical staff will refer a particular patient for PAT or patients may apply to program staff.
3. Each applicant is asked to sign the PATIENT CONSENT to PAT with program staff and is asked to bring in a medical clearance from their respective primary care physician.
4. The clinical supervisor will discuss referrals for PAT in weekly clinical peer group and review patient history with the intern in the context of weekly clinical supervision.
5. The PAT intern will review the patient chart and schedule a first appointment with the patient and assigned counselor to review and update treatment plan.
6. The PAT intern will enter all treatment activities into the system.
7. The PAT intern will receive weekly clinical supervision by the clinical supervisor.
8. The PAT intern will be encouraged to participate in all staff meetings, clinical peer group and in-service trainings.
9. The Director of The D. J. Pet Assisted Therapy University Certificate Program will provide on-going supervision to the PAT intern and will evaluate the program site on an on-going basis.
10. Only PATFs with completed Community College of Rhode Island class work in PAT will be accepted as at this agency.
11. The PATF makes current certificates, licensure, animal health, temperament test, proof of liability and malpractice insurance available to the worksite as required. This may include licensure as a PATF in the future.
12. The PATF will refrain from abusive and exploitive relationships with colleagues, patients and the therapy animal.
13. The PATF will assume a teaching and advocacy function and display behavior consistent with the highest standards of the profession.

DATE   PATF   STAFF WITNESS

PAT CODE OF ETHICS:

This CODE OF ETHICS is specifically designed for PATFs in chemical dependency programs and supplements the existing agency's CODE OF ETHICS.

1. The Pet Assisted Therapy Facilitator (PATF) will maintain certification up to date and will continuously update his/her skills and undergo regular clinical supervision. This entails a minimum of ten hours per year of PAT and/or continuing education in related fields; future licensure of PAT may set higher standards for the profession.
2. The PATF will be responsible for the health, safety and behavior of the therapy animal at all times and will not expose the animal to an emotionally or physically unsafe treatment setting.
3. The PATF will abide by the agencies policies and procedures, as well as code of ethics at all times.
4. The PATF will avoid dual relationships with patients and staff at the internship site.
5. The PATF will comply with confidentiality laws stipulated in 42 CFR Part II.
6. The PATF will establish an unconditional human-animal bond first and foremost with the therapy animal regardless of his/her potential for therapy. This commitment supersedes all other potential benefits derived from this special relationship.
7. The PATF abides by the principles of positive reinforcement and non-violent behavior modification during obedience and therapy training. Any punishment or aversive techniques, verbal or physical in nature, are abuse to both the therapy animal and patient and render the PATF unqualified for forming a therapeutic rapport.
8. The PATF educates and prepares potential worksites and patients for PATF prior to starting a program.
9. The PATF puts the needs of the therapy partner first at all times.
10. The PATF obtains the full and informed consent from all patients including an explanation of potential benefits and dangers.
11. The PATF will immediately terminate or reschedule the session if the therapy animal is injured, hurt or in any type of distress.

Patient Consent to PAT

I, the undersigned, hereby give my full and informed consent to Pet Assisted Therapy (PAT).

My participation is voluntary and I have the right to withdraw it at any time.

I am required to furnish clearance from my primary care physician in order to participate in PAT.

It has been explained to me that the therapy animal (s) have been specially screened and evaluated for this treatment modality and that the therapist is under the supervision of both, the agency's clinical supervisor and the field placement coordinator. The PATF is solely responsible for the behavior of the animal.

Staff has the right to be apprised of confidentiality laws 42 CFR Part II and patient's rights.

I agree to inform the agency's staff of any health-related conditions which may affect my continued participation in PAT (chemotherapy treatment, AIDS and other conditions which may suppress the immune system).

The PAT program operates in compliance with all licensing regulations and the agency's policies and procedures. It has been approved by the Medical Director, as well as the Board of Directors, and The Rhode Island Department of Health has received notification.

I, furthermore, understand that all PAT-related activities will be entered into the agency's chart.

I understand that any verbal/physical abuse directed at the therapy animal will result in immediate suspension from the PAT program.

_____
Date   Patient

_____
Date   Staff Witness

_____
Date   Clinical Supervisor

PAT Guidelines

I. INFECTION CONRTOL

1. Animals will have their health certificates updated twice yearly and a copy will be kept in the facilitator's personnel file.
2. Proof of rabies vaccine will be required of all cats and dogs entering the facility.
3. "Clean-up" and disinfection will be the responsibility of the facilitator. The facility will be responsible for notifying the PATF of cleaning products used and for providing an "animal-friendly" physical and emotional program site.
4. PAT staff will be subject to annual TB testing.

II. PAT SESSIONS

1. All animals will be attended and leashed at all times while at this agency. PAT staff will be provided with patient status updates as needed prior to sessions and will be alerted of any potential crisis situations.
2. The front entrance will be used, as well as a separate office in the facility.
3. PAT session will be scheduled in advance and in coordination with this agency's staff to ensure clinical back-up.
4. PAT sessions will occur as individual or group sessions.
5. The facilitator will file group and individual progress notes, following each session, into the system.
6. This agency's staff will be present at all times at the facility for supervision and support when PAT sessions take place.

III. DOCUMENTATION

1. PAT will be documented in the patients' individualized treatment plans and progress notes will be filed after each PAT contact. PAT staff will additionally add PAT as an added activity into the system to track utilization.
2. All patients will be required to sign the PATIENT CONSENT TO PAT, with their primary counselor, prior to the first session.
3. The primary counselor is responsible for referring the patient to the PAT PROGRAM.
4. The patient, counselor and PATF will schedule a treatment team meeting to update the treatment plan and to address specific goals and objectives associated with participation in PAT.
5. The facilitator will have unlimited access to his/her patients' charts.
6. All PAT staff will be treated like any full-time staff member in regards to the NEW STAFF ORIENTATION PROCEDURE

(Confidentiality, BCI check, policy and procedure review, ethics statement, etc.)

7. PAT staff are required to bring in proof of college-sponsored intern ship and proof of professional liability insurance covering them and their therapy animal.
8. This agency will request certain patients to bring a note from their primary care physician allowing them to participate in the PAT program.
9. This agency's staff and the facilitator will follow all policies and licensing requirements related to reporting all incidents.

IV. EVALUATION

1. PAT staff is evaluated in the context of their field placement.
2. The facilitator will follow routine employee performance evaluation procedures described in the personnel policy.
3. PATF's will be evaluated on the basis of their job description by this agency and the PAT Program Director.
4. PAT participants will be asked to complete a patient satisfaction questionnaire and other more specific measures.

V. SUPERVISION AND TRAINING

1. This agency's PAT program will be supervised while on-site by the Clinical Director. The Program Director of The D. J. Pet Assisted Therapy University Certificate Program will interact with the agency regarding overall program, will be available to the intern on an as needed basis and will engage in timely evaluation of the interns, as well as the internship site.
2. The PATF will receive clinical supervision by this agency's Clinical Director or his/her designee.
3. The PATF is strongly encouraged to participate in in-service trainings, staff meetings and clinical peer groups, and to otherwise comply with the continuing education standards of the PAT profession. It is recommended that PATFs attend a minimum of ten hours per year of continuing education in PAT or related fields.
4. PAT staff will undergo a full agency New Employee Orientation, and will offer a staff in-service training on PAT.

Pearl Salotto

PAT Therapist
Job Description

To assist patients in meeting their treatment needs in the context of an interdisciplinary treatment team.

Engages the patient in a task-oriented process toward meeting treatment goals by drawing out patients' internal resources and connecting the patient with external supports.

ESSENTIAL RESPONSIBILITIES & FUNCTIONS:

1. Comply with this agency's Policy and Procedures, as well as State and Federal regulations in providing services to patients.
2. Provide Pet Assisted Therapy (PAT) consistent with established policy and safety standards.
3. Comply with agency's and PAT-specific Code of Ethics.
4. Assist the treatment team in implementing treatment goals and document these services.
5. Seek supervision and consultation regarding patient progress as indicated.

DUTIES AND RESPONSIBILITIES:

1. Maintain complete and up-to-date patient records.
2. Participate in interdisciplinary treatment team meetings, staff meetings and clinical supervision.
3. Maintain a positive and professional relationship within and outside of this agency.
4. Maintain health and safety of the therapy animal and patients.

POSITION REQUIREMENTS:

1. Education: High School Diploma; GED; Associate Degree or Bachelor's Degree in human service or related field.
2. Health certificate and updated vaccinations for therapy animal.

A VISION OF A BETTER WORLD

<u>Nina Natelson</u> founded Concern for Helping Animals in Israel (CHAI) in 1984, and has been its Director since that time. She has been a vegetarian and active in animal rights issues since 1980, and has been a vegan since 1982. She lives in Annandale, VA with her husband, Murry Cohen, MD., a psychiatrist and Co-Chair of the Medical Research Modernization Committee (MRMC) and their two dogs (including Patterson) and five cats.

These remarks were originally presented in May 1995 at the Web of Hope Conference in Providence, RI. and sadly, are still timely today.

The information you've heard here today about the link between child and animal abuse is very powerful. It's powerful because it gives you the key necessary to unlock important positive changes in society. Awareness leads to understanding and understanding leads to right action.

Before I talk about the vision of the world we've come here today to seek and how we can get there from here, I'd like to explain a little bit about who I am, about the organization I represent, and about our work in Israel, because you're probably all wondering "What does helping animals in Israel have to do with a conference in Rhode Island on the child/abuse link?"

About twelve years ago, I went to Israel to visit my relatives there, and I saw many scenes of animal suffering that were very upsetting to me. I saw a tremendous number of starving stray cats and dogs in horrendous condition (blind, injured limbs from having been hit by cars, etc.) everywhere I walked — in alleys, parks, on the beaches, and even on the streets. I saw horses, donkeys, and mules hauling heavy loads, with home-made harnesses that cut into their skin and created open, infected wounds that went untreated. These animals were made to stand for hours in the hot sun with no shade or water, and were driven in heavy traffic. I learned that the municipalities strychnine poison animals to control their numbers. Pets, as well as strays who eat the poison die from asphyxiation during convulsions over a period of up to 24 hours.

I also encountered tremendous indifference to the suffering of animals. Israelis would often ask me "Why is an educated person like you wasting your time on animals? Who cares?" On one trip, I saw a white dog lying on a busy street corner in a large city, apparently hit by a car and paralyzed. I don't know for how many hours he had been lying there, unable to move, suffering, and in shock. No one payed any attention to him. I even saw one woman move her baby carriage over him, first lifting the front wheels and placing them on the sidewalk beyond his body, and then the back wheels, stepping over him without stopping to find out why he was lying there immobile. It took two hours of phone calling, while my husband sat on the sidewalk with the dog's head cradled in his lap, to finally get someone from the municipality to come and put him out of his misery.

On the first trip to visit my relatives, one of my cousins suggested we walk around the Old City of Jerusalem, where there is a market place filled with stalls of people selling a myriad of wares. There, I saw a man selling pigeons that had been stuffed into wire cages. There were so many pigeons in each cage, they were standing on each other's backs, sometimes three layers to a cage.

I was horrified, and I asked my Israeli cousin to bargain with him for all the pigeons. My cousin looked very uncomfortable, but he did as I asked, and I bought the pigeons. But my relief soon vanished when I saw the vendor begin to jam the pigeons, one after another, into a single paper bag, as though they were inanimate objects rather than living, sentient beings. I didn't know whether to be furious or to cry, but eventually we got the pigeons to a nearby open area, where we set them free.

Some flew away right away and some took off when we stomped on the ground near them, but most had never lived outside a cage, it seemed, and either couldn't fly or wouldn't fly. Pretty soon, some children, attracted by the sight of so many pigeons walking around one spot, began to pick up small stones and throw them, laughing, at the birds. I pleaded with my cousin to explain to them that they shouldn't hurt the birds, but that instead we needed their help to get the birds to fly.

The children, excited by a different kind of power they could have, dropped their stones and began to help us get the pigeons to fly. By the time that hour or so was over, I was feeling better that at least we had done something to reliever the suffering we had come upon. My cousin, on the other hand, looked **very** unhappy and said what he really needed was a beer — and he's a non-drinker! I asked him if he was mad at me for turning what he had planned as a pleasant afternoon of sightseeing into a pigeon rescue effort.

His answer surprised me. He said "There is so much suffering around that I keep my door to my heart closed to protect myself from feeling overwhelmed by it. Today, you forced me to open the door and it's painful. I prefer to keep the door closed."

I told my cousin that I didn't expect him to, Superman style, take all the world's suffering on his shoulders, but if you come upon a specific incident of cruelty, you ought to do what you can to stop it. If **you** see it, it's **yours**. And that one small step at a time, as you go about the business of your daily life, it isn't really so overwhelming. But by then, frankly, all he wanted was a beer.

Keeping the door to your heart closed is dangerous business, as we have learned today. Studies have shown that it leads to heart attacks in the person with the closed door, it hurts those around them who care about them and who are cut off from love and understanding, and in its silence, it is the ultimate betrayal of those who are being abused and whose only hope is someone with the empathy to see their plight and the courage to intervene to end it. Suffering, whether of animals or children, if left unnoticed, comes back to haunt us and to hurt us.

Because of the sights I had seen, upon my return to the States, I formed Concern for Helping Animals in Israel or CHAI (which is the Hebrew word for life) to support the Israeli animal protection community in their efforts to bring about a better world for the country's animals.

And let me clarify that Israel is not worse than other Middle Eastern or Mediterranean countries. As everywhere, it's a matter of education and cultural tradition. Israel has absorbed immigrants from all over the world and they have brought with them the attitudes toward animals of their native countries. Israelis will also ask "With all our defense and economic problems, along with problems of absorbing successive tides of immigrants, you want me to care about a stray dog?"

They don't understand that animal suffering affects people, too. Israeli mothers have told me "I'll never have a dog in the house again because I can't watch my children go through again what they went through when they came home from school and found their dog dead from poisoning or having convulsions and dying before their eyes."

Over the past eleven years, CHAI had helped get the country's first Animal Protection Law passes, provided funds and veterinary medical supplies to the few, small animal shelters, replaced strychnine poisoning at the municipal pounds with humane euthanasia methods and encouraged the government to switch from poisoning and shooting animals to humane rabies control measures.

We also held an international medical conference on alternatives to animals in laboratories that led the Israeli Army to switch from performing operations on healthy dogs to train paramedics to humane alternatives, and we co-sponsored, with the Ministry of Education, a country-wide Humane Education Contest that has now become an annual event.

Because Israel has been constantly under the threat of war, the military plays a much greater role in Israeli society than in societies that are at peace. Israeli children grow up wanting to be tough, strong, and aspiring to be fighter pilots as the highest ideal. This emphasis on the "male" side of the personality — military power — reduces emphasis on the "female" side — sensitivity and humaneness. In order to be seen as "macho" by their peers and to be accepted by them, children of immigrants to Israel sometimes commit acts of cruelty to animals.

So for our Humane Education Contest, we wanted to do something that would reward, at the highest levels, kindness to animals, rather than cruelty to animals. We had a big ceremony, with the Minister of Education present and gave prizes to the children who had done the most to help animals. The Ministry was pleased with the effort and has continued it as an annual event. Also, with the Tel Aviv area Board of Education, we co-sponsored a pilot humane education project to test humane education in the Tel Aviv area schools. And much more.

But our real breakthrough came as a result of a conference similar to this one, held in March of 1994, again with the Ministry of Education, called "Preventing Violence in Society Through Education." Once people clearly understood the roots of the cycle of abuse, doors opened to us that, until then, had been closed.

The conference came at a good time. There had just been an incident where three teenagers "from good homes" in good neighborhoods – the father of one was an attorney – had gotten into the back seat of a random taxicab and shot the driver in the back of the head and killed him, "for fun." The police quickly found the teenagers who had committed the crime because they had absolutely no remorse for what they had done and one of them had been bragging about it at school. When they searched the boy's rooms, they found written plans that they had made, for their next act, to rob a bank and shoot and kill the tellers, also "for fun." The public was shocked by this incident and began asking itself whether Israel was on its way to becoming as violent a society as the U.S. People were seeking answers on how to stem the violence.

Following our conference, which was well published in the media, the Interior and Environment Committee in the Knesset (which is Israel's Parliament) raised the problem of animal abuse in Israel for the first time and recommended to the Chief of Police that he take reported cases of animal cruelty seriously and investigate them, which he agreed to do.

The media also began asking questions about the perpetrators of violent incidents. The first violent incident involving youth that occurred after the conference concerned a car full of teenagers who drove around Tel Aviv shooting air guns at people. About twenty people ended up in the hospital. The media, now educated about the human/animal violence link, asked questions they had never asked before about what had led up to these shootings and how they might have been prevented. They discovered that the teenagers had started by shooting air guns at cats in the street, "for the fun of seeing them jump." When they got bored with that, they turned the guns on humans.

The Knesset Committee also recommended to the Ministry of Education that some classroom time be devoted, on a regular basis, to the subject of animal abuse and how to prevent it. The Ministry went much further by agreeing to disseminate and promote a humane education program that CHAI is developing throughout the elementary school system and to pay the salaries of humane education teachers trained by CHAI, who will go from school to school training other teachers in what is humane ed., why it is important in the process of building empathy, and how to teach it.

In addition, the Ministry agreed to pay the salaries of instructors who will teach a continuing education class for teachers and school psychology counselors on the child/animal abuse link and how to stop the cycle of violence. And finally, the Ministry is helping us, including financially, with our program called "Living Together" that brings Jewish and Arab children together at the SPCA to learn about animals and become active in efforts to help them.

Israel is, to my knowledge, only the second country to take the tremendously forward-looking step of introducing a program of humane education into the school system — the first was Costa Rica, as a result of the efforts of the World Society for the Protection of Animals.

The message people at our conference in Israel understood – and the message I hope people her today will understand – is that whether or not you like animals, you **must** respect them and you **must** teach children to respect them, if you expect to live in a non-violent world. As anthropologist Margaret Mead said, "One of the most dangerous things that can happen to a child is to kill or torture an animal and get away with it."

What is required to achieve the non-violent society we all seek and on which, I think we all have come to realize, our very survival depends, is nothing short of a revolution in consciousness. We must change and change quickly, from a world where one-upmanship and indifference to the feelings of others gives way to a world community, with a deep sense of knowing that we are all one in a very real, very concrete sense. We are all – plants, animals, people – all that the earth encompasses – strands in an interconnected web, and if one strand is hurting, we all suffer.

The revolution in attitudes and behavior that is required of us must and will – if we are to survive – affect all of our life's choices, from the food we eat to the clothes we wear, to the values we instill in our children. If we develop the empathy for others that we want others to feel toward us, can we continue to separate calves from their mothers at birth, lock them in wooden crates too small to allow them to stand up and turn around, feed them watered down milk to keep them anemic, and pump them full of antibiotics so they'll remain alive despite being malnourished and abused, until at sixteen weeks of age, they are slaughtered, all so that we can serve the "white veal" that is considered an elegant entree?

Can we weed our lawns with chemicals that seep into the water supply and poison the earth?

Can we catch wild animals in traps armed with jagged steel jaws that penetrate to the bone, traps in which they may lie in the cold and wet for days before they die, so that we can skin them, don their fur, and think we look chic?

Can we go on selling drugs banned in the U.S. as health hazards to people in undeveloped countries because they don't yet know any better, and why throw the stuff away when, after all, we're making money and isn't that the "bottom line?"

Can we use cosmetics and household products made of caustic substances that have burned the eyes of rabbits to the point of blindness while their heads are held immobile in stocks to color our eyelids with just the right shade?

Can we ignore the hopelessness and despair felt by poor inner-city teenagers who see no way out, as long as we're happy and safe where we live, and not expect those teenagers to turn to drugs and crime that ultimately reaches out a hand to engulf us along with them?

Can we continue to allow children to take the wings off flies, stomp on ants, and when they get older, dissect cats and frogs in school and feed mice candy bars until they sicken and die, so the children can compete for the number one prize in their local science fair?

Can we dismiss, with phrases like "boys will be boys" and "they'll grow out of it," the behavior of children who can show only hurt rather than love toward other living beings because that's all they've ever seen modeled at home?

If we have a violent consciousness and practice violent behavior toward others by the choices we make daily, is it any wonder that we live in a violent world? A vision of a non-violent future doesn't mean non-violence only for the group to which we belong. It doesn't work that way. If we want peace for ourselves, we must be ready to grant it to others also. We must, as Albert Einstein said, "free ourselves by widening our circle of compassion to embrace all living creatures and the whole of nature in its beauty."

Whether you are an educator, social worker, psychologist, administrator, or parent, there is a tremendous amount each of us can do in our daily lives to create the revolution in consciousness that will lead to the peaceful world in which we would all be happy to live. It starts with awareness of the implications of the choices we make, and ends with the behavior we model ourselves and the behavior we condone in others, one small act at a time, one day at a time.

I hope you will take the awareness about the link in the chain of violence you develop here today and turn it into new choices in your lives tomorrow. Creating a better world begins with each of us, with every unloving thought toward another we replace with a loving one, even if no one else knows what's in our mind, because thoughts have power. It begins with every unloving act we stop ourselves from making or for which we care enough to make amends.

You have the power to get awareness of the link into the training classes of police, social workers, counselors, etc., to get humane education into the school system, to convince lawmakers that acts of cruelty, whether to humans or animals, must not be condoned, to let movie makers and TV stations know that acts of cruelty or disrespect to animals are not funny, they're outrageous and won't be tolerated, to change the games children play from "king of the mountain" to "the council of living beings," for example, which celebrates diversity. This is an activity in which children make masks of their favorite animal, speak on behalf of that animal to the council of humans and humans representing animals, and each child makes one promise to do something to improve the world for the animal they represented.

We can no longer live in a win-lose world, where one can only feel good about themselves if they succeeded at the expense of someone else. Since we are truly one, we will either learn to seek situations in which everyone is a winner or we will all perish together.

In digesting what you have heard here today while you're at lunch, I urge you to open your hearts, as well as your minds to the plight of the non-human, as well as the human life forms on our planet, for as another famous Albert said, (Albert Schweitzer) "Until he extends the circle of his compassion to **all** living things, man will **not** himself find peace."

Section 6:
A VIEW FROM THE LEGAL SIDE

<u>*Maureen S. Ramirez*</u> *was a Business Education teacher at East Greenwich High School in East Greenwich, Rhode Island from 1967 to 1995. Maureen received her JD degree from New England School of Law in Boston, MA in June 1980. She was admitted to practice law in RI in November 1980. In 1982 she became a part-time associate in the law firm of Healy & Jones in Providence, RI. In 1995, Maureen became an associate with the Law Offices of Paul T. Jones, Jr. in Providence, RI. Since 1985 Maureen has been an active member of both national and local animal protection organizations including the East Greenwich Animal Protection League, Volunteer Services for Animals, World Wildlife Fund, Animal Legal Defense Fund, PETA, and others.*

The Rhode Island General Assembly recently enacted Public Laws Chapter 00-451, which amends Chapter 40-9.1 of the General Laws entitled "Equal Rights of Blind and Deaf Persons to Public Facilities." This legislation effectively extends to family therapy pets the same privileges of access and transportation accorded to personal assistance animals. Following forthwith is the text of the Act:

State of RI
In General Assembly
January Session, A.D. 2000

AN ACT
RELATING TO HUMAN SERVICES-
RIGHTS TO PUBLIC FACILITIES

2000-H 8062
Introduced By: Reps. Dennigan and Sherlock
Date Introduced: March 21, 2000
Referred To: Committee on Health, Education and Welfare

It is enacted by the General Assembly as follows:

Section 1. Chapter 40-9.1 of the General Laws entitled "Equal Rights of Blind and Deaf Persons to Public Facilities" is hereby amended by adding thereto the following section:

Family therapy pets in public places. *— The privileges of access and transportation provided to personal assistance animals in section 40-9.1-2 shall be extended to family therapy pets which shall be further defined as primary companions which are to include but not limited to dogs, cats, rabbits, and guinea pigs, that are working in the provision of pet assisted therapy treatment and education. The provisions are such* *that the pet assisted therapy facilitator is working in conjunction with the family therapy pet in a predetermined medical or educational setting with a selected clientele. Said medical interactions are to be individually planned, goal-oriented, and treatment based and said educational settings are to [be] classroom based. Throughout said interactions, the pet assisted therapy facilitator and the family therapy pet will abide by a set code of ethics and will follow professional guidelines to ensure that the actions and deeds of the pet assisted therapy facilitator reflect advocacy of [the] profession, pets, and clients, and other professionals; while simultaneously ensuring that the interactions of the family therapy pet and client remains beneficial and strives to enhance the quality of life through the animal-human bond. Prior to any interactions, the family therapy pet must first meet the immunization criteria, a current certificate of good health, which shall be issued by a licensed, practicing veterinarian, as well as the temperament criteria, a certificate of good temperament, which shall be issued from a certified or practicing dog trainer or animal behaviorist, and training criteria, in which the pet assisted therapy facilitator and the family therapy pet learn to work as a team learning together to execute safely [safe] and effective interaction, which are accepted in the field, specifically other pet assisted animal facilitators, veterinarians, dog trainers, animal behaviorists and the state of Rhode Island. Access and transportation privileges are only extended while the family therapy pet is on the way to or actively participating in a program. The animal assisted therapy facilitator, an individual who has successfully completed or is in the process of completing accepted pet assisted therapy program, shall be responsible for the control and safety of the pet, which is to include cleaning up and elimination of wastes, keeping the pet on a proper leash and collar, carrying smaller animal [in] and a travel crate, adhering to all standard rules, regulations, and laws within both the facility and the state of Rhode Island, and upholding an active insurance policy that will cover an unforeseen mishap and/or accidental occurrence which may result in causing property damage and/or personal injury while actively participating in a program.*

The family therapy pets must be accompanied by a Pet-Assisted Therapy Facilitator in all public places. The Facilitator has complete responsibility in terms of controlling interaction with clients, supervising activities, maintaining safety of therapy pet, and cleaning up after pet.

Most likely to benefit from this new legislation are public places such as nursing homes, convalescent homes, hospitals, clinics, assisted-living homes, educational institutions of all levels from day care through university, and other similar places. Prior to the passing of this legislation, many nursing homes and hospitals in Rhode Island allowed therapy pets within their facilities on an informal basis. From a legal standpoint, these facilities were exposing themselves to a certain level of liability. However, this new Act delineates the terms and conditions under which family therapy pets will be allowed in public places.

Therapy facilitators are required by the new law to obtain an insurance policy in the event of an unforeseen mishap. This would alleviate personal liability should such a situation arise.

The Rhode Island General Assembly demonstrated their awareness and understanding of the needs and concerns in this area of family therapy pets and took a progressive step forward by enacting this legislation.

A further issue to study is the matter of whether or not the Pet-Assisted Therapy Facilitators should be licensed. Since the new law classifies the therapy facilitators as professionals, it only seems natural that a licensing procedure is necessary.

To qualify for a license, the applicant should successfully complete a course within a program that has been approved and accredited by the State of Rhode Island. Personal background information, including the existence of a criminal record, should also be checked. The licensing procedure will serve as a control in the selection and qualification of the Pet-Assisted Therapy Facilitators.

Pet-Assisted Therapy Facilitators and other concerned people should now focus their efforts on upgrading the legal status of family pets. Currently, family pets are classified as personal property in the same category as furniture, motor vehicles, clothing, and the like — none of which are alive. Family pets, as well as other animals, feel and experience pain, hunger, thirst, joy, sadness, and other emotions, similar to humans. In keeping with the momentum of this progressive legislation, we must lobby for a future amendment, which will essentially classify all family pets as members of the family unit, replacing their current status of inanimate objects of property. Such legislation will pave the way to revise the criminal statutes to impose more severe penalties upon abusers of family pets, barnyard animals, and other animals as well.

Postscript:

As this book goes to press, Rhode Island Bill #1619 has just become the first state to include the word guardian, along with owner, in all of its animal care statutes. This legislation was inspired by Rita Anderson's guardian ordinance in Boulder, Colorado, and initiated locally by Feinstein High School PAT students and the Windwalker Humane Coalition.

Section 7:
PET THERAPY ANIMALS: WORKING MIRACLES WITH LOVE

__Gina Santoro__, a professional Pet Therapy Facilitator, has loved animals since she was a toddler visiting her grandparents' rabbits, cows and dogs on their farm. Her best friends are her family pet therapy dog, Spooky, rescued from an animal shelter as a puppy; an adopted greyhound named Gloria; and a terrier/sheepdog affectionately named Ragamuffin. Santoro and Spooky have worked with adults with developmental disabilities, seniors and children in Rhode Island in the Spooky's Special Friends program. Santoro has seen remarkable changes in the people who have interacted with Spooky. A professional writer with an M.F.A. in Writing and an adjunct professor at Johnson & Wales University, Santoro plans to write about these experiences.

Arthur Robbins, a successful entrepreneur and respected volunteer, once said that every segment of our population needs love and nurturing. His remarks were directed to attendees at a volunteer recognition awards dinner held in Providence where he was being honored.

Although his remarks were aimed at improving the quality of education in public school systems and helping at-risk students, his sentiment is entirely applicable to the fledgling field of Pet-Assisted Therapy.

What does needing love and acceptance have to do with Pet-Assisted Therapy? Simply put, everything. As the saying goes, love can move mountains. In a therapeutic situation, it can work miracles. Obviously, a therapist is not required or even asked to love his or her patient. That is not the intent of therapy. A therapist, like all medical professionals and everyone alike, is asked to respect their patients and treat them with dignity and caring.

So how does a person who hungers for love and a much-needed miracle receive these two gifts? A pet-therapy animal is one way. A cuddly gray kitten, a patchwork-coated goat, a retired racing dog, a floppy-eared bunny — they all have something in common because they have the ability to love unconditionally. They don't differentiate between a person's color, lifestyle, cash flow or profession. A scratch on the nose, a pat on the back and a hug feels wonderful to any animal, whether it comes from a Wall Street financier or supermarket cashier.

It's this total lack of bias and unconditional outpouring of affection that is tapped in a therapeutic situation. A good therapy dog won't shy away from a bandaged arm or sightless eyes. A suitable therapy cat won't avoid a shy student or a rubber-wheeled walker.

These animals won't stare or snicker. Instead, they will approach the afflicted person with curiosity and friendliness. After all, the animal sees them as a potential source of affection. Likewise, a pet-therapy animal's uninhibited response to a person who may feel embarrassed about his post-surgical bald head or misshapen leg will only feel delight with the caress of soft fur or a warm tongue. For some people, who are isolated from society because of their illness, age, or socioeconomic status, this friendly touch from a loving animal may be the only outreach they receive from the outside world.

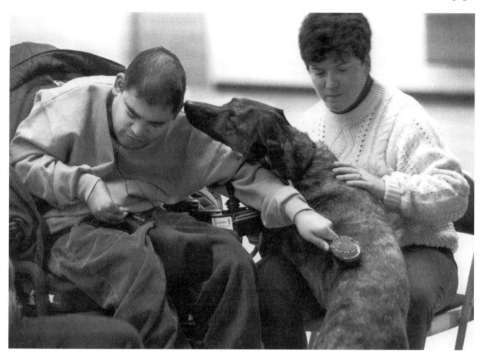

Brushing Spooky (family therapy pet of Gina Santoro) is only one of the many favorite interactive activities participants enjoy at the J. Arthur Trudeau Memorial Centers (Warwick, Rhode Island) PAT program for adults with developmental disabilities. Courtesy of the Providence Journal

As advocates of pet therapy, it is our job to open the eyes of the world to the miracle that these animals and their human assistants can achieve. We need to raise people's awareness that animals can be more than house pets or inhabitants of a zoo. Trained pet-therapy animals can be just as valuable, if not more so, to a person needing love, nurturing and attention, as the melodic notes of a piano or swirling colors of paint in other accepted expressionistic therapies. Unlike an inanimate object, the living, breathing pet can respond to a person's overture. The pet serves as a source of acknowledgment and validation that that person is there. For some people, such as children with autism or adults with Alzheimer's, this validation can coax the ill person back from a dark void into the light of reality. That, in itself, is miraculous.

Yet, for all their powers, animals cannot speak for themselves. They rely on their human counterparts to do this for them. Therefore, it is people like us who need to speak out about the power of animals. If you've ever smiled or laughed when stroking the fur of a kitten or have been tickled by the lick of a dog, consider yourself lucky. There are people in society, perhaps your neighbors, who have never, ever been touched emotionally that way. Isn't it time that they are?

CHAPTER 8

CURRICULUM/PROGRAM GUIDELINES FOR PET ASSISTED THERAPY

Section 1:
THE D. J. PET ASSISTED THERAPY (PAT) UNIVERSITY CERTIFICATE PROGRAM
CURRICULUM OBJECTIVES AND INTERNSHIP PACKET
(Pearl Salotto)

Vision:

This program is designed to provide an academic foundation for individuals who:

* Appreciate the awesome implications of pets in our lives.
* Understand our responsibility to all living things.
* See the possibilities that pets can provide for wellness, friendship, treatment, education, stimulation, motivation, and character building.

By sharing the love of our family therapy pets with others and working together with like-minded people, we can help build a "profession" and a calmer, more peaceful world.

Program Outline:

The first course in the PAT program is designed to introduce the student to the history and theory of Pet Assisted Therapy. It will also focus on ethical responsibilities, setting up and evaluating safe and effective programs for people and animals, and state-of-the-art issues such as credentialing, insurance, connections to major issues and problems in society, etc. Discussions will also focus on the strengths and needs of populations with whom PATFs will be working. Guest speakers, visiting therapy dogs, field trips, videos of model programs, as well as class interaction will be included.

The second course will provide the opportunity to learn about animal behavior and psychology, temperament evaluation of potential therapy pets, animal communication and the affect of genetic background and environmental stimulation. Although this class will include some dog training and acclimation of therapy pets to hospital/school environments [wheelchairs, PA systems, elevators, stairways, fire alarms, etc.], this class will primarily focus on understanding the potential of animals in therapy [dogs, cats, horses, rabbits, birds, etc.], as well as our responsibilities to understand and focus on the needs and care of our animals.

The third course is a professional internship experience in which the director and student will design a program based on the student's and pet's individual needs, experience and interests. Each student will gain some experience working with various populations. Following this portion of the internship experience, each student will be then challenged to set up a PAT program of his/her own, with the support of the director. Each student will also spend some time in professional advocacy activities.

Pearl Salotto

Course I Description: Introduction to Pet Assisted Therapy

The student will be introduced to the profession of Pet Assisted Therapy. Through studying the Human Companion-Animal Bond from a historical, theoretical, and practical perspective, the student will learn to apply this information in combination with his/her humanity and professional skills in developing quality ethically-based PAT programs for children and/or individuals who are elderly, who have special needs, who have chemical dependencies, as well as mental and physical challenges. Legal, safety, ethical concerns, and model programs, as well as therapeutic programming techniques and documentation procedures will be discussed. This course will also cover the link of abuse between people and animals.

Course I: Outline

I. Historical and Theoretical Perspective

1. Human-Animal Companion Bond Throughout History
2. Pet Assisted Therapy — The Big Picture
3. Research in Pet Assisted Therapy

II. Potential for Positive Change via Pet Assisted Therapy
1. Benefits to prisoners, children, and to individuals who are elderly, who have developmental and physical challenges, and mental health and chemical dependency issues.
2. Needs and strengths of special populations
3. Model Programs

III. Therapy Animal Behavior/Psychology

1. Medical — temperament profile
2. Genetic background (breed characteristics), socialization, learning, and motivation.
3. Emotional-physical responses
4. Appreciation of gifts of the therapy pet

IV. Quality Programming
1. Ethical issues
2. Safety issues
3. Legal issues
4. Rights and responsibilities of each party to the bond
5. Pre-planning -infection control, written guidelines and policies
6. Interactive programming techniques and ideas
7. Documentation and reports
8. Evaluation plan

314

9.   Quality assurance guidelines
10. Public relations
11. Confidentiality issues
12. Insurance issues
13. Dealing with problems and/or emergencies

Course I Objectives:

1. Student will become aware of the role and significance of the Human Companion-Animal Bond throughout history.
2. Student will become aware of the history, research, and scope of PAT.
3. Student will understand ethical, safety, and legal implications of PAT.
4. Student will understand issues and trends in the field.
5. Student will understand the therapeutic benefits of PAT for selected populations and the positive characteristics of quality PAT programs throughout the nation.
6. Student will gain an understanding of the strengths and needs of special populations.
7. Student will learn to appreciate the "gifts" and understand the needs of his/her therapy pet, as well as his/her personal responsibility to them.
8. Student will learn how to plan professional, ethically based, individualized treatment-based PAT programs.
9. Student will learn how The D. J. "Respect for Living Things" Elementary Program can have a permanent positive effect on the children's respect for animals, others, and themselves
10. Student will learn how The D. J. Pet Assisted Therapy Service Learning Feinstein High School Program not only has a positive impact on the student's attendance, behavior and grades, but opens up a whole new vision of each of their potential for making a difference in the world.
11. Student will learn how to use previous knowledge, values, skills and knowledge of PAT for safe and effective interactions.
12. Student will understand the client's, the pet's, the therapist's, and the institution's role in the interaction.
13. Student will understand the guidelines and requirements which will determine whether PAT is appropriate for any given individual and if so, how to make interactions safe and effective for all parties.
14. Student will begin to appreciate the awesome and life-changing implications for individuals, animals, and society

— as a result of the HCAB and the profession of PAT.

15.   Student will begin to understand each of our responsibilities to be advocates for this profession.

16.   Student will understand the link of abuse between people and animals.

Course Syllabus

Developer/Director: Pearl Salotto

Course: Introduction to Pet Assisted Therapy

Instructor: Pearl Salotto

Course Requirements: Attendance at every class is expected. If you need to miss a class, it is necessary to advise the instructor and to get notes from a fellow student. There will be weekly reading assignments and six written assignments (see below). Additionally, three field trips to professional PAT programs will be required, which need to be individually planned. Additionally, temperament testing of potential therapy pets will be held.

Site Visits: Students will visit appropriate facilities in their area, which have Pet Assisted Therapy programs.

Required Text:

Pet Assisted Therapy: A Loving Intervention and an Emerging Profession: Leading to a Friendlier, Healthier and More Peaceful World by Pearl Salotto.

Written Assignments:
* Personal Experience Essay
* Sample Code of Ethics
* Advocacy Article
* Sample Program Proposal I
* Sample Program Proposal II
* Impressions of Site Visits Essay

Final Exam

<u>Course I Outline</u>

<u>WEEK 1:</u>

Welcome — Introductions — Logistics:
>An effective way to have the student introduce themselves is to let them describe how they feel when they see a heartwarming picture illustrating the Human Companion Animal Bond.

Topics:

- *State of the Art:* **D.J.'s Legacy** <u>"We Can Build a Better World"</u>
  Seeing Pet Assisted Therapy through pictures and videos of D.J.'s work with school children (The D.J. "Respect for Living Things" Program) and with individuals in hospitals, nursing homes, psychiatric settings, and agencies for individuals with developmental disabilities.

- *What is professional Pet Assisted Therapy?*
  Professional PAT in the Field: Paving the Way for Society's Changes — Panel of local experts.

Reading Assignments: Preface, Introduction, Forward
>Part 1, Chapter 1

Written Assignment:

>*Personal Experience Essay*: Write an essay of any length on a relationship that you have or have had with a companion animal friend. Explain how this relationship affects your life and what effect this special relationship had on your enrolling in this certificate program or on your vision of PAT.

<u>WEEK 2:</u>

Topic: *History of the HCAB and PAT*

Reading Assignments: Part I, Chapter 2, Section 1-5
>Part 2, Chapter 3, Section 1, Articles 1-3

Written Assignment:

>Write a five page essay on an interesting aspect of the history of PAT. You

can use a variety of resources, including the web and personal contact.

WEEK 3:

Topics: *Research*
Introduction to PAT with individuals who are elderly

Reading Assignment: Part 2, Chapter 3, Section 2, Articles 1-5
Part 2, Chapter 3, Section 3, Articles 1-4

Written Assignment:

Develop a profile of what you would consideer to be a high quality PAT and a high quality PAT pet.

WEEK 4:

Topic: *Guest speaker* who has expertise in areas a PAT might be working, such as gerontology, development disabilities, criminal justice, mental health, regular education (national education standards)

Reading Assignment: Part 2, Chapter 3, Section 4, Articles 1-6

Written Assignment:

Sample Code of Ethics: Write a Code of Ethics that you would feel comfortable presenting to a hospital or school administrator prior to setting up a Pet Assisted Therapy Program. This can be done in outline form.

WEEK 5:

Topic: *Ethics*

Outline: *Ethical Principles*

Animal Bill of Rights
People Bill of Rights
Code of Ethics
Respect and concern for people and animals
Education and certification

Collaboration with experts
Participation in ITT
Knowledge of health care criteria
Ability to "be a friend"
Ability to work creatively with therapy animal
Involvement of families, staff and residents in planning and program
Filing of appropriate animal medical and temperament documents
Choice of individuals to relate or not and how to structure program
Protection of animals from environmental hazards, from disease of clients and inappropriate behaviors
Medical approval to prevent allergies
Frequent breaks
Ability to recognize animal stress
Provision for related activities is an alternative of animals if animal's are fatigued
Animal should only be approached by one person at a time in appropriate manner (with permission)
Maintenance of bond
Individually planned program
Appropriate language (we do not USE animals, animals are not a tool)
Ethics have assured safety of animals of life
Andrew Rowan on Ethics
Dealing honestly with problems and regular evaluation
Advocacy for animals and people
Concerns and precautions with feeding
Concerns and precautions with leashes
Expecting the unexpected

Reading Assignment: Part 3, Chapter 6, Sections 1-7

Written Assignment:

> *Advocacy Article*: Write an article that could be published in a local newspaper or professional journal advocating for the profession of PAT.

WEEK 6:

Topic: <u>*Guest speakers*</u> in the areas of mental health or developmental disabilities.

Reading Assignment: Part 3, Chapter 4, Sections 1-9

WEEK 7:
Topic: <u>*Variety of quality programs*</u>

Written Assignment:

> *Sample Proposal I*: Write a sample proposal for setting up a PAT program with a population that is health based. Include: introduction, rationale, benefits, ethics, guidelines, methodology, and evaluation. This sample proposal will help prepare student for the internship.

WEEK 8:

Topics: *The Link of Abuse between People and Animals*
    PAT in Prisons
    PAT Treatment
    Wildlife Rehabilitation
    Training Service Dogs
    Pets in

Reading Assignment: Chapter 5, Sections 1-7

Written Assignment:

> Research other prison programs from the contact list and write a critique.

WEEK 9:

Topic: *PAT as part of regular education — civics*
    PAT as part of parent education

Reading Assignment: Part 4, Chapter 7, Sections 1-8

WEEK 10:

Topic: *?? videos, field trip, speaker, role playing*

Written Assignment:

> *Sample Proposal II* : education based

WEEK 11:

Topic: Review

WEEK 12:

Topic: Final Exam

Final Exam: This particular exam for Course I is being included as a possible foundation for a future national credentialing exam in PAT.

Question 1: Name several individuals and several therapy pets who have had an impact on the history of Pet Assisted Therapy? Explain why?

Question 2: Write an essay on what you consider to be the critical ethical issues in this profession?

Question 3: What effect do you think The D. J. "Respect for Living Things" Program will have on children as they grow into adulthood? What are the critical elements that the PATF has to bring and that the pet has to bring in order to be effective?

Question 4: Why do you think that PAT is an emerging profession? What do see as the next steps, over the next decade, to bring PAT on par with other professions?

Question 5: Cite several articles from *Loving Intervention*, which have had a profound effect on you, and will stay with you as you enter this field? Explain.

Question 6: Do you think studying the link of abuse is relevant to this profession? Explain your answer?

Question 7: Choose one of the following two questions:
    a. Lady A lives in a group home. She has difficulty accomplishing ADL (Activities of Daily Living). She has difficulty communicating and difficulty moving around. Additionally, she is frequently depressed and sad. Develop a treatment plan, which would include goals to address each of these issues and the methodology by which you would meet your goals with your therapy pet.
    b. Lady B lives in an area nursing home. She has difficulty with long and short-term memory. She is confined to a wheelchair and doesn't seem to relate well to other residents and she rarely participates in programs. Develop a treatment plan, which would include goals to address each of these issues and the methodology by which you would meet your goals with your therapy pet.

Question 8: Choose one of the following two questions:
    a. Discuss the potential impact of pets in prisons?
    b. Discuss the potential impact of pets with individuals with HIV?

Question 9: Discuss the impact of any two of your guest speakers.

Course II Description: "Building on the Bond: Hands-On-Paws-On Learning"

This course teaches Pet Assisted Therapy students how to recognize, evaluate, appreciate, and work with a variety of therapy pets, including dogs, cats, horses, rabbits, etc., leading to safe and effective interaction, in which both the client and the therapy pet benefit. The course will combine lecture, discussion, observation, and training in order to help prepare Pet Assisted Therapy teams for their internship. The training component of this course is designed for therapy dogs who pass initial temperament screening and who appear to enjoy interacting with people. This course will teach some obedience skills and some PAT skills, so as to enhance the potential for safe and effective interaction.

Course II: Prerequisite — Course I

Course II: Objectives — Obedience and Therapy Skills

1. Student will learn how to teach his/her potential therapy dog how to heel on a loose leash.
2. Student will learn how to teach his/her therapy dog how to sit-stay, or down-stay, off leash, with distractions.
3. Student will learn how to teach his/her therapy dog how to "come" off leash with distractions.
4. Student will learn how to teach his/her therapy dog to stand-stay, while being petted or groomed.
5. Student will learn how to teach his/her therapy dog to wear a backpack.
6. Student will learn how to acclimate his/her therapy dog to other animals.
7. Student will learn how his/her therapy dog should approach clients in beds, wheelchairs, etc.
8. Student will learn how to teach his/her therapy dog how to retrieve reliably and gently, with distractions.
9. Student will learn how to teach his/her therapy dog, on command, to be able to be on level with the client (i.e. paws on chair, jump or climb on chair, mat, bed or table).
10. Student will learn how to teach his/her therapy dog hand signals.
11. Student will learn how to teach his/her therapy dog other commands important for therapy work (i.e. leave it, easy, wait, closer or scooch, back up and gentle).
12. Student will learn how to teach his/her therapy dog other skills, if desired (i.e. give paw, and roll over).
13. Student will learn how to teach his/her therapy dog, depending on natural abilities and interests of dog, interests of the student and needs of the population to be served (i.e. jump

through hoop, pull a cart or sit in a wheelchair.

14. Student will learn how to acclimate his/her therapy dog to hospital equipment and sounds (i.e. walkers, rollators, motorized wheelchairs, canes, geri chairs, automatic doors, etc.), fire bells and PA systems, elevators, stairs, etc.

15. Student will learn how to teach his/her therapy dog how to heel **SLOWLY AND CALMLY**, pacing himself/herself to the gait of someone frail — or pacing himself/herself to heel next to a wheelchair, including turns.

16. Student will learn how to exit buildings in an emergency with his/her therapy pet.

17. Student will learn how to evaluate and develop protocols for therapy cats, rabbits, etc.

18. Student will learn about the strengths and needs of a variety of potential PAT pets.

Course III: Internship Description:

The internship in Pet Assisted Therapy will be individually planned between the PAT student, Program Coordinator, and the facility liaison. The internship will be designed to provide the student with hands-on experience, working creatively, safely, and effectively with his/her therapy pet.

Prerequisites: Courses I and II

Course III Objectives:

1. Student will ensure that eagerness of his/her therapy pet is a prerequisite to all interactions
2. Student will learn to work creatively and effectively to enhance the lives of people and animals.
3. Student will learn to work as an effective member of the treatment team or school-based support team.
4. Student will learn to reinforce and secure skills and knowledge learned in Courses I and II and to appropriately integrate same with each individual's and pet's creative potential.
5. Student will learn to complete progress notes and reports and how to handle publicity and quality assurance protocol.
6. Student will learn to appropriately self-evaluate, accept suggestions, and evaluate overall impact of Pet Assisted Therapy services on clients and pets.
7. Student will learn to be an advocate for Pet Assisted Therapy.
8. Student will gain confidence that problems can be openly, flexibly, and cooperatively resolved.
9. Student will complete a paper assessing the benefits to the clients, his/her therapy pet, and himself/herself.

Internship Guidelines

It is recommended that each PAT intern will split their one hundred hour internship as follows:
* 25 hours: PAT in a setting of your choice within an existing PAT program.
* 25 hours: PAT in a another setting of your choice within an existing PAT program.
* 25 hours: Setting up your own PAT program
* 25 hours: Advocacy

Each twenty-five hour segment can include 75% direct contact and 25% documentation, meetings, seminars, etc.

Each placement will be approximately twelve weeks or more, depending on needs of the student, agency and therapy pet.

Prior to starting PAT treatment, each intern will have:
* Had an interview at the site of choice
* Registered at the university
* Returned to director signed internship agreement form — see page 331
* Submitted written plan to director — see page 330
* Submit to the director, PAT guidelines developed by the PAT and the agency liaison for the specific site which would include, ethics, logistics, documentation protocol, etc.
* Submit to the director treatment plan goals for each client to be served (maintain confidentiality)
* Submit proof of completion of first two courses, personal resume and pet's temperament and health evaluations to internship site liaison.
* Submit proof of insurance

Once internship starts the PAT intern will:
* Document each interaction in their own journal or in patient's chart (per facility policy)
* Be in touch with PAT director every two weeks
* Mail a copy of your documentation every two weeks
* Contact director immediately if there is any change in your internship schedule

Additional readings or monthly seminars may be required.

CODE OF ETHICS AND CONDUCT

* Provide appropriate temperament, health records, and insurance on your therapy pet.

* Have PAT written plan to benefit the clients of the affiliated agency or students in the school. This plan also needs to meet the needs of your therapy pet.

* Maintain a safe and healthy environment for clients and therapy pet.

* Provide for the respect and dignity of clients.

* Provide for the respect and proper treatment of the therapy pet.

* Keep client confidentiality at all times.

* Be an advocate for the profession.

* Be able to self-evaluate and accept evaluation of others.

* Keep abreast of professional developments in the field.

PAT DIRECTOR'S RESPONSIBILITIES

* Seek out and confirm suitable internship sites and seek signed contract between university and site.

* Approve each internship program.

* Offer guidance, support, information, and help throughout the internship experience.

* Complete at least one on-site evaluation.

* Be in touch with on-site liaison as mutually agreed upon.

PAT STUDENT INTERN'S RESPONSIBILITIES

* Complete an interview with the site supervisor and mail signed agreement to director.

* Request an orientation to the facility.

* Work with PAT site supervisor to develop guidelines and code of ethics, which are then to be approved by infection control and PAT director.

* Provide in-service to staff.

* Identify objectives based on individual's strengths, needs and functioning level. Develop PAT goals with the agency liaison.

* Maintain a PAT caseload as agreed upon by all parties.

* Design, plan, assess, implement, and evaluate individual treatment plans according to agency and PAT guidelines. (PAT treatment sessions can be documented in the charts or in separate folders per agency protocol.)

* Attend IIT meetings and staff meeting as feasible and agreed upon.

* Be in touch with director every two weeks.

* Send a copy of your documentation journal to the director every two weeks.

* Be aware of and abide by all laws as they affect PAT, as well as all regulations, policies and procedures of the affiliating agency.

* Complete established hours of internship.

* Complete required readings and assignments and participate in monthly seminars, as required.

* Complete an essay on each PAT internship experience, demonstrating benefits to the individual, the pet, the institution, society, and yourself.

AGENCY'S RESPONSIBILITIES

* Provide student intern with agency's policies and regulations.

* Provide student intern with an orientation to the institution.

* Provide student intern with a staff person to supervise internship and provide on-going evaluation.

* Provide a list of medically referred clients, who are not allergic or phobic to animals and who have no physical or mental conditions which might compromise the well-being of the therapy pet.

* Provide appropriate area (s) for the student interns' PAT program, for keeping records, for working on records and for therapy pet to rest.

* Provide a signed agreement with student intern, PAT Director, allowing for internship and specifying policy therein, i.e. acceptable entrances, exits, etc.

* Allow student intern to participate in staff development meetings and programs as agreed upon.

* Allow student intern the right to read records, with professional standards of confidentiality ensured

* Allow student intern the right to participate in health care planning or treatment team meetings as agreed upon.

* Allow student intern the opportunity to apply classroom learning, to test skills and competencies and allow for creative and innovative solutions.

* Notify PAT Director immediately in the event the intern's performance becomes unsatisfactory.

* Complete a final evaluation of the student intern's performance and submit to student intern and PAT Director.

INTERSHIP PLAN

Name: _____

Social Security Number: _____ Date of Birth: _____

Permanent Address: _____ Phone: _____

_____ _____ Zip Code: _____

Emergency Contact: _____ Phone: _____

1.   Where would like to do your internship and with what population?

        _____

        _____

        _____

2.   When will you start? _____

3.   What is your tentative schedule? (days and hours)

        _____

        _____

4.   Briefly describe your overall goals:

        _____

        _____

        _____

5. I, the PATF intern, understand that I am solely responsible for the well-being and behavior of my therapy pet at all times.

Name: _____ Date: _____

Please attach specific policy and guidelines developed for each internship site.

PAT INTERNSHIP AGREEMENT FORM

This form must be submitted for each internship site.

It is agreed between _____ and _____
                             Student   PAT Director
and _____ that the above mentioned student will complete
            Facility Liaison
_____ of PAT, with, _____, which include direct PAT, PAT pre-planning,
hours   therapy pet
staff advising and evaluating, treatment team meetings, and other related activities at

_____
  Internship Site

Start Date: _____

Anticipated Ending Date: _____

Day of Week: _____

Time:_____

Please attach a copy of policy and guidelines developed for this specific site.

I, the Pet Assisted Therapy Intern, understands that I am solely responsible for the well-being and behavior of my therapy pet at all times.

                              _____
                              Student signature

PAT TIME SHEET

Student Intern Name: _____

    <u>Date:</u>   <u>Time:</u>

Intern signature: _____

Liaison signature: _____

AGENCY/SCHOOL DESCRIPTION

Agency/School Name: _____ Date: _____

Address: _____ Phone: _____
_____ Zip Code: _____

Agency Director/School Principal: _____

Agency/School Type (please check one): Public _____ Private _____ Non-profit _____

Brief Description of Agency Function: _____

_____

_____

Contact for Internships: _____ Phone: _____

Immediate Supervisor: _____ Phone: _____

Orientation and On-site Training Planned for Intern: _____
_____
_____

Describe Available Workspace for Intern: _____
_____
_____

EVALUATION
by Site Supervisor and Program Director

KEY: U — Unsatisfactory
S — Satisfactory
E — Excellent

I. Course Requirements

_____ 1. Completion of agreed upon number of hours.
_____ 2. Attendance at seminars, client meetings, or in-services, as required.
_____ 3. Conducted staff in-servicing.
_____ 4. Mailed copy of documentation on a regular basis to director, as agreed upon.
_____ 5. Consulted with director prior to making schedule changes.

II. Therapeutic Setting

_____ 6. Demonstrates the integration of therapy pets into the individuals' treatment plan using existing needs and strengths to develop therapeutic objectives.
_____ 7. Demonstrates concern for the welfare and needs of the therapy petsl.
_____ 8. Demonstrates concern for the welfare of individuals.

III. Professional Requirements

_____ 9. Demonstrates the ability to work effectively as an active member of the interdisciplinary treatment team.
_____ 10. Completes all required written documentation in a timely manner.
_____ 11. Demonstrates the ability to deal with problems in an effective and positive manner.
_____ 12. Demonstrates the ability to adapt to changes in routines.
_____ 13. Seeks help and assistance from supervisor or staff when necessary.
_____ 14. Adheres to legal institutional and Pet Assisted Therapy guidelines.
_____ 15. Conducts oneself in a professional manner at all times.
_____ 16. Demonstrates the knowledge, principles, and guidelines relevant to the Pet Assisted Therapy program.

IV. Job Attitudes

_____ 17. Demonstrates interest, enthusiasm, compassion and humanity.
_____ 18. Demonstrates relationship with peers.
_____ 19. Demonstrates a working relationship with supervisors.
_____ 20. Demonstrates good judgment in working with individuals/clients, as well as his/her therapy pet.
_____ 21. Attends all sessions.
_____ 22. Follows safety guidelines.

V. Comments

_____   _____
PAT Director   Agency Liaison

Section 2:
SAMPLE UNDERGRADUATE UNIVERSITY CURRICULUM OBJECTIVES FOR A MINOR IN PET ASSISTED THERAPY
(Pearl Salotto)

Required Courses In Pet Assisted Therapy

I.	Overview of Pet Assisted Therapy	3 cr hr
II.	Methods & Techniques of Setting Up Pet Assisted Therapy Programs in Health Care Facilities	3 cr hr
III.	Methods & Techniques of Setting Up Pet Inspired Values Development Programs in Schools	3 cr hr
IV.	Psychology of Animal Behavior	3 cr hr
V.	Understanding, Appreciating, and Training of Therapy Animals	3 cr hr
VI.	Issues & Trends in Pet Assisted Therapy	3 cr hr
VII.	Orientation to Clinical Internship	1 cr hr
VIII.	Internship in Pet Assisted Therapy	6 cr hr

If a student taking PAT as a minor is majoring in education, counseling, social work or in human service then their program will already call for them to be taking courses where they would learn to work with various populations. However, if a student is majoring in a non " human service" profession then it would be required for them to take several courses focusing on the needs of special populations in order to round out their pet therapy minor.

I. OVERVIEW OF PET ASSISTED THERAPY

1. Student will become aware of the role and significance of the Human-Companion Animal Bond throughout history.
2. Student will become aware of history, research, and scope of PAT.
3. Student will understand the safety, legal, and ethical implications related to PAT.
4. Student will understand the therapeutic benefits of PAT for selected populations and the positive characteristics of quality PAT programs throughout the nation.
5. Student will understand profile of potential therapy pets, including eagerness to work, health, temperament, etc.
6. Student will learn how to use skills and knowledge of Pet Assisted Therapy to increase physical and mental health for children, for individuals who are elderly, who have mental health and chemical dependency issues, and who have physical challenges.
7. Student will learn about the link of abuse between people and animals.
8. Student will understand about the "big picture" of PAT and its

potential for helping to bring about a "healthier, friendlier and more peaceful world."

9. Student will learn about the potential of Pet-Inspired Values Development in schools.

II. METHODS & TECHNIQUES OF SETTING UP PET ASSISTED THERAPY PROGRAMS IN HEALTH CARE FACILITIES

1. Student will learn how to seek out appropriate facilities.
2. Student will learn how to gain approval from administration and infection control committees in hospitals and medical settings.
3. Student will learn how to work with liaison to develop appropriate medically approved referrals, assessments, objectives, methodology, and evaluation procedure for Pet Assisted Therapy and be able to participate in Interdisciplinary Treatment Team meetings in medical settings.
4. Student will learn how to seek out appropriate areas for Pet Assisted Therapy within the facility.
5. Student will learn how to plan individualized treatment-based programs for individuals in medical settings.
6. Student will learn how to "treat" clients with Pet Assisted Therapy.
7. Student will learn how to follow regulations and procedures.
8. Student will learn how to deal with emergencies.
9. Student will learn how to protect the therapy pet while at work.

III. METHODS & TECHNIQUES OF SETTING UP PET INSPIRED VALUES DEVELOPMENT PROGRAMS IN SCHOOLS

1. Student will learn what Pet Inspired Values Development (PIVD) is.
2. Student will learn about the potential of PIVD for children.
3. Student will learn about the potential of PIVD for society.
4. Student will learn about the origin of the model PIVD program (The D.J. "Respect for Living Things" Program).
5. Student will learn strategies and methodologies in PIVD.
6. Student will learn the role of the therapy pet in PIVD.
7. Student will learn the role of the PATF/Educator in PIVD.
8. Student will learn about the impact of PIVD on families.
9. Student will learn how PIVD as part of the curriculum can enhance educational standards/outcomes.
10. Student will learn how to protect the therapy pet while at work.
11. Student will learn how to work with administrators and teachers to set up Pet-Inspired Values Development programs in schools.
12. Student will learn how to develop lesson plans to empower students to respect all living things.
13. Student will learn how to work with children in an empowering

and validating manner.

14. Student will learn how to adapt programs for varying ages and abilities.

IV. PSYCHOLOGY OF ANIMAL BEHAVIOR

1. Student will learn how to select a potential therapy pet, keeping in mind that the pet's place in the family comes first, regardless of whether or not the pet turns out to be appropriate for PAT .
2. Student will learn how to effectively temperament test therapy pets.
3. Student will learn what personality, skills, and behavior should be expected of a therapy pet.
4. Student will learn the importance of early socialization and critical learning periods.
5. Student will learn the impact of genetic background on their therapy pet.
6. Student will be bonded with his/her therapy pet first and will learn how to read an animal's physical and emotional responses (eagerness to work, stress, fatigue, illness, fear, dominance, etc.) through an understanding of body language, vocalization, facial expression, physical signs.
7. Student will learn how to understand and appreciate the gifts of their therapy pets.
8. Student will learn how to understand and take care of the needs of their therapy pets.
9. Student will understand clients, pets, and facilitator's role in PAT interactions.
10. Student will understand techniques for effective interactions.
11. Student will understand guidelines and requirements for making PAT safe for pets and people.

V. UNDERSTANDING, APPRECIATING, AND TRAINING OF THERAPY PETS

1. Student will learn how to teach his/her potential therapy dog how to heel on a loose leash.
2. Student will learn how to teach his/her therapy dog how to sit-stay, or down-stay, off leash, with distractions.
3. Student will learn how to teach his/her therapy dog how to "come" off leash with distractions.
4. Student will learn how to teach his/her therapy dog how to stand-stay, while being petted or groomed.
5. Student will learn how to teach his/her therapy dog to wear a backpack.

6. Student will learn how to acclimate his/her therapy dog to other animals.
7. Student will learn how to teach his/her therapy dog how to approach clients, safely.
8. Student will learn how to teach his/her therapy dog, on command, to be able to be on level with the client (i.e. paws up on a chair, jump or climb on chair, mat, bed, or table.)
9. Student will learn how to teach his/her therapy dog hand signals.
10. Student will learn how to teach his/her therapy dog other commands important for therapy work (i.e., leave it, easy, wait, closer or scooch, back up, and gentle.)
11. Student will learn how to teach his/her therapy dog other skills, if desired (i.e. give paw, roll over).
12. Student will learn how to teach his/her therapy dog — depending on natural abilities and interests of dog, interests of the student and needs of the population being serviced (i.e., jump through hoop, sit in a wheelchair).
13. Student will learn how to acclimate his/her therapy dog to hospital equipment and sounds (i.e., walkers, rollators, motorized wheelchairs, canes, geri chairs, etc.), fire bells and PA systems, elevators, stairs, etc.
14. Student will learn how to teach his/her therapy dog how to heel SLOWLY, CALMLY placing themselves to the gait of someone frail — or pacing themselves to heel next to a wheelchair, including turns. Client should never walk therapy pet unassisted.
15. Student will learn how to teach his/her therapy dog to exit buildings in an emergency, with leash on wrist while assisting patient.

VI. ISSUES AND TRENDS IN PET ASSISTED THERAPY

1. Student will become aware of state of the field.
2. Student will become aware of Certification guidelines.
3. Student will become aware of liability/insurance issues.
4. Student will become aware of professional standards.
5. Student will become aware of research possibilities in the field.
6. Student will become aware of organizations and resources.
7. Student will become aware of legislative needs and possibilities.
8. Student will become aware of safety and legal issues.
9. Student will become aware of ethical responsibilities.

VII. ORIENTATION TO CLINICAL

1. Student will learn to write treatment or lesson plans.
2. Student will learn quality assurance procedures.
3. Student will learn governmental requirements (i.e., responsibilities to surveying bodies).

VIII. INTERNSHIPS IN PET ASSISTED THERAPY

1. Student will develop skills necessary to become a professional PAT.
2. Student will learn how to set up, run, and evaluate professional PAT programs.
3. Student will gain experience in working creatively with approved therapy pet and clients.
4. Student will learn how to adapt PAT program to individual needs.
5. Student will gain experience in working cooperatively with Interdisciplinary Treatment Team in medical settings or administrators and teachers in school settings.
6. Student will learn how to "treat" individuals with PAT in medical settings or teach respect for living things in educational settings.
7. Student will have an opportunity for the exchange of ideas with facility staff.
8. Student will be an advocate for Pet Assisted Therapy.
9. Student will learn how to handle publicity appropriately.
10. Student will learn how to handle quality assurance protocol.
11. Student will be able to self-evaluate and to accept positive suggestions.
12. Student will gain confidence that problems in PAT can be openly — flexibly — and cooperatively resolved.
13. Student will become familiar with concerns and issues of population served, through direct contact and required readings.
14. Student will write a formal paper documenting changes.
15. Student will demonstrate commitment to ethics by always being aware if his/her pet is safe and eager to work.

Section 3:
THE D. J. "RESPECT FOR LIVING THINGS" PROGRAM
(Pearl Salotto)

Program Goals:

- to build self-esteem through D. J.'s unconditional love.

- to develop concern and compassion for the well-being of animals, due to children's love for D. J. and their recognition that she is a living thing with feelings and needs.

- to develop recognition that people, as well, have feelings and needs, and that it is our responsibility to respect, love, and display kindness and empathy to those people and animals, from whom we receive it.

- to develop understanding, through learning about, and observing D.J.'s unconditional love for all, regardless of race, religion, economic or health status — that it is our responsibility as human beings, to treat individuals caringly without discrimination or stereotyping.

- to develop understanding that, just as D. J. is trained to do her job as a Pet Assisted Therapy dog, we also need training (education) to accomplish our goals in life.

- to develop understanding that, just as D. J. needs an environment in which people are calm and gentle in their voices and actions, that people as well, thrive in a peaceful environment.

- to develop understanding that, just as I would not have taken D. J. into the family unless I had the energy, resources, love, time, and commitment to see that she has a good life, that the same applies to bringing children into the world, as well.

- to develop recognition that, just as D. J. is unique and special, and that, with her own package of strengths and weaknesses, she is making a difference in the world, that we also are unique and special, that we need to protect our body, heart and mind, and that we have a responsibility to make a difference in the world, through our own unique set of talents.

Pearl Salotto

SESSION ONE: *RESPECT FOR ANIMALS*

Introduction

How does D. J. make you feel?
What animals do you have at home?
What does the name of the program "Respect for Living Things" mean?
Can we begin respecting others and ourselves by introducing ourselves?

Discussion Questions

Are animals living things?
Do all animals have feelings and needs?
Do animals deserve love and respect?
How do we show respect for animals?
Is D. J. special and unique?
Are each of you unique and special with our own special strengths and
    weakness?
In what way are each of you special and unique?
Do people have feelings and needs?
How do we show respect for people?
What respect do we deserve ourselves?
Is it our responsibility to return love from the animals and people from
    whom we receive it?
Are our companion animals members of the family?
What is the Human-Companion Animal Bond?

Essays

Write or dictate a story about someone who loves you and how you
show love back to that person or animal. Illustrate your story.

Outcomes

Children will appreciate the "aliveness" of animals.
Children will begin to internalize the concept that all living things have
    feelings and deserve love and respect.
Children will begin to internalize the concept that each of them is special and
    unique and deserves respect.
Children will begin to recognize that each of us has a responsibility to
    return the love to those from whom we receive it.
Children will understand that our companion animal friends are family.

SESSION TWO: *RESPECT FOR PEOPLE*

My sharing of D. J.'s work in pet therapy through pictures, stories, and videos serves as a springboard for discussions of the feelings of family members, classmates, neighbors, individuals who are elderly and individuals who are physically challenged. The children come to respect people of all walks of life, as they want to emulate D. J.

Discussion Questions

Pet Therapy
What is D.J.'s role as a Pet Assisted Therapy dog ?
What other animals are therapy pets?
Where do pet therapy animals work?
Do therapy pets enjoy their work?
Do they need training for their work?
What does it mean to say that D. J. has a job?
What is the career of Pet Therapy?
What ethical responsibilities do PATFs have?
Do therapy pets give unconditional love to all regardless of race, religion, health or economic status?
Why is it important that D.J.'s happiness in the family come before her jobs?

Sensitivity Building
How do you think it would feel to be elderly?
How do you think it would feel to live in a nursing home?
How do you think it would feel to face physical challenges?
How do you think your parents feel, your siblings, new friends in school or on the block?

Is D. J.'s Example a Good One for Us to Follow?
What is the Role of other Working Animals?
(seeing eye dogs, hearing ear dogs, service dogs, rescue dogs, drug prevention dogs)?

Essay
Write or dictate a story on what can we learn from D. J.

Outcomes
Children will understand what it means to be a PATFs.
Children will understand the role of therapy pets.
Children will begin to understand the strengths and needs of individuals who are elderly.
Children will begin to become sensitive to the challenges of individuals with physical disabilities.
Children will begin to "appreciate" the amazing ability of working dogs to

enhance potential for independence with individuals who are physically challenged.

Children will understand that therapy pets and other working animals need training.

Children will begin to understand the ethical considerations and responsibilities when working with therapy pets.

Children will understand the unconditional love of therapy pets can be an example for all of us.

SESSION THREE: *RESPECT FOR OURSELVES*

Life Changing Connections — Values For Life

If the children have internalized the values of respect for animals and respect for people from sections one and two, it is easy for me to facilitate their realization that it is also their *responsibility to respect themselves, (their mind, heart, and body).*

Discussion Questions

ARE EACH OF US SPECIAL AND UNIQUE AS D. J. IS SPECIAL AND UNIQUE?

What do we like best about ourselves?

Is our total package of strengths and weaknesses unique and special?

Is it OK if we are not the best on the baseball team or if we do not have perfect vision or whatever?

Is it good to be me?

HOW DO WE SHOW RESPECT FOR OUR MINDS?
(The need for education)

Did D. J. need training for her work?

Did I need an education for my work?

Do you need an education to accomplish your goals?

What are your short-term and long-term goals?

What talents and interests do you have that will lead you to your goals?

How will your education and your behavior affect your achievement of your goals?

HOW DO WE SHOW RESPECT FOR OUR BODIES?
(The need to avoid substance abuse)
(The following questions do not usually have to be asked, but rather, the answers come spontaneously from the children, when I ask how they should respect their bodies.)

Do we need proper nutrition?

Do we need proper exercise?

Do we need proper medical care?

Do we need proper rest?

Do we need to avoid substances that will harm our body, such as cigarettes, alcohol, drugs and other poisons?

HOW DO WE TAKE CARE OF OUR HEARTS?
(The need to live peacefully with others, and avoid violence in word and deed, so we can feel comfortable with ourselves)

Do we need to be quiet and calm in front of D. J.?

Do we need to act toward others in a manner in which we can feel proud?

Do we feel good when we are honest, fair, supportive, kind, dependable, cooperative, patient, helpful, generous?

How do we avoid behavior for which we feel ashamed?

How can we feel better when we feel sad, lonely, angry?

Do we need to broaden our horizons by being open to new ideas and listening to others?

How can we spread cheerfulness and be Children of Joy, just as D. J. is a Dog of Joy?

HOW CAN WE DEMONSTRATE COMMITMENT AND RESPONSIBILITY IN OUR RELATIONSHIP WITH PEOPLE AND ANIMALS?
(The need to avoid premature sexual involvement)

What commitments do we need to make before we bring companion animals into our family?

What commitments do we need to make before bringing children into the family?

Do we need to be polite and good mannered with people in our homes, schools, and neighborhoods?

Do we need to be aware of the lasting effect of our words?

Are we aware that kind words and deeds can lead to permanent positive good feelings and cruel words and deeds can lead to permanent negative feelings?

Are we aware that joy and pain are universal feelings and that we need to be advocates for ourselves and others?

Essay

Write or dictate an essay on one or more of the following topics:

How can we be Children of Joy?

What are our career goals?

How should we take care of our bodies?

Outcomes

Children will understand that we only have one body and that it is our responsibility to take care of it.

Children will understand that it is only when we respect ourselves — caring for our hearts, minds and bodies that we can find meaning in life and help others.

Children will understand that we need an education to achieve our goals.

Children will understand that we all have the ability and the responsibility to spread joy and kindness and that it is good to be just who we are.

Children will understand that we need to make a permanent commitment before we bring an animal or child into our life.

Children will understand the effect of our words and deeds on others, the universality of feelings and our responsibility to be advocates for ourselves and others.

Children will understand that we must be responsible not only for our actions, but for our words, that our words can bring joy and pain to others, and that once spoken they cannot be taken back.

Children will feel empowered, through realization that they can make a positive difference in their world through their words and deeds.

SESSION FOUR: *RESPECT FOR THE ENVIRONMENT*

The program comes full circle with our responsibilities, not only to our companion animal friends, other people, and ourselves, but to the wild animals and our earth as well. As with the first section on Respect for Animals — Respect for the Earth is a natural, peaceful, and comfortable topic for the children to "feel" and "live" and encircles the whole program in a sense of meaning.

Discussion Questions

What are the rights of wild animals, like the wolves, and the whales, the great cats, and those with whom we share 98% of our genetic makeup, the great apes, and what are our responsibilities to them?

What are our responsibilities to the rain forest, the oceans, the air and the soil?

Are plants and flowers living things?

What can we learn from how animals like the wolves live in families, share responsibilities, and care for each other?

Essay

What can I do to help save the wolves or the whales, the great apes, or great cats or other wild animals?

Outcomes

Children will realize that one person's actions can make a difference

Children will realize that they can participate in saving the earth for the next generation.

Children will realize that the Native American tradition of *respect for all living things* is the only way we can survive.

Children will realize that just as D. J. sets the example, in the first session, of the fragility and meaning of aliveness, so does the social structure and family values of many of the wild animals — inspire us — with many powerful lessons.

Supplementary Ideas:

It is easy to find creative means to include concepts of respect for animals, people, oneself, and the environment in academic areas, teacher/parent workshops, and school-wide activities. Possible ideas include:

"Respect for Living Things" reading list
"Respect for Living Things" essay writing topics
School-wide and classroom bulletin boards on respect
Teacher in-service on the link of animal abuse and child abuse/domestic violence
Parent seminar on link of abuse and Pet-Inspired Values Development programs like the D.J. Program
Family "talking time" on respectful relationships
School posters depicting respect
Mural — art projects on respecting animals, people and the environment
Kind News (Humane Society of United States publication)
Field trips
Community Service — Letters to seniors
Visit to seniors
Musical entertainment for seniors
Review Sessions

Essay Ideas

How can I show respect for animals?
How should I treat my pet at home?
How do you think zoo animals feel?
How can I show respect for my parents?
How do you think it feels to live in a nursing home?
Am I special and unique?
How can I be a child of joy like D. J. is Dog of Joy?
How can I display respect for my mind?
How did The D. J. Program affect my choices?
What is the profession of Pet Assisted Therapy?
What professions am I interested in learning about for my future?
How can I help build a better world?
What can we learn from D. J.?
How can I show respect for a new child in a classroom?

347

Pearl Salotto

What does it mean that all living things have feelings?
How can I show respect for my teacher?
How can I show respect for my body?
How can I show respect for my sisters and/or brothers?

Pledge: *The Children's D.J. Pledge for Peace and Respect*

I pledge to respect myself by doing my best in school and by avoiding drugs, alcohol, and tobacco.

I pledge to respect the feelings of my family and all people with whom I come in contact.

I pledge to treat my pet with the same respect as other members of the family.

I pledge to do my part to help make the world a better place for people, animals, and the environment.

Additional Resources:

Poem: *May You Always Outrun Me*

> *May you always be healthy,*
> *With your four paws running carefree.*
> *May you always be happy,*
> *With your tail wagging in the breeze.*
> *May you always be eager,*
> *As you smell among fall leaves.*
> *May you always outrun me,*
> *With your life and energy.*
>
> *May you always be cheerful,*
> *As you greet each new day with me.*
> *May you always be enthusiastic,*
> *With your life and energy.*
> *Whether rain or snow,*
> *Or cool sweet air so dear.*
> *As long as we're together,*
> *We'll enjoy all seasons of the year.*
>
> *May you always go bounding,*
> *Across the yard so fast.*
> *As you chase all the airplanes,*
> *As they fly so low and fast.*
> *May you always want to go home with me,*
> *Whether from the lake or park.*

As in all true relationships,
The bond is heart to heart!
So — may you always be healthy,
As you greet each new day with me.
May you always outrun me,
With your life and energy.

With your life and energy!

Booklets 1 and 2: are in Part II, Chapter 5, Section 3

Booklet 3: *Can We Follow Her Example and Build a Better World?*

   This booklet is designed with photographs following each question, so that after teachers lead a discussion of each topic, the illustrations will help the children internalize the values. As teachers use this book with the following questions, they can use their own photographs or childrens' drawing as illustrations. This booklet also includes music, some of which was developed by this author and some of which was developed by school children at Robertson School in Central Falls, RI.

- Do our pets as well as people need a home where they are safe, warm, and comfortable?

- Do our pets need good food, cool water, and enough rest to be healthy just as we do?

- Do we take the time to share joy and love everyday?

- Do our pets need good medical care, dental care, and grooming just as we do?

- Do our pets need exercise and fun to stay healthy just as we do?

- Do our pets need play time everyday just as we do?

- Do we take the time to do whatever it takes to keep our pets safe, happy, and healthy?

- Are our pets curious about what's going on just as we are?

- Can we give the same respect to everyone regardless of race, age, health or economic status just as our pets do?

- Can any animal who eagerly gives unconditional love to one and all be a therapy pet?
- Is it important that therapy pets enjoy their work just as people should?

- Can therapy pets enhance the school environment?

- Do therapy pets need a good education just as we do?

- Do our pets stay in the family through the years as children do?

Booklet 4 (Version I): *Maj-En and Me* — Children can illustrate each of these thoughts

- Maj-En has a family.

- Maj-En likes to go to school and learn.

- Maj-En likes his job. His job is Pet Therapy. He makes people happy.

- Maj-En loves everyone who is kind and gentle. He doesn't care how old you are or what race or religion you are.

- Maj-En respects me because I am special. He gives me his paw and kisses and plays with me.

- Maj-En is special too. I can be kind and gentle to Maj-En and to all living things.

Booklet 4 (Version II): *Maj-En and Me* — Children can illustrate each of these thoughts

- Maj-En has a family. I have a family too.

- May-En likes to go to school and learn. I like to go to school too.

- Maj-En likes his job. His job in Pet Therapy. He makes people happy. I like to make people happy too.

- Maj-En loves everyone who is kind and gentle. He doesn't care how old you are or what race or religion you are. I like people and animals who are kind and gentle too.

- Maj-En respects me because I am special. He gives me his paw and kisses and plays with me. I play with my friends too.

- Maj-En is special too. I can be kind and gentle to May-En and to all living things.

Booklet 5: *Maj-En Facilitated Learning: Paws on the Path to a More Peaceful World*
   This booklet is a photo essay describing the benefits of the D.J. Program

— showcasing therapy pet Maj-En. (Available through author.)

Song 1: is in Part II, Chapter 5, Section 3

Song 2: *Hooray for Family Pet Maj-En* is sung to the tune of "Bingo." It was inspired by Central Falls 3rd graders who wrote their own songs and by my granddaughter's preschool who enjoyed singing them.

Maj-ee Maj-ee goes to work
Maj-ee goes to work
MAJ-EN MAJ-EN MAJ-EN
Oh, Family Therapy Pet Maj-En

Oh, Maj-ee Maj-ee loves his job
Making people happy
MAJ-En MAJ-EN MAJ-EN
Oh, Family Therapy Pet Maj-En

Oh, Maj-ee Maj-ee loves the children
And they love him too
Maj-ee teaches children
Maj-ee inspires children
Maj-ee empowers children
To respect all living things – oh

Maj-ee is building a new profession
Pet Assisted Therapy
Pet Assisted Therapy
Pet Assisted Therapy
Pet Assisted Therapy
Pets and people together

Oh Maj-ee is very majestic
And he's enthusiastic too
Following in D.J.'s pawprints
Following in D.J.'s pawprints
Following in D.J.'s pawprints
A good job he does too oh!

Oh Maj-ee Maj-ee helps all
Build a better world
A more healthy world
A more friendly world
A more peaceful world
Oh Maj-ee help us all — oh

So Maj-ee Maj-ee goes to work
His gifts he freely shares
MAJ-EN MAJ-EN MAJ-EN
Hooray for family pet Maj-En

Song 3: *Oh, We Respect,* is sung to the tune of "Oats, and Beans and Barley Grow," where children can add a single noun to each sentence. For example:

Oh, We Respect our parents, parents
We respect our parents, parents
We respect, We respect
We respect our parents, parents....

Similarly, children can give input into the final noun, such as:

Oh, We Respect our family pets
Oh, We Respect our friends in school.

In the second component of this song, children simple add a verb. For example:

We show respect by loving, loving
We show respect by loving, loving
We show respect, we show respect
We show respect by loving, loving....

Children will be eager to add other verbs, such as:

We show respect by helping
We show respect by listening

<u>**Proposal for a PAT Room at an Elementary School**</u>

Goals, Objectives, and Strategies:

   The purpose of this proposal is to offer the children the opportunity to have a Pet Assisted Therapy (PAT) room as part of their school environment, staffed by a professional PATF and his/her therapy pet. The children will have the opportunity to grow in their recognition of their own rights and value as human beings and in their recognition of their responsibility to be aware of the feelings and needs of all living things — animals, other people, themselves, and their environment. Each participating student will need their family's concurrence for the following goals, as evidenced by a Home/School contract.

- children will come to school daily and on time.

- children will complete their school work and homework to the best of their ability and return it on time.

- children will live up to the D. J. *challenge* of treating everyone — peers, teachers, other adults, and animals, with the same respect as D. J. treats them.

- children will display self respect by avoiding conflict and having no behavioral incidents.

- children will participate in daily family discussions on respect. (This could be an opportunity to acknowledge family member's kind words and deeds. This could also be an opportunity for a discussion of concerns, resolution of conflicts, acknowledgment of each other's feelings, and joint decision-making

- children will have the opportunity to come into the PAT room for successful conflict resolution.

- children will have the opportunity to keep journals, in which they will describe their developing awareness of their responsibility toward pets, people, themselves and the environment.

- children will also have the opportunity to come into the PAT room with their classmates if their teachers would like a group discussion on respect for animals, people, themselves, and the environment.

- children will have the opportunity to come into the PAT room to learn leadership skills, which might include their being able to teach lessons on respect to younger students.

- children will learn to put the feelings of the therapy pet first.

- children with a history of behavioral problems, can come into the PAT room, when they are in control of their behavior.

In addition to the short-term goals of attendance, grades and behavior, the PAT room will offer a "safe haven" within the school for fun, relaxation, and creativity where children can display photos, art work, and essays, where children can groom, train and play with the therapy pet and where children can participate in discussions, make friends, and find support, calm and respect.

Long-term goals to be measured and documented would include: avoidance of drugs, avoidance of early sexual involvement, or any behavior abusive to people, animals and our environment. Long-term goals would also seek to document that youngsters involved in the program were better able to develop future academic goals, develop their talents, would be more likely to be able to facilitate conflict resolution among their peers and in their own families, and be involved in community advocacy projects to better the lives of people, animals and the environment.

Section 4:
FEINSTEIN HIGH SCHOOL LEVEL I PAT SYLLABUS
(Pearl Salotto)

Description:

Students will be introduced to the profession of Pet Assisted Therapy. Students will study the Human Companion-Animal Bond from a historical, theoretical, and practical perspective. Students will learn how ethically based PAT programs for individuals with special needs, individuals who are elderly, children, individuals with chemical dependency and physical challenges are set up. Legal, safety, ethical concerns, and model programs will be discussed, as well as PAT's connections to a variety of disciplines and issues.

Feinstein High School student Michael Davis, a natural born teacher, who inspired countless elementary school students to respect animals, other people, and themselves, enjoys a quiet moment with Maj-En.

Objectives:

1. Student will understand the meaning of the profession of Pet Assisted Therapy.
2. Student will understand the meaning of the Human Companion-Animal Bond.
3. Student will understand the therapeutic benefits of Pet Assisted Therapy for a various populations.
4. Student will begin to understand the history of and the research in this profession.
5. Student will understand the ethical responsibilities of Pet Assisted

Therapy.

6. Student will gain an understanding of the strengths and needs of special populations.

7. Student will learn to appreciate the "gifts" and understand the needs of therapy pets.

8. Student will begin to understand the powerful effect of Pet Assisted Therapy through learning about model programs.

9. Student will begin to understand how the profession of Pet Assisted Therapy can lead to a healthier, friendlier and more peaceful society.

10. Student will begin to understand each of our responsibilities to all living things. (animals, other people, the environment and ourselves)

11. Student will begin to understand how Pet-Inspired Values Development Programs can empower school children of all ages to grow in their recognition of their own humanity and in their recognition of their responsibilities to animals, other people, themselves and the environment.

12. Student will begin to understand the tragic link of abuse between people and animals and how using our knowledge of this link can help lead to a less violent world for people and animals.

13. Student will learn about the current state of the art, including legislation which has been introduced to acknowledge the rights of therapy pets, RI Health Department Pet Therapy Guidelines, and state commissions to study the link of abuse.

Class Outline

Class One:

Topics:

* *Introductions — D.J.'s legacy — "We Can Build a Better World"*

* *Definitions of the Human Companion Animal Bond and Pet Assisted Therapy*

* *History*

Assignments for Next Week:

Assignment 1: Search the Web and find an individual or therapy pet who is famous in the history of PAT and write an essay on his/her contribution to the field.

Assignment 2: Read one of the vignettes from *Animals and Individuals Who are Elderly: Can Pets Fill the Void?* (from *Loving Intervention*) and write a paragraph on the relationship between the individual you read about and D. J.

Class Two:

Topics:

* <u>Model Programs with children, individuals who are elderly, and individuals with mental and physical challenges</u>

Assignment for Next Week:

Reading Assignment: *"Is Holly Working Today" — Barbara Wood*

Writing Assignment: *Write an essay or outline describing our responsibilities to therapy pets, as well as the clients.*

Class Three:

Topic: <u>*Ethics, Standards, and Guidelines*</u>

Assignments for Next Week:

Reading Assignment: *Quadruped Conquers Culture — Barbara Wood Everybody Rides: Therapeutic Horseback Riding — Sue Epstein*

Writing Assignment: none

Class Four:

Topic: <u>*The D. J. "Respect for Living Things" Program (Pet-Inspired Values Development) taught by Level II PAT Students*</u>

Assignment for Next Week:

Reading Assignment: none

Written Assignment: *Write an essay on your impressions of what Pet Assisted Therapy is, based on meeting the family therapy pets, watching videos, completing your readings and listening and participating in class.*

Class Five:

Topic:
* *Pet Assisted Therapy and Violence*
> PAT with Prisoners
> Link of Abuse Between People and Animals

Assignment for Next Week:

Reading Assignment: none

Written Assignment: *Advocacy Essay*
> Imagine that you were invited to write a guest editorial for another high school's newspaper on the topic — How can the profession of Pet Assisted Therapy Help to Bring About a "Healthier, Friendlier and More Peaceful World."

Class Six:
Topic:
* *Pet Assisted Therapy Impacting on Society's Issues and Problems*
Assignment for Next Week: review for final

Class Seven:
Topic: *Final Exam*

Students who successfully complete Level I PAT will have the opportunity to build on their interest in this field through Level II Service Learning PAT in a nursing home.

Level II PAT:
THE COMMON BOND IS CARING: FEINSTEIN HIGH SCHOOL INTERGENERATIONAL PROGRAM AT ST. ELIZABETH'S HOME

<u>*Todd Williamson*</u> *following a traumatic brain injury back in October of 1989, and the subsequent three year rehabilitation, he pursued a master's level degree in Therapeutic Recreation Management and graduated three years later from Springfield College in Springfield, MA. After graduation, Todd entered the nursing home field, where he is now the director of Therapeutic Recreation at the St. Elizabeth's Home in Providence, RI. Mr. Williamson is certified by the National Council for Therapeutic Recreation Certification. He has developed an intergenerational program of Pet Assisted Therapy for the residents of the St. Elizabeth's Home and some very gifted students from Feinstein High School who have helped to make this program a success. Though Todd has recently passed away the program continues.*

Program Description:

- This program will give Service Learning Credit for students who have completed PAT I at Feinstein High School.

- This program will take place two times a week at St. Elizabeth's Home with up to six students in each PAT group.

- This writer, a staff person at St. Elizabeth's, who is nationally certified in therapeutic recreation, and who is in the process of completing the University PAT program, will supervise the morning program. He will work with his sister's therapy dog, Molly, a 2 ½ year old chocolate Labrador Retriever.

- On Tuesdays, sessions include room visits and on Fridays there are group sessions in the beautiful solarium. In the room visits the students bring PAT treatment to individuals with physical and cognitive impairments who present at a reduced functional level. Group sessions take place with individuals who are much more functionally independent.

Orientation of Students: 4 ½ hours of orientation for Feinstein High School students

- History of St. Elizabeth's Home
- Overview of population

- Infection Control

- Fire and Emergency Procedures

Benefits to Residents:

- Increased affect following the program.

- Talking about therapy pet Molly, up to several days after the program.

- Positive comments about the high school students up to several days after the program.

- Increased socialization with the pet, staff, students and other residents.

- Opportunities to increase physical movement of the upper extremities.

- Some individuals chose PAT who seldom participate in other group leisure programs.

Benefits to Students:

- Learn about feelings, needs, and abilities of individuals who are elderly.

- Learn about how PAT impacts individuals who are elderly.

- Learn how to integrate classroom learning in PAT with real life.

- Learn how to work with therapy pets.

- Observe nonverbal behavior.

- Join with the residents and the therapy pet in an intergenerational program.

Benefits to the Therapy Pet:

- Enjoys all the attention, including petting and treats.

- Seems to enjoy having a "job to do."

- Enjoys loving comments such as "You're beautiful" and "I love you."

Methodology:

- Each PAT session is unique in that there is a particular theme.

    * Some days are reminiscent programs, others are filled with trivia about Labrador Retrievers.

    * A therapy rabbit is occasionally substituted for Molly. While the therapy pet remains in his basket, the residents still feel like they are cradling him,

when the basket is placed on their laps.

 * Occasionally, we make it a totally social event, with refreshments being served to residents by the students.

- The students help to transport the residents back to their respective destinations.

- Students then gather together to process the experience.

- The students are given homework to assist them with their observation techniques. The individual program response form, which the students fill out, is the same form which this author uses to document and post in the resident's chart.

- On the days when neither therapy pet is at work, the students are actively engaged, by this writer, in alternate programming activities such as development of a mission statement for the program or making charts with photographs and captions.

Ethics:

- The responsibilities of the PATF are indeed many. In this particular program the PATF is not only the responsible clinician serving the residents of the St. Elizabeth's Home, the caretaker of the therapy pet, but also the "educator" challenging young minds eager to learn.

- The PATF must treat the residents as he/she wishes to be treated.

- The therapy pet, Molly, is dependent on this writer to make sure that she is always treated fairly and no harm will come to her. Potential concerns to look out for include: intriguing smells in a trash can, meal trays being traversed down the hallways, and chemicals for many applications. The PATF must be certain that the therapy pet is protected at all times from being allowed to sample anything that may be potentially damaging.

Therapy pets, Molly and Percy, enjoy bringing out the best in people, consistently, time after time, session after session. They have the power to light up a room with smiles. As Molly and Percy work their magic, amidst the gathering of residents in the solarium, the students and their facilitator watch and study facial expressions and listen to the many pleasant comments. They strive to make each and every session special.

The program at the St. Elizabeth's Home is educational and beautiful in the manner in which the young and old share common feelings. The students have learned to be more appreciative and the residents have learned that friendships can be formed between people of differing ages. ***The common bond is caring!***

Section 5:
THE D. J. PET ASSISTED THERAPY/SERVICE LEARNING CURRICULUM FOR MIDDLE SCHOOLS
(Pearl Salotto)

Mission:

The mission will be to include education about Pet Assisted Therapy (PAT) in the sixth grade curriculum and to provide follow up opportunities in PAT/Service Learning. In the follow up PAT/Service Learning component, students, under the guidance, supervision, and mentorship of a professional PAT/Educator, can experience sharing therapy pets with individuals who are elderly and or children, while at the same time recognizing that they are making a difference in their community and their world. (The pets the students will be working with are temperament tested, trained, and family members of the professional PAT/Educator.)

Logistics:

PAT/Service Learning Curriculum at Calcutt Middle School has been developed by Pearl Salotto, who has over the past thirteen years, developed and taught nationally recognized PAT programs for elementary, high school, and university students. She will supervise the program and teach, along with two other PAT/Educators who have successfully completed The D. J. Pet Assisted Therapy University Certificate Program, currently run at CCRI. Linda Jones, Service Learning Coordinator for the Alan Shawn Feinstein High School, and the only nationally recognized Service Learning Educator with an expertise in professional PAT, will provide an invaluable resource to the successful implementation of this unique sixth grade model of the integration of PAT with Service Learning.

In the first year, each of the PAT/Educators will be responsible for the education and follow-up Service Learning experience for one of the three sixth grade teams. The fall semester will be spent in planning between the PAT/Service Learning staff, school administration, teachers, parents, and nursing home personnel.

In January, all sixth graders will receive PAT/Service Learning education once a week within their instructional block for seven weeks. Following the successful completion of these seven weeks, students will be referred to a Service Learning site. The sites will include an area nursing home or at an educational site (preschool, daycare, kindergarten, first or second grade).

Students participating in PAT/Service Learning at a nursing home will assist the PAT/Educator in delivering PAT treatment to residents. Students participating in PAT/Service Learning at an educational facility, will assist the PAT/Educator in teaching The D. J. "Respect for Living Things" Program (respect for animals, oneself, and others).

Rationale:

The proposed plan described above is modeled after The D. J. Pet Assisted

Therapy/Service Learning program at Alan Shawn Feinstein High School for Public Service in Providence, developed by Pearl Salotto and Linda Jones. (see page 160)

Curriculum

Class One:

I. Learning/Educational Objectives:

a) Students and family therapy pet, Maj-En, will become acquainted. (Maj-En is a four-year old Samoyed who has been working in the field for three years.)

b) Students will be introduced to the meaning of terminology in the field, including *Human Companion Animal Bond (HCAB)* and *professional PAT.*

c) Students will learn about the variety of pets who can work in this profession and how they are evaluated and trained.

d) Student will be introduced to individuals and pets who are part of the history of this profession.

e) Students will be introduced to the benefits of professional PAT for individuals who are elderly.

II. Methodology:

a) Students will introduce themselves by describing their family, including their pet, special interests, and talents.

b) Students will discover the meaning of the words PAT and HCAB through studying and talking about photographs demonstrating various PAT experiences with different populations.

c) Students will be introduced to historical leaders in the field, as well as pets, including Dr. Boris Levinson, Dr. Leo Bustad, Dr. Aaron Katcher, Dr. Dick Dillman, as well as to therapy pets, Jingles, Bumper, Jake, and D. J.

d) Students will be introduced to research in the field which documents the benefits of pets to people.

e) Students will view two videos:
1) Medical Benefits of PAT at Rochester General Hospital
2) Companion Birds.

III. Assignment:

Students will write one paragraph describing one of the following topics:
Definition of HCAB and PAT
A leader in the field or a pioneering therapy pet
The benefits of PAT to individuals who are elderly

IV. Outcomes:

a) Students will have had an opportunity to open up their minds and hearts, sharing their feelings and ideas, as a result of interacting with family therapy pet, Maj-En, and ensuing discussion.

b) Students will have learned that PAT is a profession that enriches the lives of others.

c) Students will have learned basic vocabulary in the field.

d) Students will have learned the protocol for therapy pets being included in the field.

e) Students will have learned that it is our responsibility, in the study of any discipline, to recognize and acknowledge the leaders of that field.

f) Students will have begun to appreciate the benefits of professional PAT to individuals who are elderly.

g) Students will have become excited about a discipline in which they can make a difference in their world through Service Learning.

Class Two:

I. Learning/Educational Objectives:

a) Students will learn about various effective PAT programs with children.

1. The D. J. "Respect for Living Things" Program — Pearl Salotto
2. The Companion Animal Dropout Prevention Program of Florida — Dr. Dillman

b) Students will learn about the potential impact of professional PAT with individuals with developmental challenges.

II. Methodology:

Students will learn about the philosophy and short and long-term goals of these programs through studying materials and resources, viewing videos, and engaging in class discussions.

1) Farm on the Move
2) Classroom Canine Companions Opening Doors to Learning

III. Assignment:

Students will begin a reading assignment to be given as an oral report on class six. Details TBA.

IV. Outcomes:

a) Students will have realized the extent, breadth, and scope of this profession.

b) Students will have begun to recognize that PAT education in schools can help future generations to respect animals, others, and themselves.

c) Students will have begun to recognize that PAT can have a positive effect on individuals with developmental challenges.

d) Students will have realized that this discipline can be easily integrated into a variety of academic areas, including reading, writing, health, science, social studies, ethics, etc.

e) Students will have begun to realize that PAT Education can help them develop a new view of the world in which they feel empathy and compassion for all.

f) Students, through PAT education, will have become better able to set personal and academic goals.

Class Three:

I. Learning/Educational Objectives:

a) Students will begin to appreciate that all professions have standards, ethics, and guidelines.

b) Students will begin to understand standards, ethics, and guidelines in PAT.

c) Students will recognize that most of life's situations and scenarios not only in PAT, but in families, schools, neighborhoods, and communities require responsible, thoughtful, ethical judgments and choices.

II. Methodology:

a) Students will learn about Code of Ethics in a variety of professions.

b) Students will each be given an index card describing a situation in which ethical principles are involved. Students will be asked to describe how they would ethically handle a given situation that will likely occur in PAT.

III. Assignment:

Students will complete an activity sheet matching specific ethical situations with Pearl Salotto's Code of Ethics, which reflects general ethical principles.

IV. Outcomes:

a) Students will have learned to recognize that all professions have Code of Ethics and guidelines.

b) Students will have learned to appreciate the dual ethical principles in PAT (our responsibilities to the individual, as well as the pet).

c) Students will have learned to appreciate all of our ethical responsibilities to each other.

Class Four:

I. Learning/Educational Objectives:

   a)   Students will begin to understand the effect of professional PAT on prisoners.
   b)   Students will begin to appreciate how PAT can have a significant effect on preventing violence in society.

II. Methodology:

   a)   Students will learn about how PAT can effect prisoners by viewing several videos of model programs.
       1)   Pets for Freedom at Lorton Prison
       2)   A Bridge of Love at Purdy Prison
   b)   Follow-up discussion will focus on possible ways that the profession of PAT can lead to a more peaceful world.

III. Assignment:

   Students will prepare for their oral book report due next week. (The oral report will include reference to principles learned in class, such as relationships between pets and children, pets and individuals who are elderly or challenging situations dealing with ethical responsibilities.) More details TBA.

IV. Outcomes:

   a)   Students will have recognized that PAT programs in prisons have a positive effect on the prison milieu, in which prisoners can work cooperatively and respectfully toward a common goal.
   b)   Students will have begun to recognize that prisoners, through PAT, can have a positive impact on society. (For example, the training of service dogs for individuals who are physically challenged.)
   c)   Students will have begun to recognize that through PAT programs in prisons, that prisoners, who are released, have a better chance of becoming responsible citizens.
   d)   Students will have begun to appreciate that, in a society where animals are acknowledged and respected, that similarly, individuals will also be acknowledged and respected.

Class Five:

I. Learning/Educational Objectives:

   Students will begin to understand the issues and challenges surrounding PAT/

366

Service Learning experiences in nursing homes.

II. Methodology:

Students will learn about the strengthens and needs of individuals in nursing homes through guest speakers — TBA.

III. Assignment:
Students will write a paragraph on their interest in doing their PAT/Service Learning in a nursing home or teaching The D. J. "Respect for Living Things" Curriculum to a daycare, kindergarten, first or second-grade. (This program is easily adapted to any age group.)

IV. Outcomes:

a) Students will have learned of the issues and challenges of individuals who are elderly.
b) Students will be more prepared to enhance the lives of individuals who are elderly through PAT/Service Learning.

Class Six:

I. Learning/Educational Objectives:

Students will learn how PAT can have a positive impact on many of society's issues. (i.e. violence, substance abuse, loneliness, school dropout, early sexual involvement, suicide, domestic violence, abuse, environmental issues, among others.)

II. Methodology:

a) Students will each note on an index card what they consider to be society's most serious problems.
b) Students, through discussion, will recognize how PAT can help ameliorate some of these problems.

III. Assignment:

Students will prepare a word search using a list of vocabulary words that pertains to the profession. This word search will be designed to help students study for the final.

IV. Outcome:

Students will have learned to recognize that PAT can have an impact on many of society's issues, thus leading to a *friendlier, healthier, and more peaceful world.*[5]

<u>Class Seven:</u>

Word Search

Final Exam

Therapy pets bring joy into the classroom and enhance learning as well. Sixth graders: Ligella, Katrina, and Marjorie enjoy the interaction between Maj-En and their teacher, Gina Furtado.

Section 6:
HOW TO SET UP A PROFESSIONAL PAT PROGRAM IN A MEDICAL/TREATMENT FACILITY

__Cheryl Ginsberg__ has a BA in Psychology from Hunter College and a MA in Early Childhood Education from Lehman College, both in NY. She taught elementary school for many years then retired to raise a family. Because of her love for animals, Cheryl sought a 2nd career in PAT and earned a certificate in this new profession at Mercy College in 1987. She was actively involved in PAT with several client hospitals and long-term care facilities in NY and NJ with her faithful friend and partner Pippin, a yellow lab retriever, as well as an assortment of bunnies. For lack of funding and insurance Cheryl had to start another career, this time as a groomer of cats and dogs. She has successfully started and continued a thriving business in mobile pet grooming in NJ called Cheryl's Animal House. Cheryl's two sons, Mark and Eric are very proud of her perseverance in finding a career which involves her love for animals and rewarding for her personally. Through-out her second and third career, she has maintained a deep, caring and supportive friendship with the author of "Loving Intervention," Pearl, who, according to Cheryl "is a shining jewel in the field of PAT." While common interest in pets and people brought them together as a team, at a time when acknowledging the validity of this profession was in its initial stages, they wish to thank their pet partners, D. J. and Pippin, for their devoted service, in helping to lay the groundwork for this emerging profession. Cheryl would also like to thank all those involved in her training and active involvement in the field, especially the patients and staff who shared in the many rewards of the program.

> *The following was an abstract submitted by Cheryl to the Delta Society following her graduation from Mercy College in 1987, envisioning PATF as a formal profession.*

Before a PAT program can actually run in a facility, specific steps must be taken.

All animals must be carefully selected and temperament tested. One must consider sources for obtaining acceptable animals, the variety of species of animals which will work with the population you deal with, the health and well-being of your animals, and the veterinary costs involved. One must also consider the fatigue of animals due to overuse, and the working conditions, which can include room temperatures of 78 degrees or more in some nursing homes.

Fee schedules must be established before you have your initial interview with a facility. This schedule must be based on your overhead, potential yearly work schedule, and the amount of profit you wish to earn and must be carefully balanced with and consideration given to the going market rate your facilities are willing or able to budget for a PAT program. You can charge an hourly fee or a per person fee. The important thing to remember is that you are offering your clients a professional service and your fees should be based on the same principals as any professional therapy or health related service. Facilities will respect you for your professional attitude if you present one to them.

A professional PAT program must offer its clients a program, which is goal-oriented and has forms for charting or recording the reactions and progress of each individual who is included in the program. Time must be allowed during each visit to complete this vital aspect of your program and during any preliminary interviews this must be discussed with your potential client facility.

Familiarity with your states' health codes in regard to visiting pets must be considered and adhered to at all times. You must also have a set of guidelines to present to your client facility in regard to the facilities' policy about any animals participating in your program or any animals working in the facility or any animals brought into the facility by staff. This is to protect both you, your animals, and the facility from any potential danger or problems with sick or unsafe or undesirable animals. Be prepared to change this initial set of guidelines to meet the specific needs of a facility, but to be professional you must have these guidelines on hand, to present at one of your initial interviews.

Insurance to cover your liability within the institution and in running your program is very important to acquire. Insurance companies, though, are quite reluctant to insure a PAT business, because both working with animals and working with people in a health related capacity are high risk.

Once a facility is interested in your services, you must conduct at least one and possibly several interviews. It is important that you are very clear in what you can offer your potential client facility and their particular resident population, and how you can meet their specific needs by custom designing a program for them considering the physical make-up of the building, and also considering the needs you might have of them in regard to resident, staff, therapist, and animal requirements.

Fee schedules must be discussed with consideration for time required for any record keeping or charting the facility desires, as well as when and how you should be paid for your services.

As part of the program, you might wish to offer your potential clients, one or more staff orientation meetings. These meetings could be held in order to help staff fully understand a PAT program, the need for animal guidelines, cleanliness of animals regarding custodial staff concerns, staff role in making the program a success and finally to discuss any questions staff might have for you.

Before selecting from the resident population for the program, both you and the facility must inquire about each potential clients allergies, animal phobias, and general health. Also, social worker staff might want to find out if families of particular clients have any input as to whether a particular client should or should not be included in the program. In this way the program activities may be carried over into an area of a resident's life outside of the facility.

As part of the initial interview, take a walk around the facility to find out where you would be conducting the program. Take into consideration and make clear to your client the physical needs your animals and your program require. Such things as adequate space for wheel chairs, geri chairs and beds, room for both you and your animal to move around in, get between or play in, are important. Your animals will require a rest area and a supply of clean water. Areas where food is prepared are off limits for use in your program, although areas used as dual dining/recreation areas may be considered depending on the state health code. If your program includes visits to clients in their rooms in a resident facility, check the room setting for hazards, space and cleanliness.

Setting up a visitation schedule for several months in advance is helpful for both you and your client. The frequency of visits should be determined by both your availability, the budget, the client population, and the goals of the facility.

Do not forget to allow time for rest or vacation for you and your therapy animals, and scheduling for seminars or out-of-town meetings. Your client facility will appreciate knowing in advance any interruptions of a set schedule.

You may wish to write up a contract with your client facility for either short-term or yearly term work. Know which department you will be directly working with and with whom you should talk whenever problems arise.

SAMPLE FORMS – Pearl Salotto

Planning Professional PAT Programs:

• Complete a professional certificate program in PAT, building on a human service background.

• Set up administrative meeting to secure administrative approval.
   ⇒ appointment of a Pet Assisted Therapy liaison
   ⇒ PAT policies and Code of Ethics in place
   ⇒ gain infection control committee approval
   ⇒ contract signed with provisions for salary, vacation days, professional development and sick days

• Complete staff education to:
   ⇒ share information on PAT.
   ⇒ gain input on planning the PAT program.

• Conduct resident meetings to:
   ⇒ share information on PAT
   ⇒ gain input on planning the PAT program

• Conduct family meetings to:
   ⇒ inform about PAT
   ⇒ gain input on patient's background with pets with regard to interests, allergies and phobias
   ⇒ seek input on planning the PAT program

• Participate in Health Care Planning meetings or Interdisciplinary Treatment Team meeting.

• Establish an appropriate area(s) for the program and additionally an appropriate area for therapy pet to rest, and for documentation.

• Establish a medically referred PAT client list, schedule and treatment plan.

• Work with PAT liaison to establish forms for documentation and for permission to photograph.

Sample Initial PAT Assessment:

Name:_____ Date of Assessment: _____

Reaction to the therapy pet:
    joy and enthusiasm:_____
    fear or anxiety:_____
    hostility:_____
    no effect: _____

*Response to staff direction in PAT:*_____
_____
_____
_____

*Behavior toward the therapy pet:*_____
_____
_____
_____

Possible benefits:

Opportunity to nurture: _____
_____
_____
_____

Enhancement of quality of life: _____
_____
_____
_____

Gross motor/Fine motor: _____
_____
_____
_____

Social/Communicative: _____
_____
_____
_____

Educational/Cognitive: _____
_____
_____
_____

Pet Assisted Therapy recommended:_____Conditions: _____

_____

_____

Pet Assisted Therapy not recommended: _____ Explain: _____

_____

_____

Signature of PATF: _____

Signature of Agency Liaison _____

Referral Form:

Personal and Social History:

Name:_____ Facility: _____ Room #: _____

Date of Birth:_____ Place of Birth:_____

Admit Date:_____ _Doctor:_____

Photo release on file:_____

Date of Health Care Planning Meetings:_____

Educational Level: _____

Former Occupation:_____

Primary Language:_____ Secondary: _____

Interests: _____

Attitude to Placement:_____

Religious Affiliation:_____

Organizational Affiliation:_____

Medication:_____
_____

Family:

Children:_____
_____

Grandchildren:_____
_____

Other:_____

Frequency of Family Contact:_____

By Whom:_____
_____

Pearl Salotto

Strengths and Needs:

Physical diagnosis:_____
_____
_____

Does patient have a physical condition that could be contagious to the therapy pet?
If yes, please explain:_____
_____
_____

Functional ability:

Ambulatory: _____
Ambulatory: (walker/wheelchair): _____
Lack of mobility:_____
Lack of range of motion: _____
Activities of Daily Living Skills:_____
_____
_____
_____

Potential for rehabilitation and/or independence:_____
_____
_____

Sensory States:

Vision:_____
_____

Hearing: _____
_____

Emotional States:

Is behavior predictable?_____

Is patient responsive or passive? _____

What does patient enjoy?_____
_____

Describe emotional state? _____
_____

Cognitive Awareness:

Level of awareness? _____
Aware that animal is a living being? _____
Aware of who he/she is? _____
Oriented to person, time, and place? _____
Judgment? _____

Communication Level:

Can patient understand verbal communication: _____
_____

Is patient able to express himself (verbally, signing, communication device)? _____
_____

Can patient follow directions? _____
_____

Pet Assisted Therapy Goals:

Psychological: _____
Educational - Cognitive: _____
Social - Communicative: _____
Quality of Life: _____
Overcoming Fear of Animals: _____
Recreational: _____
Physical: _____
Mobility - Independence: _____

Past experience with animals: _____
_____
_____

Allergies to dogs: _____
            cats: _____
            birds: _____
            other: _____

Responsible Professionals:

Physician: _____

Nurse: _____

Occupational Therapist: _____

Recreational Therapist: _____

Social Worker: _____

Physical Therapist: _____

Speech Therapist: _____

Pet Assisted Therapy Liaison: _____

Is your institution willing to provide staff support to whatever extent is needed to provide for safety of the therapy pet despite an individual's emotional or developmental abilities?

Is your institution willing to inform PATF on an on-going basis of any changes in the mental, physical or emotional states of individuals, which might have an impact on the safety of the therapy pet?

Staff person responsible: _____

Signature: _____

Date: _____

Approved by PAT: _____

PAT treatment goals can be developed per individual needs from a wide variety of potential PAT benefits — some of which are listed below.

Psychological/Emotional Benefits:

Attitude: Friendships — human and canine
Opening of trust
Increased empathy
Transfer of trust
Improved attitude
Improved participation
Increased social acceptance
Anticipation of joyous experiences
Being praised for appropriate behavior
Increased motivation for Activities of Daily Living
Motivation to control behavior
Decrease in sleep during the day and decreased boredom
Building of values and morals — enhanced respect for people, animals and the environment
Possibility of new understanding and respect for rules, due to seeing pets having to obey rules too, for their own safety
Enhanced potential for appropriate choices (i.e. staying in school, avoiding drugs, premature sexual involvement and violence).

Feelings: Relaxation
Sense of normalcy
Feeling better
Therapeutic touch
Laughter and humor
Opportunity to express emotions
Homelike atmosphere
Feelings of intimacy
Reawakening of memories
Fun — Joy — Pleasure
Sense of well-being
Opportunities to connect with nature
Feeling special, proud, and unique
Unconditional and non-judgmental love
Possible partial distraction from worry, sorrow, and pain
Feeling needed and useful
Feeling its okay to mess up and still be loved (as animals can)
Gives meaning, interest, and enthusiasm to life

Skills: Concentration
Reality focusing

Facilitating creativity
Potential for increased leadership
Decreased fear of animals
Potential for increasing eye contact
Increased self-esteem and self confidence
Potential for improved decision making

Social/Communicative Benefits:

Increased language stimulation
Increased communication with family due to enthusiasm for pet
Increased desire to come out of room and participate in program
Development of relationship with others due to common interest in pet
Possibility for the initiation of language after long periods of silence
Development of increased status with staff due to common connection of pet
Increased potential for expressive language due to enthusiasm over the therapy pet
Increased potential for auditory language and following directions due to focusing and concentrating on therapy pet
Elevated status in the eyes of the staff

Quality of Life:

General increase in physical and emotional well-being, thereby, quality of life, due to multiple positive therapeutic effects of bonding with therapy animals.
Better ability to cope with and adapt to difficult and painful situations, as well as motivation to reverse inappropriate behavior.

Physical Benefits:

Increased ambulation
Increased independence
Decreased blood pressure
Increased functioning of immune system
Increased exercise through walking the dog with assistance
Increased motivation to walk, i.e. down the hall
Increased possibility of survival after a serious illness, due to relationship to the therapy pet
Tactile sensory stimulation

Cognitive/Educational Benefits:

Learning difference between living and non-living things
Learning about life cycle
Learning about personal hygiene from learning appropriate pet care
Stimulation of a myriad of interests, academic and leisure, due to bonding with therapy pet
Learning respect for all living things

Rating Scale Criteria for documenting PAT Treatment Sessions:

Rating of 1:	no reaction
Rating of 2:	smiles, reaches and responds to questions
Rating of 3:	smiles and pets the therapy pet
	pleased to see therapy pet and facilitator
	responds to conversation, but does not initiate it
Rating of 4:	true joy with pet (enthusiastic and affectionate interaction)
	beginning to open up to facilitator
	initiates conversation
	beginning to share
Rating of 5:	considerable time spent in the visit
	recognizes dog and facilitator
	bonds with facilitator, as well as therapy pet
	high level of comfort with facilitator
	initiates conversation
	sharing of the past
	cares for the dog as a unique and special being

Circle all reactions that apply.

Reaction to facilitator:
- remembers facilitator
- responds to facilitator verbally
- initiates conversation
- shares memories
- discusses needs and joys
- high level of enthusiasm
- high level of comfort and openness with facilitator

Overall rating: 1   2   3   4   5
Comments:

Reaction to therapy pet:
- remembers the pet
- remembers other visits
- smiles
- initiates talking and stroking or allows assistance in stroking
- displays feelings of nurturing
- displays high level of enthusiasm

Overall rating: 1   2   3   4   5
Comments:

Photo release: I give permission for my photograph(s) to be used for the purpose of educating the public about Pet Assisted Therapy.

_____

Signature of PATF

_____

Signature of Client/Patient/Resident

_____

Signature of Witness

_____

Signature of Witness

Follow Up: Assessment Form to be completed, by staff liaison, between PAT sessions

Please check if each individual spoke of therapy pet, the facilitator or the PAT program. We welcome any comments that the staff may have.

Week of _____

Clients/Patients	Remark sabout Therapy pet	Remarks about Facilitator	Other Relevant Remarks

Section 7:
THE RHODE ISLAND GUIDELINES FOR PETS IN HEALTH CARE FACILITIES AND PET ASSISTED THERAPY
(Rhode Island Department of Health)

The following document, which was initially facilitated by the Windwalker Humane Coalition, went out to all Rhode Island Department of Health licensees.

I. Philosophy of Pet Assisted Therapy

The Department of Health supports and encourages the concept of pets being a part of patients'/residents' lives in both the acute and long term healthcare settings. The presence of pets can enhance the quality of life of individuals and be a motivator to the accomplishment of treatment goals. The success of a program depends on the individual bringing the program, whether it be a professional Pet Assisted Therapy Facilitator or a volunteer being overseen by an organization.

Our philosophy is founded on the premise that all individuals, whether they be volunteers or professionals or whether they are family members or staff responsible for resident pets, need a deep and abiding respect for the pets and people involved.

II. The Professional Pet Assisted Therapy Facilitator and the Volunteer: Difference and Similarities

In general, what distinguishes the volunteer and the professional are the level of education required, as well as the role that the individual bringing the program plays in the residents'/patients' lives. The professional, in other words, delivers an individually planned treatment based intervention. The professional requires a medical referral, and PAT would become part of the patient's care plan, approved by an appropriately licensed individual. The professional would provide documentation of professional liability insurance. A professional has obtained education in PAT from a university or national organization specializing in PAT, with ethical and educational standards in accordance with professionals in the field of PAT.

The volunteer should be a member of a humane organization where instruction and supervision in PAT are given. The volunteer would be covered by the organizations insurance.

III. Whether a professional or volunteer, the following global standards should apply.

a)   A PAT folder will be maintained including the following material
      1) health certificate, regularly updated in the pet, including all legally required vaccinations
      2) a statement of good temperament for the therapy pet
      3) a personal resume for the person delivering the program
      4) statement documenting inservice

b) A facility liaison will be designated to work with the PAT professional or volunteer to develop written policies with approval of infection control, including scheduling of visits, acceptable areas for PAT, rules and regulations, manner of referrals, contra-indications including phobias, allergies, physical or psychological conditions of client which might be harmful the pet, etc.

c) Liaison will accompany PAT volunteer and professional, unless otherwise agreed upon.

d) Therapy pets will be on short leash or carrier, unless otherwise agreed upon.

e) Patient confidentiality will be maintained and photos will only be taken with appropriate releases.

f) All incidents will be reported.

g) Individual bringing in the pet will be responsible for any necessary clean up and will, additionally, notify appropriate individual.

h) The Pet Therapy team will be part of the evacuation plan.

i) Residents will wash their hands before and after PAT.

j) ID will be worn per facility policy.

k) Wild animals will not be part of PAT program unless accompanied by Wildlife Rehabilitator, Zoo personnel or similarly qualified individual.

IV. Resident Pets

Specific written guidelines for the safety of the resident pet and the patient/residents will be developed to address the following items.

Specify who is responsible for the safety of the pet.

Informed the Health Department, in writing, about your resident pet.

Developed a protocol to protect the resident pet from environmental hazards such as doors, windows, elevators, medicines, chemicals, physical/emotional conditions of individuals, etc.

Attempt to include the pet in treatment plans.
It would be advisable for the person who is responsible for the pet to become educated in PAT from a university or agency.

Evaluate the pet on an ongoing basis, for overall quality of life, willingness to relate, good health, temperament, safety and contentment to the surroundings? Is this documented.

A plan must be in place to protect the pet in the event the pet can no longer remain in the facility?

Note: The pet will be part of the on-site inspection of facilities regarding health and safety.

Note: Global guidelines apply as appropriate.

V. Family Pet Visits

Facilities need written policies for family pet visitys – detailing such items as staff liaison to the family members, scheduling of visit, protocol for approval of visit, including temperament and health documentation, area for visit, safeguards such a short leash or carrier, reporting of any incident or clean up issues, etc.

VI. Summary

In conclusion, we trust that whether people/pet interactions involve professional, voluntary, family pet visits or resident pets, that the individuals lives are enhanced, while the pet is also enjoying himself/herself.

If there is any way we can assist toward this goal, please contact the Dept. of Health.

Section 8:

STATE OF RHODE ISLAND

IN GENERAL ASSEMBLY
JANUARY SESSION, A.D. 1997

SENATE RESOLUTION

CREATING A SPECIAL LEGISLATIVE
COMMISSION TO STUDY THE ASSOCIATION
BETWEEN AND AMONGST DOMESTIC VIOLENCE,
CHILD ABUSE, AND ANIMAL ABUSE

97-S 0462

Introduced By: Senators Perry, Graziano, Cicilline, Nygaard, Sosnowski, et. al.
Date Introduced: February 6, 1997
Referred To: Senate Committee on Special Legislation

1   WHEREAS, Members of most societies have long believed that a
2   person's treatment of animals reflects his or her treatment of other
3   human beings; and
4   WHEREAS, Scientific, social service, medical, judicial, and law
5   enforcement communities are beginning to recognize violent behav-
    ior
6   often first reveals itself in the form of cruelty to animals; and
7   WHEREAS, Some of this recognition has come about through
8   detailed profiles of violent criminals. There exists compelling cir-
9   cumstantial evidence linking serial and mass murderers with earlier
10   acts of cruelty.
11   WHEREAS, Acts of animal cruelty are very likely predictors of
12   both domestic and societal violence; now, therefore, be it
13   RESOLVED, That a special legislative commission be and the same
14   is created consisting of fifteen (15) members: two (2) of whom shall
15   be from the senate, not more than one (1) from the same political
16   party, to be appointed by the majority leader: one (1) of whom shall
17   be a member of the Windwalker Humane Coalition; and one (1) of whom

1   shall be the State Veterinarian, or designee; one (1) of whom shall be
    the
2   director of the Department for Children, Youth and Families, or desig-

3   nee; one (1) of whom shall be the director of the Department of

4   Health, or designee; one (1) of whom shall be a member of the Rhode

5   Island Animal Legislative Coalition (R.I.A.L.C.); one (1) of whom

6   shall be a veterinarian; one (1) of whom shall be a mental health pro-

7   professional; one (1) of whom shall be a member of the Animal Con-

     trol

8   Officers Association; one (1) of whom shall be a member of the Rhode

9   Island Veterinary Medical Society; one (1) of whom shall be a mem-

     ber of

10   the Volunteers In Service to Animal Society; and, three (3) of whom

11   shall be members of the general public to be appointed by the major-

     ity

12   leader.

13   In lieu of any appointment of a member of the legislature to a

14   permanent advisory commission, a legislative study commission, a

15   legislative study commission, or any commission created by a gen-

     eral

16   assembly resolution, the appointing authority may appoint a member

     of

17   general public to serve in lieu of a legislator, provided that the

18   majority leader or the minority leader of the political party which is

19   entitled to the appointment consents to the appointment of the mem-

     ber

20   of the general public.

21   The purpose of said commission shall be to study the association

22   between and amongst domestic violence, child abuse, and animal abuse

     to

23   produce legislation to require cross reporting between DCYF and

     Animal

24   Control Officers (SPCA).

25   Forthwith upon passage of this resolution, the members of the

26   commission shall meet at the call of the senate majority leader and

27   organize and shall select from among the legislators a chairperson.

28   Vacancies in said commission shall be filled in like manner as the

29   original appointment.

30   The membership of said commission shall receive no compensa-

     tion

31   for their services.

32   All departments and agencies of the state shall furnish such

33   advice and information, documentary and otherwise, to said commis-

     sion

1   an its agents as is deemed necessary or desirable by the commission

2   to facilitate the purpose of the resolution.

3   The joint committee on legislative services is hereby authorized

4	and directed to provide suitable quarters for said commission; and be
5	it further
6	RESOLVED, That the commission shall report its findings and
7	recommendations to the general assembly on or before January 22, 1998
8	and said commission shall expire on March 22, 1998.

PD330/2

EPILOGUE

A Gift Called D. J.

A magnificent six year old Samoyed named D. J. has not only brought joy to family, friends and neighbors all her life, but since she was temperament tested at Mercy College in 1987, she has been eagerly working as part of treatment and education, as well.

Loving bonds established with D. J. have motivated patients to say that first word after a stroke and to propel their own wheelchair.

Comfort received when D. J. sleeps across one's feet, has encouraged individuals to share feelings, long held deep within. Feelings expressed by D. J.'s interaction with schoolchildren have empowered them to grow in their respect for all living things.

D. J. has brought countless smiles - allowed individuals to overcome deep-seated fears and has allowed nurturing to take place.

D. J. is truly a shining example of a therapy dog.

Whether D. J. works as part of treatment in an agency or nursing home, whether she calms otherwise noisy teenagers as she walks with me down the halls of Franklin High School or whether she delights innocent first graders at Crane School, Rochester, New York, waiting with outstretched hands as my granddaughter Stacey proudly walks with her up and down the aisles - **she always shares her gifts of love.**

It is my hope and truly the purpose behind this book that duly educated Pet Assisted Therapy teams will someday take their rightful place in healthcare and educational settings across this land and that D. J. will take her rightful place in the history of this profession following in the paw prints of Jingles and Jake.

As I watch D. J. with her many friends, and as I watch this profession unfold, I am in awe, amazement, and appreciation that gifts so freely given - can do so much.

D. J., DOG OF JOY, recently passed away peacefully within the loving arms of her family. The smiling face of this big white dog is synonymous with professional Pet Assisted Therapy (PAT), locally and nationally, because of the countless people of all ages whose lives she touched, because of the many programs, as well as social reform initiatives that she inspired, because of the many dreams that she helped turn into reality.

Anyone who recognizes that pets and people are good for each other can turn this moment of sadness into a celebration of D. J.'s life and commit to carrying on her legacy, recognizing that she did more than her part in bringing about a healthier, friendlier, and more peaceful world simply by being herself.

D. J. showed me, at a New York nursing home in 1988, how residents could find a renewed joy of life through her loving touch and thus, inspired not only my university program, but also my vision that all universities should have PAT degree programs so that ultimately all facilities could have professional PAT as part of their treatment team.

D. J. showed me, in my granddaughter's first-grade class in New York in 1991, how a dog's strolling up and down aisles and interacting with children could open up their hearts and minds to their responsibilities to pets, people, and themselves.

D. J. showed us all the profound and life-changing impact that her freely given love could have on Feinstein High School students, giving them the "heart-opening" opportunity to learn of the positive impact that animals can have in all of our lives through their one-of-a-kind PAT curriculum and the subsequent follow up opportunity to share their love with others through PAT Service Learning.

D. J. showed me from the first day of our experiences together that the bond between the therapy pet and the professional is the ethical foundation of this profession, protecting the pet in the field and providing the example from which all else flows.

D. J. and D. J.-inspired programs have led to schoolchildren writing and singing songs about respecting animals, other people, and themselves; Rhode Island Health Department guidelines for pet therapy; an official state commission; annual D. J. "Respect for Living Things" days on her birthday, May 8th; several Rhode Island agencies having professional PAT programs; the integration of PAT with Service Learning; and Windwalker Humane Coalition for Professional Pet Assisted Therapy, among other programs.

Won't you join my children, grandchildren, friends and colleagues, elementary school students of Central Falls, Woonsocket, Providence, and Feinstein High School students, and individuals of all ages who knew and loved D. J., in doing all in our power through all our words and deeds to help this magical profession earn its rightful place in health care, education, social services, and society as a whole, spearheaded over the past thirteen years by the smiling face and extended paw of a big white dog named D. J.

Hands of love: D.J. loving the loving touch. Photo credit: Cindy Wilson

Pawprints of a Pet-Assisted Therapy Legend
by Roberta Preziosi

D. J. was a friend of mine;
A sincere, loving canine.
Her eyes were honest and kind.
Like a meteor's impact into Earth leaves a crater behind,
The light of D. J.'s life's impact here on Earth shall always shine.

Pawprints of a pet-assisted therapy legend
are forever engraved in my mind

Unconditional love exists in non-human creatures.
Like D. J., they all possess pure and innocent features.
D. J. proved to us that animals are our best teachers.
She taught young and old about love,
Inspired us all to rise above.
Extend your paw to everyone you meet.
Make the children's faces smile cheek to cheek.
She leaves this world a better place
Because her sweet paws walked our space.
Respect, compassion were her traits.
Hail D. J., white dog of true grace.
D. J. you will be missed.
Though gentle winds still whisper your kiss.
Saying your name brings about such bliss.
Everlasting afterlife to D. J. is my wish.

BIBLIOGRAPHY

Articles:

Allen, Karen (1996, April 3). The Value of Service Dogs for People With Severe Ambulatory Disabilities. <u>Journal of American Medical Association,</u> 275(13), 1001-1006.

Bernstein, Emmanuel (Ed.) (1978). Humane Innovations and Alternatives Newsletter. <u>Psychologists for the Ethical Treatment of Animals.</u>

Burke, Sarah (1992, February 24). In the Presence of Animals, <u>U.S. News & World Report.</u>

Campbell, Virginia (1990, Summer). Mending Hearts and Minds. <u>Our Health.</u>

Cohen, Susan Phillips (1991). Hugs that Help. <u>Newsweek.</u>

Friedmann, Erika, Ph. D., and Sue A. Thomas, RN (1995, December, 15). Pet Ownership, Social Support, and One Year Survival After Acute Myocardial Infarction in the Cardiac Arrhythmia Suppression Trial (CAST). <u>The American Journal of Cardiology,</u> 76, 1213-1217.

Gadbois, Mary (1992, December). Pet Therapy: An Assessment. <u>AlphaBits.</u>

Gadbois, Mary (1993, March). Pet Visitation in Hospitals. <u>AlphaBits.</u>

Gadbois, Mary (1993, June). Using Therapy Dogs in Physical Therapy Visits. <u>AlphaBits.</u>

Gadbois, Mary (1993, December). Therapy Dogs and Traumatic Injury Patients. <u>AlphaBits.</u>

Gordon, Crystal (1994, October 5, 1994). The Cat Who Walks Through Walls. <u>Cat Fancy.</u>

Grant, Anne (1994, October 5). Animal Abuse Can Spawn Human Torture. <u>Providence Journal Bulletin.</u>

National Institute of Health (1987, September). Health Benefits of Pets. (Author)

Kuttner, Beth (1996, Fall). The Web of Hope Moves On. <u>The Latham Letter.</u>

Morrone, Jaclyn (1991, October). Special Birds. <u>Bird Talk.</u>

Preziosi, Roberta (1997, Spring). Code of Ethics. <u>The Latham Letter.</u>

Reynolds, Rita (1992). In Appreciation of all Animals Newsletter. <u>la Joie.</u>

Rosen, Ellen (1991, May 17). Therapist's Best Friend. <u>Democrat and Chronicle.</u>

Ryan, Michael (1992, March 22). Where Saving Animals Save Others. <u>Parade Magazine.</u>

Pearl Salotto

Rowan, Andrew and Alan Beck (1994). The Health Benefits of Human Animal Interactions. <u>Anthrozoos</u>, 7(2), 85-89.

Salotto, Pearl (1996, January). D. J. - Dog of Joy. <u>Rhode Island Veterinary Medical Association Newsletter</u>.

Salotto, Pearl. (1994, Winter). A Call for Professional Accreditation of PAT Facilitators: Paws on the Path to a Profession. <u>The Latham Letter</u>.

Salotto, Pearl (1995, Spring). The D. J. "Respect for Living Things" Program: Rhode Island Conference <u>Weaves a Silver Web of Hope from the Tangled Threads of Violence</u>," <u>The Latham Letter</u>.

Salotto, Pearl (1996, Summer). Profile of D. J. Winning the RIVMA Award. <u>The Latham Letter</u>.

Salotto, Pearl (1998, Spring). Rhode Island Commission Sets Example for Other States - How a single comment benefits thousands of children and animals. <u>The Latham Letter</u>.

Salotto, Pearl (1996, June). Sharing the Love: D. J. and Mag-En - Teachers, Friends and Motivators. <u>Tailwaggers</u>.

Salotto, Pearl (1998, Spring). Making Respect Part of the Curriculum: Linking the Circles of Compassion: Preventing Child Abuse, Animal Abuse, and Domestic Violence, <u>Hayworth Press</u>.

Salotto, Pearl (1998, Spring). Healthy Babies are brought up by Healthy Parents. <u>Healthy Mothers, Healthy Babies</u>.

Sandler, Roberta (1990, October). The Puppy That Didn't Know How to Quit. <u>Good Housekeeping</u>.

Tannenbaum, Jerold, Esq. (1985, December). The HCAB: Cliché of Challenge. <u>Veterinary Practice</u>.

Delta Society (1989, Summer). Terrior Helps Take the Terror Out of Dental Visits. <u>People, Animals and the Environment</u> (now called InterActions).

Temple, Tara, Dr. (1996, July). The Windwalker Humane Coalition Celebrates its 1st Year. <u>Rhode Island Veterinary Medical Association Newsletter</u>.

Books:

Arkow, Phil (1995). <u>Breaking the Cycles of Violence: A Practical Guide</u>. Alameda, CA: Latham Foundation Publications.

Angel, Deborah, K. (1991). <u>And Now I Walk</u>. Debili Enterprises Co.

Anderson, Robert K., with Benjamin L. & Lynette A. Hart (1984). The Pet Connection: Proceedings of the Minnesota - California Conferences on the Human Animal Bond. University of Minnesota's Center to Study Human Animal Relationships and Environments at the University of Minnesota.

Arkow, Phil (1995). Breaking the Cycle of Violence. Alameda, CA: Latham Foundation Publications.

Arkow, Phil (1997). The Loving Bond. Saratoga, CA: R&E Publishers for the Latham Foundation.

Arkow, Phil (1985). Resource Guide for the Use of Companion Animals in the Helping Profession. Colorado: Humane Society of Pikes Peak.

Barrie, AneMarie, Esq. (1990). Dogs and the Law. Neptune City, NJ: P.F.H. Publications, Inc.

Benjamin, Carol Lea (1988). The Secondhand Dog. New York: Howell Publishers.

Bustad, Leo Dr. (1987) . Compassion - Our Last Great Hope. Renton, WA: Delta Society.

Church, Julie Adams (1987). Joy in a Woolly Coat. Oakland, CA: Canticle Publishers.

Cusak, Odean (1984). Pets and the Elderly. New York: Hayworth Press.

Cusak, Odean (1985). Pets and Mental Health. New York: Hayworth Press.

Salotto, Pearl (1994). The D. J. "Respect for Living Things" Program. Warwick: Rhode Island (Author).

Dillman, Dick Dr. (1981). A Comprehensive Community Companion Animal Program for Dropout Prevention. Florida: Miami Dade Community College.

Fogle, Bruce (1991). Interrelations Between People and Pets. Illinois: Charles C. Thomas Publishers.

Hart, Benjamin L. and Lynette A. Hart (1988). The Perfect Puppy. New York: W.H. Freeman & Co.

Hines, Linda (1991). Pet Partners Manual. Renton, WA: Delta Society.

Houston, Edens, et.al. (1989). Caring Critters - Animal Assisted Therapy Volunteer Handbook. Houston: Caring Critters.

Jones, Linda Tellington, with Sibyl Taylor (1992). The Telling TTouch. New York: Viking Press.

Katcher, Aaron, Dr. and Dr. Allen Beck (1983). New Perspectives on Our Lives with Companion Animals. Philadelphia:University of Pennsylvania Press.

Katcher, Aaron, Dr. and Dr. Allen Beck (1983). <u>Between Pets and People</u>. New York: Putnam Publishing Group.

Lee, Ronnal, with Marie Zeglan, Terry Ryan, Clover Gowing, and Linda Hines (1985). <u>Animals in Nursing Homes</u>. Renton, WA: Delta Society.

Levinson, Boris (1962). <u>Pets and Human Development</u>. Illinois: Charles C. Thomas Publishers.

Levinson, Boris (1969). <u>Pet Oriented Child Psychotherapy</u>. Illinois: Charles C. Thomas Publishers.

Lorenz, Konrad (1952). <u>King Solomon's Ring</u>. New York: Signet Books, New American Library.

The Monks of New Skete (1978). <u>How to Be Your Dog's Best Friend</u>. Cambridge, NY: New Skete Monastery.

Mooney, Samantha A. (1983). <u>A Snowflake in My Hand</u>. New York: Dell Publishing.

Nebbe, Linda Lloyd (1991). <u>Nature as a Guide</u>. Minnesota: Educational Media Corp.

Pfau, Holli (1990). <u>PAT at Huntington Hospital</u>. Pasadena, CA: Huntington Memorial Hospital.

Reynolds, Rebecca (1995). <u>Bring Me the Ocean</u>. Vander Wyk & Burnham Publishers.

Rowan, Andrew (1988). <u>Animals and People Sharing the World</u>: Massachusetts: University Press of New England for Tufts University.

Russman, Marion (1985). <u>Pets and the Family</u>. New York: Hayworth Press.

Ryan, Terry (1990). <u>The Puppy Primer</u>. Pullman, WA: People-Pet Partnership at the College of Veterinary Medicine at Washington State University.

Schoen, Allen M., DVM, and Pam Proctor (1995). <u>Love, Miracles and Animal Healing</u>. New York: Simon & Schuster.

Vaughan, Sherry, with Larry Peterson, Dr. Leo Bustad, Terry Ryan, and Linda Hines (1990). <u>Learning and Living Together - Building the Human Animal Bond</u>. Pullman, WA: People-Pet Partnership at the College of Veterinary Medicine at Washington State University.

Ward, Robert and Dolly Ward (1985). <u>The New Complete Samoyed</u>. New York: Howell Publishers.

Yates, Elizabeth (1973). <u>Skeezer - A Dog with a Mission</u>. New York:Avon Publishers.

Conference Abstracts:

HABAC International Conference - Saskatchewan, Alberta Canada - 1992

6th International Delta Conference, "Animals and Us" - Montreal, Quebec, Canada -1992

10th Annual Delta Conference, "People, Animals and Nature" - Portland, Oregon- 1991

9th Annual Delta Conference - Houston, Texas, 1990

8th Annual Delta Conference, "Living Together in Cities" - Parsippany, New Jersey - 1989

7th Annual Delta Conference, "Exploring Our Interdependence" - Orlando, Florida - 1988

Videos:

A Man Who Loved Animals (a video made by Jane McCulloch in honor of her deceased husband, Dr. Mike McCulloch) [Film]. (Availability unknown. Contact the Delta Society, 289 Perimeter Road East, Renton, Washington 98055-1329.)

Breaking the Cycle of Violence. [Film]. (Availability unknown. Contact the Latham Foundation, Latham Plaza Building, Clement and Schiller Streets, Alameda, CA 94501.)

Canine Companions Opening Doors to Learning - Sally Brockett . [Film]. (Availability unknown. Contact the Delta Society, 289 Perimeter Road East, Renton, Washington 98055-1329.)

Children's D. J. Song - Can We Follow Her Example (1994). [Film]. (Available from Pearl Salotto, 173 Easton Avenue, Warwick, RI 02888.)

Companion Animal Drop-Out Prevention Program [Film]. (Available from Dr. Dick Dillman, 4000 S.W. 128th Avenue, Miramar, FL 33027.)

Companion Birds - Marilyn Larkins [Film]. (Availability unknown. Contact the Delta Society, 289 Perimeter Road East, Renton, Washington 98055-1329.)

D. J. - A Dog of All Seasons (1997). [Film]. (Available from Pearl Salotto, 173 Easton Avenue, Warwick, RI 02888.)

Farm on the Move [Film]. (Available from Dr. Dick Dillman, 4000 S.W. 128th Avenue, Miramar, FL 33027.)

From Pound to Hearing Ear Dog [Film]. (Availability unknown. Contact the Delta Society, 289 Perimeter Road East, Renton, Washington 98055-1329.)

Gardening with Special Children [Film]. (Availability unknown. Contact the Latham Foun-

dation, Latham Plaza Building, Clement and Schiller Streets, Alameda, CA 94501.)
The Health Benefits of Pets [Film]. (Availability unknown. Contact the Delta Society, 289 Perimeter Road East, Renton, Washington 98055-1329.)

HIV Population [Film]. (Availability unknown. Contact the Latham Foundation, Latham Plaza Building, Clement and Schiller Streets, Alameda, CA 94501.)

Innovations [Film]. (Availability unknown. Contact the Delta Society, 289 Perimeter Road East, Renton, Washington 98055-1329.)

Lorton Prison [Film]. - Dr. Earl Strimple) (Availability unknown. Contact the Delta Society, 289 Perimeter Road East, Renton, Washington 98055-1329.)

Maj-En: A Loving Bridge to a Better World (1998). [Film]. (Available from Pearl Salotto, 173 Easton Avenue, Warwick, RI 02888.)

Medical Benefits of Pet Assisted Therapy (1992). [Film]. (Available from Pearl Salotto, 173 Easton Avenue, Warwick, RI 02888.)

Molly [Film]. (Availability unknown. Contact Monroe County New York BOCES).

Clinical Benefits of Pet Assisted Therapy (1992). [Film]. (Available from Pearl Salotto, 173 Easton Avenue, Warwick, RI 02888.)

Nika and the Elephant - Jingles Award [Film]. (Availability unknown. Contact the Delta Society, 289 Perimeter Road East, Renton, Washington 98055-1329.)

The PACT: Animals Coming Together [Film]. (Availability unknown. Contact the Delta Society, 289 Perimeter Road East, Renton, Washington 98055-1329.)

Pet Therapy in Continuing Care - St. Mary's Hospital, New London, Ontario [Film]. - (Availability unknown. Contact the Delta Society, 289 Perimeter Road East, Renton, Washington 98055-1329.)

The Rainforest [Film]. (Availability unknown. Contact World Wildlife Foundation.)

Son - The Service Dog [Film]. (Availability unknown. Contact the Delta Society, 289 Perimeter Road East, Renton, Washington 98055-1329.)

INDEX

* only the kindest thoughts go to our wonderful Therapy Pets, but for lack of space, we have eliminated all the names of each, except for D. J.

** denotes first appearance only of people or programs which appear frequently throughout the book.

Gadbois,
>   Bob, 83
>   Mary, 83
Gallucci, Ruth, 56, 209,
Garden Therapy Project (Sonora County, CA), 116, 119
Geraldine L. Dodge Foundation (Middletown, NY), 115-116
Ginsberg, Cheryl, 369
Green Chimneys (NY), 114
Guildford County Humane Society (Greensboro, NC), 115

Hall, Judy, 81
Harkum College (Bryn Mawr, PA), 8
Harris, James, 234
Hart, Lynette, 6
HCAB (Human Companion Animal Bond), 4-9, 169
Hearne, Vicki, 242-243
Hellman, D., 115
Hindley, Jan, 53, 215
Hines, Linda, 242
Hodge, Guy, 115
Horses, 63-66
HSUS (Humane Society of the United States), 4, 8-9
Humane Coalition Against Violence, 116
Humane Society News, 115

IDEA (Individuals With Disabilities Education Act), 56-59
IEP (Individual Education Plan), 56-59
Introduction, xiii
International Association of Human-Animal Interaction Organizations, 8
Israel, 259, 301-306

Jingles Award, 8, 219-227
Joachim, Marion, 291
Jones, Linda Passarelli, xviii, 160
Journal of Nervous and Mental Disease, 8
Journal of Personal and Social Psychology, 8

Katcher, Aaron, 6-8

Lariviere, Marie, 228
Latham, Edith, 4
Latham Foundation, 4, 8-9, 115
Latham Letter, 4, 261
Latham, Milton, 4
Lee, David, 7, 108
Legislations, State of Rhode Island, 307-308, 386-388
Levinson, Boris, 5, 11
Loar, Lynn, 116